The Media at War

Second Edition

Susan L. Carruthers

palgrave
macmillan

First edition 2000
Second edition 2011

Published by
PALGRAVE MACMILLAN

Palgrave Macmillan in the UK is an imprint of Macmillan Publishers Limited, registered in England, company number 785998, of Houndmills, Basingstoke, Hampshire RG21 6XS.

Palgrave Macmillan in the US is a division of St Martin's Press LLC, 175 Fifth Avenue, New York, NY 10010.

Palgrave Macmillan is the global academic imprint of the above companies and has companies and representatives throughout the world.

Palgrave® and Macmillan® are registered trademarks in the United States, the United Kingdom, Europe and other countries

ISBN 978-0-230-24456-6 hardback

ISBN 978-0-230-24457-3   ISBN 978-0-230-34535-5 (eBook)
DOI 10.1007/978-0-230-34535-5

This book is printed on paper suitable for recycling and made from fully managed and sustained forest sources. Logging, pulping and manufacturing processes are expected to conform to the environmental regulations of the country of origin.

A catalogue record for this book is available from the British Library.

A catalog record for this book is available from the Library of Congress.

10   9   8   7   6   5   4   3   2   1
20   19   18   17   16   15   14   13   12   11

For John Hardie Carruthers, again

Contents

Acknowledgements

This book began its life long ago and far away. I wrote the first edition in the late 1990s, while teaching at the University of Wales in Aberystwyth. At the time, few people had heard of Osama bin Laden or Al Qaeda and even the most prescient observers didn't venture to predict anything so rash, or unlikely, as a US-led decade-long war in Afghanistan. Instead the talk was of major conflict's 'obsolescence' and cyber-war's 'virtualization'. Likewise, digital media were still in their infancy back then. No one had yet dreamt up Facebook or YouTube, and Tweeting was something only birds did. That so much has changed in the intervening years has made me wary of offering too many hostages to fortune in this new version.

Rapid changes in the geopolitical landscape and in the development of 'new media' have also meant that the second edition required a much more thorough overhaul than initially anticipated. I duly, and appreciatively, acknowledge the patience with which Steven Kennedy and Stephen Wenham at Palgrave Macmillan have waited for this book's deferred delivery. Helen Caunce gracefully oversaw the transformation of manuscript into book, while it fell to Keith Povey and Joy Tucker to straighten out my transatlantic punctuation. I'm also grateful to the anonymous reviewers who read the manuscript, and to instructors at many institutions in various countries who have assigned *The Media at War* to their students over the past decade. I hope they'll be pleased with its new incarnation.

This edition has been written in a very different setting from its predecessor. For the last eight years, I've been fortunate to enjoy the academic community and institutional support of Rutgers University in Newark, New Jersey. A semester of sabbatical leave in the fall of 2009 gave me the opportunity to overhaul the manuscript in its entirety. I'm grateful to both my students and colleagues for keeping me on my toes intellectually and socially. In particular, thanks are due to Fran Bartkowski, Karen Caplan, Marvin Chochotte, Jon Cowans, Eva Giloi, Steven Kuza, Neil Maher, Reyther Ortega, Allison Perlman, Gary Roth, Doris Sher, Rick Sher, Mara Sidney and Christina Strasburger. Kaete O'Connell deserves special thanks for her assistance with the picture research and procurement. I'd also like to acknowledge good friends off-campus, especially

Mary Nell Bockman, Andy Buchanan, Tom Doherty, Matthew Shurtleff and Marilyn Young, who invariably supply good cheer and great conversation.

Finally, I pay tribute to the caring support of my family in Galway – my parents and my sister and family – who've grown accustomed to my spending far too much time writing books and not enough time visiting Ireland. The first edition of *The Media at War* was dedicated to my father, John Hardie Carruthers. It remains so again, with much love and many thanks for all the things, large and small, you've fixed, made and done for me over the years.

Newark, NJ   SUSAN L. CARRUTHERS

The author and publishers would like to thank the following who have kindly given permission for the use of copyright material; Anne Telnaes for Illustration 1.1; Ohio State University Billy Ireland Cartoon Library and Museum for Illustrations 1.2 and 3.3; The Imperial War Museum for Illustrations 2.1, 2.2, 3.2 and 3.4; The US National Archives for Illustrations 2.3 and 3.1; *The Daily Mail* for Illustration 2.4; AP/Wide World Photos for Illustrations 4.1 and 6.3; *The Daily Telegraph* for Illustration 4.2; Corbis for Illustration 5.1; N. Garland/*The Independent* for Illustration 5.2; Cox & Forkum for Illustration 6.1; *The Evening Standard* for Illustration C.1.

Abbreviations

ABC	American Broadcasting Company (United States)
AP	Associated Press
BBC	British Broadcasting Corporation
BBFC	British Board of Film Censors
BMP	Bureau of Motion Pictures
CBS	Columbia Broadcasting System (United States)
CIA	Central Intelligence Agency
CNN	Cable News Network
DOD	Department of Defense (United States)
DORA	Defence of the Realm Act
ETA	*Euskadi Ta Askatasuna* (Basque Homeland and Liberty)
IED	improvized explosive device
INLA	Irish National Liberation Army
IRA	Irish Republican Army
ITN	Independent Television News
JIB	Joint Information Bureau
MACV	Military Assistance Command, Vietnam
MIA	missing in action
MOD	Ministry of Defence (United Kingdom)
MOI	Ministry of Information (United Kingdom, World War II)
MRT	Media Reporting Team (Gulf War, 1991)
NBC	National Broadcasting Company (United States)
NGO	non-governmental organization
NLF	National Liberation Front (Vietnam)
NPR	National Public Radio (United States)
OKW	*Oberkommand das Wehrmacht* (Army High Command, Germany, 1933–45)
OWI	Office of War Information (United States, World War II)
PAO	Public Affairs Officer
PK	*Propaganda Kompanien* (Propaganda Companies, attached to German *Wehrmacht*)
PRO	public relations officer
RFK	*Reichsfilmkammer* (Reich Chamber of Film, Germany, 1933–45)

RKK	*Reichskulturkammer* (Reich Chamber of Culture, Germany, 1933–45)
RMVP	*Reichsministerum Für Volksaufklarung und Propaganda* (Reich Ministry for Popular Enlightenment and Propaganda, Germany, 1933–45)
RPF	Rwanda Patriotic Front
UFA	*Universum Film Aktiengesellschaft* (Universal Film Studio, Germany)
UNITAF	United Task Force (Somalia)
UNOSOM	United Nations Operation in Somalia
UNPROFOR	United Nations Protection Force (in Former Yugoslavia)

List of Illustrations

Introduction

Shooting war

Since the late nineteenth century, war and mass media have enjoyed a long, intricate relationship. Like many lengthy relationships, their entanglement has been at once supportive and conflicted: replete with recriminations and declarations of independence on the part of soldiers and reporters, followed by acknowledgements of mutual need. The very technologies with which war is fought have also shaped the means of communication through which distant observers apprehend warfare. The kinship between the gun and the camera – both instruments that bring subjects into sharp focus prior to shooting – has often been remarked (Virilio, 1989). Few books about war and the media lack a dustjacket image that shows men with guns being shot by men with cameras. As this emphasis on sighting and scoping mechanisms suggests, mechanized warfare placed a premium on the ability to pinpoint distant targets with ever greater precision, supplanting more intimate forms of combat in which soldiers clashed at close quarters.

At the same time that modes of destruction became more attenuated, industrial-age war also encouraged the growth of technologies that would hasten the relay of information across distance. Whether traveling on foot, horseback or by armored car, humans made slow messengers between strategists at HQ and men at the front. Modern militaries thus sought to accelerate the transmission of orders down the chain of command and, in the opposite direction, the dispatch of battlefield situation reports back to base. Telegraphy, radio broadcasting, digital computers and the internet have all been catalyzed by military investment (Edwards, 1996).

It's hardly surprising, then, that the history of communications technology is often pegged to a succession of wars. The popularization of still photography is commonly related to Mathew Brady's astonishing photographs of the American Civil War, which for the first time revealed the aftermath of battle not with flourishes of artistic embellishment but as the camera's unflinching eye captured it. In the opinion of the *The New York Times*, his photography worked a powerfully instructive effect, dispelling civilians' ordinarily cavalier attitude towards death. In an

1

editorial about Brady's gallery in New York, where a selection of his prints of 'The Dead of Antietam' was on display, the *Times* noted:

Crowds of people are constantly going up the stairs; follow them, and you find them bending over photographic views of that battlefield, taken immediately after the action. Of all objects of horror one would think the battle-field should stand pre-eminent, that it should bear away the palm of repulsiveness. But on the contrary, there is a terrible fascination about it that draws one near these pictures, and makes him loth to leave them. You will see hushed, reverend groups standing around these weird copies of carnage, bending down to look in the pale faces of the dead, chained by the strange spell that dwells in dead men's eyes.

Brady might not have laid fresh corpses at New Yorkers' doorsteps but he had 'done something very like it' (*The New York Times*, 1862b, 5).

Film-makers' attraction to combat has also been frequently noted, though film scholars rarely ascribe their pioneering efforts the same didactic force as Brady's photographs. Photographers strove to be taken seriously as artists and moral tutors. Early purveyors of moving images, on the other hand, were more content to see themselves primarily as entertainers whose productions drew on the same popular traditions as freak shows and vaudeville: amusements that made neither a requirement of literacy nor any pretence to ethical edification. Where Brady sought to create a somber photographic memorial to places and people ruined by war, film-makers' interest in conflict tended to be more prurient or opportunistic – lured by the thrillingly kinetic spectacle of *action* not the sobering sight of corpses incapable of motion. Cinematography required drama, and clashing human bodies or armed forces fit the bill perfectly. It's not coincidental that one of Thomas Edison's very first productions in 1894, 'Barroom Scene,' depicted men engaged in a drunken brawl.

In 1898, with commercial cinema just two years old, the Spanish–American war in Cuba provided film-makers with conflict on a much grander scale, posing the twin challenges of reducing epic events to screen-size dimensions and capturing distant action in intelligible ways – two enduring challenges for cinematographers of war. In the many short kinescopes that emerged from this brief war, much of what purported to be authentic battlefield footage was actually mocked up or recreated far from the scene. The Biograph company shot figures in uniform charging on horseback towards the camera in Tampa, Florida, for its film *Roosevelt's Rough Riders* (1898). Edison's team did much the same thing in West Orange, New Jersey, while the French pioneer of 'trick films' George Méliès exploded toy ships in an aquarium that he passed off as Havana harbor. 'The movies became so identified with war news,' observes media scholar Robert C. Allen, 'that Edison renamed his Projecting Kinetoscope the "Wargraph" for the duration of hostilities' (quoted by Castonguay, 2006, 99). With this militarizing move, he made a bid for cinema to be taken more seriously as a 'visual newspaper,' albeit one with the added benefit of showing bodies and objects in motion.

In later decades, Hollywood studios would repeatedly capitalize on war to enhance their patriotic credentials while expanding the domestic and international market for their offerings. What the film industry successfully essayed in World War I – selling movie tickets in record numbers while lending its star power to official recruitment efforts and bond sales drives – it reprised to yet greater effect in World War II. Amidst pervasive rationing, shortages, and conscription, Hollywood secured protected 'war industry' status for itself. As a result, it managed to churn out films at an almost undiminished rate throughout the war, emerging in 1945 as the world's preeminent purveyor of motion pictures. Studio bosses repaid the government by lending their most talented directors to the Army Signal Corps and other branches of the military to help produce instructional films and combat documentaries. With this felicitous wartime partnership in mind, the White House summoned Hollywood executives to Washington, DC, shortly after the attacks of September 11, 2001, to discuss the studios' contribution to the newly declared 'war on terror.' Several executives cited Frank Capra's famous *Why We Fight* series as a possible model. World War II, noted *New York Times* reporter Jim Rutenberg, was the 'era to which executives are now looking for guidance' (Rutenberg, 2001a).

For all its ability to distract, uplift, amuse and inform, cinema was less the pre-eminent medium of World War II than radio. Broadcasting had taken off in the interwar years, its growth encouraged by Europe's ascendant totalitarian states – Stalin's Soviet Union and Hitler's Third Reich – drawn to broadcasting's immediacy and accessibility. Radio programs created the illusion that the listener was being spoken to directly, though the potency of the 'wireless' was enhanced by collective participation in the act of listening. Like cinema, radio could be enjoyed irrespective of literacy. But unlike other more tangible media – newspapers required physical distribution; reels of film needed bulky projection equipment and screens – wireless transmissions could be picked up on cheaply manufactured receivers, traveling through space unimpeded by state borders. All the major combatant powers involved in World War II made extensive use of radio to reach domestic, neutral and enemy audiences. Some of these networks, like the BBC World Service and Voice of America, remain in existence today.

Radio's invisibility also made it the perfect medium for *covert* attempts to corrode enemy morale since broadcasts could, and did, easily mystify their creators' identities and whereabouts. Trying to encourage surrenders on the opposite side, Allied propagandists thus broadcast to *Wehrmacht* soldiers in the guise of disgruntled German officers – a ploy the Axis powers in turn employed to corrode Allied troops' morale. Whether these stratagems actually caused many enemy personnel to break ranks remains a moot point amongst historians, uncertain as to how much credence we should place in what POWs tell their captors about their reasons for giving up (Doherty, 2000; Howe, 1982; Lerner, 1971). But the allure of radio to psychological warfare operatives, 'pyswarriors,' has remained undiminished.

At home, however, the decades following World War II indisputably belonged to television. Temporarily interrupted by the war, television's meteoric rise was facilitated by postwar America's growing affluence. Over the course of the 1950s, television ownership increased rapidly in the United States, trailed by Britain and other European countries whose recovery from the war was slower, shallower, and complicated by messy imperial divestments. By the mid-1960s, a majority of Americans owned at least one television and had come to rely on it as their principal source of news. That this development coincided with the Vietnam War ensured that television would forever be associated with that conflict – and, in many influential quarters, blamed for America's defeat. Since, stalemate in Korea aside, the United States had never lost a war before, it stood to reason that its failure to prevail against a third world peasant military must be tied to a new and unwelcome war zone presence: that of television cameras. Television news, its critics lamented, had nightly depicted war in all its blood-stained viciousness, ignoring more optimistic portents. Poisoned against the war by television's slow drip of negativity and its increasing emphasis on atrocity, Americans withdrew their support. And without it, the war couldn't be prosecuted to a successful conclusion.

Or so the story goes. The fact that it happens to be unsupported by historical evidence hasn't prevented this received wisdom from coloring attitudes towards television news in many subsequent wars – a view of television's potency shared by such unlikely bedfellows as Saddam Hussein and George Bush, Osama bin Laden and Margaret Thatcher. All of them, at different moments, have espoused the notion that western civilians, lacking any stomach for casualties, will recoil from the sight of human suffering and demand a precipitate end to war. To secure victory it's thus necessary either to curtail images of damaged and dead bodies or to give them the widest possible exposure, depending on one's strategic vantage-point. In the twenty-first century, this battle over images has expanded beyond television onto the internet: today's pre-eminent site for the display and exchange of visual imagery. Echoing Vietnam's description as the first 'television war,' the Iraq war (begun in 2003) has been dubbed the first 'YouTube war.'

Selling war

War sells. This truism is well worn, and given the long history of media thraldom to war its wisdom might seem indisputable. One British observer noted after World War I that 'War not only creates a supply of news but a demand for it. So deep-rooted is the fascination in war and all things appertaining to it that ... a paper has only to be able to put up on its placard "A Great Battle" for its sales to mount up' (Lasswell, 1927, 192). The sentiment, if not its precise wording, wouldn't be out of place coming from the lips of a Ted Turner or a Rupert Murdoch. The Gulf War of 1991 reaffirmed the pertinence of an adage coined in 1919. Twenty of America's twenty-five biggest selling newspapers enjoyed circulation gains during that conflict, while Turner's Cable News Network (CNN) experienced a ten-fold increase in audience size (Hallin and Gitlin, 1994, 149).

But like almost every generalization concerning media and war, the opposite of this oft-repeated proposition is also true. That's to say, war doesn't *always* sell and may sometimes be a major turn-off – as producers of war-themed films in the United States have recurrently found in recent years. Although wartime's initial flurry of agitation often generates additional newspaper sales and boosts TV audiences, this craving for words and images of war tends to diminish over time. The degree to which a 'war sells' depends on whose war it is, how long it lasts, and how great a sense of popular involvement it generates. 'Other people's wars' may not grip the attention of distant media, which often presume a lack of interest on their audience's part in remote conflict. The words of Evelyn Waugh's fictional press baron Lord Copper, proprietor of *The Beast*, still resonate: 'The British public has no interest in a war which drags on indecisively. A few sharp victories, some conspicuous acts of personal bravery on the Patriot side, and a colourful entry into the capital. That is *The*

Beast policy for the war' (1943, 42). The phenomenon of flagging interest isn't restricted to others' wars in faraway places. 'Our' wars too may
be subject to a similar law of diminishing returns. The 1991 Gulf War
provided dramatic action by the side with the suggestively named Patriot
missiles, not to mention a colorful entry into Kuwait city, spearheaded by
journalists in advance of the UN Coalition's advancing forces. But by day
three of the ground campaign journalists started to complain that the war
was 'dragging on,' just as they did in April 2003, when the US military's
vaunted 'shock and awe' bombing of Baghdad failed to reduce Iraq to
instant submission.

If this impatience for victory is true of short campaigns, the tendency
for media to disengage is more pronounced during long wars of uncertain
outcome. The size of the US press corps in Vietnam shrank dramatically
after President Nixon announced that the United States was on its way out
– even though ending the war took several years to accomplish. Nixon's
policy of 'Vietnamization' was in fact accompanied by a major escalation
of the war into Laos and Cambodia. Where there had been 637 accredited
correspondents in Vietnam during the 1968 Tet offensive, by 1972 there
were 295, and in 1974 – one year after US troops pulled out, and one year
before Saigon 'fell' to the North – just five foreign reporters remained
(Rid, 2007, 56). To take a more recent example, the war in Afghanistan
was the most covered news story on the CBS, ABC and NBC networks in
2001. Two years later, although the fighting was far from over,
Afghanistan received just 80 minutes of coverage from the three
networks combined over the course of twelve months – 20 per cent of the
attention this story had claimed in 2002 (Sweeney, 2006, 219–20). If war
is a saleable commodity, then, it suffers the same fate as other products
whose market value rises and falls.

What broader observations, other than to beware generalizations,
might we derive from the inconsistency with which war sells? First, we
might note that war has to *be* sold – not just by its news media purveyors
but, in the first instance, by its architects. Since the resort to armed force
doesn't simply sell itself, political leaders generally take great pains to
generate support for waging war, enlisting mass communications media
to help bolster the case. Ruling elites do so regardless of whether or not
the citizens being sold on war are simultaneously being called upon to
fight it, and irrespective of whether or not they can vote the leaders of an
unpopular war out of office. In other words, while they may take more
heavyhanded steps to quash dissent, autocratic regimes court popular
consent just as much as parliamentary democracies. Making war is, after
all, the most consequential activity a state can embark on beyond its

borders. War is liable to be costly in terms of 'blood and treasure,' and so potentially squandrous of political capital too. The recourse to force is also, under many circumstances other than self-defense, *illegal*. To launch an aggressive war is to invite international condemnation and risk prosecution should the gamble fail. (It's worth recalling that the principal charge against the Nazi defendants at Nuremberg in 1945 wasn't genocide but planning, initiating and waging a war of aggression that constituted a 'crime against peace.')

Since statesmen and stateswomen invariably seek to justify their actions in the loftiest terms, every war – if we credit their pronouncements – is defensive or fought for the noblest and most altruistic of reasons. For similarly self-serving reasons, liberal states often resist acknowledging that they engage in censorship or propaganda in wartime, preferring to suggest that the enemy alone seeks to manipulate opinion. Where Nazi Germany boasted a well-staffed Ministry of Popular Enlightenment and Propaganda under Josef Goebbels' directorship, the United Kingdom established a Ministry of Information and Washington an Office of Facts and Figures that later became an Office of War Information during World War II – agencies hastily demobilized in 1945. More recently, British and US policy-makers have coined a variety of euphemisms, such as 'security review,' to describe the oversight that journalists' stories and images are subjected to in war zones prior to transmission.

We shouldn't be misled by anodyne phrases, however. Over the past 100 years, 'opinion management' has become a central preoccupation of states at war, with civil and military leaders devoting ever more attention to the task. Their efforts to shape popular perceptions and attitudes encompass both slanting and suppressing news. Censorship, the active withholding of information, constitutes the state's most blunt implement, and as such one to be wielded with discretion. More subtle forms of influencing what's now referred to as the 'information environment' are generally preferred. For political elites, setting the news-agenda and framing events in favorable terms, 'spinning' in other words, is more desirable than striking a blue pencil through undesirable material, demanding post facto corrections, or attempting to snatch back newspapers that have already been distributed. But though it's commonly claimed that policy-makers have become ever more sophisticated practitioners of spin, hiring professional public relations experts to help promote particularly troublesome policies (of which war is undoubtedly one), outright suppression of proscribed material is far from a thing of the past. Hence, for example, the Bush administration's ban on photography of coffins returning to the United States with the bodies of soldiers killed in action in Iraq and Afghanistan. This prohibition remained in place from 2003 to 2009, uncannily echoing the Kremlin's insistence that dead soldiers returning from Afghanistan during its war there from 1979 to 1988 be sealed in zinc coffins, bolted shut to prevent images of Red Army fatalities gaining public currency (Alexievich, 1992).

As these bans suggest, states at war are acutely concerned to shield their publics from war's single most irrevocable fact: namely, that people die – not just on the other side, but our people, 'us.' How death and injury are represented forms an enduring, sometimes overriding, concern of wartime leaders. As a result, they tend to scrutinize visual media (photography, film, television or the internet) with particular vigilance, seeking to screen out material considered likely to agitate anti-war sentiment. But as we'll see, this generalization isn't an unwavering constant any more than the dictum 'war sells.' On occasion, leaders choose openly to acknowledge and valorize their soldiers' wartime death with a view to galvanizing renewed public support for a flagging war effort. As historian George Roeder has observed of World War II, US 'officials perceived pictures of the American dead as extremely hazardous material during the war's early years. Before it ended they considered them the most powerful weapons in their motivational arsenal' (1993, 25).

The larger point is that states take uncommonly invasive measures to shape what can be said and shown of war, armed with a battery of justifications. Sensitive information must be kept from enemy hands; bereaved relatives must be protected from the sight of their loved ones in bodily anguish or as corpses; 'morale' must be maintained – on the home front as at the frontline. And while these represent genuine concerns for those in the business of winning a war, such rationalizations are also liable to abuse. The 'fog of war' hints at more than the atmospheric and perceptual murk that envelops battlefields. It also alludes to the haze of deception that commonly masks why war is waged and how it is fought. As Arthur Ponsonby presciently observed in 1928: 'War is fought in this fog of falsehood, a great deal of it uncovered and accepted as truth. The fog arises from fear and is fed by panic. Any attempt to doubt or deny even the most fantastic story has to be condemned at once as unpatriotic, if not traitorous' (1928, 26).

According to liberal theory, it's the media's job to pierce this blanket of obfuscation and bring clarity to the confusion and chaos of war. At least, that's what the organs of opinion-formation *ought* to do if they're to discharge their pivotal role in sustaining democracy. By subjecting the words and deeds of policy-makers to critical scrutiny, news organizations hold the powerful to account. Tenacious reporters expose lies as falsities, cutting exaggerated boasts down to size. They insist elected representatives make good on their electoral pledges and spend taxpayers' money wisely. In this watchdog role, the media constitute what's often referred to as a 'fourth estate:' a check on executive power. Futhermore, by keeping citizens informed, news media stimulate the informed debate without which deliberative democracy would degenerate into partisan mudslinging – an endless litany of 'he said' versus 'she said,' with no one outside this loop sufficiently well-informed to adjudicate the veracity of either claim.

That, at any rate, is the theory. Wartime invariably prompts fresh reminders to media personnel – often by concerned colleagues – of their critical function in keeping the wheels of democracy spinning by satisfying the public's 'right to know.' Scholars are also given to issuing pleas for informed debate and vigorous watch-dogging. Indeed, much of the literature on 'war and the media' takes these assumptions as its normative foundation. Yet in wartime we're apt to see how starkly media practice contradicts liberal theory. Far from subjecting patriotic jingoism to withering critique, skewering xenophobic or outright racist representations of foreign antagonists and challenging whether it's necessary to tackle an international dispute with guns and bombs, media outlets often appear positively eager to act as war's cheerleaders. Just when deliberative democracy cries out for vigorous debate, media may seem at their most supine and credulous.

Why is this? That question forms a core concern of this book and it has multiple answers. But one fundamental issue at the heart of the discrepancy between theory and practice is that, while 'watchdog' notions of the press ascribe it a public service role, most media in North America, in much of Europe and elsewhere are *commercial* enterprises, while ostensibly public broadcasters are subject to mounting market pressures. In other words, they exist in order to generate profit. Not only, then, do news-media face pressure from policy-makers looking for favorable coverage, they must also satisfy advertisers looking for high circulation figures, ratings or hits. Profitability thus depends on providing consumers with a product that delivers their desired quotient of information, opinion and entertainment. Media organizations must continually appraise the vagaries of shifting public moods, responding to (but surely also shaping) what their customers might want. These revenue-raising imperatives tend to constrain the range of opinion offered by large circulation newspapers, radio and television networks.

If news-making is a cutthroat business at the best of times, war generates additional pressures from above, below and within, forcing questions of loyalty to the fore. Objectivity, impartiality and balance between alternative viewpoints may be ideals that at least some news organizations customarily strive for. But when a nation is at war these professional goals can appear – to commercial sponsors, readers, viewers, and policy elites – suspect at best, and treasonous at worst. Freedom of expression in wartime is a perilous proposition. Where should the boundaries around dissent be drawn? Should balance extend to depicting the war from the opponent's point of view – from the vantage point of 'their' civilians as well as 'our' soldiers? Is there a place for public expression of anti-war sentiment or does anything less than unanimous conviction jeopardize victory by demoralizing the troops and heartening the enemy?

The obvious rejoinder to arguments against free speech in wartime is that they assume the war in question is just: that it's being fought for unanimously agreed (and laudible) goals, and that it's prosecuted in a way that employs force proportionate to the ends at stake, without gratuitous or excessive violence. Arguably, though, there never was and never will be a war in which these are not legitimate issues for public deliberation.

Yet the voices calling for suppression of dissentient opinion and disruptive information generally prevail. After all, they have one especially powerful weapon in their arsenal: the cudgel of patriotism. In wartime, whether or not lawmakers have proscribed certain forms of utterance as seditious, self-proclaimed vigilantes often spring into action to stigmatize – and silence – those whose views they deem injurious to the war effort, and hence 'disloyal.' Members of the public duly rebuke the media when they fail to display sufficient support for 'our troops,' question the wisdom of strategy or appear too sympathetic to the plight of an enemy population. Accusations of disloyalty are also a form of discipline that media exert over one another. BBC reporter John Simpson, for example, noted during the 1991 Gulf War that many of his colleagues were 'loudly demanding a curb on free reporting,' in headlines that echoed the Nazi '*Volkischer Beobachter*, sniffing out traitors' (1991a, 12). This book is called *The Media at War* – rather than, say, *The Media in Wartime* – precisely to signal the *intranecine* conflict that wartime produces within and between media organizations themselves.

To sum up, war poses special challenges – as well as opportunities – for media: logistical, financial and political. It is at once costly and contentious to cover. States require allegiance in the name of 'national security' that may mask narrow political interest; militaries demand 'security-mindedness' that often seems tantamount to a blanket ban on criticism; and publics push for both more and less exposure of battlefield conditions, and greater or lesser discussion of war's objectives, modus operandi, and likely outcomes. With war constituting a state of emergency, peacetime rules appear suspended while new terms of engagement apply. One reason to study media in wartime is precisely to scrutinize these pressures and contradictions: where they come from, and how different individuals and organizations negotiate them.

But wartime, itself an elastic category, isn't *completely* aberrant. While some wars entail a wholesale reorientation of society and industry to military production, others do not, just as some impinge deeply on civilian consciousness while others pass relatively unheeded. Wartime in the United States in 1918, for example, had a very different character than wartime in 1968 or in 2008.

It's also worth noting that much news- and image-making about war emerges far from the scene of conflict. Given the distinctive niche that war correspondents occupy in popular culture, to say nothing of journalistic lore, we might imagine that war reporting is their exclusive domain. But in many cases the production of news about foreign relations closely corresponds to domestic peacetime routine – assembled from press handouts, news briefings, and off-the-record conversations with elite sources close to the policy-making process. For example, of 414 stories on Iraq broadcast on NBC, ABC and CBS from September 2002 to February 2003, all but 34 originated at the White House, Pentagon and State Department (Cunningham, 2003, 26). To study media in wartime is thus also to contemplate the everyday processes by which we come to know the world second-hand thanks to certain information having acquired the status of 'news.'

Overview

The Media at War offers an interpretive overview of a huge, disparate and ever-expanding field. It draws on scholarship in a range of disciplines – international politics, history, communications and cultural studies – as well as media sources themselves. Going back to read old newspapers or watch the films of an earlier historical moment invariably adds nuance to any blanket generalizations one might make about 'the media,' and is increasingly easy to do as ever more content is digitized and posted or streamed online.

A book of this length is necessarily more synoptic than exhaustive in its coverage. It can't possibly deal with *all* wars since the birth of mass media, nor does it pretend to. Although this study ranges as far afield as Rwanda, Nazi Germany, the Soviet Union and postwar Japan, the United

States and United Kingdom loom large throughout. These happen to be the two states with which the author is personally most familiar. More importantly, though, Britain and America have been frequent wartime allies, and even when they have not fought alongside one another – as, for example, in Vietnam – their militaries have consistently traded operational wisdom and informed one another's thinking on matters of 'media management.' Thus the British Ministry of Defence (MOD) fashioned its restrictive press plan for the 1983 Falklands campaign in the firm belief that Vietnam had been lost on and by television. The MOD's self-proclaimed victory over the press during that shortlived war in the South Atlantic was one that the Pentagon, in turn, tried to emulate in Grenada, Panama and the Gulf War of 1991.

The larger objective of this book is to stimulate reflection on how media operate at distinct moments in the life-cycle of wars of different durations and degrees of intensity: variously serving as midwife, mythologizer and memorialist, among many other things. To appreciate the media's complex investments in war, we must contemplate not only wartime 'proper' but how media approach the onset of hostilities and how they deal with wars past – since the work of interpretation and re-examination is never done. At times of crisis, historical conflicts are often disinterred and dusted down with particular alacrity by those seeking to press past wars into present-day service: a source of inspiration, analogy or warning. With this end in mind, the chapters of *The Media at War* are arranged not in strictly chronological sequence but in a rather more circular and thematic fashion. In some cases, particularly with regard to the 'war on terror' – treated here as both an ideological formation and as discrete wars in Afghanistan and Iraq – discussion is split between more than one chapter.

Chapter 1, Mobilization, considers the role that media play in marshaling popular energies for war and in framing the political issues at stake such that force comes to appear the most desirable method of resolution. Addressing a central question of this book – why mass media commonly seem far more enamored of war than of its alternatives – this chapter offers illustrations drawn from Rwanda in 1994, the United States prior to its war with Spain over Cuba in 1898, the Gulf War of 1991, and the British and American media's treatment of the Weapons of Mass Destruction claims prior to the launch of 'Operation Iraqi Freedom' in 2003. To explain the media's supportive posture, the analysis concentrates on the close relationship between news-making and elite sources, exploring how journalists practice 'objectivity' in a way that often seems to guarantee coverage that's far from neutral.

The next chapter, Total War, traces the development of techniques of 'opinion management' from World War I to II. In these wars of total mobilization, political leaders sought to shape popular attitudes – at home and overseas – to an unprecedented degree, seeking to harness new media like cinema and the radio to war-winning ends. In part, the story here is of how states developed extensive machineries of control: some heavy-handed and dictatorial in their prescriptiveness, others resting on the principle of 'voluntarism' but no less pervasive for that. Yet the experience of total war wasn't simply one of *repression*. Not only did many news and entertainment outlets relish their role as flagwaver for the national cause – a feature of both sides in both wars – for some, wartime also effected a paradoxical liberalization of expression. Forcing the pace of social change, total war generated contradictory effects in its unsuppressible magnitude.

Chapter 3, Television Wars, focuses on the Vietnam War and its aftermath. If World War II provided British and US policy-makers with an idealized image of press–state cooperation in wartime, Vietnam supplied its antithesis: a warning of what could go wrong if 'uncensored' media were left to their own devices. Underpinned by a set of assumptions about the power of television, this interpretation of America's loss in Vietnam quickly solidified into unshakeable commonsense, informing transatlantic military-media doctrine for a good two decades after US troops left Vietnam in 1973. Subsequent conflicts in the Falkland (or Malvinas) Islands, Grenada, Panama and the Persian Gulf saw the British Ministry of Defence and the Pentagon make concerted efforts to limit television cameras' access to the scene of combat. But, as this chapter argues, the conventional wisdom is highly selective in what it remembers about US media performance in Vietnam, what it fails to recall about official 'spin,' and unconvincing in its estimation of pictures' pacifistic power.

Chapter 4, Other People's Wars, extends the analysis of television news imagery into the 1990s, focusing on debates over the so-called 'CNN effect.' Soon after the conclusion of the Gulf War in 1991 – as the Cold War ended and pundits began to interrogate the ensuing 'new world disorder' – CNN and other purveyors of real-time news footage found themselves in the spotlight. In the opinion of some, such networks were a globe-shrinking force to be welcomed: agents of a cosmopolitan, postnational consciousness based on wider exposure to the predicament of fellow humans in far-off places. Others, however, saw CNN as a threat to rational policy-making. These critics charged CNN's rolling 24-hour coverage of distant crises with shaking up priorities, forcing instant responses, and animating emotional mood-swings among viewers. This chapter tests the validity of various hypotheses about 'real-time' TV in a number of post-Cold War crises: Kurdistan, Former Yugoslavia, Somalia and Rwanda. Taking issue with CNN's admirers and detractors alike, it concludes by examining how some distant conflicts become constituted as global crises while others do not, and how over the course of the 1990s militarized 'intervention' came to be associated with humanitarianism – endowed with an unexamined aura of virtue.

Wars on Terror, the fifth chapter, takes us back to the late nineteenth century and then forward to the present to explore how and why terrorism came to be understood primarily as attention-seeking behavior and hence a phenomenon to be combated with psychological weapons. Terrorists are now routinely viewed as skillful 'event promoters' who gain 'disruptive access' by 'somehow crashing through the ongoing arrangements of news-making, generating surprise, shock, or some more violent form of "trouble"' (Molotch and Lester, 1997, 201–2). Many critics have posited a 'symbiosis' between publicity-hungry terrorists and the sensation-driven media, who can't help but give the former what they want. This chapter challenges that orthodoxy, suggesting that states are far less at a disadvantage in their counterterrorist campaigns than they routinely paint themselves. Their central predicament isn't so much media complicity with terrorists' agendas as the violence of official initiatives to win 'hearts and minds' – psychological campaigns that often become brutally coercive in targeting obdurate bodies that refuse to submit.

The final chapter, War in the Digital Age, considers elements of both continuity and change in the mediated representation of the wars in Afghanistan and Iraq. Here, the focus is largely on US official efforts to control what appears to be an increasingly uncontrollable 'information environment' – given the rapid proliferation of new digital media in their multiple manifestations and the unmistakable salience of Arabic-language media in the Middle East and beyond. For the Pentagon, the challenge now lies not just in shaping what commercial media show and say of war but in regulating American soldiers' capacity to act as alternative chroniclers of combat, whether by sharing digital images, creating blogs or uploading video clips to YouTube. Although much agonized discussion in recent years has focused on the spread of 'jihadi' websites, many of the most disruptive moments for Washington during these wars have been occasioned by pictures taken by military or defense industry personnel – the Abu Ghraib photographs forming a particular case in point.

Declarations of the state's incapacity to control the media appear premature. After all, control has never been a straightforward function of the physical capability to block information and censor uncongenial viewpoints. Rather, as *The Media at War* strives to show, states exercise power over media through multiple forms of persuasion, cooptation and coercion that do not look set to wither away. But, as these increasingly unpopular wars suggest, policy elites don't always succeed in molding opinion in the desired direction for the desired duration.

Chapter 1

Mobilization: The Media Before War

When Senator Hiram Johnson observed in 1917 that 'the first casualty when war comes is truth,' he expressed a sentiment that was already familiar. As early 1758 the English essayist and lexicographer Samuel Johnson had noted 'among the calamities of war ... the diminution of the love of truth, by the falsehoods which interest dictates and credulity encourages.' Replete with lies, half-truths and obfuscations, two and a half centuries of war have amply attested the wisdom of Johnson's judgement.

Less commonly remarked, however, is that dissimulation tends to begin well before the first exchange of fire. War is not, after all, a malign act of fate – an unexpected volcano eruption or a tornado that spirals up from nowhere. Rather, wars 'begin in the minds of men,' as the UNESCO preamble puts it. Since organized violence requires planning, civilians' psychological mobilization is as necessary a precursor to war-waging as logistical preparedness. Media organizations play a crucial role in this process as conduits through which the case for taking up arms is advanced and sometimes contested. If we're to understand how media behave in wartime, first we must examine their contribution to processes of militarization.

To do so, this chapter ranges broadly from the United States's confrontation with imperial Spain over Cuba in 1898 to Rwanda in the 1990s and the contemporary wars in Afghanistan and Iraq. Even a cursory survey of this field makes one point very clear. Rarely (if ever) does a combatant state or warring faction announce bluntly that its recourse to violence is motivated by greed, vengeance or prejudice. The use of force may indeed be directed towards securing territory, expropriating resources, reaping profits, punishing foes or annihilating despised populations. But war-makers prefer to present their cause as defensive, just and unavoidable: an overdue rectification of past wrongs and/or a pre-emptive aversion of future assault by an enemy whose malignance is clear but whose inferiority will ensure rapid defeat. In short, every war is just and victory is always certain – if combatants' claims are to be believed.

A second point also soon becomes evident: that journalists often become de facto, if not more ardent, champions of military solutions to perceived threats, lending support to the justifications for force offered by policy-makers and other war-minded parties. This is not to say that media organizations *never* endorse alternative policy options in times of international or internecine tension. But history provides comparatively few examples of prominent newspapers, radio stations or television companies adopting firm anti-war positions in the face of regimes that appear eager for combat. Ironically, perhaps, since we have come to think of World War II as the 'good war' that commanded universal support in the Allied nations, the case for entering that conflict was vigorously protested by many elements of the press in the United States – an isolationism gradually worn down by force of circumstance, FDR's persuasive efforts, and the Japanese attack on Pearl Harbor (Casey, 2001). But that instance of concerted nay-saying to war is a historical rarity. Rather than dissecting aggressors' justifications for employing force, media organizations often fan the flames of animosity. As the first half of this chapter shows, journalists have long played – and continue to play – a prominent part in the process of rallying opinion for war, whether by heightening a sense of imminent threat, animating outrage against barbarous violators of civilized morality or constraining debate over non-military responses to insecurity.

If we understand the press, at least in liberal polities, as a 'fourth estate' whose function is to check abuses of power by the executive organs of state, journalists' readiness for mobilization requires explanation. Surely news organizations should play a particularly vigilant role in scrutinizing policy-makers' rationales for deploying force and in probing the intelligence on which claims of endangerment rest? Never is a free press more critical than during the prelude to war since, as political scientist William Dorman proposes, '[t]here is no action of the state that can have a more immediate or dramatic impact on the lives of its citizens than the use of military force against an external foe.' Moreover, if the recourse to war isn't debated *before* hostilities commence, the condition of being at war will likely foreclose debate thereafter. 'The thoughtful consideration of alternatives simply is unacceptable, suffocated as it were by nationalism and patriotism, not to mention fear and rage.' This being so, 'the only meaningful time to debate the need for war is before one begins' (Dorman, 2006, 11).

Why, then, do media often appear to fall short in playing their watch-dog role at such crucial moments? The second half of this chapter addresses that question, examining the variety of reasons why media seem more often to 'manufacture consent' for war than to foment dissension.

Inciting violence: slaughter as 'self-defense'

In December 2003, the International Criminal Tribunal for Rwanda made history when it found Ferdinand Nahimana, Jean-Bosco Barayagwiza and Hassan Ngeze guilty of 'genocide, direct and public incitement to commit genocide, conspiracy to commit genocide and crimes against humanity (persecution and extermination)' (Thompson, 2007, 9). The three convicted Rwandans had not personally participated in the slaughter that swept across Rwanda in April and May 1994, leaving between 800,000 and 1 million people dead. Rather, as directors of *Radio Television Libre des Milles Collines* (RTLM) and editor of the extremist newspaper *Kangura*, they had taken a vocal lead in whipping Rwanda's Hutu population into a state of homicidal fury against their Tutsi neighbors, turning the media into a 'tool of genocide' (Destexhe, 1995, 29). Journalists, as this guilty verdict made clear, could also be war criminals.

Largely unaware that what they saw was the result of mass media advocacy of mass killing, the western reporters who flooded into Rwanda in May 1994 encountered scenes of raw carnage. Churches filled with dozens of corpses and thousands of mutilated bodies strewn by roadsides and clogging the rivers bore witness to a blood-thirsty frenzy of killing. There was nothing clinical or industrialized about this process: no gas chambers or firing squads. Men, women and children had been hacked at with *pangas* – curved blades that made messy, laborious work of killing. Perpetrators had accosted victims in the most brutally intimate way, leaving journalists to explain how mass slaughter had occurred at the tail-end of the twentieth century when Europeans and North Americans, in exultant post-Cold War mood, liked to imagine that glob-alization would steadily float all boats on a rising tide of peace and pros-perity (Hilsum, 1995; F. Keane, 1996).

Many reporters reached for what seemed the most obvious answer: that Rwanda's genocide was a particularly vicious expression of African atavism, of bloodletting that has stained the 'dark continent' since time immemorial, with ancient hatred between two ethnic groups suddenly flaring into an orgy of killing. Tribalism apparently offered the key to events in Rwanda. But lazy ethnocentrism of this kind offers no clue as to *why* Rwanda's Hutu population hated the Tutsis with such murderous passion. If these two groups really had bristled with mutual loathing since the dawn of time, what triggered a rash of killing in April 1994 rather than years earlier? Surely something more specific than eternal animosity must explain how Hutu, having lived side-by-side with Tutsi, turned on their neighbors, hacking at them with sharpened knives before tossing their bodies aside (Carruthers, 2004).

Any more nuanced explanation of Rwanda's genocide must reckon with the role of mass media. Some months later, reporters and human rights activists began to document what had already been apparent to international monitors attuned to Rwandan radio broadcasts for some years. Namely, that a particular clique around President Juvénal Habyarimana was deliberately urging Hutus to take up arms against both Tutsis and those Hutu who favored power-sharing political arrangements. Far from representing a spontaneous eruption of pent-up hatred, the killings were planned by an elite that, fearing the erosion of its power, saw a chance to reconsolidate its position through manipulating current tensions and historic inequities, and deliberately set out to organize a campaign of extermination through local militia, the *Interahamwe*. These Hutu death-squads were not only galvanized by Radio Rwanda and RTLM broadcasts but actively instructed on why they must kill, when to do so, and whom to attack (Des Forges, 2007, 48–50).

In a country isolated from foreign media, RTLM – the mouthpiece of 'Hutu Power' extremists – cultivated a sense of imminent threat to Rwanda's majority population from Tutsis who were systematically represented as 'outsiders,' and dehumanized as 'dogs,' 'snakes,' and 'cockroaches' (*inyenzi*) to be stamped upon. According to RTLM broadcasters, Tutsi invaders planned to turn Hutus into 'beasts of the field' (F. Keane, 1996, 8–9; Chrétien, 2007, 56). To forestall calamity, Tutsis must be dispatched to Ethiopia, whence they allegedly came, via the Nayabarongo River (African Rights, 1994, 71). With scant euphemistic disguise, RTLM presenters urged Hutus to kill their Tutsi neighbors, dumping their bodies in the river that feeds into Lake Victoria. This duly occurred after President Habyarimana's helicopter was shot down in April 1994 and the signal for killing to commence was transmitted.

Rwanda offers a particularly stark case of media incitement. But if this instance seems unique, it's worth recalling that Rwandan broadcasters plied a set of themes commonly found in mobilization propaganda – a genre in which aggressors invariably cast themselves as victims. Architects of Rwanda's campaign of annihilation represented the *panga* as an instrument of self-defense. Playing on communal grievances cultivated under

Belgian colonial rule, RTML broadcasters informed audiences that Tutsi rebels, rushing in from neighboring Uganda, sought to pauperize, displace and subjugate Rwanda's majority population. The *inyenzi*, warned one broadcast, were 'going to exterminate you [Hutu] until they are the only ones left in the country so that they can keep for a thousand years the power that their fathers had kept for four hundred years' (Des Forges, 2007, 48). Taking up arms against these invaders – people who had come only belatedly into the Great Lakes region from north Africa, Hutu propagandists asserted – represented the only way to stave off looming catastrophe. 'Strike them before they strike you' was RTML's blunt and relentless message. Once the killing began, the station broadcast repeated appeals to its listeners to keep up their 'work' of uprooting the Tutsis, not resting until the job was done. With rousing music to keep their spirits aloft, listeners were prodded to 'clear the bushes,' 'separate the grass from the millet' and 'pull out the poison ivy together with its roots' (Li, 2007, 96; Mironko, 2007, 133).

To historians of propaganda, this sounds eerily familiar. In Hitler's Third Reich, state-controlled newspapers, radio stations and feature films consistently depicted Jews as Aryan Germans' eternal enemies: a rapacious, vengeful race apart, hell-bent on world domination. The National Socialists' own exterminationist goals were thus ascribed to the targets of their genocidal program. In this endlessly reiterated construction, *Germans* were the victims and Jews the perpetrators. Without directly informing audiences of what fate awaited Jews in the camps, Nazi propaganda presented the SS as agents of 'purification' whose job it was to isolate and quarantine a lethal threat to the Aryan body politic. By implication, whatever steps proved necessary to eradicate such a noxious pathogen were wholly necessary acts of national prophylaxis. To lend emotional resonance to this paranoid projection, Nazi opinion-formers invoked a historical sense of grievance, attributing German ruination in World War I to Jewish financiers, while peddling crude caricatures of the Jew as leering, slovenly, hook-nosed Other – the antithesis of the idealized blue-eyed Aryan citizen (Herf, 2006).

Hutu supremacists employed similar tropes and stereotypes. They too summoned history to substantiate visions of persecution. Under Belgian colonial rule, Hutus had been marginalized and Tutsis elevated to positions of greater privilege – set apart by their ostensibly lighter skin tone and sharper features. When Hutu ideologues announced that the Tutsi RFP sought to dispossess Rwanda's dominant ethnic group, returning it to subordinate status familiar from the days of colonialism, they struck a resonant chord. This vision of ineradicable difference between two clearly distinct peoples was itself an imperialist construction, deliberately fostered by Belgian administrators and anthropologists who took Tutsis to be Nilotic migrants to central Africa, arriving centuries after the indigenous Hutu. Long-standing patterns of intermarriage made a nonsense of this myth of racial purity, but it nevertheless served imperial purposes to treat the Hutus as an ethnic group whose history was separate, separable and subordinate to that of the Tutsis – 'proto-European pastoralists' whom the Belgians sought to co-opt (Destexhe, 1995, 36). The higher status and greater wealth Tutsis subsequently achieved left a bitter after-taste sharpened by Hutu agitators, whose propaganda attempted to elevate a 'historical outcome into a primordial difference' (Destexhe, 1995, 28; Mamdani, 1996, 6).

'Killing is very discouraging if you must decide to do so yourself,' observed one participant, reflecting back on the genocide, 'but if you are obeying orders from the authorities, if you are adequately conditioned, if you feel pushed and pulled, if you see that the carnage will have absolutely no adverse effects in future, you feel comforted and revitalized. You do it without shame' (quoted by Chrétien, 2007, 55). This, then, was the work of radio in Rwanda during the period from 1990–4. In conjunction with a power-seeking faction, it worked to ease social prohibitions that surround killing by making slaughter seem as necessary and neutral as stamping on roaches or pulling out weeds – the routine business of good housekeeping. Radio's 'conditioning' and reassurance clearly proved effective. Even by a conservative estimate, 'over three-quarters of the entire population registered as Tutsi were systematically killed in just over 100 days' (Caplan, 2007, 28).

Animating outrage: the galvanizing role of atrocities

During the early 1990s in Rwanda, as in the Third Reich some 60 years earlier, media prompted citizens to embrace purgative violence as a necessary form of self-defense from enemies within and without bent on tormenting, driving out or annihilating blameless Hutus or Germans. In both cases, architects of violence conjured a fearful imagined future. Whether projected ahead or unfolding in the present, atrocities have long assumed a commanding position in pre-war mobilization efforts.

Even a cursory examination of US media in periods preceding direct American engagement in war yields numerous examples of how atrocities – some real, some embellished, some invented outright – have been artfully publicized to bestir public opinion. One of the most widely cited examples stems from press baron William Randolph Hearst's efforts to instigate a war between the United States and Spain in the late 1890s. When Frederic Remington (an artist working for Hearst) cabled from Cuba in 1897, 'there will be no war,' the press baron is apocryphally said to have cabled back: 'You furnish the pictures and I'll furnish the war.' To that end, Hearst's newspapers spent months crusading against the cruelty of Spanish rule over Cuba, hoping to incite an American intervention.

Editorials thundered against 'Butcher' Weyler, a Spanish general depicted as the brave Cuban nationalists' most villainous oppressor. But the *pièce de resistance* of Hearst's campaign was the story of 17-year-old Evangelina Cosio y Cisneros, the beautiful daughter of a jailed Cuban patriot. Languishing in Havana's notorious house of correction for women of ill repute, this 'Cuban Joan of Arc' had been imprisoned without trial by Weyler for her alleged role in an assassination plot against a colonel whose advances Evangelina had rebuffed. Virtuous, virginal and imperiled, Senorita Cisneros made a beguiling emblem of Cuban patriotism. In what one historian later termed a 'paroxysm of typography,' Hearst determined to rescue the girl whose plight symbolized the whole island's unhappy fate. If Hearst could rescue this lustrous 'rose of Cuba,' then US forces must rescue the islanders at large – and Americans should accordingly press for action (Millis, 1931, 84; Brown, 1967, 93–102).

Hearst's *New York Journal* duly urged 'the women of America' to lobby 'Butcher' Weyler, Pope Leo XIII, the Spanish minister in Washington, and Spain's Queen Regent on Evangelina's behalf. Many prominent female figures responded, while thousands more added their names to a petition for Cisneros's release. Meanwhile, Hearst dispatched a young reporter to Cuba to intervene directly. After many weeks' suspense, Karl Decker orchestrated a jailbreak in October 1897: 'the greatest journalistic coup of this age' (Millis, 1931, 84). With fellow prisoners drugged into oblivion and guards bribed into inertia, Evangelina made good her escape disguised as a man in a large sombrero, chomping a fat cigar. When she reached New York City, a crowd estimated at 75,000 swarmed around Madison Square Garden to greet this 'timid, shrinking girl.' Within months the United States was at war with Spain, fervor having been heightened by fresh stories of insults to American honor, culminating in the sinking of the battleship *Maine* – an alleged act of Spanish barbarism that historians now suspect was more likely caused by an accidental explosion.

This exercise in yellow journalism could be discounted as an idiosyncratic example of Hearst's megalomania. But that would be to neglect several elements that recur with striking regularity in pre-war reporting. In the American context, it's noteworthy that Hearst centered his efforts on a *captivity* story – a genre popular since Puritan days when sermons elaborating the 'horrible sufferings' of Euro-American settlers at the hands of marauding Indians formed a staple of pulpit oratory, giving rise to America's first unique literary genre. As many critics have pointed out, captivity narratives proved a stimulus to Indian-hating. By depicting God-fearing Christians as perpetually menaced by barbarous others, retaliatory violence came to appear not only necessary for survival but also socially regenerative (Slotkin, 2000; Strong, 1999).

More noteworthy yet is the fact that this genre privileges *female* captivity. Surveying the history of modern warfare, it's hard to miss the overwhelming emphasis on atrocities perpetrated against women and children in exhortations to fight. World War I provides numerous examples. For months before the United States joined the fray in 1917, America's public sphere was choked with stories of dreadful brutalities conducted by 'the Hun' as he raped and rampaged his way across Europe. Prominent among them were tales of Belgian nurses whose breasts had been sliced off and babies wantonly bayoneted to death or left abandoned with their tiny hands severed. Given the prior strength of popular sentiment that the United States should stay out of the Great War, refusing to let Wall Street financiers' assistance to the Entente powers trap the country in a distant conflagration, such stories played a significant role in reorienting public attitudes. At any rate, isolationism was steadily abandoned – not just by President Woodrow Wilson, who had fought and won an election campaign in 1916 on the basis that he had 'Kept America Out of The War,' but by citizens at large (Ross, 1996, 145–213). A wave of anti-Germanism that swept urban America suggests that 'fighting spirit' wasn't, for some recruits at least, grudgingly mustered but reflected a more active enthusiasm for quashing German brutishness – even if the misery of trench warfare later extinguished the flames of avenging ardor.

World War I threatened to discredit atrocity-mongering permanently. In its wake, it became clear that many of the most gruesome atrocity stories had been of dubious provenance: unreliable hearsay, unsupported witness testimony, or fabricated outright (Ponsonby, 1928; Read, 1941; Squires, 1935; Peterson, 1939). The revelation that allied opinion-formers had peddled anti-German stories whose basis in fact was questionable at best – and non-existent at worst – served to cement an equation between atrocities and propaganda, propaganda and lies. We might note here too another family resemblance between Hearst's story about the teenage 'rose of Cuba' and atrocity stories more generally. Crucial elements were essentially made up.

After 1918, popular disillusionment with a war that had neither ended all wars nor made the world safe for democracy, coupled with bitterness over the way in which Americans had been suckered into fighting, engendered lingering skepticism. Some scholars suggest that Americans were slow to credit reports of Nazi criminality in the 1930s and during World War II because they assumed such reports to be no more reliable than tall tales of the beastly Boches from the last war (P. Taylor, 1995, 197). In the months preceding US entry into the war in 1941, German atrocities appeared less visible in American news-media than they had been in 1917. While dedicated anti-fascists struggled to turn opinion in favor of intervention, with Hollywood studios producing a handful of features set in or satirizing Nazi Germany, such as Frank Borzage's *Mortal Storm* (1940) and Charlie Chaplin's *The Great Dictator* (1940), opinion polls showed that most Americans remained resolutely against participation in the war throughout 1941. It took Japan's attack on the US Navy at Pearl Harbor to override this popular reluctance (Casey, 2001, 3–45).

When allied troops liberated the Nazis concentration camps three years later, the celluloid footage they captured, more graphic than anything shown before in American cinemas, helped dissolve the nexus between atrocities and falsehood. Only a handful of immovable skeptics continued to quibble that the visual evidence of genocide caught by Russian, American and British photographers and cameramen must have been faked (Zelizer, 1998). Thereafter, 'Hitler' became a byword for atrocity, and analogies with him a staple of campaigns to discredit dictatorial adversaries.

This 'Hitlerizing' phenomenon was especially pronounced in US media treatment of Saddam Hussein from 1990 until his execution in December 2006. After August 1990, when Iraqi troops invaded and occupied neighboring Kuwait, the White House repeatedly explained events in the Gulf with reference to Hitler's aggression in 1930s Europe. Television and press reports seized on a comparison President Bush made so frequently that some reporters saw fit to comment on occasions when he *failed* to do so (Dorman and Livingston, 1994, 71). While Bush assembled the largest multinational coalition of armed forces since World War II in Saudi Arabia, the rallying of civilian sentiment continued apace. Aided by elite sources on Capitol Hill, news organizations detailed Iraqi atrocities in occupied Kuwait. In this regard, the most memorable testimony was delivered by a teenage Kuwaiti girl, introduced simply as Nayirah, who offered tearful testimony to the US Congressional Caucus on Human Rights about scenes she claimed to have witnessed in a hospital where Iraqi troops had thrown babies from their incubators in an orgy of looting (MacArthur, 1993, 51–66).

It would be pleasing to think that the days when propagandists manipulatively deployed the figure of violated womanhood as a symbol of virtue abused were long gone – if only it were true. But Hearst's 'rose of Cuba' story looks less antiquated if we compare it to the saga of Jessica Lynch, a US Army private first class who became headline news in April 2003 during 'Operation Iraqi Freedom.' Lynch, the headlines announced, had been taken captive by Iraqi fighters and held for a week in hospital before being rescued by US forces: a story she later claimed in a 2007 Congressional hearing had been 'hyped' for propaganda purposes (Talev, 2007). The notion that women as a sex are both blameless and defenseless – politically innocent and physically incapable in ways that men are not generally taken to be – remains an enduring cross-cultural, trans-historical motif. Thus opinion-formers continue to present atrocities against 'innocent women and children' as more outrageous than abuses of men, and hence more deserving of preventative and/or punitive action.

Who is the target audience for gendered atrocity material? We might imagine that World War I's Belgian nurse stories were angled primarily towards a male audience. Titillating images of female violation, while charged with a voyeuristic frisson, offered aroused male ardor a 'chivalrous' outlet. Similarly, to emphasize Spain's violation of female virtue in 1898 was to endow military intervention with ennobling overtones – protective, not offensive. Teddy Roosevelt's 'splendid little war' was thus redeemed from any taint of imperialistic aggression. And if the Rough Riders' campaign against the Spaniards appeared punitive, it was punitive only in the interests of chastening and disarming enemies of civilization.

Nearly a century later, gendered constructions of women's endangerment are differently encoded. The idea that the sanctity of hearth and home – the cherished space of femininity – requires armored protection may strike us as archaic. It's hard not to look at World War I mobilization posters and be struck by the discrepancy between womanhood's idealized veneration as guardian of domesticity or totem of national purity and women's debarred access to political participation and numerous forms of paid employment. But the notion that soldiers should fight to protect or liberate imperiled women hasn't vanished in the twenty-first century. It has simply been supplanted by a contemporary variant: war for women's rights. No longer is femininity or domesticity the object to be secured, but rather the opposite. We go to war to ensure that girls can go to school and that women can enjoy equal access to public space and the ballot box.

Nowhere was this justification for war more evident than during the launch of 'Operation Enduring Freedom,' as the 2001 war with Afghanistan was dubbed. 'The fight against terrorism is also a fight for the rights and dignity of women,' announced Laura Bush in a radio address on November 1, 2001, having just stressed that, 'Only the terrorists and Taliban forbid education to women. Only the terrorists and the Taliban threaten to pull out women's fingernails for wearing nail polish.' The US-led campaign would thus free Afghan 'women of cover' (as President Bush termed them) from their burkas and end honor killings. It would ensure girls' right to schooling. In both the US and UK, news stories documenting the plight of Afghan women proliferated in October 2001 (Hammond, 2007, 163). This sudden stress on Taliban outrages against women and girls wasn't accidental, but a calculated pitch to liberal audiences less likely to endorse war as 'payback' for 9/11 or a manhunt for bin Laden and his fellow 'evildoers' (Shepherd, 2006; Dubriwny, 2005).

'Liberal violence' to emancipate Muslim women from their burkas might seem a far cry from calls to halt the rapacious Hun in 1917. Yet both projections function to reassure their audience that war can serve to civilize. Kept in abeyance are the troublesome implications of 'saving' women whose lack of agency is taken to be absolute, and whose absolute oppression is deduced from her Islamic dress. Does the desire to 'unveil' not contain seeds of cultural and sexual violence? Might these rescue missions themselves be less than moral in their underlying motives (Abu-Lughod, 2002, 783–90)? The power of atrocities lies in keeping such questions under wraps. And though *The Independent*'s Robert Fisk bluntly asserted in December 2001 that 'we did not go to war in Afghanistan to make the world free for kite flyers or cinema lovers or women in veils,' few followed his lead (quoted by Hammond, 2007, 163). Indeed, his own paper gave notably short shrift to those who protested the war.

Giving peace less of a chance: constrained debate on the 'war option'

Peace researchers have long discerned a militarist bias in mainstream media: a reflexive predisposition to favor military force over non-violent methods of conflict resolution (Roach, 1993). This point was made

Illustration 1.1 'Network Sheep and War' by Ann Telnaes , 2003

Source: Ann Telnaes and the Cartoonist Group.

explicit in the 1984 UNESCO-funded MacBride Report, *Many Voices, One World*, which prompted media to 'remember that, beyond national interests, there is the supreme interest of humanity in peace' (quoted by Spencer, 2005, 166). Yet at precisely the time when vigorous debate over policy options is most necessary, media often do more to constrain rather than facilitate discussion, muting cautionary voices and allowing the rationales of leaders intent on war to pass largely unchallenged. Media thus acquiesce to the 'war option,' if they don't more ardently embrace it. The recent past provides two vivid examples that seem to corroborate the case: first, the US media's performance in the 'establishing phase' of the 1991 Gulf War; and second, during the build-up to what the Bush administration termed 'Operation Iraqi Freedom' in March 2003.

In 1990, following Iraq's invasion of Kuwait, and throughout 2002 and early 2003, the respective administrations of Bush senior and junior appeared to favor using force against Iraq. This preference was scarcely disguised. Although in each case war was preceded by diplomatic efforts to garner supportive UN resolutions, the concurrent mustering of an international 'coalition of the willing' signaled a determination to use force to effect the desired outcomes: Iraq's eviction from Kuwait in the first instance, and Saddam Hussein's removal from power in the second. Costly to sustain, large-scale military deployments generate their own momentum for war sooner – not least when everything from porta-loos to bottled water has to be freighted in to support uniformed men and women sweating out miserable desert conditions. In the months after August 1990, the Pentagon presided over the deployment of some half million personnel amassing in the Saudi desert near Iraq's border and on carriers in the Gulf. On a lesser scale, the same phenomenon recurred in late 2002, as US forces took up positions in Saudi Arabia. Since troops can't remain poised for action indefinitely while sanctions bite or weapons inspectors unearth stockpiles of weapons that may not exist, it was plain to see where these mobilizations would lead.

However, it would be naive to believe that logistical momentum alone carried the US and its allies into war in January 1991 and again in March 2003. In both cases, the president clearly preferred the use of force, ideally with a measure of international legitimacy but without if necessary. After the fact, White House insiders revealed to investigative reporters that George Bush senior had decided on war with Iraq from as early as August 1990, and that his son was already discussing the possibility of 'taking out' Saddam on the night of the September 11 attacks – even when informed by his central intelligence director that Osama bin Laden, not Saddam Hussein, was the culprit. On November 21, 2001, Bush instructed Donald Rumsfeld to begin planning for war with Iraq in earnest (Western, 2005, 192). As we'll see in greater detail later, the two Bush administrations subsequently made intensive efforts to sell war with Iraq at home and abroad.

So much for the White House. What of mainstream US media? In the aftermath of the 1991 Gulf War, which ended Kuwait's occupation by Iraq, left Saddam Hussein in power in Baghdad, and saw repressed uprisings (encouraged by the US) put down by his troops, critics assailed journalists with numerous sins of omission and commission. Why hadn't news organizations scrutinized Washington's aid to Baghdad during Iraq's eight-year war with Iran in the 1980s? Why didn't they probe the green light that US ambassador April Glaspie allegedly gave the Iraqi ruler to invade Kuwait, without US obstruction, on the eve of Iraq's move. A clearer signal that invasion was unacceptable might, in other words, have averted the crisis altogether, while a firm stance against Iraq earlier yet, in the 1980s, would have trimmed Saddam's claws before he did so much damage to his own citizens as well as neighboring states.

Other media critics adopted a different stance. Rather than criticizing Bush and his predecessors for alleged appeasement, they pointed to the function that 'Hitlerizing' Saddam Hussein served in the months before the Coalition's ground war against Iraq began in January 1991. Far from being an empty rhetorical flourish, this analogy implied a clear policy prescription. After all, the abiding 'lesson of Munich' was that aggressors' territorial greed is never satisfied by swallowing just one country. Since conquest and concessions merely whet the dictatorial appetite, such rapacity can be halted only by war. If Americans accepted the parallel with events in Europe 50 years earlier, they were thereby encouraged to see war as the fitting response to Iraqi aggression. 'With Saddam-as-Hitler, "compromise", or any other alternative policy option, was effectively eliminated from debate well before the actual debate got under way' (Dorman and Livingston, 1994, 74; Peer and Chestnut, 1995). By the time Congress came to deliberate America's response to the invasion, the direction had already been set. And while US media did report a range of views aired on Capitol Hill, they nevertheless marginalized opinions conflicting with the president's.

Similar patterns were again evident before the invasion of Iraq in March 2003. US journalists did much to bolster the administration's claim that Saddam Hussein still harbored a significant cache of weapons of mass destruction (WMD), outlawed under the terms imposed on Iraq after its defeat in 1991. Prominent opinion-formers, echoing the Bush administration, insisted that Saddam was planning to use these weapons against the United States and its allies. Although White House rationalizations for the war would later shift when no secret arsenal was subsequently unearthed, in the months before 'Operation Iraqi Freedom' Iraq's defiance of the international weapons inspection regime formed the central bone of contention between Bush, Blair, and Baghdad. In Britain, anxiety centered on the claim that Iraqi missiles could be readied to hit targets within 45 minutes of an order being given (Edwards and Cromwell, 2004, 210–14). Meanwhile, in the United States more attention focused on the question of whether Saddam was actively pursuing a nuclear missile program – or, in the most alarmist terms, whether he might in fact already possess a nuclear bomb.

The most high-profile reporter to lend credence to these claims was *The New York Times*'s Judith Miller, later imprisoned for refusing to divulge the source who had disclosed that Valerie Plame, the wife of former ambassador Joseph C. Wilson (a critic of administration assertions that Iraq had sought uranium in Niger) was a CIA operative. In several front-page articles run in September 2002, Miller detailed the state of Iraq's alleged weapons capability and intentions. Her focus on the import of high-strength aluminum tubes of a sort that could potentially be used in centrifuges to enrich uranium bolstered the worst-case claims of Bush's inner circle: that Iraq had 'stepped up its quest for nuclear weapons and [had] embarked on a worldwide hunt for materials to make an atomic bomb' (Miller, quoted by Massing, 2004, 33). As Miller's critics later pointed out, there was in fact significant dispute within the US intelligence community and amongst weapons experts about the likely use of this tubing, and more generally about Iraq's nuclear ambitions. A handful of journalists, notably investigative reporters working for the Knight Ridder group, pointed this out at the time. But without the institutional clout of *The New York Times* or the *Washington Post*, these reporters failed to shift public debate in a more skeptical direction. Miller herself barely acknowledged that many defense analysts disputed whether Iraq posed a clear and present danger to national security at all (Massing, 2004, 36–44).

Failing to alert US audiences to the serious doubts many experts had over the status of intelligence that administration officials presented as clear-cut evidence of Iraq's malevolence, news channels also contributed to the growing popular conviction that Iraq was connected with Al Qaeda, and that Saddam was thus somehow responsible for 9/11. Of all the reasons why US troops should invade Iraq – a secular state with no firmly documented ties to Islamic terrorism – this was undoubtedly the most emotionally resonant (Robinson and Livingston, 2006, 23–37). But it took some doing to establish this belief in American audiences. A poll conducted on September 24, 2001, found that just 6 per cent of respondents thought Saddam Hussein had anything to do with the recent attacks on the Pentagon and World Trade Center. More than 50 per cent held Osama bin Laden responsible (ibid., 28). Yet three years later, in September 2004, 42 per cent of respondents to a *Newsweek* poll believed that Iraq was 'directly involved' in the terror attacks – this shortly after publication of the *9/11 Commission Report* which explicitly *refuted* any link between Saddam Hussein and Al Qaeda (ibid., 25).

This turnaround can be attributed to both the Bush administration, which assiduously worked to establish the linkage, and key sectors of the media – Fox News most notably. Since evidence of this alleged link was tenuous at best, its existence was generally implied through verbal cues that elided the 'terrorists' responsible for 9/11 with the 'terror state' Iraq. As Robinson and Livingston point out, this rhetorical strategy conjured a 'syllogism of associative blame:' 'Terrorists are bad guys. Terrorists attacked the United States on September 11, 2001. Saddam is a bad guy. Ergo, Saddam is a terrorist; Saddam must have been behind 9/11' (Robinson and Livingston, 2006, 34, 25). With terrorism the central preoccupation of public discourse after September 2001, numerous commentators hypothesized that Saddam Hussein, America's principal nemesis, must surely be a sponsor of terrorism. And even if Iraq was not a *direct* ally of bin Laden, many press columnists, television pundits and talk-radio hosts nevertheless speculated that the two of them might easily be in cahoots, given their shared animus against the US, or could well prove to be in the future – aligned in the nefarious 'Axis of Evil.' Iraq's possession of WMD thus became all the more alarming when yoked to the prospect of Saddam supplying such weapons to terrorist organizations.

In the volatile atmosphere of anger, vigilance and hyper-patriotism that engulfed the United States after 9/11, compounded by a nationwide anthrax scare and a series of sniper-shootings in the capital, it's perhaps not surprising that Americans who protested the quick-step march to war with Iraq in early 2003 found themselves marginalized, if not more actively demeaned, in the press. Reporters regularly treated peace protestors as anachronistic throwbacks to an earlier age of flower power, campus-takeovers and mass demonstrations: 'professional pacifists' resurrecting 'the moldy clichés and self-righteous pieties of the 1960s,' in the words of the *Boston Herald*'s Don Feder (quoted by Bishop, 2006, 48). Often, news stories focused on the *activity* of protest, barely considering the protestors' animating reasons for opposition to the invasion of Iraq, and giving prominent play to opponents who insisted that anti-war sentiment not only disrespected but actively endangered US troops. A Pew Research Center poll conducted in March 2003 found that 48 per cent of respondents thought they'd heard 'too much' about the views of Americans who opposed the war, while only 17 per cent protested that they had heard too little. Meanwhile, a CBS News poll that same month found that 32 per cent of those questioned believed the very fact of holding protest marches 'hurt the war effort' and should not be allowed (Pew, 2003; CBS News/NYT, 2003).

When not stigmatized altogether, protest was treated as performative behavior – an expression of nostalgic, regressive, or self-indulgent impulses – rather than taken seriously for its political content: a trend also evident in the reporting of protest during the 1991 Gulf War and, two decades earlier, during the Vietnam War (Reese, 2004; Hallin, 1989). While anti-war groups made intensive use of new media to mobilize and coordinate their activities, 'old media' tended to gloss over the fact that an identifiable subset of Americans rejected the prevailing wisdom that Iraq posed a clear and present danger to the US. The grounds on which dissent rested were similarly sidelined. Anti-war demonstrations were trivialized when peaceful and relatively small as a pale imitation of their Vietnam era antecedents, lacking the passion and vigor of those more consequential protests. But at the same time, when anti-war marches in 2003 attracted larger and more assertive throngs, they were castigated as the unruly behavior of a disorderly element – drawn to protest for protest's sake (Bishop, 2006, 39–63). Consumers of mainstream US news-media learnt similarly little about the huge anti-war protests held across five continents on February 15, in which over 8 million people marched, leaving the administration's claims to have garnered international legitimacy for the attack on Iraq looking more plausible to many US citizens than they would have done to many elsewhere around the world.

Explaining media performance before war

Graham Spencer opens his book *The Media and Peace* with a blunt assertion: 'The news media is not well disposed to peace.' As we've just seen, it is not hard to catalog historical and contemporary instances in which mass media have embraced the call to arms. Explaining why this is so takes rather more effort. If peace is a 'more socially desirable' state of affairs than war, as Spencer puts it, how do we account for this predilection (Spencer, 2005, 1)?

One obvious rejoinder to Spencer's claim is to point out that, all too commonly, states and other actors do *not* regard peace as preferable to violence. War is often depicted as irrational – the overtaking of reason by more primal, blood-thirsty impulses – but it is nevertheless *interested*, calculating behavior. Whatever individual or collective psychological pay-offs war may provide, combatants employ violence in pursuit of tangible ends: to secure territory, resources and markets or to disarm enemies who may or may not, in fact, be poised to attack. The outcome frequently disappoints those aspirations. When fighting stops, societies may confront shattered cities, devastated landscapes, wrenching loss of life, psychological and bodily damage – for victor and vanquished alike. Yet in the early twenty-first century military force remains widely accepted as a way to pursue 'politics by other means.' Many cultures continue to valorize the soldier as warrior and the warrior as hero. In western societies, attitudes conducive to war are deeply engrained in childhood games. Khaki-clad boys are still given toy soldiers and plastic guns to play with. If anything, war-play has become more prevalent as computer games provide social sanction to older boys (aka men) to hone their trigger reflexes and develop their strategic acumen. In US culture, guns readily appear not as a lethal menace to urban life but as essential tools of personal expression: firearm ownership an inalienable right of citizenship. Shooting is how you earn respect, establish authority, and vaporize problems.

We can, then, explain media 'war bias' in ethno-cultural terms. If media seem to endorse military force more readily than other conflict-resolution options that's because society at large places less value on negotiation, compromise and diplomacy. But such macro-level explanations only get us so far. The remainder of this chapter offers more specific analyses of why media organizations, and individual journalists, behaved as they did in the scenarios just outlined.

State direction

A tight alignment between states intent on violence and supportive journalists would seem to offer the simplest answer as to why media, in certain situations, have actively encouraged the use of force. Regimes intent on upending the current status quo, like Hitler's Third Reich and the 'Hutu Power' movement around President Habyarimana in Rwanda, used state-controlled media to cultivate popular enthusiasm for their genocidal projects. But how do states come to dominate organs of popular expression? Does compulsion – the threat of retaliation or joblessness – suffice to explain why media workers lend themselves to the objectives of ruling parties? Or do we need to consider more active ways in which reporters' and journalists' consent is solicited, co-opted or volunteered?

In both the Third Reich and Rwanda, the ruling group used censorship and personnel purges to marginalize, if not altogether expunge, dissentient viewpoints from state-controlled media. As Chapter 2 shows in greater detail, the National Socialists began monopolizing Germany's public sphere as soon as they came to power in 1933: a campaign to ensure Nazi ideology saturated every channel of communication that took years to complete. Similarly, in Rwanda in the early 1990s, broadcasters who opposed the increasingly dominant Hutu Power movement around Habyarimana were ousted from their jobs. But this clique, engineering a campaign of genocide, didn't trust state-controlled media to effect the necessary psychological mobilization unassisted, especially after the ruling party was forced under mounting internal and external pressure to share power with other Hutu groups and potentially also with the Tutsi RPF. Fearing the end of its privileged position, the circle around the president, his wife and her family set out to reconsolidate Hutus as a homogeneous ethnic front – united in hatred and fear of the minority Tutsis.

To achieve this objective, the *genocidaires* placed their greatest faith in radio. RTLM was the creation of the faction around Habyarimana: a channel calculated to stir up anti-Tutsi feeling. For the engineers of genocide, radio held great appeal in a country where, according to the 1991 census, 44 per cent of the population could neither read nor write. At a time when wages were plummeting and prices skyrocketing, few literate Rwandans could afford newspapers that cost the equivalent to the average day's salary of a rural migrant worker (Higiro, 2007, 81). Conditions of economic crisis, occasioned by a sharp drop in world coffee prices and by IMF structural adjustment policies (which mandated the privatization of public assets and diminution of state welfare services and subsidies), increased impoverished Hutus' receptivity to extremist messages (Pottier, 2002, 21–2). More accessible than print media, radio also represented a potent mechanism to activate group feeling, kindle solidarity and cement ethnic allegiance in the face of what broadcasters represented as an imminent threat of annihilation by 'outsiders'.

As Joseph Goebbels also well appreciated, radio tends to be a social medium. While newspapers are commonly read alone, broadcasts lend themselves to collective listening – a phenomenon encouraged in both Rwanda and the Third Reich. RTLM quickly came to dominate public space, its populist style fostering a sense of collective belonging, with chatty presenters, catchy music and a good deal of direct audience participation in the form of call-in requests and vox-pop interviews. Accessible to illiterate audiences, RTLM also established a broad base of support: a phenomenon that helps explain how not only peasant militias but businessmen, teachers, NGO workers and clergy took part in the genocide, as 'killers, lookouts, informants, looters, logisticians and cheerleaders' (Li, 2007, 91). RTLM was not, then, a *government*-run station per se. Rather, it was the creation of a certain clique who found a like-minded group of broadcasters to perform a clearly delineated function – to mobilize popular energy for slaughter – which they did with indisputable success.

Manipulation

'We were lied to!' forms a common refrain of journalists whose stories have been discredited during or after war. And it's true that, time and again, reporters have been misled by policy-makers and their spin doctors, professional public relations officers inside and outside government, and by foreign states and their agents. As I. F. Stone once memorably observed: 'If you want to know about governments, all you have to know is two words: governments lie' (quoted by Schell, 2004, v). So, it should come as no surprise that interested parties fudge facts, withhold salient details, bluster, fib, and lie with particular persistence and determination when making the case for war. Electoral outcomes aside, rarely does it matter so much to incumbents of power what citizens think of their leaders' actions. Will they accept costs of war – financial and human? Only if persuaded war is necessary and victory assured.

Manipulation forms a dominant theme in the history and study of war reporting. Tellingly, the scholarly discipline of communications studies emerged in the 1920s with studies of the propaganda techniques that had been used to sell interventionism to American audiences and to sustain public commitment to a war of unparalleled enormity. Prompted by scholars like Harold Lasswell and others keen to prevent guileless citizens from falling for emotionally manipulative propaganda again, Americans learnt how British agents had actively cultivated interventionist sentiment (Gary, 1999, 55–84; Ewen, 1996). 'There must have been more deliberate lying in the world from 1914 to 1918 than in any other period of the world's history,' wrote one of propaganda's first systematic analysts (Ponsonby, 1928, 19). The most notorious atrocity story of the war, concerning a German corpse factory which melted down German soldiers' bodies for glycerine, was exposed as a deliberate fabrication circulated in 1917 by British officials with a view to stirring anti-German feeling in China (Read, 1941, 38; Ponsonby, 1928, 111; Squires, 1935, 32).

Not all atrocity stories were manufactured, however, and those that proved exaggerated weren't all invented by British propagandists. Some stories were probably battlefield exaggerations of behavior which Allied soldiers had actually witnessed. Others, including the tale of a crucified Canadian soldier, were popular soldiers' rumors, though civilians could also manufacture equally blood-thirsty tales (Ponsonby, 1928, 67–9, 91–3; Read, 1941, 37). But even if British propagandists concocted few stories, the government undeniably gave extensive currency to battlefield embellishments, distortions and outright fabrications with the publication in 1915 of the Bryce Report (the *Report of the Committee on Alleged German Outrages*). This 60-page document resulted from an official investigation into German conduct in occupied Belgium, with bulky appendices of eye-witness testimony. But its authors avoided any attempt to evaluate the veracity of these accounts – to distinguish between rumor and half-truth, or to ensure that testimony had not been given in response to leading questions (Read, 1941, 202–8; Peterson, 1939, 53–61; Wilson, 1979, 369–83). By virtue of their reproduction in an official report, the stories were given greater credence than they might otherwise have received, as the Westminster government undoubtedly hoped. Publication helped quell initial US doubt over German atrocities in Belgium. American journalists who visited Belgium in September 1914 inclined to disbelieve anti-German stories, having personally found no corroborating evidence (Read, 1941, 29–30).

When the Bryce Report appeared British propagandists noted with satisfaction that: 'Even in papers hostile to the Allies, there is not the slightest attempt to impugn the correctness of the facts alleged. Lord Bryce's prestige in America put skepticism out of the question, and many leading articles begin on this note' (Peterson, 1939, 58). *The New York Times* greeted the publication with the headline 'German Atrocities are Proved' (Ross, 1996, 53). Thus the report itself was either 'one of the worst atrocities of the war' or Britain's 'stroke of genius,' depending on one's perspective (Peterson, 1939, 58; Lasswell, 1927, 88).

Following these revelations American journalists vowed never again to be so deceived – a vow reaffirmed after almost every war. We find echoes of similar foreign interference after the Gulf War of 1991. In this case, postwar investigative reports revealed that the emir of Kuwait and his exiled regime had hired the services of a leading US public relations firm Hill and Knowlton, at a cost of some $10.8 million, to kindle greater support for war on behalf of an oil-rich emirate the size of New Jersey (MacArthur, 1993; Kellner, 1992).

Hill and Knowlton's initial attempts to work on 'positive' themes, stressing for example that Kuwaiti women could drive even if they couldn't vote, fell on unreceptive ears polling subcontractors found in their telephone surveys and focus groups (Manheim, 1994, 142–3). Since negative attacks provoked stronger responses, Hill and Knowlton concentrated their efforts on demonizing the Iraqi leader. In this regard, the incubator story – as told by the Kuwaiti teenager, Nayirah – represented their trump card. President Bush claimed to have been so moved by her testimony that he retold the story of Iraqi soldiers tearing babies from their incubators five times in the space of five weeks (MacArthur, 1993, 65). The credibility of her account was further enhanced by Amnesty International, which repeated allegations that over 300 babies had died in this way in its own report on Iraqi violations of human rights in Kuwait (ibid., 66). After the war, however, it came to light that Nayirah was in fact the daughter of the Kuwaiti ambassador to the US, and that her tearful testimony was less that of a traumatized witness than of a well-coached actress carefully rehearsed for her moment under the Congressional spotlight by Hill and Knowlton's handlers (ibid., 59).

Foreign governments are far from alone as culprits where media manipulation goes. Indeed, one striking feature of the 1991 Gulf War was the US administration's *own* use of PR firms, including Hill & Knowlton and the Wirthlin Group, to conduct opinion polls and engage in 'issue development.' Their job, in other words, was to test-drive justifications for war as though branding a new commercial product, developing an attractive package that would move prospective consumers decisively towards purchase.

In 1991, this was a novel development. Ten years later, with the younger Bush in office, the tight relationship between the executive branch and corporate PR companies had become firmly entrenched. To promote the 'war on terror,' Bush not only turned to PR companies but appointed professional marketing executives to key positions within his strategic communications machinery. Pentagon spokeswoman Victoria Clarke, former director of Hill and Knowlton's Washington office, was charged with bringing together 'a group of Beltway lobbyists, PR people and Republican insiders' to work on selling war with Iraq (quoted by Western, 2005, 202). Many members of this group were drawn from the same team that had framed 'Operation Enduring Freedom' in Afghanistan as a humanitarian venture, considering their 'greatest hit' to have been 'exposing the Taliban's treatment of women' (Martha Brant, quoted by Rampton and Stauber, 2003, 38–9).

Since 2003, numerous accounts have elaborated the Bush administration's efforts to manufacture a casus belli with Iraq – their titles leaving little doubt as to the authors' chagrin that journalists were, once again, both lied to and lying: *Embedded: Weapons of Mass Deception, When News Lies, The War in Iraq and Why the Media Failed Us*, and *Tell Me Lies* (Schechter, 2003; Schechter, 2006; Dadge, 2006; Miller, 2004). 'Never before in the annals of contemporary American foreign policy,' notes William A. Dorman wryly, 'was so much evidence accumulated so quickly that the assumptions leading to a war were so questionable' (2006, 12). While commentators more generously inclined towards the Bush administration continued to maintain that the president and his advisors were themselves misled by faulty intelligence, most critics soon found little room to doubt that the principal fault with US intelligence stemmed from the president's insistence that evidence be found – fabricated if necessary – to consolidate the case against Iraq. As one analyst put it on a Public Broadcasting Service *Frontline* documentary, he and his colleagues had been required to produce 'faith-based intelligence' (Massing, 2004, 25).

There is no question that the administration worked vigorously to reanimate the WMD issue, to insinuate a connection between Baghdad and Al Qaeda, and draw attention to Saddam Hussein's dismal human rights record. According to President Bush, planning for war had to be top secret because he knew 'what would happen if people thought we were developing a potential or a war plan for Iraq' (quoted by Western, 2005, 193). But with intensive efforts underway to bestir popular opinion, this planning

Illustration 1.2   'Iraqerjack' by Steve Sack

Source: *Minneapolis Star-Tribune*/Ohio State University Billy Ireland Cartoon Library and Museum.

was hardly a well-kept secret. Bush's chief of staff, Andrew Card, convened a White House Iraq Group to coordinate the 'daily message on Iraq,' also creating a website, *Iraq: A Decade of Deception and Defiance*, to corroborate the case that Hussein had long been violating terms of UN disarmament resolutions imposed on Iraq after 1991. Bush began using the phrase 'Axis of Evil' to further consolidate the imagined nexus between Saddam and bin Laden, framing conflict with Iraq in terms redolent of World War II – the 'good war' waged against the Axis of Japan, Germany and Italy (Western, 2005, 195).

Case-building against Iraq involved heavy promotion of the administration's preferred themes, frames, analogies and circumstantial evidence that, for example, Mohamed Atta (the alleged hijacker of American Airlines Flight 11) had met an Iraqi intelligence official in Prague some months before the September 11 attacks: a claim later discounted in the *9/11 Report* (Robinson and Livingston, 2006, 31). But the culmination of these efforts didn't lie in an off-the-record whispering campaign but the highly public presentation regarding Iraq's intentions and capabilities made by Colin Powell at the UN on February 5, 2003: a speech the former

Secretary of State would later repudiate as the nadir of his career. The next morning, the *Washington Post* pronounced Powell's evidence 'irrefutable,' while *The New York Times* concluded that while he 'may not have produced a smoking gun,' the Secretary of State left 'little question that Mr Hussein tried hard to conceal one.' Other leading US newspapers, including the *Chicago Tribune, Los Angeles Times, USA Today*, and *Wall Street Journal* all chimed in with editorial endorsements (Dorman, 2006, 17). According to one subsequent scholarly study, there was a '30-point jump in the number of Americans who felt convinced of a link between Saddam Hussein and al Qaeda after he spoke' (Gershkoff and Kushner, quoted by Dorman, 2006, 16).

Reporters and editors were not, of course, *obliged* to provide such effusive endorsements. Rather, this gushing response to Powell illustrates the power of trusted executive personnel to set the agenda, and how much credence is invested in seemingly authoritative pronouncements – most later discredited. But White House spin also assumed a more bullying aspect. 'Their management is far greater than that of any administration I've seen,' observed John Walcott of the Knight Ridder group of the Bush administration's communications team. To 'domesticate' the media, they rewarded sympathetic reporters with 'leaks, background interviews, and seats on official flights,' while freezing out those who didn't play along. As media critic Michael Massing notes: 'In a city where access is all, few wanted to risk losing it' (2004, 46). By dint of controlling that most vital of strategic assets, Bush's information managers not only impeded investigative reporting but neutralized tough questioning with the threat of cutting off troublesome reporters from the sine qua non of their business: sources who make news.

News routines and the habits of deference

If manipulation is a fact of life and political leaders routinely embellish the case for wars they're committed to fighting, why do journalists let them get away with it? After all, the self-image of many reporters in democratic polities is built around a notion that journalists are tenacious watchdogs who regularly sink their teeth into mendacious politicians, refusing to let go until they've received a satisfactory response to the question, 'Why is this lying bastard lying to me?' (This interrogative, often attributed to BBC *Newsnight* presenter Jeremy Paxman, was originally expounded by Louis Heron, a former deputy editor of *The Times* (Wells, 2005).) In the months prior to 'Operation Iraqi Freedom' in 2003, this spirit of dogged pursuit was somewhat more evident in the United Kingdom than in the US. In what quickly became a *cause célèbre*, BBC reporter Andrew Gilligan repeated the opinion of an unnamed government weapons expert (later revealed as David Kelly, who committed suicide in the subsequent furor) that intelligence claims about Iraq's WMD capability had been purposely 'sexed up' by 10 Downing Street (Lewis and Brookes, 2004, 283–4). Yet in a country where, in January 2003, 75 per cent of polled opinion opposed war with Iraq, the two biggest circulation broadsheets and the most popular tabloid (*The Times*, *Daily Telegraph* and *Sun* respectively) nevertheless favored the line on Iraq pursued by Bush and Blair (Couldry and Downey, 2004, 274).

Journalistic timorousness, gullibility or belligerence can be explained in different ways – depending in part on how active or passive a role one thinks media played in the process of manufacturing consent in 2003. Some commentators, including journalists themselves, attribute a good deal to the overwrought mood of post-9/11 America, which discouraged them from posing tough questions of a then enormously popular president. Noting the reaction when the *Washington Post* published criticism of Bush, reporter Dana Priest recalled, 'We got tons of hate mail and threats, calling our patriotism into question' (quoted by Massing, 2004, 46). Leery of being deemed traitorous by Fox News or conservative radio hosts like Rush Limbaugh, journalists ducked and cowered.

In the wave of apologetics that soon followed the invasion of Iraq, media organizations partially exonerated themselves in this way, also stressing the power of an efficient system of threats and rewards in ensuring that journalists show due respect towards those who wield the carrots and sticks. However, they also directly faulted certain individual journalists for lapses of professionalism. Thus *The New York Times*'s ombudsman took Judith Miller to task for basing several articles from the fall of 2001 to 2003 on 'controversial' information, 'insufficiently qualified or allowed to stand unchallenged' (quoted by Western, 2005, 214). In a July 2004 editorial the *Times* offered regrets that America's paper of record did not 'do more to challenge the president's assumptions' and that it hadn't listened carefully to those who disputed Iraq's possession of a WMD stockpile. 'We had a "group think" of our own,' the paper confessed (quoted by Dorman, 2006, 18).

But these explanations do not offer a complete explanation of behavior that was not unique to the post-9/11 era nor isolated to a handful of prominent reporters who temporarily let standards slip. After all, the same cycle had been played out little more than a decade earlier during the 1991 Gulf War: a largely uncritical embrace of the administration case for war, followed by a wave of hair-tearing, accusations of manipulation and postwar mea culpas. Rather than attributing these symptoms to random outbreaks of group-think, we need a deeper structural account of how media organizations *make* news – and how they see the function of the news they make.

Clearly, news-making is a process that cannot be explained in the singular. What counts as news, and who counts as newsworthy, differs according to context – from one historic period to another, one national context to another, and from one news outlet to the next within the same place at the same time. Here, we'll confine ourselves to a preliminary understanding of how mainstream US media construe their task to better appreciate the habits of deference already noted.

Two points are immediately clear: first, the hierarchical value news organizations attach to elite sources, according a privileged position to the president at the apex of political power, closely followed by the Pentagon and State Department: the so-called 'golden triangle' of newsbeats. That news media are so attuned to executive power affords considerable latitude to the White House to set the agenda and frame debates in congenial ways – as we've already seen. It also helps explain why access is such a powerful tool in the administration's news-management arsenal. After all, if journalists regarded a wider range of individuals and organizations as authoritative news-makers, the threat of being frozen out of official briefings wouldn't be nearly such an effective disciplinary tool.

As many communications scholars point out, mainstream US news media have increasingly come to define the function of news not as offering the widest possible spectrum of views on topical issues, but rather as a barometer tracking the mercury of policy deliberation on Capitol Hill (Bennett, 1990; Entman and Page, 1994; Zaller and Chiu, 2000). In the language of communication scholar Lance Bennett, media coverage is 'indexed implicitly to the dynamics of governmental debate' (Bennett, 1990, 108). By the lights of his 'indexing hypothesis,' it was to be expected that in both 1990 and 2003 US news-media would fail to broaden public discourse over a putative war with Iraq. Instead, they adhered closely to dominant viewpoints on the Hill, and since Democrats in both houses failed to enunciate forceful opposition to the war, the press didn't either. By calibrating attention so precisely to policy elites, news media claims to 'balance' must therefore be understood to operate within narrowly confined parameters.

A second key issue regards 'objectivity': another cherished principle of reportorial practice. In lay terms, we might imagine objectivity would involve reporters in scrutinizing personal biases, blind-spots and preferences, while subjecting sources' statements to close scrutiny, fact-checking and cross-referencing (Cunningham, 2003). How else to ascertain the validity of contending truth-claims? But as we'll see in later chapters, this commonsense understanding of what it means to be objective does not in fact underpin journalistic practices of objectivity. Tellingly, Judith Miller defended her WMD stories – many of them based on dubious intelligence supplied by Iraqi exiles with a vested interest in US intervention to topple Saddam Hussein – on the grounds that: 'My job isn't to assess the government's information and be an independent analyst myself. My job is to tell readers of the *New York Times* what the government thought about Iraq's arsenal' (quoted by Massing, 2004, 62).

Bearing this in mind, the largely uncritical coverage of presidential war policy in 1991 and 2003 appears less an anomalous breach of journalistic procedure than the predictable outcome of a set of professional norms more concerned with following the policy-making flow than disrupting it. In short, journalists didn't so much fail to do their job in these cases as fail *because* they were doing a job they understand in a very particular way – one that elevates elite sources as 'primary definers' of news (Couldry and Downey, 2004, 275).

To regard media as hapless victims of manipulation is to overlook the complex symbiosis of a two-way relationship of mutual need. News organizations are not compelled to place such a high valuation on executive power. In 2003, they could, for example, have reflected a broad range of opinion, drawing on the oppositional viewpoints of liberal think-tanks, academics, area specialists and anti-war activists. But consensus occupies its own privileged niche in US mainstream news-making. A deeply embedded tendency to ignore or ostracize those beyond the inner policy-making world produces a self-fulfilling prophecy: those outside that charmed circle remain beyond its circumference, while those at the core are duly empowered to police its boundaries.

Conclusion

Pity the poor journalist:

> Our newsrooms are marketing-driven and profit-oriented, our staffs are poorly trained and dispirited. We dread being called liberal, we hate to be seen as unpatriotic. We fear making our readers unhappy, we don't want to insult powerful people – indeed we seem to yearn for their favor. (G. Overholser, quoted by Dorman, 2006, 20)

Among US journalists, it would seem that the most unprintable four-letter word is 'lies.' Dependent on elite approval for access to the corridors of power, they can't bring themselves to state outright that politicians, let alone presidents, might mislead the public.

If all this is true *before* war, the prohibitions against full-throated criticism surely only increase once states are actively engaged in conflict – or so it would certainly seem. Several trends encountered thus far will feature again in later chapters: news organizations' tendency to allow political elites to set the agenda; the potency of patriotism to muffle dissent and curb debate; the willingness of media to discipline one another; and professional norms of objectivity and balance that appear to institutionalize, rather than eliminate, certain forms of bias. In short, much of what we conceive as behavior unique to war isn't confined to wartime at all, and hence can't be explained with reference to the special emergency conditions. Reporters' hesitancy to articulate alternative viewpoints and attacks on anti-war opinion are both prominent features of war's 'establishing phase': a phrase that itself indicates how war becomes naturalized as inevitable in certain circumstances, rather than being regarded as the outcome of particular human choices that might have been otherwise.

As we've also seen, media obviously *matter* as critical agents of opinion-formation. How they report conflicts – how they frame what disputes are about, why they have arisen, and how they might be addressed – influences popular perceptions. Whether before US entry into World War I, the Gulf War of 1991 or Operation Iraqi Freedom in 2003, mass media did much to move opinion towards greater enthusiasm for war. Even in Britain, popular reluctance to invade Iraq dwindled on the eve of Operation Iraqi Freedom.

If policy elites and compliant media often succeed in rallying support for wars, they do not always manage to sustain it, however. Things have a habit of falling apart in war. Even the best-laid plans unravel, as assuredly do shoddier schemes. Not every war remains popular war even if it began with a burst of popular enthusiasm and, as we'll see, few remain uniformly popular throughout.

Chapter 2

Total War

'There is no question but that government management of opinion is an unescapable corollary of large-scale modern war,' Harold Lasswell observed in a pioneering study of propaganda (1927, 15). His judgement was based on experience of what was then called the Great War – the most destructive conflict in human history to date – in which every combatant state had bombarded its own population as well as neutral and enemy nations with relentless appeals, injunctions, warnings and threats. Writing in 1927, Lasswell doubtless hoped that his assertion would not be put to the test in the future. World War I was meant to be 'the war to end war,' after all. But with hindsight his words seem all the more apt. Many techniques of state opinion-management pioneered between 1914 and 1918 were adopted and adapted during the yet more lethal conflict of 1939–45.

Why did popular attitudes matter in unprecedented ways in 'large-scale modern war'? It certainly wasn't the case that the major protagonists were democratic polities whose leaders felt compelled to keep citizens informed about foreign affairs and domestic decision-making. In Germany, with its vigorous socialist movement, sedition – a catch-all offense – was punishable with imprisonment. Tsarist Russia, after a revolution in 1905, was teetering towards collapse: a crumbling autocracy with extremely limited representative institutions. In none of the combatant states could women vote, and in many the electorate excluded the poor, the illiterate, immigrants and ethnic minorities. These were not, then, states in which any notion of a public 'right to know' prevailed. Far from it.

They were, however, societies in which new media were reshaping patterns of consumption, habits of leisure and means of communication. In Britain, France, Germany and the United States, cinema emerged as an intoxicating form of mass entertainment in the early years of the twentieth century. Radio, still in its infancy during World War I, developed radiply in the 1920s and 1930s, whether as a state-run monopoly or a profit-oriented enterprise. Taking advantage of these powerful channels through which millions of people could be reached simultaneously with standardized messages, professional ad-men – another new species of the early twentieth-century – cultivated the art of popular seduction, selling people products they didn't necessarily need but suddenly couldn't live without.

And so it was with war. In the summer of 1914, there was no great popular enthusiasm to fight. On the contrary, many German newspapers gave vocal expression to anti-war sentiment, while in Britain a large-scale European war was neither wanted nor expected. Most newspapers were too preoccupied with the imminent prospect of war over Irish Home Rule to devote serious attention to the crisis looming on the continent (Thompson, 1999, 18). For most ordinary people in France, Russia, Germany and Britain, Serbian nationalism, imperial rivalries and the death throes of the Ottoman empire appeared far less pressing than immediate questions about workplace conditions, wages, food, housing, women's emancipation and popular representation. The early years of the twentieth century were marked by widespread labor unrest, strikes, suffragist protests and by swelling radicalism in autocratic Germany and Russia.

Tumult of a different sort gripped Europe after the assassination of Austro-Hungarian Archduke Franz Ferdinand by a Serbian nationalist in June 1914. As alliance commitments clicked into place, binding Britain, France and Russia to war against Germany and Austria-Hungary, the two opposing camps faced an immediate need for manpower. Industrialization and mechanization meant that warfare no longer resembled the cavalry-dependent engagements fought by professional soldiers in the nineteenth century. In this all-out confrontation, vast armies deployed new weapons of destruction: submarines, torpedoes, tanks, zeppelins, bombers, shells, rockets, and poison gas. Meeting the voracious need for manpower and materiel of these military machines required that men were hustled en masse into uniform – some 70 million all told. Women, meanwhile, were conscripted to 'man the factories' and sustain the war effort in multiple other ways.

Total war redefined traditional gender roles. It also blurred pre-existing distinctions between combatants and non-combatants. All-out war left civilians vulnerable to attack – a function of the conflict's vast scale, with the battleline stretched across continental Europe into the Middle East, and of new military technologies and tactics that turned civilian society into a distinct arena of conflict. Cities and towns faced bombardment as enemy aircraft sought simultaneously to destroy strategic installations and shatter civilian nerves. Ports were subject to blockade, exposing their inhabitants not only to shelling but starvation. Peasants and farmers saw their land ravaged, crops commandeered or destroyed, and livestock slaughtered. Total war, in short, meant just that: no one lay untouchably beyond its ambit, including the colonial subjects of European empires, millions of whom were also called up to serve in this inter-imperial showdown. For many combatant states national survival itself appeared to be at stake. And even in those countries facing no imminent danger of invasion, notably the United States, fears of civilizational collapse nevertheless thickened the air after 1917.

With the 'home front' vital to military success, civilian morale became a factor of unprecedented significance. General staffs devoted much energy to strategizing how they could corrode fighting spirit on the enemy side while boosting it at home and among the troops. Total war appeared to demand total conviction: whole-hearted participation and unswerving commitment to the cause. Only if everyone enthusiastically joined up – or, at the very least, joined in – could victory be assured. The war of 1914–18 thus saw a proliferation of state-supported channels of communication in the form of newspapers, newsreels, posters, and pamphlets. But political leaders were also convinced that esprit would shatter if people perceived the brutal realities of trench warfare too vividly. As British Prime Minister, Lloyd George put it to C. P. Scott, editor of the *Manchester Guardian*: 'If people really knew, the war would be stopped tomorrow. But of course they don't know and can't know. The correspondents don't write and the censorship would not pass the truth' (quoted by Knightley, 2004, 116–17).

Claiming between 50 and 70 million lives (of whom more than half were civilians), leaving millions more refugees, and decimating the Jewish population of central Europe, World War II surpassed the enormity of its predecessor in almost every way. State machinery to control mass media, shape opinion and monitor its vagaries became yet more pervasive. This was true not only in Nazi Germany and the USSR, where radio, film and the press served as instruments of political control and ideological uniformity in peace and wartime alike, but also in Britain and the United States where free speech ostensibly prevailed. All sides looked to derive lessons from the perceived propaganda failures of World War I and from their adversaries' supposedly superior success in marshaling popular will.

Yet despite intrusive governmental efforts to mold perceptions on all sides – variously to inspire, demonize, and demoralize – historical verdicts cast on media performance in World War II are typically much more positive than for its predecessor. Judgements about the 'Great War'

Illustration 2.1   'Meet John Londoner': a BBC program that allowed ordinary Britons to air their attitudes on the radio, 1941

Source: Ministry of Information Photograph Division/Imperial War Museum.

have tended to be uniformly harsh. 'More deliberate lies were told than in any other period of history,' notes Philip Knightley, lamenting a singularly 'discreditable period in the history of journalism' (2004, 84, 103). Contrast that blunt assessment with the much fonder recollections that surround the media of World War II. Many American commentators deem that conflict the 'the best reported war, ever,' recalling the radio broadcasts of Ed Murrow from London during the blitz, the frontline dispatches of Ernie Pyle, the darkly humorous cartoons of Bill Mauldin, and vivid photographs of Margaret Bourke-White (Ambrose, 2001, xv). Hollywood's wartime offerings are remembered with similar fondness, as too (by a certain demographic at least) are Britain's stiff-lipped melodramas of stoical endurance and sacrifice. Meanwhile, in Russia the frontline reportage of journalists such as Ilya Ehrenburg and Vassily Grossman has found enduring admiration.

How do we make sense of these divergent appraisals of the twentieth century's two total wars? Perhaps every aspect of the Allied war effort against the Axis powers is simply bathed in the rosy glow of nostalgia bestowed by that conflict's retrospective construction as the 'good war,' while World War I suffers from its postwar reputation for futility and immoralism. Or did states and mass media indeed behave differently in World War II? How, then, do we explain the paradox of total war producing what's often seen as a golden age of media liberalization even as state control reached unprecedented heights?

News media and the state in World War I

In July 1914, none of the statesmen leading their countries into war anticipated a conflict that would last more than four years and claim in excess of 15 million lives. But despite optimistic expectations that it would all be over by Christmas, military and civilian leaders in Britain and Germany did not take any chances with wartime communication. Neither state had gone so far as to plan a dedicated ministry to censor and release news, but traditions of official secrecy ran sufficiently deep in Wilhelmene Germany and Edwardian Britain that formal sanction already existed for tight control over the publication of information. Both were states with flourishing newspaper industries and vigorous labor movements in which politicians feared popular radicalism and generals reviled journalists. Not surprisingly, at the onset of war, policy-makers in Berlin and London placed far greater emphasis on prohibition of speech and curtailment of communication than on ways in which mass media might be actively enlisted to help rally popular sentiment and raise revenue through the sale of war bonds. Such 'positive' uses of reporters, photographers and film-makers – as well as opinion-formers drawn from academia and the arts – developed only after it became clear that this would be a long, largely static, war of attrition. The habitual military preference, evident in Germany and Britain alike, to say nothing until the war ended clearly couldn't be maintained.

Germany thus began the war with a well-worn expedient, announcing a State of Siege on July 31, 1914 which entailed suspension of 'the right to express opinion freely by word, print or picture.' Chancellor Bethmann-Hollweg simultaneously issued the press with 26 prohibitions 'to prevent unreliable information from reaching the public' (Marquis, 1978, 470–1). Eight days later, General von Kessel reminded the press that 'the printing of news regarding military affairs is prohibited.'

However, it was most unlikely that the press would come into possession of any hard and fast news from the high command. The sole wire service in Germany was the semi-official Wolff Telegraph Bureau (WTB), through which all official news was transmitted, any 'politically sensitive material' having already passed through Foreign Office clearance. Once war began, the German press was completely reliant on the censored-at-source WTB for frontline news. Should a newspaper manage to send one of its correspondents into the field, their reports were subject to censorship by the local military command (Marquis, 1978, 476). Although the purpose of censorship was ostensibly to prevent damaging information reaching the enemy, its remit in practice was much broader: governing the tone of news presentation and eliminating criticism of how the war was being waged.

After 14 months of fighting, the German government established a *Kriegspresseamt* (War Press Office) to suppress and release news. It disseminated its own publications aimed largely at troops, held regular press briefings, and twice- or thrice-weekly conferences at which editors were hectored and showered with a welter of 'recommendations.' In one historian's judgement: 'The tenor of government dealings with the press generally was that of a long-suffering and kindly – but stern – parent dealing with a wilful, malicious, unruly and potentially murderous child' (Marquis, 1978, 480). Newspapers were strictly warned, amidst a deluge of other repressive instructions, to desist from informing their readership of the censorship measures. But it's hard to conceive that readers could have remained ignorant of state interference. Newspapers which refused to conform were shut down, and those still in circulation adopted a uniformly defensive tone and evasive approach.

The situation worsened as the war lengthened and prospects of German victory faltered. Convinced that civilians were succumbing to defeatism, the military high command assumed an increasingly prominent role in news-management. General Ludendorff, the Chief of Staff, established a new press service, the *Deutsche Kriegsnachrichtendienst*, under his own personal direction. This move predictably angered politicians who feared that these uniformed press officers were inspiring political stories to serve their own agenda: refusal to sue for peace and determination (in the face of civilian opposition) to achieve a complete German victory (Messinger, 1992, 18).

According to many authors, Germany's downward curve was reversed in Britain. After a clumsily amateurish start, British sophistication at news-management grew steadily throughout the war – initial reticence caused by a squeamish distaste for the ungentlemanly business of propaganda coupled with a sense that patriotically minded editors could be left largely to censor themselves. Or so the received wisdom has it. But gentlemanliness hadn't prevented Westminster from devoting consideration to future wartime censorship arrangements before 1914 as rivalry between Britain and Germany intensified (Towle, 1975, 103–16). As early as 1904, a draft Bill had been placed before Parliament to 'provide for the control of the publication of Naval and Military Information in Cases of Emergency.' This was followed by an Official Secrets Act in 1910 which determined that the press would not be told anything deemed contrary to the 'public interest' – a term whose definition remained imprecise (Rose, 1995, 7). The next year, a committee was convened, with representatives from the War Office and Admiralty together with five press delegates, to determine what information could reasonably be withheld from the public during times of military emergency (Rose, 1995 11). Given this ten-year history of legislation, it was hardly true that wartime press censorship was 'as unfamiliar as it was unwelcome' – a claim later made by Edward Cook, the chief wartime censor (1920, xiv).

In August 1914, the British military exhibited the same impulse as their German antagonists, hoping to thwart the press 'bias in favour of publicity' by simply suppressing war news altogether (Cook, 1920, 18). The British state enjoyed certain advantages in this regard. While the German government controlled traffic flowing through the Wolff Telegraph, Westminster used powers reserved in the International Telegraph Convention to suspend telegraph and radio services throughout the empire. Although a diminished telegraph service continued, all ingoing or outgoing traffic had to pass through a Press Bureau whose existence was announced by Winston Churchill (then First Lord of the Admiralty) on 7 August 1914, with the promise that it would ensure a 'steady stream of trustworthy information' (Haste, 1977, 30). With Germany's transatlantic cables severed, Britain enjoyed a monopoly over national and international cable services.

Under the Defence of the Realm Act (DORA), instituted on August 8, 1914, the British state imposed wide-ranging prohibitions against the collection or publication of information about the war or any material which might directly or indirectly be useful to the enemy. False statements or utterances 'likely to cause disaffection to His Majesty' were also proscribed (Cook, 1920, 25). These sweeping powers undermine the claim that the slow evolution of the official Press Bureau and other home front propaganda agencies resulted from government confidence that a patriotic press could be left to its own devices (Haste, 1977, 21). The penalties attached to infringing DORA's terms – editors initially faced the prospect of court martial and a possible life sentence for severe infractions – suggest less than complete certainty that voluntarism would produce the desired compliance (Cook, 1920, 27–8).

DORA's terms were as broad as they were vague. Forbidding publication of information that might be useful to the enemy, the Act omitted any definition of how utility might be gauged. The most charitable explanation for this elasticity is that no one in Whitehall knew exactly what *would* aid the enemy in this new type of warfare. Consequently, policymakers erred on the side of caution. More skeptically, one might suggest that the very open-endedness of DORA's provisions pushed the press towards self-censorship for fear of transgressing a poorly demarcated boundary. Subjects such as German air raids on Britain were, understandably, particularly vexed. But while most editors appreciated the sensitivity here and agreed to wait until after an official communiqué had been released, at which point air raids could be written up according to individual editors' taste, other suppressions – such as weather forecasts – were 'never understood.' In this regard, 'much sarcasm was expended on us,' the Press Bureau's chief censor later moaned (Cook, 1920, 142).

Many editors sought Press Bureau guidance on stories (acquired from sources other than the official wire service) which they feared might contravene the nebulous rules. This was 'voluntary' self-censorship in operation. And in this way, as chief censor Cook pointed out, the Bureau 'became a shield for the Press. It was no offence not to submit an article or an item of news to the Press Bureau, but to do so was a sure defence … Submission thus relieved one of responsibility' (1920, 43). 'If in doubt, ask the censors,' became the editors' unwritten rule at a time when the margin for doubt was wide and penalties for miscalculation severe. But there was another reason besides editorial wariness why prosecutions of editors were fairly rare, with only 12 referrals to the Director of Public Prosecutions in 1915 (Haste, 1977, 31). Some editors did in fact infringe DORA and, to the chagrin of their scooped rivals, got away with it. This happened on occasions when the Director of Public Prosecutions judged that a prosecution would only compound the initial damage by drawing greater public – or enemy – attention to the offending article. As Cook observed, the system engendered the 'anomaly that the more serious the indiscretion was, the more reason there might be for letting it go unpunished' (1920, 83–4; Rose, 1995, 19).

The Press Bureau also issued but did not *originate* frontline news. However, as frequent scapegoat for military reticence, it formed the butt of much press criticism. The Bureau, its employees protested, was the mere conduit through which official news flowed. It took no responsibility for vouching the accuracy of the military's 'steady stream' of information, which was more commonly a slow trickle, given that the most experienced censor could process only around 110 incoming telegram messages in an eight-hour shift (Cook, 1920, 53). However, much as Cook might deny that the Bureau's job was to color news, undoubtedly the military attempted to slant information. Thus the Naval censor later recalled that Churchill at the Admiralty would 'hold on to a bit of bad news for a time on the chance of getting a bit of good news to publish as an offset' – a technique evident in many subsequent wars (quoted by Lasswell, 1927, 203). Newspapers, complained the press baron Lord Northcliffe, were being made 'part and parcel of a foolish conspiracy to hide bad news' (quoted by Messinger, 1992, 151).

Correspondents at the front

In every war, most reporting is done far from the scene of battle. Invariably, though, the relationship between soldiers and journalists in the field generates the greatest friction. In the thick of things, careless revelations appear most liable to cost lives. Journalistic criticism of military tactics or of shortfalls in manpower and equipment, no matter how constructively intended, is likely to elicit furious displays of martial temper. Even the most patriotically inclined journalistic boosterism can rankle by striking an insultingly breezy note. Tensions between soldiers and 'scribblers' were particularly pronounced during the early months of World War I as the British military first sought complete distance from the press, then cultivated an intimacy that some reporters found suffocating and others flattering.

Distaste for the 'jumpy profession,' as one military censor put it, typified attitudes towards journalists among the top brass who regarded pressmen as 'badly bred, ill-mannered, uneducated' fellows who 'revelled in indiscretion' (Major A. N. Lee, quoted by Grieves, 1996, 721; Lytton, 1921, viii). For their part, journalists brought to bear an unrealistic set of expectations derived from reporting colonial wars of much shorter duration and smaller scale: exotic 'spectacles' – almost always victorious – written up in the breathless register of war correspondence, somewhere between exotic travelogue and ripping *Boy's Own* yarn (Farish, 2001, 274). 'Looking back at that time,' mused Philip Gibbs, perhaps the best-known British correspondent of World War I, 'I find a little painful amusement in the thought of our immeasurable ignorance as to the meaning of modern warfare. We knew just nothing about its methods or machinery, nor about its immensity of range and destruction' (1923, 232).

Editors initially assumed that this new war would resemble 'the South-African affair' (the Boer War of 1899–1902): a confrontation 'remote, picturesque, romantic,' in which the reporter considered himself a blithe spirit who went where derring-do led, 'trott[ing] about on a pony with a pocketful of gold, purchasing his food or rations and making his own cabling arrangements' (Lytton, 1921, vii). War correspondents of the old school accordingly prepared for their new assignment by taking riding lessons in Hyde Park, 'believing that they would need horses in this war on the western front.' But while they cooled their heels waiting months for the War Office to make formal arrangements for accreditation, younger journalists simply dashed across the English Channel to France and Belgium.

When they arrived at the front, their reception was several degrees below frosty. Treated 'as if they were criminals let loose, war correspondents were locked up in stalls by a corporal's guard' (Cook, 1920, 178). Indeed, until May 1915 reporters and photographers were officially excluded from the war zone altogether. Official secrecy was so severe that newspapers were prohibited even from announcing the dispatch of a British Expeditionary Force across the Channel. Such obtuse rigidity could not be maintained indefinitely, however. Various considerations forced a relaxation. It soon became clear that the press would fill the vacuum of official silence with rumor, speculation and embellishment. Those reporters who weren't confined to stalls in France and Belgium filed copy that told of successive bold victories against the advancing Hun – stories that were simply invented, as Germany's rapid westward advance soon made apparent. From an official point of view, far greater danger lay in these wild fabrications than in a measured release of news and a professional accommodation with the press. If newspapers were to exert the desired 'steadying effect' on nerves, it did no good to risk a massive collapse of morale when a bleaker picture emerged.

Gradually, the military relented. Their initial approach to news, other than staying mum, had been to appoint a senior officer – with a 'tincture of letters' – in a capacity approximating that of official war artist. This uniformed 'eye witness,' Lieutenant Colonel Sir Ernest Swinton, would produce 'word painting' from the front to offer civilians an aestheticized vision of martial endeavor. His reports were submitted for Field Marshall Kitchener's approval to ensure that they corresponded with Swinton's instructions: to 'avoid helping the enemy;' to 'tell as much of the truth as was compatible with safety;' 'to guard against depression and pessimism, and to check unjustified optimism which might lead to a relaxation of effort' (Swinton, quoted by Haste, 1977, 32; Farrar, 1998, 24). As many historians point out, little truth escaped this thicket of restrictions – as Kitchener surely intended, given his legendary 'contempt for the "public" in all its moods and manifestations,' to say nothing of his repugnance for journalists as 'drunken swabs' (Haste, 1977, 33). No wonder one editor proposed that '"Eyewash" would have been a better pseudonym' for the author of these mollifying reports' (Knightley, 2004, 91).

When the 'eye witness' was retired in the spring of 1915, the War Office finally allowed five seasoned British correspondents and one American reporter to join the military at the front, an experiment that soon evolved into a wider scheme of official accreditation (Sweeney, 2006, 40). The need to persuade the United States to abandon its neutrality constituted a compelling argument for greater press freedom, not least when former president Theodore Roosevelt (now an active champion of intervention) insisted that there was a 'very striking contrast between the lavish attention showered on war correspondents by the German military authorities and the point-blank refusal to have anything to do with them by the British and French governments' (quoted by Knightley, 2004, 100). His criticism chimed with one made by British newspapers: namely, that the United Kingdom lagged behind the enemy in the propaganda war – a call to arms repeatedly sounded in later conflicts.

What emerged on the western front might be considered an embryonic experiment in 'embedding': the practice of nestling reporters alongside soldiers somewhat redolent of the system employed during the Gulf War of 1991 and 'Operation Iraqi Freedom' in 2003. For the military, this arrangement allows not only for easier scrutiny of copy but also more subtle shaping of journalists' perspective – a cosying-up that promises certain benefits to all parties. While reporters gain access to the frontline, officers achieve greater supervision over what the press says about the progress of the war and morale of soldiers engaged in it. Civilians, meanwhile, are brought closer to men in combat by timely access to reports fresh from the front. Everyone wins, at least according to this benign version of the theory.

By 1918 officers had come to look on reporters 'with affection, confidence and admiration,' noted former military censor Neville Lytton (1921, viii). Reporters didn't necessarily view the relationship quite so rosily, though. Sometimes they chafed against the intrusive presence of officers who chaperoned their movements – 'a kind of jailer and spy, eating, sleeping, walking and driving together,' in the words of Philip Gibbs (quoted in Grieves, 1996, 719). However, the arrangement did at least afford them access to the front, a site to which daily excursions were laid on. Briefings by senior officers at GHQ were followed by accompanied sorties, as Lytton later explained:

> After these lectures, the correspondents would go to their rooms, take an early dinner and a few hours of sleep, and then proceed by motor to some hill-top just behind the battle-line. After zero hour some would go on to the battle-fields, others would go 'corps-crawling', i.e., collecting information from corps headquarters, and they would all return to their mess by two o'clock. A conference would then take place among themselves, and all information gathered, from whatever source, was pooled, and they retired to their rooms to write their despatches. This pooling was initiated by the British correspondents, as they thought, quite rightly, that the war was too big to admit of 'scoops'. (Lytton, 1921, xi)

The fruits of this toil were then subject to a curious form of anticipatory censorship, since nothing could be passed at variance with an official communiqué that, in Catch-22 style, wasn't issued until *after* the despatches had been couriered to the nearest telegraph location for transmission to London. There the stories were censored once again.

Appraising how inadequately World War I was reported, many critics have passed damning verdicts on the military's domestication of the press, noting the ease with which reporters were turned into propagandists by receipt of a green uniform, the honorary rank of major and luxurious billets at chateaux far from harm's way. 'By stationing the reporters at the various army headquarters, and by making them personal friends, they became apologists for the British cause,' noted H. C. Peterson in 1939 (26): an opinion echoed in Knightley's classic history of war correspondence, *The First Casualty* (Knightley, 2004, 101–3).

Some war correspondents were more apologetic than others, however. And though some were certainly amenable to spreading false reports in the interests of misleading the enemy, others had a different sense of why their reports from the front were necessarily partial – both incomplete and engagé. Consider this passage from Philip Gibbs's *Adventures in Journalism*, published in 1923:

> Some of us, as least, did not spare ourselves to learn the truth and tell it *as far as it lay in our vision and in our power of words*. During the course of the battles it was not possible to tell all the truth, to reveal the full measure of slaughter on our side, and we had no right of criticism.

But day by day the English-speaking world was brought close in spiritual touch with their fighting men, and knew the best, if not the worst, of what was happening in the field of war, and the daily record of courage, endurance, achievement, by the youth that was being spent with such prodigal unthrifty zeal. (271–2; emphasis added)

Gibbs conveys a conflicted sense of duty. He clearly endorses a sense that the journalist is at the front to 'learn and tell the truth.' However, this aspiration clashes not only with the demands of operational security, which abridge the 'right of criticism,' but with another objective that Gibbs depicts as the war correspondent's higher calling – namely, to keep English-speakers 'in spiritual touch with their fighting men.' In short, producing an unvarnished account of combat mattered less than demonstrating emotional fealty with men at war: to be there and bear witness, a conduit between frontline and home front. This conception of the correspondent's function as essentially *affective*, not instructive, is one that has reverberated through many subsequent wars, fueling an impetus towards self-censorship.

But while reporters may have seen themselves as the ordinary Tommy's kith and kin, soldiers frequently viewed the relationship much less sentimentally. One frontline journalist related the view of a subaltern in the London Rifles who 'wanted the blood of all war correspondents – seemed to want to paddle in it' (quoted by Grieves, 1996, 723). Numerous other accounts relate the disdain infantrymen felt for reporters who experienced the privations of trench warfare in the most fleeting fashion, trivializing the misery of life and death at the front with jaunty accounts that treated battle as something between a football match and a Sunday picnic.

H. M. Tomlinson, a leader writer for the *Daily News*, recorded the troops' sarcastic repartee during one of his excursions to the front:

'I'd love to see GHQ. Really, what is it like? Is it true you have parlour-maids?' 'And is it true,' added another fellow, 'you don't reckon we are men, but only insufficient numbers?' They always rubbed it in like this. It was a privilege of theirs. (Tomlinson, quoted by Grieves, 1996, 723)

Then as now soldiers complained that civilians in general, and journalists in particular, had no business commenting on what they didn't know and couldn't possibly understand, not having been in the firing line themselves. Tomlinson acknowledged the point. Far from being seduced by

Illustration 2.2 'The German Spring Offensive on the Western Front': a German Army cinematographer films infantry marching along a road near Albert, 1918

Source: German First World War Official Exchange Collection/Imperial War Museum.

officer status and chateau accommodations, he was uncomfortably aware that proximity to the officer class – with the attendant ability to 'go home' at the end of each day or even leave the war zone altogether – distanced journalists from the trenches' conscripted population.

This wasn't the only problem of differently angled visions. One central impediment to narrating the war with any kind of detachment (had reporters wished to do so) was the issue of perspective – hinted at in Gibbs's comment that journalists endeavored to tell the truth *'as far as it lay in our vision.'* But from what vantage point could they gain sufficient elevation to apprehend clearly what was unfolding along the vast front-lines of this war? As Matthew Farish points out, World War I presented a profound challenge to ocularity, occasioning a 'crisis of representation' (2001, 276). Its scale was too enormous to be taken in whole. British offi-cer-minders tried to treat it as a show that could be viewed as though by theater-goers seated in a lofty box, observing the stage through opera-glasses. Yet the battles of World War I defied 'spectacularization' of this kind – none more so than the Somme offensive of July 1916, which claimed 57,420 British casualties, including 19,240 dead, on the first day alone. Once the smoke lifted, it was 'too late to see our men actually moving from the trenches,' recalled one reporter who had been driven that morning to a nearby hill-top. Another expressed amazement at 'the utter absence of any visible human being ... in a world which was being broken into chaos' (Robinson, quoted by Farish, 2001, 285). As William Beach Thomas concluded, despite new-fangled aids to sight, 'all combined could scarcely penetrate the fog of war' (ibid., 283).

Accustomed to regarding this phrase as metaphorical, critics have tended to overlook obstacles to perception that weren't the product of state censorship but of the war's immensity: its resistance to apprehen-sion either when viewed from afar or by those caught up in its nerve-shattered confusion.

Film and World War I

If the 'fog of war' hampered correspondents' perceptual abilities, how did photographers and cameramen fare in World War I? For state opin-ion-managers, visual media were a source of especial concern. The visceral realism of photography was potentially more affecting than verbal depictions of war, as well as more accessible to a greater number of people. Vivid portraits of men at war, especially of those *fallen* in war, threatened civilian sensibilities. And then there were moving images – projected frames of celluloid film that showed animate life in motion, a thrilling new phenomenon of the early twentieth century.

In Britain, Germany, and the United States alike film formed a partic-ular target of state intervention, though not until the war's latter stages. Policy-makers found themselves simultaneously attracted and repelled by this parvenu medium of the masses. Many who staffed the official propaganda agencies that each combatant state developed – Wellington House and then the Ministry of Information in Britain, the *Kriegspresseamt* in Germany, and the Committee for Public Information in the United States – lacked expertise in film, an ignorance tinged with snobbish disdain. Cinema-going was, broadly speaking, a class-specific recreation. Along with music halls and pubs, the picture palace was a preserve of the working class. 'Vulgar and without serious importance' was how Lucy Masterman (wife of the director of the British propaganda agency, Wellington House) characterized her peers' attitude towards cinema (quoted by Reeves, 1993, 188; Haste, 1977, 45). But in 1914, Britons bought 20 million theatre tickets, and a medium of such popularity could scarcely be ignored indefinitely. As the press baron Lord Northcliffe, charged by Lloyd George with responsibility for overseas propaganda, rather reluctantly averred, 'Not everyone reads the newspapers, and those who do forget what they have read, but no one can forget what he has seen happen on the screen' (quoted by Haste, 1977, 45).

Political and military leaders set out with the supposition that images of wounded and dead bodies would ignite a firestorm of pacifist protest and must accordingly be kept altogether from the realm of public inspection: a position replicated in numerous successive conflicts. Kitchener debarred photographers from the front until 1915, when the War Office sanctioned the presence of two. But images of mortality and maiming were not, of course, the only possible depictions of war. And even stark pictographic acknowledgement of war's human toll was not *bound* to occasion a collapse in morale. On the contrary, formal memorialization of sacrifice also promised to galvanize popular determination to see the war through to a successful conclusion. Lost life could form its own justification for continuing to prosecute a war – even (or perhaps especially) a war in which formal justifications no longer seemed, or had never unanimously seemed, sufficient. By this logic, victory alone stood to vindicate loss. 'Death in all its grim nakedness' would stiffen public resolve, claimed film director Geoffrey Malins (quoted by Ferguson, 1999, 237).

Over time, intuitions of this kind began to color official thinking. In the first instance, however, British propagandists received prodding from gung-ho newspapers, berating governmental slowness to tear a leaf from their enemy's book. In Germany, complained the *Daily Mail* in April 1915, 'every man, woman, and child knows what the war means and how the nation is fighting,' thanks to 'brilliant war correspondents and constantly changing kinematograph films and photographs' (quoted by Farrar, 1998, 66). The enemy's apparently superior speed and skill in producing propaganda formed a compelling reason to rectify the deficit. Germany, in turn, would establish a *Bild-und Filmamt* (Picture and Film Department) and then a film company UFA (*Universum Film Aktiengesellschaft*), in 1917, believing it had fallen behind the British (Curry, 1995, 140–2). By then, British propagandists had produced a number of films. The first, *Britain Prepared*, appeared in 1915 and was screened in 'practically every country which possesses cinematograph facilities,' Wellington House boasted (Reeves, 1986, 15). Twenty-seven short subjects followed in the next six months.

In 1916, the best known film of World War I was released, *The Battle of the Somme*: a production that merits discussion for what it reveals of difficulties surrounding both the production and reception of wartime film. In Britain, audiences were struck by its realistic representation of trench warfare. Some 13 per cent of its 77 minutes' running time contained shots of the dead and wounded. In light of the antiseptic character of many verbal and visual renderings of combat to date, a scene depicting a soldier going 'over the top' before collapsing back into the trench was especially striking in its candor. However, as many film historians have noted, this sequence – like many others – was in fact staged. Just as reporters struggled to piece together what had occurred during the Somme offensive, so cameramen were afflicted by the smoky, vaporous confusion of the battlefield. How could they possibly hope to capture events strung across such an expansive landscape of wreckage, or render dramatic a conflict in which *inaction* often typified soldierly experience, without resorting to fakery? Reconstructing scenes, a common expedient in the film industry, was necessary to render combat footage intelligible and to convey a sense of emotional, if not literal, realism – making battle conform with civilians' expectations of what warfare looked like (Badsey, 1983, 106; Hüppauf, 1995, 102).

Contemporary audiences seem to have accepted such scenes at face value. But perhaps more tellingly, they were not unanimously in favor of being shown so much of what they assumed was the reality of war. A London paper, *The Star* reported:

> There is no doubt that the Somme pictures have stirred London more passionately than anything has since the war. Everybody is talking about them. Everybody is discussing them. Everybody is discussing whether they are too painful for public exhibition. (Quoted by Reeves, 1997, 17)

Private individuals' scruples about *The Battle of the Somme* sprang from different sources. Some felt that images of the dead and wounded trespassed on private grief. Others believed that it was simply wrong to turn soldiers' pain into 'a spectacle for the pleasure of those who like to gloat, in perfect safety themselves, over the agonies of others' (letter to the *Manchester Guardian*, August 15, 1916, quoted by Reeves, 1997, 17).

The Battle of the Somme fueled the anti-war convictions of some while gratifying the anti-Germanism of others. 'Praise God, from whom all blessing flow, A few more Germans gone below,' chorused one viewer after watching it (quoted by Reeves, 1997, 19). Audiences in some neutral countries were left unmoved; bored by what Britons found variously gripping, inspiring or galling. In the United States, by contrast, the film was censored after complaints that its horrors were impacting recruitment in a harmful way. But if the film didn't move everyone in the same way, as images invariably do not, official propagandists nevertheless believed *The Battle of the Somme* had fulfilled a vital purpose. At a time when almost every British family had at least one member in uniform, the film offered a prop to imagination – one exhibited at 2,000 cinemas across the country (Ferguson, 1999, 236). As such, it fortified a sense of identification between civilians and soldiers, 'showing,' as Lloyd George put it, what 'our men at the Front are doing and suffering for us, and how their achievements have been made possible by the sacrifices made at home' (quoted by Badsey, 1983, 99).

However hard it is to chart the gradations in popular response to wartime film, one thing is clear. Wartime not only boosted the circulation figures of many newspapers, even as their size dwindled due to paper and print shortages, it also elevated the popularity and prestige of film. This

Illustration 2.3   Charlie Chaplin promotes the Third Liberty Loan in Washington DC on the first anniversary of US entry into WWI (1918)

Source: Still Pictures Section, US National Archives.

was true in both Germany and Britain, but nowhere more so than in the United States where Hollywood emerged as the Great War's greatest beneficiary.

American film studios, production companies and distributors had been poised for dominance even before 1914, capturing a weekly domestic audience of 80 million. But war simultaneously helped open overseas markets and established the movie industry as a patriotic institution with a broadened appeal to middle-class audiences attracted to the auditoriums by newsreels and more high-minded wartime fare. During the 19 months of America's formal involvement in the war, Hollywood rehearsed the role it would play with greater aplomb in World War II. Teaming up with the government Committee on Public Information, Hollywood's own Committee of the Motion Picture Industry (chaired by D. W. Griffith, director of the notorious classic, *Birth of a Nation*) urged the studios to manufacture such gleefully anti-German fare as *The Hun Within* (1918), *The Kaiser, Beast of Berlin* (1918) and *The Claws of the Hun* (1918). With theater lobbies doubling as bazaars for war bonds, the stars of the silver screen helped simultaneously sell *and* finance the war effort, while also raising Hollywood's own stock. By personal example, on- and off-screen, movie stars encouraged Americans to emulate them in new roles – as soldiers, nurses, production-line workers or simply as committed supporters of the war (DeBauche, 1997).

Legacies and lessons

Retrospective judgements on the media's contribution to World War I have been damning. At their most extreme, critics have charged the press with kindling a global conflagration from which ordinary people would have recoiled had newspapers not beaten the drum for war so clamorously and to such hypnotic effect. The case was trenchantly put by Viennese satirist Karl Kraus:

> Through decades of practice, the newspaper reporter has brought to us that degree of impoverishment of the imagination which makes it possible for us to fight a war of annihilation against ourselves. Since the boundless efficiency of his apparatus has deprived us of all capacity for experience and for the mental development of that experience, he can now implant in us the courage in the face of death which we need in order to rush off into battle ... His abuse of language embellishes the abuse of life. (Quoted by Ferguson, 1999, 240–1)

Would the war have been possible at all without the press, Kraus mused in his play *The Last Days* – 'possible to begin or possible to continue?' Some took a different view. Early twentieth-century critiques of capitalism, notably those of V. I. Lenin and the English liberal J. A. Hobson, had predicted that predictable inter-imperial rivalry would ultimately lead to war: a product of capitalism's incapacity to find adequate domestic markets and its ceaseless need to find new sources of raw commodities and sites to reinvest surplus capital. These structural dynamics had fueled the furious scramble for colonial markets and materials of the late Victorian and Edwardian eras that heightened tension between the European great powers. A human catastrophe the war certainly was, but neither an unfathomable accident nor the straightforward result of hate-mongering propaganda.

Yet it remains common to find World War I treated as an epic folly – a 'meaningless act of slaughter' blundered into by inept politicians, goaded by a bombastic press and then prosecuted by headstrong generals with fatally outmoded tactics, 'until a state of exhaustion set in because no one knew how to stop it' (Knightley, 2004, 83). This conception of the war as a needless tragedy born aloft on vast quantities of hot air has heightened criticism of the media, encouraging counterfactual speculation along the lines ventured by Kraus. Had newspapers reported events following Franz Ferdinand's assassination in less frenzied terms, conflict would have been averted. And had reporters, photographers, and film-makers but shown the war's fatalities and futility, it would never have lasted as long as it did. Such hypotheses not only overlook the more profound structural forces productive of war, but rest on two other often unquestioned assumptions. First, that the wartime media engaged *solely* in militaristic tub-thumping; and, second, that contemporary newspaper reports, newsreels and films dictated popular attitudes, which in turn were uniformly pro-war. Neither assumption, however, is entirely warranted.

As a number of historians have pointed out, many leading newspapers in both Britain and Germany, far from urging statesmen to declare war, counselled just the opposite in the summer of 1914. The *Berliner Tageblatt* insisted on July 30 that the German people were 'absolutely peaceful,' and should do nothing more than secure the border in response to Russian mobilization, while the conservative *Norddeutsche Allgemeine Zeitung* argued for localization of the dispute between Serbia and Austria. Similarly, in Britain the *Manchester Guardian* warned that war would 'risk everything of which we are proud.' The *Daily Mail* urged a posture of strict neutrality. The *Daily News* went so far as to carry an article bluntly headlined, 'Why We Must Not Fight' (Ferguson, 1999, 215–17). Once battle began many editors and reporters adopted a supportive stance – as is commonly the case in wartime. But amidst the hurrahing columns, penned with that 'bank holiday touch' so distasteful to many frontline soldiers, criticism did not wither away entirely (Grieves, 1996, 728). That an establishment paper such as *The Times* could carry a report in November 1914 announcing that 'war has become stupid,' bemoaning the sacrifice of thousands of lives for 'a few hundred yards' of territory, the 'butchery of the unknown by the unseen,' gives the lie to blunt assertions that the 'wastage [of human life] went completely unreported in Britain until after the war was over' (Ferguson, 1999, 218; Andersen, 2006, 13).

It's also misleading to imagine, as some critics propose, that entire populations were 'led to madness' in 1914, and remained in a blind fury for four years thereafter, by brilliantly successful propaganda to which an obsequious press contributed (Andersen, 2006, 16). The reasons why millions of men and women contributed to the war effort varied greatly, often having little to do with a burning hatred of the enemy instilled by mendacious press reports, flagwaving films or lurid recruitment posters. Amongst these reasons, and by no means the least significant, was a massive expansion of state power that accompanied the war, especially in the United States. Enlistment was ostensibly voluntary but maintaining principled opposition demanded a good deal of personal courage. The lot of conscientious objectors was nowhere a happy one, often involving jail sentences for those who refused to serve even in non-combat capacities.

In the United States, pacificists and anti-war protestors found it extremely difficult to air their views without incurring the wrath of federal authorities or outraged fellow citizens. Patriotism assumed a viciously xenophobic edge. As historian Susan Brewer notes, the CPI's slogan '100% American,' making support for the war a badge of national belonging, was 'turned into a weapon against Americans suspected of being traitors because of their ethnic heritage.' German Americans faced severe harassment, or worse, from self-appointed patriotic vigilantes. A St Louis mob attacked a man called Robert Prager in April 1918 when he attempted to enlist in the navy. His name sounded worrisomely German, as did that of sauerkraut which became 'liberty cabbage' for the duration. Prager met a more irrevocable fate, however. Wrapped in the stars and stripes, he was lynched – a 'patriotic murder' following which the perpetrators were acquitted (Brewer, 2009, 69). Over the course of the war, at least 70 Americans were killed as a result of mob violence (Capozzola, 2008, 6, 10).

Murderous actions of this kind weren't simply spontaneous products of nativist zeal. US federal authorities did a good deal to harness popular animosity towards recognizable 'outgroups' – whether Germans, socialists, or African Americans – using it to drive dissent underground and encourage public displays of loyalty. Supported by the Justice Department, the American Protective League, an organization of some 250,000 citizens, spied on neighbors and colleagues, opened mail, broke into homes, intercepted telegrams and advocated assault (Brewer, 2009, 70). Not content with encouraging vigilantism of this kind, the US government also enacted legislation – the Espionage Act (1917), Trading with the Enemy Act (1917), and Sedition Act (1918) – which ensured that Americans could be arrested, tried and jailed for discouraging men from enlisting or for any criticism of either how the war was being conducted or of its aims, amongst a welter of other new wartime offenses (Sweeney, 2006, 50–2). Still, not all Americans thought such measures went far enough. A group of New York women urged Congress to make defacement of war posters a federal crime.

And yet despite this massive expansion of the state's coercive power, the inescapable imprint of official propaganda and sometimes lethal venom of a public licensed to assail perceived traitors, not all Americans supported the war. (Nor, for that matter, did all Britons. A wave of strikes and protests swept the country in 1917.) As Christopher Capozzola's history of US citizenship and World War I points out:

> Some 337, 000 men successfully avoided the draft, antiwar neighborhoods consistently failed to meet their Liberty Loan purchase quotas, and at the battle of the Meuse-Argonne Valley in September and October 1918, more than one hundred thousand men fled the front lines and refused to fight. (2008, 9–10)

While some soldiers may have been fired up with hatred of the enemy, propaganda did less to keep troops in line than harsh military discipline. Court-martials and executions formed a routine part of frontline life.

At root, why people enlist or resist in wartime may owe relatively little to prompts from commercial media or state propaganda – a point many studies of wartime media fail adequately to stress. Take the Anglo-Welsh poet, Edward Thomas, for example. In a poem entitled 'This is No Case of Petty Right or Wrong,' penned in December 1915, he insisted:

> I hate not Germans, nor grow hot
> With love of Englishmen, to please newspapers.
> Beside my hate for one fat patriot
> My hatred of the Kaiser is love true.
>
> (Thomas, 1979, 165)

And yet despite his scruples, Thomas joined up, dying at the Battle of Arras soon after arriving in France in April 1917. In wartime, as in peacetime, individual motivations spring from multiple, sometimes contradictory, sources. Thomas ultimately enlisted as a result of his preservationist attachment to rural life, which he believed endangered by the war. Others enlisted from a sense of obligation, duty or fatalism – sometimes irrespective of whether they accepted the justice of the cause. Behavior, in short, is not always straightforwardly prompted by belief, a disconnect that state opinion-managers have trouble accepting, preferring to imagine that citizens fulfill their allotted wartime roles with complete conviction in a spirit of willing obedience, not grudging compliance or defeated resignation.

Preparing for the next war

One individual convinced that propaganda made *the* decisive contribution to molding opinions and thus to determining national destinies in the Great War was Adolf Hitler. He maintained that the British campaign to demoralize their opponents – an 'inspired work of genius' – had effected the collapse of German morale, and he was far from alone in this conviction. German soldiers, announced General Ludendorff, had been 'hypnotized … as a rabbit by a snake.' During the interwar Weimar era the notion steadily gained ground that the 'German people were not beaten on the battlefield but were defeated in the war of words,' as Nazi propagandist Eugen Hadamovsky put it (quoted in Ferguson, 1999, 213). Of course, it served Nazi purposes to kindle the idea that Germans had been stabbed in the back by psychologically manipulative foes from within and without, heightening a sense of national victimization and vengefulness. But however self-serving this *Dolchstoß Legende* (stab-in-the-back myth) may have been, Hitler was a true believer in the power of propaganda, as *Mein Kampf* made abundantly clear.

As soon as the National Socialists assumed power in 1933, they set about establishing complete Party control over the state, and state control over every conceivable outlet of individual and collective expression. The aim, Goebbels announced, was to effect what Josef Goebbels termed a 'spiritual mobilization' of German life. The Third Reich had no place for waverers: to be a good German was to be a devout Nazi. Uniformity of belief would be achieved by compulsion and terror where necessary, but by preference because the Aryan *Volk* would see how perfectly State and Party represented their interests: an organic unity Rudolph Hess captured in his slogan 'The Party is Hitler, but Hitler is Germany, just as Germany is Hitler!' (Taylor, 1979, 170). 'It is not enough to reconcile people more or less to our regime, to move them towards a position of neutrality towards us,' Goebbels further elaborated before press representatives on March 15, 1933, 'we want rather to work on people until they are addicted to us' (cited by Welch, 1983a, 5).

Media in the Third Reich would thus become syringes pumping ideological serum into German veins. But how to ensure that only authorized material entered the national bloodstream? To this end the Nazi state established multiple layers of filtration. Goebbels occupied the position of purifier in chief, simultaneously head of the Reich Ministry for Popular Enlightenment and Propaganda (RMVP), President of the Reich Chamber of Culture (*Reichskulturkammer*, RKK) and Director of the Central Propaganda Office of the Party.

Through the Chamber of Culture, conditions of employment were established and undesirable personnel purged. Since journalists, filmmakers, writers and artists were all compelled to belong to the appropriate Chamber whose gate-keeper was a fervent Party functionary, potential members with racial or political 'impurities' were screened out. The Third Reich thus marginalized potential dissidents without making Party membership itself a *sine qua non* of professional activity. Historian of Nazi propaganda, David Welch suggests that the RKK's purgative activities allowed the regime largely to dispense with formal censorship since the remaining personnel needed little coercion (1993, 27). Yet despite their likely docility, German media were not free from further scrutiny. On the contrary, the state took ever more radical steps to eliminate what little latitude for maneuver still remained. This took time to accomplish, but the Nazis worked at it steadily both before and during the war.

The German press posed the most complex problem. In the 1930s, Germany boasted 4,700 newspapers – more per capita than any other state. Of these, the Nazi Party owned only 59 titles in 1933, with a fairly paltry circulation of 782,121 (Welch, 1993, 38). The obvious solution was to reduce plurality by acquiring newspapers for the Party's own publishing house, *Eher Verlag*, headed by Max Amann, an important party functionary who also served as the Press Chamber's president. While Amann's underlings expunged unsuitable personnel, undesirable content shrank as editors experienced mounting pressure to follow daily directives issued by the official press agency, the *Deutsches Nachrichtenburo*. From October 1933 onwards, editors were compelled to excise anything 'calculated to weaken the strength of the Reich abroad or at home' (Welch, 1993, 37). Editors who disobeyed were likely to find their newspapers either shut down or bought out by the Party.

By 1939, *Eher Verlag* controlled two-thirds of the German press. But it was the war which really enabled the state to consolidate its grip. Wartime privations meant that press circulation would have fallen irrespective of state policy as paper, print and personnel shortages bit (Hale, 1964, 275). However, the Nazi regime exploited these practical difficulties for political purposes, rationing paper and newsprint in such a way as to reward Nazi papers at the expense of the last remnants of a semi-independent press. As more and more titles were shut down, Amann could at last proclaim in 1943, 'The Party Commands the Press' (ibid., 289). By February 1945, however, newspapers scarcely existed, reduced to little more than a handbill on which was printed the daily military communiqué and desperate appeals of the party elite.

Radio, on the other hand, was ripe for *gleichschaltung*. The German broadcasting network had been state-owned since 1925, albeit with the Weimar state exercising relatively little say over program content. By a decree of June 1933, the network's nine former regional stations were placed under the control of the RMVP. The next step was to bring this 'magnetic' medium closer to the people. To boost listenership the state set about producing cheap radio sets: the 'people's receiver.' These sets were heavily subsidized so workers could afford what was still a relatively new innovation. Since they were manufactured to pick up frequencies from a limited range, German listeners struggled to tune into foreign broadcasts (Welch, 1993, 32–3). Consequently the 70 per cent of German homes which owned a set by 1939, the highest percentage anywhere in the world, were almost obliged to listen to home-grown fare whether they liked it or not – and Goebbels found plenty of evidence as the war progressed to suggest that they did not. For those without, the state also encouraged 'community listening,' complete with local party functionary, the *Gau* radio warden, to monitor audience reaction.

Hitler modeled Nazi policy on what he believed was British propaganda practice from World War I. Meanwhile, as Germany swallowed up one neighboring country after another, British policy-makers adopted the view that if Britain was going to fight the Germans again, it should have exactly the same weapons as Germany now boasted, though, as historian Michael Balfour observes, 'there was not an equal recognition, particularly in the Services, as to what exactly those weapons were.' Ironically, then, when Chamberlain's government tentatively began planning for a future information war, 'the British imagined they were copying from the

Germans something which the Germans imagined they had copied from the British' (1979, 54).

In different ways, British, Soviet and American officials all tended to minimize the prospect of war until their state was actually in the thick of it. In Westminster, fitful talk of resuscitating the Ministry of Information (MOI), disbanded in 1918, rumbled on from 1935 until September 1939 when Britain declared war on Germany after it invaded Poland. While Chamberlain had desperately hoped that appeasement would assuage Germany's territorial ambitions, his advisers assumed that the worst-case scenario – should Hitler fail to back down – would pit the RAF against the Luftwaffe in a short, intense aerial confrontation. In such a war, it would be imperative to maintain civilian morale, for it was feared that bombing would quickly shatter British nerves (McLaine, 1979, 26). Maintaining morale was at a premium, but no one quite knew what it was nor how to sustain it, although many planners assumed that working-class Britons did not possess the desired esprit in natural abundance. Recognizing that high morale would partly hinge on carefully rationed news, plans for the MOI's relations with the BBC and newsreel companies nevertheless remained extremely fluid as the 'Phoney War' began and British officials awaited the drone of German bombers overhead.

In September 1939, British official policy towards the media remained so shambolic that reporters feared a return to the 'Dark Ages' of 1914–15. In an echo of August 1914, the military imposed a total news blackout on the British Expeditionary Force's dispatch to France – doing so only *after* newspapers had already gone to press. This resulted in 'a farce which saw Fleet Street offices occupied by Scotland Yard and the offending newspapers seized from startled early morning commuters before the ban was lifted again shortly afterwards' (Taylor, 1995, 212). In France itself, censorship was so draconian that one American reporter in Paris lamented that 'News does not arrive, or maybe it does not exist' (Mathews, 1957, 180). Meanwhile, the BBC suspended regular programming to crank out hours of organ music, an unedifying diet which listeners couldn't escape by seeking refuge at the cinema. These had all been closed down for the duration in anticipation of an airwar that would turn picture palaces, filled with flammable film stock, into death-traps: a decision soon reversed as the war confounded all expectations (Aldgate and Richards, 1994, 1). No wonder, then, that Lord John Reith (founder of the BBC and one of three men to serve as Minister of Information in the first two years of war) wondered what Goebbels would have made of all this mess, could he have 'believed a tenth of what was happening here' (quoted by Balfour, 1979, 109).

The Soviet Union approached unfolding events in central Europe with a different set of blindspots, evasions and miscalculations. After signing a Non-Aggression Pact with Germany in August 1939, the Soviet Union prosecuted a parallel war from 1939 to 1940 – not against Hitler, with whom Stalin had colluded, but against Finland which the Red Army invaded in November 1939. This Winter War lasted until March 1940, when Finland ceded portions of territory to Moscow. But these Finnish concessions hardly represented the ringing victory that Stalin had led his population to expect. Determined resistance by Finnish fighters dealt a powerful blow to Red Army prestige and to the credibility of the Soviet press.

The Kremlin's refusal to appraise Soviet security realistically led to a yet more disastrous crisis of confidence on June 22, 1941, when German troops poured across the Soviet Union's western border. Since Stalin had staunchly maintained that there would be no war with Germany, while simultaneously hailing the invincibility of the Red Army, Hitler's launch of 'Operation Barbarossa' was a stunning blow. The USSR's state-run media were left scrambling since the Kremlin's state of denial had precluded any serious planning for an eventuality that couldn't be publicly contemplated. Thus on the night of June 22, no radio correspondents were present on the Ukrainian and Belorussian fronts as German panzer divisions charged east into Soviet territory. At first Radio Moscow, the state broadcasting network with an estimated 30 million regular listeners, greeted this catastrophic turn of events with silence. Normal programming continued as though nothing untoward had occurred (von Geldern, 1995, 47). But clearly an event of this scale could not be covered up indefinitely – even in a country where misrepresentation and mendacity were routine.

Within two days the Kremlin created a new agency, *Informbiuro*, to centralize the censorship, release and presentation of wartime news. But, as in Britain, it took time for this opinion-molding bureaucracy to iron out organizational glitches and make good the harm done by Stalin himself. After a two-week disappearance from public view, his early wartime utterances continued to offer increasingly implausible assurances of early victory, even as vast tracts of Soviet territory fell to the advancing *Wehrmacht*. Three weeks after the Kremlin had relocated from Moscow to Kuibyshev, Stalin continued to insist that 4.5 million German soldiers had already been taken out of action, terrified by the Soviet cavalry (von Geldern, 1995, 49). Yet many Soviet citizens knew from first-hand experience of German occupation that this couldn't possibly be so.

Like Stalin and Chamberlain, Roosevelt also initially maintained that the United States would remain aloof from conflict – a declaratory posture of neutrality that looked ever less credible as the president authorized large-scale assistance to the beleaguered western allies in the form of Lend-Lease. This incremental progression from non-involvement to wholesale commitment required a major public relations campaign to sell reluctant Americans on the need for war. But given the mistrust that continued to surround war-mongering propaganda, FDR and his advisors had to tread gently (Casey, 2001). Exhortations that seemed too obviously aimed at creating interventionist sentiment threatened to backfire. Hence, while censorship was imposed in December 1940 on the reporting of certain topics – such as the movement of US planes and ships (already supporting British transport in the Atlantic) or the development of secret weapons – no overt state agency could be created devoted to propaganda so long as the US was formally neutral (Sweeney, 2006, 67).

Instead, a series of innocuously named offices sought to rally opinion for war without appearing to do so. In September 1939, the Office of Government Reports was established to keep track of domestic opinion, which pollsters found to be markedly against war and tinged with pro-Germanism. An Office of Civilian Defense, headed by New York's pugnacious Mayor La Guardia, was tasked with promoting public safety and boosting morale, while the division of information of the Office for Emergency Management pumped out numerous daily press-releases on the build-up of America's arsenal. Nelson Rockefeller, as Coordinator of Inter-American Affairs, led US efforts to rally foreign opinion. In parallel with these efforts, Colonel William Donovan served as Coordinator of Information – an agency that became the Office of Strategic Services (OSS, later mutating into the CIA), tasked with conducting psychological operations at the enemy. To coordinate this proliferation of agencies, FDR then established an Office of Facts and Figures in October 1941. Its remit, as a jaded *New York Herald Tribune* put it, was to 'explain what those who explain what the explainers of the explanations mean' (quoted by Brewer, 2009, 93–4).

Despite all this preparatory groundwork, Japan's attack on Pearl Harbor on December 7, 1941 wrongfooted US officials in much the same way that 'Operation Barbarossa' confounded the Kremlin, and that the invasion of Poland – followed by Chamberlain's declaration of war – caused institutional lock-jaw in Britain. Washington's initial impulses also ran in the direction of suppression and evasion. The US army and navy imposed martial law on Hawaii, censoring communication by telephone, radio and cable between the islands and the mainland. Roosevelt requested that FBI director J. Edgar Hoover coordinate censorship, which he did with relish – suppressing a report by Drew Pearson and Robert S. Allen on the extent of devastation that official statements had wilfully minimized, and even threatening Pearson with jail (Sweeney, 2001, 31,139–41).

At the outset, then, Germany seemed to enjoy every advantage in the war of words and weapons alike. Not only did the Third Reich boast the best-oiled propaganda machine and most tightly disciplined media, the *Wehrmacht* also scored a series of lightning victories that gave Nazi propagandists much to brag about and little reason, unlike their dazed antagonists, to lapse into silence and obfuscation.

The 'shock troops of propaganda'

News, as the BBC's founder Lord John Reith put it, was the 'shock troops of propaganda.' Differently phrased but similarly formulated, this point was also made by Goebbels, who noted in his diary in May 1942 that, '[n]ews policy is a weapon of war; its purpose is to wage war and not to give out information' (quoted by Doob, 1995, 203). In other words, news represented a commodity to be dispensed, withheld or manipulated in pursuit of victory. News was central to the maintenance of home front esprit, just as it was critical in attempts to sway neutral nations and undermine enemy morale.

An instrumental attitude towards news had been evident in World War I – after the various national high commands overcame their inclination to keep mum for the duration. But in this second global conflict news appeared a yet more critical front in the battle for opinion. The stakes were higher as more people now enjoyed access to a greater range of media, including those (namely film and radio) that did not depend on literacy. And for the first time millions also lay within range of *enemy* broadcasts thanks to the development of a new medium utterly unmindful of national boundaries. States could attempt to secure a monopoly for their own national radio networks only by jamming enemy broadcasts – a resource-intensive technical undertaking that wasn't always successful – or by imposing draconian penalties on citizens caught listening to foreign transmissions. This too proved an ineffective way of curbing people's curiosity to tune in to illicit programs, whether because these stations played better music, were more humorous, entertainingly preposterous or provided more credible news.

Technological developments placed radio at the center of this information war. The transformed communications landscape also encouraged states and their militaries to approach media in a more dynamic way – as active producers and sculptors of news, not simply its suppressors. As Goebbels recognized, the popular 'hunger for news must somehow be satisfied' or Germans would be 'compel[ed] to listen to foreign and enemy broadcasts' (quoted by Doob, 1995, 203). World War II thus saw a vast proliferation of media, spanning the gamut from state-issued posters, pamphlets, comics and films to military newspapers and radio stations. The Soviet Union boasted no less than 757 separate military titles by the war's end (McReynolds, 1995, 29). As for radio, the BBC increased its foreign language services from ten in 1939 to 45 in 1943 (Briggs, 1995, 18). The US government inaugurated the multilingual Voice of America network in 1942, while at home the amount of radio airtime devoted to news rose from an estimated 5 to 20 per cent – with nine out of ten Americans listening to four hours of radio daily (Brewer, 2009, 102).

That all sides regarded information as a vital strategic commodity generated intense competition between the Axis powers and their opponents to dominate the news cycle by releasing information as speedily as possible, or suppressing it with as little evidence of burial as possible. The importance attached to news also produced pressures *within* combatant states as they developed complex, overlapping agencies to manage the concurrent release and censorship of information. Tension arose not simply between media and state but between civilian personnel and military officials as they tussled over what to release, what to stifle and how to deal with the most vexed issue in wartime news-management: reversals, losses and defeats likely to demoralize the home front.

In Germany, internal conflict over news policy assumed personalized form in the struggle between Goebbels and the *Wehrmacht* high command, and more specifically between the Reich's propaganda minister and the Führer himself. Goebbels' authority had never been total, thanks to Hitler's insistence on duplicating functions within his inner circle – the better to rule over them in 'calculated chaos' (Balfour, 1979, 35). Since wartime elevated the military to a position of primacy in newsmaking, Goebbels found himself battling with the *Wehrmacht* high command's propaganda division (OKW/Wpr) and against Reich Press Chief Otto Dietrich, who accompanied Hitler on his peregrinations to the various fronts. Hitler was the final arbiter of OKW press releases: a review process that bypassed Goebbels' machinery altogether. If OKW communiqués met Hitler's approval, they were released directly through the state news agency in time for the two o'clock radio bulletin (Balfour, 1979, 105). If they did not, they were amended accordingly, often privileging the fantastical at the expense of the factual. On one typical occasion, reading that the Army had taken 30,000 POWs, Hitler insisted that the figure be altered: 'Don't put 30,000 but 30,723 and everyone will believe an exact count has been made' (quoted by Balfour, 1979, 122).

Hitler saw no problem with deception – so long as people swallowed the bait. As *Mein Kampf* made clear, its author regarded lying as an essential element of successful propaganda. Being believed was, of course, helpful. But in Hitler's opinion the more audacious the lie, the less liable it was to scrutiny. Goebbels, with whom the 'Big Lie' became synonymous, adopted a rather more nuanced position. Since he discerned a correlation between credibility and accuracy that Hitler discounted altogether, their working relationship wasn't free from friction (Baird, 1974). Moreover, as the war progressed and the *Wehrmacht* suffered a devastating reversal of fortune at Stalingrad – where the eastern front's most bitterly contested battle ended in German defeat in February 1943 – the divergence between their approaches became yet more apparent. Having predicted victory, the fallible Führer shunned the public spotlight, while tightening his grip on the press so ferociously that even Goebbels' own column in *Das Reich* wasn't free from censorship. But if Hitler usurped some of his propaganda minister's powers, the latter simultaneously assumed some of the Führer's, striding into the limelight to fill the sudden and embarrassing leadership void (Kershaw, 1987).

As the war reached its climax, Goebbels moved center stage to encourage, exhort and threaten a dispirited German populace. In the most significant speech of his career, at the Berlin *Sportspalast* on February 18, 1943, he warned that Germany could lose the war if the Aryan *Volk* didn't respond in the fervent affirmative to his call for a war effort 'more total and radical than ever imagined' (Balfour, 1979, 321). This unprecedented intimation of defeat chimed with Goebbels' avowed policy of 'total frankness.' But, not surprisingly, frankness only extended so far. Despite his insistence that propaganda's function was 'not to make predictions but to report facts,' Goebbels indulged wild flights of fancy. Bouts of irrational mysticism, during which he would conjure a 1,000-year Reich for eternity, were interspersed with boasts about miraculous secret weapons poised to deliver victory (Welch, 1983a, 6).

The Third Reich's media war shared certain similarities with that of the Soviet Union, albeit with fortunes reversed. Both were polities in which rigid state control over all forms of communication – the apparatus of ideological instruction and hence of opinion's homogenization – was intrinsic in peace and wartime alike. Both also accorded the military greater dominance over news-making than did the British or US administrations.

Illustration 2.4 'Nothing Much in the Paper This Morning': British cartoonist NEB (Ronald Niebour) mocks Goebbels' desire to mollify Hitler by snipping offensive material from the newspaper in its entirety, 1943

Source: *The Daily Mail.*

One manifestation of these trends was the parallel emergence in Germany and the USSR of a new kind of war correspondent who was a trained member of the armed services. Germany's state-produced newsreel, the *Deutsche Wochenschauen*, was shot by specially enlisted *Propaganda Kompanien* whose cameramen were expected to throw themselves wholeheartedly into battle, an innovation which the propaganda minister boastfully extolled (Welch, 1983c, 206). With exhilarating close-up scenes carefully edited to eliminate bloodshed and commentaries supervised by Goebbels himself, these newsreels proved appealing to German cinema-goers in the early months of the war: a popularity achieved at the expense of the PK cameramen (ibid., 208–12). Since a higher premium was placed on dramatic footage than on their lives, over 1,000 PK men were killed or missing in action by October 1943 (Hoffmann, 1996, 95).

Similarly, in the USSR a new breed of *voenkor* (war correspondent) was mobilized, drawn primarily from the officer corps, trained at the military's Lenin Institute and licensed to criticize his peers in order to improve overall performance (McReynolds, 1995, 28–9). Already tenuous lines of demarcation between the Communist Party bureaucracy, the Soviet literati and the Red Army – itself under the tight ideological surveillance and discipline of a Communist Party commissariat known as the *Glavnoe Politicheskoe Upravlenie* (GPU) – became yet more blurred. Red Army officers assumed editorial positions at leading state publications, while prominent journalists and writers joined units at the front to report for military newspapers. The latter, most notably *Red Star*, also attracted a civilian following drawn to their vivid vignettes of soldierly life penned by well-known authors such as Vassily Grossman, Ilya Ehrenburg, Mikhail Sholkhov and Konstantin Simonov (Brooks, 2000, 16–18).

As their German counterparts later would, Soviet news managers struggled with military setbacks: a topic that resisted candid treatment in a society steeped in Stalin's triumphalist personality cult. Well-worn prewar slogans like 'Where Stalin Is, There is Victory!' quickly vanished from *Pravda*. In the face of defeat the great leader was little evident – a strategic retreat that foreshadowed Hitler's vanishing act when the two enemies' battlefield fortunes were reversed. Given the inescapability of Stalin's image in Soviet public culture before 'Barbarossa,' his greatly diminished presence was all the more striking. Throughout the war newspapers never showed him visiting army units, inspecting war damage or conferring with his generals. 'Stalin knew he had to lie low,' noted Ehrenburg. And when he did surface, his mode of address was markedly altered. For the first time he spoke to Soviet citizens as 'brothers and sisters,' and 'my friends,' invoking love of country rather than faith in communism as the pre-eminent source of wartime motivation (Brooks, 2000, 161–5). During what quickly became known as the 'great patriotic war,' sentimental representations of the motherland and of the noble Russian soul – with its boundless capacity for suffering and steely commitment to vengeance – dominated official framings of the war.

Where Hitler's retreat was felt as a loss in Germany, Stalin's reduced role in public life had an energizing effect in the Soviet Union. Reporters who had initially shrouded defeat in vague euphemisms – fighting 'in the direction of' served as shorthand to refer to areas abandoned to German troops in 1941 – developed a more forthright tone. Far from dealing a mighty blow to truth, war pried the lid off a hitherto tightly sealed communication system, allowing air to circulate in a stiflingly repressed society that had come to mistrust official information during the purge era of the 1930s, when flagship Soviet media had offered wholly incredible accounts of the crimes of Stalin's victims and their subsequent fate. Permitted greater latitude for realism, writers like Vassily Grossman dared hope, however fleetingly, that Stalinist victory culture would shatter forever on contact with the 'ruthless truth' of war (Grossman, 2007, 114).

War was the 'arbiter of all fates, even that of the Party,' Grossman later observed in his epic novel *Life and Fate*. As the Soviet Union battled for survival, it experienced suffering and devastation so enormous as to make a cover-up impossible. Needless to say, however, there remained dimensions of wartime experience too unpalatable for forthright treatment – or any treatment at all. As one might expect, the most unspeakable actions weren't those inflicted by the 'bloody Hitlerite hordes,' but rather the collaboration of Soviet citizens with the German occupying forces, including the mass desertion of Red Army soldiers to the ranks of the *Wehrmacht*. A 'great patriotic war' it may have been, yet the upsurge in nationalism occasioned by Germany's invasion didn't prevent looting, food riots, arson and signs of public panic. Nor did it prevent Stalin's regime from ruthlessly punishing both soldiers and civilians suspected of disloyalty or cowardice – offenses so vaguely defined that those who turned up late for work were liable to find themselves sentenced to years of hard labor in a *gulag* whose population exponentially expanded during the war (Stites, 1995, 3). At the front, martial resolve was 'stiffened by the most terrifying discipline,' military historian Anthony Beevor observes. The Red Army executed no less than 13,500 of its own men during the five-month battle of Stalingrad alone: their crime, 'betrayal of the Motherland' (Grossman, 2007, 141).

British and American wartime news-managers self-consciously set themselves apart from their German foe and Soviet ally by cultivating a 'strategy of truth:' an approach espoused both by the Ministry of Information (MOI) and its Washington counterpart, the Office of War Information (OWI). The phrase is telling. Openness affirmed liberal polities' self-image as societies in which information flowed freely with only minimal state interference. Freedom of speech was, after all, one of the 'Four Freedoms' for which the war was being fought, as FDR and Churchill framed Allied purposes in 1941's Atlantic Charter. But truthfulness was a *strategic* choice as much as an ideological imperative. A degree of candor would encourage citizens to feel that their leaders trusted them to accept even bad news with unruffled equanimity. The truth dividend would thus be felt in higher national morale – or so experts advised. A report to the British Ministry of Information in September 1939 had advised that 'Distrust breeds fear much more than knowledge of reverses. The all-important thing for publicity to achieve is the conviction that the worst is known' (quoted by McLaine, 1979, 28). A nation of grumblers should be given sufficient to grumble about.

But what did this approach entail in practice? In both Britain and the US, censorship rested, as it had in World War I, on a principle of 'voluntarism,' backed by the threat of stiff legal penalties. Neither government established the unwieldy bureaucracy that would have been necessary to review *all* news stories prior to publication. Instead, they issued lengthy lists of 'security sensitive' topics whose publication was prohibited, ranging from weather reports to details of troop movements and stories relating to strategic wartime industries. On these matters, editors could print nothing that might aid the enemy under pain of prosecution. Since the official prohibitions' parameters were exceedingly vague – Britain's D-Notices 'covered just about every conceivable human activity,' in the words of the retired rear-admiral who served as Chief Censor – editors were encouraged to submit to the censors any stories about which they were in doubt (Thomson, 1947, 6). As during World War I, editors lifted the threat of arrest by transferring to the censors the job of arbitrating what material the enemy might find useful, or they sidestepped the red tape by simply not publishing anything that Hitler or Hirohito might conceivably care to read (Sweeney, 2001, 40–70).

Editors and reporters became their own censors. They also became one another's censors, as the architects of this voluntaristic system surely intended. Wielding the mallet of patriotic security-consciousness, journalists frequently took aim at colleagues on other publications who didn't seem adequately mindful that there was a 'war on.' State officials barely needed to threaten media personnel with legal action when the latter policed their colleagues' speech with such relish, checking for any infractions of the official rules with hawk-like vigilance.

Events surrounding Germany's surrender on May 7, 1945 offer an especially striking illustration of the internal discipline exercised within the US press corps. One correspondent, Edward Kennedy of Associated Press, transmitted word of this epic occurrence before a SHAEF (Supreme Headquarters Allied Expeditionary Force) public relations embargo had been lifted. Much ink was spilt on this topic by the US press, with the critical mass of opinion weighing heavily against Kennedy's unilateral action. Some went so far as to suggest that his recklessness endangered soldiers' lives – though the Germans had already broadcast news of the armistice several hours earlier. Yet, as the *New Yorker*'s A. J.

Liebling observed, it was surely more striking that SHAEF had chosen to permit only three representatives of the US press to witness 'one of the memorable scenes in the history of man, and they only on condition that they promise not to tell about it until the brigadier general in charge of public relations gave them permission.' Moreover, the three in question all represented news *syndicates* (AP, Hearst's International News Service, and the United Press) – not particular newspapers or radio stations.

In Leibling's interpretation, the venom heaped on Kennedy resulted from his having broken a corporate 'combination' whereby the wire services, together with prominent US news outlets, had ganged up against smaller titles, monopolizing access to the military and elbowing less powerful players aside. Having flagrantly disregarded the rules of this privileged members-only club, Kennedy was roundly abused by its disgruntled members. For their part, SHAEF public relations officers announced that they would retain control over correspondents in Europe, despite Germany's surrender, vexed by the breakdown of a system which had served both parties well hitherto. (Favorable coverage of the military was, after all, the price of admission media representatives paid to gain exclusive access.) SHAEF censors duly undertook to suppress anything they considered unauthorized or inaccurate and 'false reports, misleading statements and rumors, or reports likely to injure the morale of the Allied forces (or nations).' Liebling offered this up as a cautionary tale of corporate jockeying meeting its comeuppance (Library of America, 2001, 646–55).

What he didn't mention, however, was that most US newspaper readers also took umbrage at Kennedy's 'premature' release of the surrender news. A Gallup poll taken ten days later found that just 35 per cent of respondents believed he was right to have done so (Gallup Organization, 1945). In insisting that everyone play by the big boys' rules, journalists who disciplined fellow reporters could thus legitimately claim to be reflecting the mood of their readership.

This fractious episode didn't occur until May 1945. As the belated character of this spat suggests, the voluntary system adopted in Britain and the US functioned with little disruption throughout most of the war, based on a distinction cherished in liberal journalistic practice between 'fact,' which could be censored on security grounds, and 'opinion,' which was free from interference – at least up to a point (Pronay and Spring, 1982, 177–8). But that point lay sufficiently far from zero-tolerance of criticism that newspaper readers in the US and UK did encounter scathing commentary on various aspects of the war's management, including, on occasion, censorship stops that seemed primarily designed to protect military reputations or to conceal the marital digressions of President Roosevelt (Sweeney, 2001, 165–87).

The biggest threat to this self-regulating system came not from editors keen to push the parameters of free speech – only one editor was prosecuted in the US during the war – but from political leaders irked by niggling press criticism. The latter sometimes found it hard to accept that wartime didn't offer them *absolute* immunity from negative opinion, just as they struggled to concede that personal criticism wasn't in itself injurious to the war effort.

Churchill, despite his prodigious oratorical talent for propaganda, was an especially reluctant adherent to the 'strategy of truth.' On several occasions he had to be dissuaded by the MOI and Home Office from suppressing the Labour-inclined *Daily Mirror* outright. The Prime Minister also harbored a profound suspicion of the BBC. Although the Corporation was undoubtedly the British public's most trusted wartime medium, its 9pm news bulletin reaching an estimated 43–50 per cent of the entire population, this approbation wasn't shared by Churchill (Briggs, 1995, 43). As the most important source of national news, the BBC also faced especially stringent oversight by the state – with Churchill repeatedly threatening to take it under direct control (Balfour, 1979, 82–5). This never happened, as the MOI (headed by Churchill's ally, Brendan Bracken) appreciated in a way the former Admiralty officer did not that *overt* government control could only dent public confidence in the veracity of BBC reports.

As it was, most listeners were quite unaware of how far-reaching censorship was in wartime Britain. Incoming cables of the Press Association and Reuters were routed directly into the Ministry of Information's Bloomsbury headquarters, allowing MOI censors to excise 'damaging' material before wire service subscribers received the cabled dispatches on which many press stories and radio broadcasts were based (Pronay and Spring, 1982, 177–8). While editorial comment in the press was left unrestricted, radio scripts of every conceivable sort – from children's programs to current affairs talks – were subject to precensorship. Speakers whom the government feared were dangerously radical, communists in particular, were kept from the airwaves altogether (Calder, 1969, 246–7). As a further precaution against 'hysterical outbursts either by announcers or artists,' BBC studios contained a 'switch censor' who could bleep out offensive words should speakers depart from approved scripts during live transmissions (Nicholas, 1996, 19).

The Ministry of Information's News Division may have aspired to 'tell the truth, nothing but the truth and, as near as possible, the whole truth,' as Ivone Kirkpatrick put it, but undoubtedly the very worst was neither always told openly nor without delay (quoted by Taylor, 1995, 213). Dispiriting developments were generally released in 'driblets' over a protracted period. The worst casualty statistics from the Battle of the Atlantic were never divulged and the British Air Ministry later confessed that it had exaggerated German losses by some 55 per cent, even though its 'cricket score' was generally believed to be accurate (Nicholas, 1996, 199). In Washington, the manipulation of casualty statistics – actual and projected – developed into a fine art. For a period in 1944, the US Army inflated the casualty figures to include those who had been discharged from the services or suffered non-combat accidents or diseases, along with the wounded and the dead. This counterintuitive move sprang from a perceived need to assure Americans – and, more particularly, their allies – that US forces were pulling their weight, despite the inordinately higher casualties sustained by the Red Army and British forces. But padding the figures by conflating different kinds of casualties was necessarily a short-lived ploy since it risked demoralizing the home front and inhibiting recruitment. This method of accountancy was dropped in February 1945 (Giangreco, 2004). By then a new imperative had arisen: to prepare the public for the staggeringly high losses projected when US troops invaded the Japanese islands, a public relations campaign also angled to dampen prospective criticism over use of the atomic bomb.

As these maneuverings might suggest, British and US officials were at their most evasive on matters of grand strategy, especially where military tactics were bound to produce heavy civilian casualties – and, most specifically, where civilians were not the 'collateral' victims of Allied bombers but calculatedly in their sights. That the carpet bombing of German cities was designed to shatter German civilian morale by destroying residential neighborhoods was obscured by press reports that stressed the Allies' scrupulous targeting of war-related facilities alone: *strategic* bombing. Likewise, the Manhattan Project remained off limits to American journalists – as details of the atomic bomb's development also was to the Soviet leadership. After the bombs were dropped in August 1945, their existence was clearly no longer any secret, but the deadly effects of radiation and horrific burns suffered in the firestorms that engulfed Hiroshima and Nagasaki remained shrouded in silence, with the cities initially sealed off from journalists' inspection.

Such strategic evasions lend an air of complacency, if not outright deceit, to the MOI's boast that its News Division told the 'the truth, nothing but the truth and, as near as possible, the whole truth.' As historian Ian McLaine has noted, British officials and their American opposite numbers were not above 'stretching the truth to the threshold of lying' – or indeed some way beyond (1979, 137).

Feature films and World War II

If news was the shock troops of propaganda, cinema was its stealth weapon. Total war undoubtedly sharpened the public appetite for news – dispatches from the front, details about individual loved ones and their military units, anything that provided reassurance or from which speculative conclusions about the war's likely duration could be drawn. But the grinding character of this protracted struggle with all its privations, large and small, also animated a deep desire for distraction. Nothing offered such a relaxing 'vacation from the present' as cinema. Leaders in Germany, Britain and the United States alike all prized cinema as a uniquely valuable stimulant to morale. That it occupied a less privileged niche in the USSR was due to the physical devastation suffered by the Soviet film industry rather than a different appreciation of a medium that the Bolsheviks had, from the Revolution's earliest days, especially valued for its ability to instruct entertainingly.

For wartime opinion-shapers, one primary attraction of film lay in its aura of utter innocence. As Elmer Davis, the CBS journalist who headed the OWI, noted: 'The easiest way to inject a propaganda idea into most people's minds, is to let it go in through the medium of an entertainment picture when they do not realize they are being propagandized' (quoted by Koppes and Black, 1987, 88). Goebbels agreed: 'The best propaganda is that which as it were works invisibly, penetrates the whole of life without the public having any knowledge of the propagandist initiative' (quoted by Kaes, 1989, 5). Feature films appealed to state opinion-managers because they seemed the very antithesis of propaganda – namely, entertainment. In practice, though, there was no dichotomy. 'Film propaganda will be most effective when it is least recognisable as such,' advised the MOI's Programme for Film Propaganda in 1940, and where better to catch audiences unawares than at the picture palace?

Since German, British and US officials regarded cinema-going itself as a fillip to high morale, we in turn could regard *all* wartime film-making as essentially propagandistic in intent, even when not overtly didactic, preachy or flagwaving in style. Indeed, heavy-handed message films, overburdened by cumbersome ideological baggage that viewers recognized as such, remained everywhere in the minority. This was true even in a society as thoroughly saturated with state ideology as Nazi Germany, where film historian Irwin Leiser claims there was no such thing as a 'non-political' film (1975, 17). On the surface, filmmaking in the Third Reich appeared to contradict his claim. Only an estimated 15 per cent of the Ufa studios' total output during the entire *Hitlerzeit* from 1933–45 contained obvious Nazi propaganda (Herzstein, 1979, 272; Reuth, 1995, 284; Hull, 1969, 100). But this was because Goebbels, a subtler strategist than the Führer, recognized that 'conveyor-belt brownshirt epics were box-office poison.' He duly insisted, not always successfully, that 'ideology must never be allowed to become obtrusive bias' (Grünberger, quoted by Rentschler, 1996, 9). Instead, Goebbels aspired to a 'cinema of pleasure' in which citizens so thoroughly participated in the fantasy world offered on screen as not to recognize the higher ideological purpose cinema culture served (Rentschler, 1996, 12; Herzstein, 1979, 272). The success of his aspirations is attested by one German who noted in 1938: 'A really clever person might claim that even if there are no propaganda films, there is still propaganda tucked away beneath film's surface details. This person, though, will have a hard time finding examples to prove his point' (quoted by Rentschler, 1996, 19).

While no feature film in wartime Britain, America or Germany could be released theatrically without at least some prior official approval, the latter exercised the tightest control. 'From the script to the final print – every single filmmaking process must be disciplined,' proclaimed RMVP film impresario, Fritz Hippler (quoted by Rentschler, 1996, 16). To ensure that this was so, the Nazis established the *Reichsfilmkammer* in July 1933, with ten separate branches encompassing every aspect of production and distribution. Meanwhile, a *Reichsfilmsdramaturg* censored scripts and administered a ratings system for films in distribution (Welch, 1983b, 6–38). Goebbels enthusiastically adopted the task of script censorship, brandishing his 'Minister's pencil' with the relish befitting a keen cinéaste, who additionally boasted an intimate knowledge of several stars of the German screen, not all of pure Aryan stock (Reuth, 1995, 195). Even if fewer than 10 per cent of the films made during the Nazi era were directly commissioned by the RMVP, 'no film appeared on the German screens without intense analysis of its contents by the censorship people of the ministry and the RFK' (Herzstein, 1979, 273). With most productions reliant on the state film bank for finance, film-makers were doubly beholden to a regime whose values many personnel internalized (Weinberg, 1984, 121).

In Britain and the US, control was less absolute but hardly unobtrusive. Since its inception as a commercial medium of mass entertainment, the cinema has been carefully surveilled by states fearful not only of films' subversive political potential but also of the licentiousness that darkened auditoria seemed positively designed to encourage amongst unscrupulous patrons with light fingers or otherwise roving hands. As historians Nicholas Pronay and Jeremy Croft point out, the British government's failure to make adequate plans for the wartime film industry was really neither here nor there, since 'film producers were entirely accustomed to working under conditions of practically total censorship.' In many regards war 'made little difference' (Pronay and Croft, 1983, 146). After September 1939, British film-makers were still obliged to submit their creations to the British Board of Film Censors (BBFC), which for years had scrutinized films on grounds of 'public decency' and political seemliness before issuing the certificates necessary for theatrical release. In wartime, ten new categories of sensitive topics – including bomb disposal incidents and treatment of prisoners of war – supplemented its injunctions against indecorous female attire, undue displays of passion, offensive expletives, irreverent portrayals of the Royals and matters likely to aggravate labor relations (Chapman, 1998, 16–17).

While the BBFC continued to be mindful of bad language and loose morals in wartime Britain, the MOI assumed greater supervision over the broad contours of film-making than tentative prewar plans envisaged. Ministry personnel, not the censors, liaised with film companies at the pre-production stage, deliberating over appropriate cinematic themes and contemplating how best to project 'the positive virtues of British national characteristics and the democratic way of life' (Aldgate and Richards, 1994, 11–12).

Reserving the ultimate right to ban a film *in extremis*, the MOI never actually exercised this prerogative. Its control was so pervasive that no project could even enter production without prior sanction. In 1940, the Board of Trade reached an agreement with the MOI's Films Division that the distribution of film stock (a strictly rationed strategic commodity) to commercial film production companies would be carried out only in consultation with the MOI (Aldgate and Richards, 1994, 11–12). Prior to allocation, the Board of Trade required a film scenario, which it then passed to the MOI for vetting. In practice, production companies learnt that the speediest way of proceeding was to submit film treatments to the MOI in the first place and also engage a script consultant, or even writer, appointed by its Films Division (Pronay and Croft, 1983, 152).

Hollywood also cooperated more closely with government and the military than in peacetime. Having made a strong case to Washington that motion pictures could variously distract Americans from the war and educate them about it, while providing morale-boosting fodder to celluloid-starved allies – to say nothing of how it could boost GIs' fighting spirit – Hollywood was rewarded with 'Essential War Industry' status. The US government, impressed by the argument that 'a Gary Cooper in the heroic screen role of a Sergeant York can contribute more to the success of America's war effort than this same Gary Cooper as a member of the American Army,' agreed that Hollywood's least dispensable 1 per cent of personnel would be exempt from conscription (Short, 1985, 99). With studios additionally guaranteed peacetime quantities of film stock, Hollywood continued to produce movies at a rate almost undiminished by war: approximately 440 features per annum compared with some 500 annually in the 1930s (Sklar, 1975, 250).

In return, the OWI expected and generally received Hollywood's willing participation in the war effort. The price for freedom from burdensome OWI control was that Hollywood willingly shackle itself closely to the state – a practice the industry termed 'voluntary self-discipline' (Short, 1985, 91). Studio executives recognized the scale of their indebtedness. In allowing Hollywood to continue business as normal during wartime, Washington effectively perpetuated the monopoly status of the big studios. For them, war meant new markets and increased trade: soldiers to be instructed and entertained, civilians looking for diversion, and allies with ailing film industries (Sklar, 1975, 250–1; Doherty, 1999).

The wartime marriage of convenience between Washington and Hollywood was not without its strains, however. In particular, filmmakers bridled at the temerity of the OWI Bureau of Motion Pictures (BMP) in pushing propaganda themes which were obviously dictated far more by the exigencies of policy than an informed knowledge of what worked on screen. Nelson Poynter, who fronted the BMP's Hollywood office, had 'no previous film experience,' as unimpressed producer Walter Wanger pointed out (Doherty, 1999, 47). Even a cursory perusal of the *Information Manual for Hollywood*, circulated just prior to the OWI's formal constitution in June 1942, illustrates why film-makers bristled at its high-minded defence of US democracy and its stipulation that movies show allies in a positive light – 'the Chinese are not little people who run laundries, they are a great nation, cultured and liberal' – while avoiding racism in depictions of the enemy. Its abstract insistence that 'militarism' was the enemy, not particular nations or races, was hardly the stuff to fuel a gripping plot. Nor was the admonition that film-makers 'picture and dramatise the tax programme.' Little wonder, then, that Hollywood had a 'sardonic name for the pushy cues' emanating from the BMP: 'poynters' (ibid., 47). When the maligned Poynter proposed that his office receive preliminary screenplays of all prospective Hollywood features, he received a predictably hostile response before backing down. Thereafter, only military-themed films were subject to compulsory pre-production review by the OWI. With regard to every other genre, 'voluntary self-discipline' remained the order of the day.

In all wartime states, cinema served to sharpen national identity: to show audiences who they collectively were, what they were fighting to preserve, and from what depredations. The task of explaining the war appeared particularly pressing in the United States. Where Britons experienced the Nazi threat in the form of regular bombing raids, Americans remained ill-informed regarding the whys and wherefores of the war in Europe and were liable, the OWI feared, to see entry into the war as simply a retaliatory response to Japan's raid on Pearl Harbor. To many US citizens, the Pacific theater was, or ought to have been, the first priority – not North Africa or Europe, where the western allies concentrated their efforts initially. In the summer of 1942, after six months at war, one third of respondents to a poll affirmed willingness to sign a separate peace with Germany. Many acknowledged ignorance as to why their country was fighting or expressed hostility towards America's new allies (Weinberg, 1968, 78). Others, while they might support the war, were adamant that peace must bring not just a new world order but a new dispensation within the United States itself. African American citizens could hardly fail to be struck by the discrepancy between FDR's rhetoric of freedom and their everyday experience of discrimination – not least in the US military, where black soldiers fought in separate units and even blood banks were segregated, as though blood itself weren't red but black or white. Launching a 'double V' campaign, for victory at home and overseas, the *Pittsburgh Courier* announced its intention to 'make this a people's war and we mean all the people' (Washburn, 1986).

Concerned by copious evidence of less than whole-hearted commitment to achieving the 'unconditional surrender' of Germany and Japan, the OWI encouraged film-makers to project both the nature of the Axis enemies and the necessity for combating them alongside allies who were reliable and worthy partners – their Bolshevism or imperialism notwithstanding. The most significant set of instructional propaganda films of this kind was undoubtedly Frank Capra's *Why We Fight* series, which skillfully spliced animation, graphics and archive footage (from Leni Riefenstahl's *Triumph of the Will* amongst other sources) to expose and indict the enemy (Culbert, 1983, 173–91). In turn, US servicemen's contribution to the war effort was impressed upon civilian America through the documentary record of many of Hollywood's most celebrated directors, including John Ford, William Wyler and John Huston, who temporarily enlisted with the armed forces' photographic units (Meyerson, 1995, 225–59).

Explaining the war was, then, in part a matter of self-representation. 'In total war, nations in their entirety confront each other, and all expressions of national life become weapons of war,' opined Fritz Hippler (quoted by Rentschler, 1996, 202). But this broad attitude wasn't confined to Germany, for in defining nationhood, wartime cinema generally sharpened the contours of national identity by projecting it in opposition to enemy Others. In British and American films, this Other was generally an Axis national or a treacherous fifth columnist, working to subvert their own state from within. The OWI was insistent, though, that Hollywood refrain from undue racial stereotyping of the enemy. Given Washington's bid for the moral highground on matters of race, the OWI hoped to instil a 'properly directed hatred' of 'militarism' – the essence of Axis belligerence – than of enemy peoples as such (Short, 1983b; Doherty, 1999, 122–48).

But this was one issue on which the Bureau of Motion Pictures and the studios never saw eye to eye. Anti-Asian racism was too deeply engrained in American culture, on screen and off, to be eradicated at the stroke of Nelson Poynter's pen. Vicious Japanese caricatures thus continued to people the movies much as before, remaining a staple of print media too. By depicting the Japanese as a pestilential menace – 'See why the villainous Japs have simply got to be *exterminated*!' ran the promotional posters for *Behind the Rising Sun* (1943) – Hollywood did far more to promote racial hatred than instil disgust with militarism (Doherty, 1999, 133–9). The 'eliminationist' character of the Pacific war thus found its counterpart back home. Asked in December 1944 what they thought the US government should 'do with the Japanese people' when the war ended, 13 per cent responded 'kill them all' (Berinsky, 2009, 38). After the atomic bombing of Hiroshima and Nagasaki, the liberal New York paper *PM* carried a simple – yet highly telling – cartoon. From an empty page, a speech bubble appeared with the words, 'So Sorry.' Presumably, this image intended to denote not just Japan's complete obliteration but the spuriousness of any apology the Japanese might be minded to make for the war, the catchphrase 'so solly' having regularly been used since 1941 to mock Japanese hypocrisy (and Japanese English). Inflected with an American accent, the words assumed a sarcastic tone, for as Melville Bernstein's cartoon implied, few Americans exhibited any remorse for dropping the bomb whatsoever (Schiffrin, 2009, 18, 267).

In Germany, the Aryan *Volk* was defined not only in opposition to foreign foes – barbaric Bolshevik subhumans and effete English imperialists – but also to enemies within (Welch, 1983b, 238–79). Nazi propaganda, as Hannah Arendt recognized, made anti-Semitism 'a principle of self-definition.' Germans would recognize themselves as everything the Jew was not, their own negative characteristics having been disowned and projected onto this odious Other (Arendt, 1958, 355–6; Rentschler, 1996, 159–64). In very different modes, respectively typifying Hitler's and Goebbels' divergent preferences in film propaganda, both quasi-documentaries such as *Der Ewige Jude* (*The Eternal Jew*) and narrative features demonized and dehumanized Jews, none more notoriously than the costume melodrama *Jud Süß*, which was required viewing for SS guards. With its gallery of Semitic grotesques and affirmative portrayals of Aryan valor, German mass culture 'became a crucial precondition for mass murder,' Eric Rentschler points out, 'serving as a shield and a blindfold' (1996, 222).

Where German films projected an exclusive Aryan identity, British and American cinema, on the other hand, strove to foster an inclusive sense of domestic belonging that encompassed different classes, multiple races and both sexes. Women's contribution to the home front was lauded and promoted in such films as *Millions Like Us* (1943) and *Swing Shift Maisie* (1943) (Chapman, 1998, 201–15; Doherty, 1999, 149–79; Harper, 1988, 168–202; Lant, 1991). Ethnic inclusiveness formed another prominent theme of Hollywood's wartime output. In the United States, the OWI encouraged cinema to exemplify the 'melting pot' ideal by depicting America as 'a nation of many races and creeds, who have demonstrated that they can live together and progress' (Short, 1983b, 175). Similarly, though with considerable circumspection, Army films sought to celebrate the contribution of the 'Negro soldier' – efforts that generally left African Americans feeling more slighted than affirmed, while riling segregationists who bridled at the very idea of inclusion (Doherty, 1999, 205–26; Cripps, 1983, 125–45).

In Britain, the emphasis was less on ethnic inclusiveness than on the distinct national and regional communities of the United Kingdom, along with its stratified social classes, pulling together in the war effort. Features dealing with the development of an *esprit de corps* amongst disparate recruits to the armed forces were particularly well suited to the task, such as Noel Coward's *In Which We Serve* (1941) and Carol Reed's *The Way Ahead* (1944). The notion of a singularly *British* national character, as distinct from a Scottish, English or Welsh identity, was thus perpetuated through film, and the positive attributes with which this character was identified – the MOI singling out 'sense of humour,' 'tolerance,' and 'stoicism' – threw into stark relief the enemy's contrasting traits.

Besides emphasizing the odiousness of the antithetical enemy, national propaganda also offered a positive sense of what was being fought *for*. Wartime productions projected a peculiarly rural, and distinctly English, version of what Britain represented, though it is questionable what viewers in Scotland or Wales (or even factory-working city-dwellers in industrial northern England) made of the British nation imagined as Ruritanian demi-paradise. One such film, *This England*, required a tactful name-change to *Our Heritage* before release in Scotland, and films exemplifying the 'rural myth,' such as Powell and Pressburger's *A Canterbury Tale* (1944), didn't always prosper at the box office (Richards, 1988, 50; Richards, 1997). But British cinema increasingly combined its fanciful depiction of 'olde England' with a more controversial vision of a remodeled Britain that ordinary people were fighting to realize, as well as more realistic portraits of present-day working-class life (Stead, 1988, 62–83).

In constructing national characters, myths, and archetypes all national cinemas plundered the past. Nazi cinema was especially wedded to the historical epic (Taylor, 1979, 164; Welch, 1983b, 164–85). German films of the era made very little attempt to transfer daily life in the Third Reich onto the screen – perhaps because ordinary existence was itself so suffused with Nazi propaganda as to frustrate Goebbels' preferences (Rentschler, 1996, 19). Instead, film-makers furthered the Nazi project by displaying the historical greatness of Germany, depicting situations and characters from the past which audiences would properly read as analogs for the present. Consequently, biopics of legendary Germans, such as Frederick the Great and Bismarck, were less concerned with eulogizing their eponymous heroes than, as Hippler acknowledged, lauding the Führer himself (Weinberg, 1984, 115). As fictional films were forbidden from representing Hitler's likeness, and as he showed an increasing distaste for public display, these hagiographic portraits played a necessary role in filling the void where the Führer's face should have been (Rentschler, 1996, 172).

Historical films generated unmistakably contemporary messages. But as film-makers could mask any propagandist intent by trumpeting their films' 'facticity', such fare, along with escapist musicals, comedies, and romances, remained popular as audiences tired of war and its on-screen cinematic reflection. Although some war-themed films, such as *In Which We Serve* and *The Way to the Stars*, were also contemporary box-office hits, evidence (patchy and impressionistic though it is) points towards a growing preference – in every combatant state – for more lighthearted fare and 'fewer war films' (Richards and Sheridan, 1987; Aldgate and Richards, 1994, 11).

If this was the view on the home front, it's even less surprising that those actually fighting should have preferred entertainment to combat movies, 'tinsel' to 'realism.' According to a 1944 *Time* poll, American GIs rated 'musical comedies best, comedies next best, then adventure films and melodramas' (Costello, 1985, 180). Soldiers apparently craved 'the three L's' – 'laughs, lookers, and letters.' And Hollywood, as film scholar Thomas Doherty points out, could deliver two and 'make kith and kin feel mighty guilty about not mailing off the third' (1999, 180). Movies served as uplifting distraction, alleviating soldiers' immediate burdens while reconnecting them with those back home. As one Marine private observed after six months' active service in the Pacific, entertainment movies 'stop us from thinking of ourselves and our surroundings ... [and] remind us that there are such things as pretty girls, gay music, and a civilization worth living for' (Costello, 1985, 181). For some soldiers, then, the war was about fighting to keep everything just as it was. For others it was about ensuring everything changed.

Total war as golden age?

In public memory on both sides of the Atlantic World War II radiates an aura of virtue: a war fought with unusual unity of purpose against an enemy whose malignance required no embellishment. This remembered felicity extends to the realm of media relations. World War II is thus recalled as a conflict in which, on the whole, British and US citizens were satisfied with how much news they received, and political leaders were gratified by how uncomplainingly editors, reporters and film-makers lent their talents to the war effort. As Thomas Doherty points out, even the 'incompatible couple' – Washington and Hollywood – 'worked together fairly smoothly for common ends,' bound by the studio executives' recognition that war was not only good for business but that failure to meet government expectations was likely to lead to more vexatious oversight (1999, 39).

Total war was not, of course, uniformly good for media business. In the Third Reich, Germans lost confidence in newspapers that by the end of the war were little more than pap-sheets printing only the official OKW communiqué and exhortations to believe in deliverance. When Max Amann finally declared victory over the press in 1943, it was a pyrrhic victory, as he himself recognized. 'How could an editor publish a good paper when he sat with one foot in jail and the other in the editorial room?' (Hale, 1964, 323). Under state dictation newspapers became uniform and, in their collective singing from the state hymn sheet, uniformly mistrusted – a fact attested by the satirical slogan '*Ein Volk, ein Reich, eine Zeitung,*' 'One People, One State, One Newspaper' (Balfour, 1979, 35).

After the first heady rush of intoxication, many Germans came to feel bludgeoned by state-controlled media and bullied into enforced exposure to them. The fate of the newsreels exemplifies this phenomenon. In May 1940, at the height of *Wehrmacht* military success, the newsreel's length increased to 40 minutes and the number of prints of each issue doubled to 2,000 (Welch, 1983b,197). But as lightning victories gave way to lingering stalemates and then to decisive defeats, the newsreels lost their popularity – even though cinema attendance doubled. Receiving intelligence from local Party surveillance officers that patrons were dawdling in cinema foyers rather than watching the newsreels, Goebbels initiated legislation in 1943 obliging proprietors to lock their patrons into the auditorium before the program commenced. Dilatory cinema-goers hoping to avoid the newsreel found themselves debarred from the main feature. But if they could no longer vote with their feet, disgruntled Germans could still cast a vote of no confidence 'with their voices ... by laughing and jeering at the newsreels they had once applauded,' observes Richard Taylor (1979, 163–4). As radio listeners couldn't be ensnared quite so readily, Goebbels resorted to other means of trapping listeners when he realized that endless hectoring speeches were a turn-off. A decree of 1942 compelled radio stations to devote 70 per cent of their airtime to light music, a move which Goebbels hoped would deliver an audience for the important political broadcasts (Welch, 1993, 34).

As historian Z. A. B. Zeman observes, 'military success is the best propaganda in a war' (1973, 172). German media suffered when the blitzkrieg victories of 1939 and 1940 turned into stalemate and defeat – a reversal of fortune compounded by the state's reluctance to acknowledge the scale of military disaster.

In Britain, the USSR, and the United States, on the other hand, mass media enjoyed rising popular esteem. With the exception of newspapers, which suffered from growing shortages of paper and ink, this boom was reflected in enlarged workforces, audiences and budgets. The BBC grew from a staff of 4,800 in September 1939 to some 11,663 in March 1944. Output trebled in hours and quintupled in transmitter power. The ten foreign-language services of 1939 had, by 1943, become 45 (Briggs,

1995, 18). Hollywood, meanwhile, generated 'unprecedented profits,' despite the OWI exerting an influence 'never equalled before or since by a government agency' over an American medium (Koppes and Black, 1977, 103). As an Essential War Industry, the studios in fact did better business than usual. And even the British film industry, which saw its studios dwindle from 22 to nine, its film stock rationed, two-thirds of its technicians called up and tax-inflated ticket prices, experienced a wartime boom in attendance and boost in critical reputation. With average weekly audiences increasing from 19 million in 1939 to over 30 million in 1945, the war, conclude Aldgate and Richards, 'was definitely to prove a "golden age" as far as domestic films were concerned' (1994, 3).

How do we account for this golden age? That there were Allied victories to report, at least after the tide turned at Stalingrad and in North Africa, surely helped. But the apparent paradox of rising popular trust in media under conditions of more complete state control also requires fuller explanation.

Was public esteem a form of false consciousness, proving the success with which systems of control (in the US and UK at least) persuaded people that a 'strategy of truth' prevailed? Certainly, some historians have suggested that only because they didn't appreciate the full extent of what was being withheld were British and American citizens 'artificially' satisfied with national media that fudged crucial dimensions of Allied strategy, consistently downplayed domestic casualties and then, in the final stages of the Pacific war, circulated alarmist projections of the Allied fatalities that would be entailed in an invasion of Japan.

All this is true. But the argument that public confidence in media rested primarily on delusion isn't entirely convincing. For one thing, publics in the US and UK were well aware that state censorship existed and hence that all manner of information – some seemingly trivial, such as weather forecasts, and some more obviously consequential, such as graphic depictions of wounded and dead soldiers – was withheld as a matter of course. Censorship occasioned a good deal of disgruntled comment in the British and US press, with cartoons regularly lampooning the MOI and OWI. Arguably, the wartime state's toleration of such mockery constituted one of the liberal system's strengths: a pressure valve for frustration that, while drawing attention to censorship, also underscored its limits. If cartoons attacking the censors made it into print, how repressive could restrictions on free speech really be?

The notion that wartime popularity of the media rested on public ignorance is also off-base in another way, for it implies that civilians clamored to know more than their states were prepared to divulge. But this was by no means always the case. A US Gallup poll conducted in January 1944 found that while 56 per cent of respondents thought newspapers and newsreels should 'show war pictures with men dead or wounded on battlefields,' 36 per cent did not agree, while 8 per cent had no opinion on the subject – hardly a clarion call for greater pictographic realism (Gallup Organization, 1944). Mass-Observation, an organization that conducted numerous ethnographic surveys of the British home front, found similarly mixed attitudes. Some viewers were no keener to see graphic representations of war in the newsreels than they were to watch combat movies for entertainment. 'Cannot the censor prevent the issue of these pictures which only bring pain and suffering to those with loved ones on active service?' inquired one cinemagoer after witnessing bomb damage in Belgium. 'After all we go to the cinema to be carried away from our troubles' (Richards and Sheridan, 1987, 405–6).

We should also beware minimizing the degree to which World War II liberalized what could be said and shown in Britain, the United States, and the USSR. This relaxation of official constraint wasn't so much a paradox of total war as a direct outgrowth of its destructive enormity. War on this scale couldn't simply be hidden, however much states might seek to obscure their losses. Sometimes, though, the imperatives lay in just the opposite direction. Publicizing casualties and depicting soldierly suffering, far from denting morale, came to be seen by American leaders as a way to transform sacrifice into a renewable source of wartime energy (Giangreco, 2004; Roeder, 1993).

Conflict of such magnitude functioned as a particle accelerator of social change, generating pressure for states to be (or at least appear to be) responsive to citizens' aspirations for postwar transformation. A 'people's war' couldn't be prosecuted in too obviously patrician or autocratic a style – as those advising Churchill, FDR and Stalin all recognized in different ways.

In the Soviet Union, writers experienced a surge of optimism that war would sweep away Stalinism as it had hitherto existed. As the novelist Boris Pasternak noted: 'when the war broke out, its real horrors, its real dangers, its menace of real death were a blessing compared to the inhuman reign of the lie, and they brought relief because they broke the spell of the dead letter' (quoted by Brooks, 2000, 173). The most popular Soviet reporters adopted the point-of-view of the regular infantryman. So did celebrated American correspondents, most notably Ernie Pyle, whose syndicated reports, with an estimated readership of 14 million, focused on the daily grind of GI experience rather than the war's macro-strategic management. Pyle's column found a visual counterpart in 23-year-old Sergeat Bill Mauldin's hugely popular cartoons drawn for *Stars and Stripes*, featuring the tribulations of his dogface protagonists Willie and Joe (Brewer, 2009, 127). Where journalism from the trenches of World War I had wilfully or otherwise adopted the purview of the officer class, a grittier perspective now emerged – one in which soldiers' (and journalists') commitment to the war effort didn't preclude grumbling about red tape, lousy food, overbearing or inept officers, and the treachery of girl-friends back home. In this more three-dimensional reportage, fear, boredom and courage all found a place. The men who never fired weapons were as central to this human-interest drama as the adrenalin surge of combat.

Visual representations of death and suffering also became more graphic as the war lengthened. The novelty of this policy was especially pronounced in the United States, where photographs of dead American soldiers had been banned during World War I, along with the British film, *The Battle of the Somme*, as likely to 'foster the anti-war spirit' in the words of the War Department's Major Kendall Banning (cited by Brewer, 2009, 73). In August 1943, Elmer Davis, head of the OWI, threatened to resign if the military maintained its refusal to offer civilians even a glimpse of the toll war was taking on American soldiers. With FDR's blessing, General Marshall ordered photographers to send back pictures that 'vividly portray the dangers, horrors, and grimness of War' (quoted by Roeder, 1993, 12).

The point, of course, was not realism for realism's sake, but a bid to galvanize home front commitment to the war effort, coupled with an attempt to encourage awareness among civilians that thousands of men would return from the war irreparably maimed, and others not at all. As with the release of casualty statistics, officials feared they might exceed a notional tipping point at which such disclosures, far from stiffening resolve, produced just the opposite effect. Hence visceral depictions of 'grimness' – like the broader Allied 'strategy of truth' – only extended so far: to an aestheticized representation of GI's corpses 'at rest' rather than bloodily maimed. Close-up portraits of soldiers in bodily or mental anguish remained unseen (Roeder, 1993, 27–42). But from a twenty-first-century vantage-point, it's nevertheless striking that from 1943 to 1945 US citizens were permitted to see things now excised from war's imagistic record, *Life* magazine's issue of July 5, 1943 featuring six servicemen carrying a flag-draped coffin (Brewer, 2009, 122).

Similar trends towards greater openness were evident in other media and other Allied states. In wartime Britain, the BBC emerged as a much more respected and popular source of information and entertainment. For the first time, its news broadcasts were permitted to scoop evening newspapers when the government tore up an agreement that had given the press a permanent advantage over its broadcast rival. Other programming also received an injection of fresh energy as the Corporation self-consciously sought to reach a more diverse listenership, recognizing that it would have to tone down the improving aspirations of its founder Lord Reith, who regarded radio as a mechanism to elevate the cultural standards of ordinary Britons. With a new Listener Research Department attuning broadcasters to audience preferences, wartime programming incorporated more comedy and light entertainment, as well as a greater diversity of regional accents and political opinions. Even left-wing commentators such as George Orwell, who loathed the interwar BBC's stuffiness and 'the unbearable voices of its announcers,' noted its 'truthfulness' and remarked that the Corporation was 'generally regarded here as more reliable than the press' (West, 1987a, 16). Only one constituency grew markedly *more* mistrustful of the BBC during the war: Conservative politicians who charged that the Corporation, by giving voice to socialist commentators like Orwell and J. B. Priestley, had been a trojan horse for Attlee's landslide electoral victory, elbowing Churchill aside at his hour of triumph in July 1945.

Since 1945 states have looked back longingly at the 'good war' as a time of harmonious cooperation: when everyone pulled together in a spirit of complete commitment to achieving victory. But if total war represented a golden age for mass communications, it's necessary to recall what brought about this loosening of wartime expression and how repressive the peacetime controls had been that war swept aside. No subsequent war has generated the same degree of popular support as World War II. But nor has any conflict since then exacted such a heavy toll on human life, which suggests that nostalgia for wartime's felicitous union of state, media and citizenry may also be tinged with myopia. It was the very *totality* of World War II that produced this liberality. The conditions that made this an era of popular confidence in wartime leaders, reporters and dramatists can hardly be replicated – and who would want them to be?

Chapter 3

Television Wars: Vietnam and After

Americans continue to disagree about almost every aspect of the Vietnam War more than 30 years after it ended. What purpose intervention in Indochina served, why America's military commitment escalated, how the war was fought, whether it could have been won, and if it should have been waged at all are questions that still generate vehement dispute. On one issue alone has something akin to consensus emerged: namely, television's pivotal role in turning American opinion against the war. Television, it's widely believed, lost the Vietnam war – for better or worse (Hallin, 1989, 105–6).

Although television ownership became widespread in the United States in the early 1950s, precisely as US forces were engaged in an unpopular and unsuccessful 'police action' in Korea, Vietnam was the first war to receive sustained TV news coverage. In technological terms, the Korean War (1950–3) resembled World War II more closely than it foreshadowed the war in Vietnam. About one third of American homes possessed a television set by the early 1950s, but this new medium's existence barely dented military consciousness in Korea. Weighing some 50 pounds and requiring three men to carry the necessary cables, batteries and sound equipment, cameras weren't readily transported onto the battlefield. In the main, network news relied on moving imagery supplied by the Army Signal Corps for stories from Korea, if they were illustrated at all. When venturesome reporters attempted to procure more graphic glimpses of combat they generally came up empty-handed (Casey, 2008, 312–13).

By the time that Vietnam began to attract regular attention from US news media in the mid-1960s television had advanced considerably as a medium. The introduction of communications satellites made footage fresher than in the early days when tapes of film had to be flown from the location of shooting to the point of broadcast transmission. With up-to-date images more readily available television news evolved from a staid recitation of daily happenings – delivered by a sedentary, studio-bound talking head – to a more dynamic format that incorporated video clips transporting viewers to the scene of action. For the first time television news assumed a half-hour format in the 1960s. Not surprisingly, given that 90 per cent of US households now boasted a television set, this new medium came to supplant newspapers as Americans' primary source of news (Brewer, 2009, 181). Television's primacy, coupled with its visual potency, strengthened the widespread impression that television coverage of the war *must* explain declining popular support for it. The first 'living room war,' as Michael Arlen termed it, was also America's least successful, most unpopular engagement. For many observers, television had to be the culpable variable that explained defeat (Arlen, 1982; Hallin, 1989, 105).

Such assertions mounted while the war was still in progress. Richard Nixon's Vice President Spiro Agnew frequently blasted the media for conspiring to 'sell the liberal ideology of the New York–Washington axis' – in other words, for pushing an anti-war agenda (Gans, 1970, 222). But it was a British broadcaster, Robin Day, who delivered the most memorable prognosis about conflict in the television age at the height of the Vietnam War. In *Encounter* magazine's April 1970 issue, Day offered a speculative judgement that would be widely repeated:

> One wonders whether in future a democracy which has uncensored television in every home will ever be able to fight a war, *however just.* However good the cause – self-defense, resisting aggression, or even fighting under the United Nations flag – the brutal details of military action may be there on the television screen to shock and to horrify, sapping perhaps the will of the nation to resist the forces of evil or even safeguard its own freedom. (Quoted by Sulzberger, 1970, 39)

'Blood,' he continued, 'looks very red on the television screen.' The implication was obvious. A war screened 'uncensored' on television could not be won – a point Nixon reiterated in his 1978 memoir when he mused whether 'America would ever again be able to fight an enemy abroad with unity and strength of purpose at home' (quoted by Hallin, 1989, 3).

Keen not to put this hypothesis to the test, the US and British militaries have sought to constrain coverage of every subsequent war they have prosecuted, formulating media groundrules with television imagery uppermost in mind. During the conflict over the Falklands/ Malvinas islands in 1982, the British Ministry of Defence (MOD) determined not to repeat what it understood to be the Pentagon's great mistake in Vietnam: namely, allowing reporters unfettered access to the battlefield. In this brief confrontation between British and Argentinian forces, the MOD kept print and broadcast journalists on an extremely tight rein. A quick military victory, reported in words and images over which British officials exercised complete control, ensured that the Falklands model would shape future US media-management doctrine. With the MOD's 'success' firmly in mind, the Pentagon excluded reporters altogether during the 1983 Grenada invasion, introducing a modified pool system during the intervention to topple Panama's General Noriega in 1989 (Mercer, Mungham and Williams, 1987; Young and Jesser, 1997).

For planners in the British and US defense communities, these brief campaigns of the 1980s proved that war in the television age was still both thinkable and winnable, but only by imposing restrictions that effectively kept TV out of the picture. Belief in the public's 'casualty aversion' remained a fixed point of military thinking. Television thus remained the primary adversary, and relations between soldiers and reporters were conceived in openly adversarial terms. As the preface to the MOD's pressbook for the Falklands campaign put it, 'The essence of successful warfare is secrecy; the essence of successful journalism is publicity' – an aphorism that risked turning a presumption of professional incompatibility into a self-fulfilling prophecy.

The 1980s adduced numerous examples of military hostility towards the media. 'Some look on news as just another four-letter word, but I believe it is more useful to look at it as a C-letter word: chaos, confusion, contradiction, crime, corruption, color, catastrophe,' opined Major General Patrick H. Brady, a one-time chief of Army Public Affairs (Browne, 1991, 227). Yet every article of faith underpinning such attitudes – about television's promiscuous desire to show and tell, and the public's squeamish aversion to images of bloodshed – is open to serious challenge.

Contrary to the received wisdom, Vietnam was a war in which television news was 'lopsidedly favorable' to Washington's geostrategic ambitions in South East Asia just as long as policy-makers on Capitol Hill themselves remained seized of that vision (Hammond, 1998; Hallin, 1989). And though Vietnam is often regarded as American military history's great aberration, the one war in which journalists ranged freely and reported at liberty, it was in fact a conflict that US public relations personnel made extensive efforts to package for domestic and international consumption. If their promotional efforts ultimately failed, it wasn't for want of trying. Nor was it the fault of television.

Uncensored, unpopular, unvictorious: the conventional wisdom about Vietnam

Precisely when America's war in Vietnam started is a matter of debate. 'You couldn't find two people who agreed about when it began,' observed Michael Herr in *Dispatches* (1978, 46). Washington established a Military Assistance and Advisory Group to train and equip the new South Vietnamese Army as early as 1955, one year after French troops withdrew, having failed to reassert colonial rule over Indochina after its wartime occupation by Japan. Without any formal Congressional declaration of war against North Vietnam, the Eisenhower, Kennedy, and Johnson administrations steadily increased this commitment over the latter 1950s and 1960s, with US troop strength reaching its peak of 543,000 men in April 1969 (Library of America, 2000, 783). But if it was impossible to say decisively when this undeclared war began, the North's victorious march into Saigon in April 1975 represented a decisive full-stop. The reunification of Vietnam under Hanoi's communist regime left Nixon's 'peace with honor' looking very much like defeat. There was little honorable in the televised scenes of Vietnamese and American civilians frantically scrambling to board the last US helicopters from Saigon.

Since defeat wasn't any more familiar than it was welcome to many Americans, apportioning blame became a protracted national preoccupation. The media provided a compelling scapegoat. By the early 1980s, 'stab-in-the-back' charges had become commonplace. According to conservative critics like Robert Elegant, television had precluded the possibility of victory through 'graphic and unremitting distortion' of the facts, combined with an unvarnished depiction of America's youthful casualties and equally unflinching exposure of atrocities inflicted by GIs on Vietnamese peasants (Elegant, 1989, 73–90). Sensational and unbalanced coverage undercut civilian determination to shore up democratic South Vietnam against communism, fueling an increasingly vociferous peace movement.

For these critics, Vietnam was a war that could have been, and *should* have been, won – had the military been empowered to apply preponderant force. In their opinion, intensive bombing of North Vietnam, Laos and Cambodia would have produced an outright victory, but the media effectively ruled this out by showing bombardment's human costs, which an increasingly restive US public refused to sanction (Kimball, 1988, 433–58). As Ronald Reagan put it, Vietnam was a war from which American soldiers 'came home without a victory, not because they'd been defeated but because they'd been denied permission to win' (quoted by Kimball, 1988, 439). US forces had been compelled to fight with one hand tied behind their back. By harnessing public squeamishness, the media had served to limit strategic options to the point at which victory became untenable.

Belief that the media 'lost the war' in Vietnam has numerous variants. Often it functions as a hostile critique of engagé journalism: of reporters with an anti-war agenda. For their part, journalists have adopted a range of positions on their contribution to the war. Some, like columnist James Reston, may agree that 'the reporters and the cameras were decisive in the end,' but few concur that they *wilfully* set out to undermine the war effort (quoted by Hallin, 1989, 3). Some maintain that they simply held a mirror to unpleasant wartime truths. If journalists revealed the ineptitude and escalating inhumanity of America's war effort, responsibility for defeat resides not with the press but those directing and prosecuting the war. Others embrace a more active conception of journalism, without endorsing culpability for a lost war. Thus David Halberstam (a young *New York Times* reporter in Vietnam who famously aroused Kennedy's ire) protested that, in their watchdog role, reporters were obliged to ferret out things that US government officials and military personnel attempted to conceal. According to Halberstam, he and his colleagues, 'carrying no excess psychological or political baggage,' simply sniffed out '*the story*' – a story that comprised a good deal of incompetence, corruption and hubris (quoted by Hallin, 1989, 6).

In critics' eyes, however, the issue appears one of active culpability. The problem wasn't that journalists passively reported things as they were; rather, they misreported events as they were not. Reporters' inexperience, ignorance, and craving for professional advancement all contributed to a distorted image of the war. General William C. Westmoreland, former commander of the Military Assistance Command, Vietnam (MACV), noted with hindsight that some 51 per cent of US reporters in Vietnam had been in their 20s. Eager to make a name for themselves, these cub reporters had done so in the easiest way possible: by criticizing authority. In the early 1960s, Saigon was 'one of the world's less desirable assignments for newsmen,' Westmoreland continued:

> A faraway, alien place, it had little attraction for American readers, so that nothing short of the sensational was likely to gain space in the newsman's home newspaper. Finding fault was one way to achieve the sensational, and finding fault with an Oriental regime with little background in or respect for Western-style democracy was easy. (Quoted by Thayer, 1992, 91)

In the eyes of Westmoreland and other like-minded critics, the media's muck-raking preferences compounded the importunate tendencies of these young men (for the critique invariably, if erroneously, gendered all reporters male). The Vietnam War coincided with the rise of investigative journalism, in which straight reporting – of the old 'just the facts' model – was abandoned in favor of a deliberately confrontational attitude. Westmoreland's complaint that 'American newsmen in Saigon ... confused reporting with influencing policy,' found many civilian proponents. In an influential *Encounter* article of 1989, Robert Elegant (a former *Los Angeles Times* reporter) lambasted his own profession for becoming 'less objective than partisan.' Instinctively 'agin the government,' the press was 'at least reflexively, for Saigon's enemies,' Elegant charged, extending the indictment to an accusation of treachery (Elegant, 1989, 138).

Journalists' inexperience lent further volatility to this unstable compound of personal immaturity and professional provocation. It didn't help that many reporters remained in country for little longer than their GI counterparts – 18 months at most (Elegant, 1989, 140). Unversed in the Vietnamese language and culture, their knowledge of military matters was equally woeful. Few 'understood the differences between, say a mortar and a howitzer, brigades and divisions, logistics and tactics,' lamented Peter Braestrup, former *Washington Post* Saigon bureau chief (1994, 12). From the military perspective, these callow youths were a far cry from the well-informed, favorably disposed old journalistic hands of World War II and Korea. No wonder, then, that the Pentagon took to offering 'official "gilt-edge" invitations to veteran correspondents of two wars back,' who duly rebuked their young colleagues for wanting to see America 'lose the war to prove they're right' (Marguerite Higgins, quoted by Arnett, 1995, 34).

Charges against journalists were legion. But amid the welter of recriminations, television attracted particular opprobrium from those convinced that Vietnam was lost in the living rooms of America. Complaints about sensationalism applied with singular force to a 'thrusting and simplistic' medium that privileged dramatic footage at the expense of the context and nuance that were (at least theoretically) possible in serious broadsheet journalism. If pressmen sometimes invented headline-grabbing material, television reporters didn't even have to bother. All they had to do was show up for people's behavior to alter. As one print correspondent wryly noted in 1966: 'Some persons will do things in front of a camera that they would not do in front of a pad and pencil' (Raymond, 1966, 34). Led by vivid images and human interest vignettes, television news delivered a far greater emotional charge than its print and broadcast rivals. Partly for that reason, the least informative medium was also the most widely trusted. As Elegant rhetorically mused: 'Who could seriously doubt the veracity of so plausible and so moving a witness in one's living room' (1989, 77–8). More tartly, C. L. Sulzberger, doyen of foreign policy commentators at *The New York Times*, observed that 'few Americans actually seem to remember how to read' (Sulzberger, 1966, E12).

Worse yet, the war that Americans saw on television was, Westmoreland claimed, 'almost exclusively violent, miserable, or controversial: guns firing, men falling, helicopters crashing, buildings toppling, huts burning, refugees fleeing, women wailing' (quoted by Thayer, 1992, 93). Television news delighted in scenes like a Marine taking his Zippo lighter to the grass roof of a Vietnamese hut, burning down a village that had resisted an order to evict the snipers in their midst – a sequence so enraging to LBJ that he phoned the president of CBS to complain that the network had 'shat on the American flag' (quoted by Sweeney, 2006, 144).

Although presidential threats, curses and imprecations multiplied over the years, they did little to reform television's bad habits. With a vampiric fondness for blood, television had no appetite for *good* news, critics insisted. 'Only scant attention was paid to pacification, civic action, medical assistance, the way life went on in a generally normal way for most of the people much of the time,' Westmoreland lamented (quoted by Thayer, 1992, 93). Since the enemy remained largely hidden from view, television offered a necessarily lopsided picture of the action. As a February 1966 *New York Times* article bitterly noted:

> American television can show the 'inhumanity' of the war without censorship – burly Marines towering over blind-folded, half-naked little men in shorts, wailing children and battered children. They cannot, however, match these scenes with pictures of the Vietcong and North Vietnamese terrorism. For this, the Vietcong field commanders and the authorities in Hanoi do not cooperate. (Raymond, 1966, 93)

Television's nightly diet of death and destruction necessarily fueled anti-war sentiment, critics insisted, for how else could such images be interpreted but as an indictment of US operations in Vietnam? Some television journalists concurred. CBS's Morley Safer (the reporter responsible for the infamous Zippo story) stated in 1966 that:

on its own every piece of war film takes on a certain antiwar character, simply because it does not glamourize or romanticize. In battle men do not die with a clean shot through the heart; they are blown to pieces. Television tells it that way. (Quoted by Fox, 1995, 141)

To mitigate this innate negativity, television news required not only more positive images of US efforts to win Vietnamese hearts and minds but a reassuring interpretive framework to neutralize disturbing images. Nixon singled out lack of context as a particular problem:

In each night's TV news and each morning's paper the war was reported battle by battle, but little or no sense of the underlying purpose of the fighting was conveyed. Eventually this contributed to the impression that we were fighting in military and moral quicksand, rather than toward an important and worthwhile objective. (Quoted by Hallin, 1989, 3)

Nixon's was not the common complaint that correspondents ceased to be objective. Instead, he obliquely attacked a fundamental tenet of objective journalism – the rigid separation of fact and comment – to suggest that the accretion of numerous details may produce a misleading impression when individual facts lack adequate explanation. For Nixon, the missing context was an optimistic spin on events which would encourage Americans to recognize that, even if the pictures *looked* grim, the war itself was not going badly. 'Pacification' – the slow, patient winning of Vietnamese peasants' trust – would necessarily take time. But television was poorly suited to taking the longer view and accordingly discouraged its viewers with pessimistic daily round-ups (Hooper, 1982, 115).

For many critics, the failings of the media reached their peak during the Tet Offensive that began on January 31, 1968. During celebrations for the new lunar year, forces of the People's Army of Vietnam (North Vietnam's Army) and the National Liberation Front (or Viet Cong as the latter was derisively dubbed by Ngo Dinh Diem, the South's US-backed leader) launched a series of uprisings in more than 100 towns and cities across the south. Their aim was to spark a popular uprising against the Saigon regime that would bring the war to a decisive conclusion. For the first time, war exploded onto the streets during daylight. Hitherto, in the words of Michael Herr 'night was the war's truest medium; night was when it got really interesting in the villages, the TV crews couldn't film at night' (1978, 40). 'Search and destroy' operations, in pursuit of an elusive and usually invisible enemy, did not lend themselves to filming –

Illustration 3.1   Walter Cronkite and CBS camera crew use a jeep as a dolly to film an interview during the Battle of Hue (1968)

Source: Still Picture Section, US National Archives.

at night or otherwise. During Tet, however, reporters (of whom there were now some 464 as against 20-odd in 1964) had only to step from their hotels to experience fighting at close range. The offensive begged to be covered.

But what to report? It was hard to discern large patterns in this mosaic of country-wide attacks, though a coordinated offensive of this kind did nothing to corroborate official projections of 'light at the end of the tunnel.' Struggling to make sense of the whole, reporters generally treated Tet as evidence that the Viet Cong and North Vietnamese had American and ARVN forces on the run. But once the smoke cleared, military analysts were adamant that Tet – despite appearances to the contrary – actually represented 'a severe military-political setback for Hanoi in the South.' The media had got it wrong. As Peter Braestrup remarked, 'the dominant themes of the words and film from Vietnam ... added up to a portrait of defeat for the allies ... a continuous black fog ... a vague, conventional "disaster" image, which few newsmen attempted to re-examine and which few managers at home sought to question' (1989, 153–4).

What did this (mis)reporting of Tet reveal? Braestrup attributed it more to the pervasive pessimism that had come to envelop the American press corps in Vietnam by 1968 than to an ideologically driven attempt to undermine domestic support for the war (Braestrup, 1994). For Westmoreland and Elegant, however, the tendentious reporting of Tet was more calculated and malicious, confirming journalists' implacable hostility to America's ally. '[M]ost South Vietnamese units fought well, but it was not the "in thing" in media circles to say anything good about the South Vietnamese,' complained Westmoreland. 'The media misled the American people by their reporting of "Tet," and even a number of officials in Washington were taken in' (1979, 38). Arguably, President Johnson was among those so deceived. In Halberstam's view, Vietnam was 'the first time in history a war had been declared over by an anchorman' (quoted by Hallin, 1989, 168).

The man in question was Walter Cronkite, and his verdict ran as follows: 'To say that we are mired in stalemate seems the only realistic, yet unsatisfactory conclusion.' Delivered on February, 27 1968, this judgement helped persuade LBJ to withdraw from the 1968 presidential race (Hallin, 1989, 170; Seib, 1997, 19). Since Cronkite was America's 'most trusted man,' if the administration had lost CBS's avuncular anchor then it had lost middle America. White House press secretary George Christian later related that 'shock waves rolled through the government' after the broadcast. On March 31, Johnson duly announced his decision not to run for a second term (Turner, 1985, 232). In a speech to the National Association of Broadcasters delivered the following day, LBJ made clear to the crowd of television professionals that they were largely responsible for his decision:

As I sat in my office last evening, waiting to speak, I thought of the many times each week when television brings the war into the American home. No one can say exactly what effect those vivid scenes have on American opinion. Historians must only guess at the effect that television would have had during earlier conflicts on the future of this nation: during the Korean war, for example, at that time when our forces were pushed back to Pusan; or World War II, the Battle of the Bulge, or when our men were slugging it out in Europe or when most of our Air Force was shot down that day in June 1942 off Australia. (Quoted by MacArthur, 1993, 133)

By implication, victory in previous wars would have been similarly jeopardized by television's 'daily barrage of bleakness and near panic.'

Johnson was scarcely alone in such counterfactual musings about television's power to shape the political landscape. 'Imagine what Goebbels would have done for Hitler with TV as well as radio to hand,' hypothe-sized C. L. Sulzberger in *The New York Times* (Sulzberger, 1970, 39). With an enemy like CBS, who needed the NLF? No wonder US forces couldn't prevail when the former effectively did the Viet Cong's job for them. If MACV had erred, it was only in failing to constrain the forces of disorder and defeatism on the ground: namely, the US press pack. For, unlike both world wars and the recent war in Korea, Vietnam was America's first long engagement fought without the imposition of formal military censorship.

From this perspective, the lesson for the military was clear. Given carte blanche to go where they pleased, write what they liked and film whatever caught their eye, journalists would eagerly bite the hand that fed them. And since politicians had tied the other hand behind the military's back, defeat was inevitable.

Lopsidedly favorable: the 'guilty media' thesis challenged

So the conventional wisdom goes: an uncensored war became increas-ingly unpopular and hence, lacking public commitment, unwinnable. The logic is familiar. It may also sound compelling. But in almost every particular this well-worn story about the media and the war in Vietnam is misleading if not downright mistaken – a syllogistic chain of reasoning strung together with unwarranted assumptions that scholars have spent the last 30 years unpicking and decoupling.

Let us begin, then, with the central charge against television news: that it fed Americans a steady supply of bloodied flesh, murderous Marines, napalmed infants and weeping peasant women. Detailed content analysis of network coverage reveals that commonplace assertions about televi-sion's visceral treatment of war in Vietnam are widely off base. As Daniel Hallin's seminal study *The 'Uncensored War'* shows, much of the networks' nightly coverage, for a considerable part of the war, eschewed exposure of war's human costs, and was particulary hesitant to cover atrocities committed by US forces. Until around the time of Tet in early 1968, television news was 'lopsidedly favorable to American policy in Vietnam,' often explicitly so (1989, 110). Hallin's research found that just 22 per cent of all film reports in the pre-Tet period depicted actual combat; around 24 per cent contained shots of the dead or wounded, but usually only briefly; and less than 10 per cent offered more than one shot of the dead or wounded (1989, 129–30). It's also worth bearing in mind that while blood 'looks very red on the television screen,' as Robin Day famously pointed out, it does so only if the viewer possesses a color TV set, which a majority of American households did not until after 1972 (Brewer, 2009, 181).

Hallin concedes that the tenor of US reporting was not unwaveringly supportive throughout the war. In 1968, television's tone began to alter, and thereafter stories were more commonly accompanied by graphic images. The networks devoted greater attention to the peace movement and anti-war sentiment, while passing more critical comment on the South Vietnamese regime and its armed forces – this at a time when the war effort was being 'Vietnamized,' which meant (at least in theory) that the ARVN played a dominant role in combat operations, with US forces providing tactical support. The question, then, is how we account for the networks' shifting register. Did the media, as commonly charged, adopt a stridently adversarial role as the war progressed, abandoning old rules of journalistic objectivity along the way, or are there other explanations for TV's growing negativity?

Technology and logistics certainly played some role in the changing look of television news. In the early and mid-1960s, the guerrilla tactics employed by the National Liberation Front didn't lend themselves to filming. 'In the past,' noted Jack Raymond in *The New York Times*, correspondents 'chose a unit and arranged to spend days or weeks or even months with it.' But unlike World War II or Korea, this was a war without battle fronts and 'relatively few battles':

> The insurgency by the Vietcong supported by the North Vietnamese Army units is designed to harass the people and shake their confidence in Government security. Despite the increasing number of military clashes, most of the war consists of relatively small-scale attempts to counter Vietcong propaganda, arson, kidnappings, terror raids, murders and various forms of sabotage.

Even the most patient reporter couldn't 'afford to spend a month in a village, waiting for a terrorist attack to study how its people react to Communist propaganda, although that is the substance of the war,' Raymond concluded (Raymond, 1966, 219).

The Tet offensive resolved the issue of nothing much appearing to happen in Vietnam. With fighting taking place in broad daylight and in urban locales camera crews had plenty to film and easier means to transmit their material back to the US. Earlier in the 1960s, it took roughly 48 hours to fly footage from Vietnam via Japan. This long lag meant that much of it was 'timeless' – images that served primarily to evoke a certain milieu rather than depicting highly topical events that would be stale on arrival. Thus Michael Arlen characterized the television war, at least until 1968, as 'a nightly stylised, generally distracted, overview of a disjointed conflict which was composed mainly of scenes of helicopters landing, tall grass blowing in helicopter wind, American soldiers fanning out over a hillside on foot' (Arlen, 1982).

But ultimately technology shaped news content less than journalistic framing practices and the values and norms supporting them. According to Hallin, the explanation for both television's initially supportive coverage of the war and its gradual swing towards a more oppositional – though still by no means anti-war – stance, lies in news organizations' 'constant commitment to the ideology and the routines of objective journalism' (Hallin, 1994a, 52). Thus television's apparent shift to oppositional journalism is somewhat chimerical. Journalists did not deviate from professional norms so much as their sources radically reappraised the war; and this elite reappraisal in turn triggered an adjustment in reportorial mode to accommodate dissensus.

To elaborate, Hallin suggests that we imagine the reporter's world as divided into three regions, 'each of which involves the application of different journalistic standards.' The first he terms the 'sphere of consensus' – the 'region of motherhood and apple pie' – wherein lie 'those social objects not regarded by the journalists and most of the society as controversial' (1989, 116). In this comfort zone, journalists do not feel obliged to act as impartial 'balancers' between alternative points of view but can instead celebrate consensual values. The dissident minority with a distaste for apple-pie or motherhood can be safely banished to the 'sphere of deviance,' which lies beyond the purview of routine journalism – a repository for views beyond the pale of mainstream society (ibid., 117). However, between the 'sphere of consensus' and this neglected netherworld lies an intermediate realm, the 'sphere of legitimate controversy,' and it's in this zone that the rules of objectivity reign supreme. Here, 'neutrality' and 'balance' are the prized journalistic virtues, with equilibrium sought among contending mainstream voices (ibid., 116).

Using this model, Hallin proposes that the recalibration of Vietnam coverage can best be explained by the war's movement from one sphere to another, not by any countercultural jettisoning of objectivity by journalist-provocateurs. In its early phase, US commitment to South Vietnam was widely viewed as essential to America's overall Cold War strategy of containing communism. The necessity of protecting a beleaguered ally in South East Asia from the menace of communism was a 'motherhood and apple pie' issue. Everyone was in favor, and those who disagreed were so marginal as not to register in mainstream news. The wisdom of containment duly went unquestioned, even if Saigon-based reporters did query whether Ngo Dinh Diem – with his habit of expelling journalists that wrote unflattering things about him – was the best possible 'democratic' leader for Washington to support in Saigon.

Over time, America's ruling elite came to question whether the south could in fact be 'saved' and whether this operation could succeed at a cost US taxpayers would accept. By 1967, elite dissensus in the capitol was plainly visible. The war had become a matter of 'legitimate controversy' – a topic on which reasonable people disagreed, and disagreed with increasing vehemence. 'Nobody "jabs" at the Administration these days; it's more like a bomb for a bomb,' wrote Tom Phillips in *The New York Times* in October 1967 (Phillips, 1967, SM7). Since lawmakers and prominent opinion-formers no longer concurred over either the underlying geostrategic logic of defending South Vietnam or the military strategy employed to that end, news media were obliged by the rules of objective journalism to report this fracturing of elite opinion. As Hallin points out: 'Not only did the media report the growing debate over the war, they were also affected by it. As the parameters of political debate changed, so did the behavior of the media: stories that previously had been reported within a consensus framework came to be reported as controversies; subjects and points of view that had been beyond the pale in the early years came to be treated as legitimate news stories' (1994a, 54–5).

As elite fissures deepened, journalists began reporting as atrocities actions which had previously received minimal attention so long as consensual anti-communism fixed the war in the 'sphere of consensus.' Prior to Tet, stories revealing the war's toll on Vietnamese villagers rarely reached the pages of the *Washington Post* or *The New York Times*. Martha Gellhorn, for example, found it impossible to persuade an American newspaper to run a series of first-hand accounts written in 1966–7 of what 'winning hearts and minds' actually entailed (Knightley, 2004, 427–8). Similarly, reports about the rape, murder and mutilation of more than 300 Vietnamese villagers at My Lai in March 1968 were initially blocked by editors leery of calling America's purposes and practices in Vietnam into question. Not until November 1969, some 18 months after they occurred, did the events at My Lai received sustained press attention, initially in the *St. Louis Post-Dispatch*, thanks to the efforts of investigative journalist Seymour Hersh. His series of articles exhumed buried reports of the massacre and drew attention to the army's investigation into the actions of Lt William Calley, the only soldier later to be convicted of war crimes (Library of America, 2000, 413–27). With publication of Ronald Haeberle's chilling photographs of the massacre's victims in December 1969, My Lai became stamped as an 'American tragedy,' in *Time* magazine's phraseology. Its exposure paved the way for other such episodes, of which My Lai was neither the first nor the last, to become newsworthy.

As dissatisfaction with the war deepened, television began to accommodate hitherto marginalized issues previously banished to the sphere of deviance, notably the peace movement. However, anti-war demonstrations became domestic news without the protestors themselves becoming legitimate *commentators* on the war. Clamorous protests on streets and campuses across the country could hardly be ignored. On May 4, 1970, as Nixon announced his approval for an 'incursion' into North Vietnamese base areas in Cambodia, National Guardsmen shot dead four student protestors at Kent State University in Ohio – evidence of domestic escalation that underscored how far the war had moved from the 'sphere of consensus.' But if Vietnam was now unmistakably a matter of legitimate controversy, that didn't mean protestors enjoyed authority to speak on matters of policy or strategy on TV news. Protestors might now *appear* on the news more than hitherto, but often in ways that tended to stigmatize them as disruptive hippies and rebels thumbing their noses at authority for protest's own sake (Hallin, 1989, 191–201; Gitlin, 1980; Small, 1994).

Even after Tet, Hallin contends, the boundaries of controversy remained largely defined by the debate raging on Capitol Hill. What media coverage of the Vietnam War demonstrates, then, is how narrow a notion of balance network news operates with, such that the very practices of 'objectivity' (often taken as a byword for impartiality) work to inscribe a routine bias in favour of power elites. Only when that elite itself became riven with dissent did television news reflect this divergence, 'contribut[ing]' to the public war-weariness that eventually made Vietnam a political albatross' (Hallin, 1989, 7). But if television was a partisan force, it wasn't activist in the ways its critics have charged. As MIT sociologist Herbert Gans pointed out in 1970, news producers constitute 'part of the middle-class culture that dominates America.' As such, they

> accept most of the economic and social values of that culture, and often judge other societies by these values. Thus, they generally see what goes wrong in Socialist countries more easily than what goes

right, and are more aware of propaganda in Russian pronouncements than American ones, consider protestors more militant than insistent lobbyists, and deem marijuana-smoking more of a social problem than alcohol consumption. (Gans, 1970, 33)

In short, professional objectivity – carefully calibrated to maintain equilibrium between views ultimately not so dissimilar – reinforced the status quo bias of a worldview unselfconsciously shared by news professionals. But the media's allegedly hostile relationship with authority is only one element in the orthodox equation. The other is an insistence that television's graphic representation of the war corroded popular support for it. Here too academic research has gone a long way to demolishing the conventional wisdom that not only misremembers the dominant character of TV images but insists that those images could only have been processed by viewers in one way: as fuel for anti-war sentiment. By this logic, exposure to 'negative' images – a wounded GI or a VC suspect's corpse – can't help but induce anti-war sentiment. Yet it's quite possible for different individuals to interpret an identical newscast or photographic image in divergent ways. What depresses one individual as irrefutable evidence that their country is fighting an unwinnable and immoral war will strike another as gratifying confirmation that VC terrorists had it coming to them.

Images are inherently unstable and indeterminate – open to multiple interpretations. But only in the aftermath of war do they tend to float free of contextualizing clues that prompt particular readings of what the picture shows. Photojournalism and news broadcasts routinely surround images with verbal commentary, disproving the popular adage that images speak for themselves. On the contrary, they're routinely spoken for. As Susan Sontag has observed, 'all photographs wait to be explained or falsified by their captions' (2003, 10). If what the pictures show is ambiguous, then 'it seems a reasonable hypothesis that most of the time the audience sees what it is told it is seeing,' proposes Hallin (1989, 131; Schudson, 1995, 113–23). During the war, those same images which retrospectively came to serve as its iconic signifiers – emblems of the pity of war or of 'Vietnam' distilled to essence – were often surrounded by text that neutralized their potential impact. Even a photograph sometimes credited with single-handedly shattering public faith in the war, Eddie Adams's shot of Colonel Nguyen Ngoc Loan executing a 'Vietcong suspect' at pointblank range, appeared with commentary that resisted drawing the more obvious conclusions about this extrajudicial murder (Hamilton, 1989, 171–83; Culbert, 1988, 253–67).

Americans as a whole undoubtedly *did* become more hostile to the war. A majority considered it a mistake by 1967: a year in which more than 9,300 American service personnel were killed in combat. But they lost confidence in the military venture in Vietnam for multiple reasons. As costs rose and casualties escalated – in 1968 more than 14,500 US troops died in Vietnam, the single worst year for American fatalities – the prospect of victory appeared to recede, prompting questions about the war's ethics and efficacy alike. If the conventional wisdom were correct, we might expect to find that those who watched more TV were more likely to oppose the war. Yet there's no overwhelming evidence to support this hypothesis. In fact, some opinion polls conducted in the late 1960s found just the opposite: individuals who paid greater attention to TV news tended to be *more* supportive of the war. Other studies suggested that television viewers turned to the news for confirmation of their *pre-existing* attitudes, interpreting broadcasts accordingly. Thus hawks were more likely to regard Walter Cronkite as a hawk, while doves tended to see him as one of their ilk (Hallin, 1989, 107).

Many Americans, however, were far less mindful of the war than retrospective recollection of a nation seething in discontent might suggest. Although most households possessed a TV set by the mid-1960s, owning a television and following network news closely were not one and the same. In fact, network news was watched by fewer than half of all television-owning households on any given night (Thayer, 1992, 99). Some of these individuals, we might imagine, remained indifferent to the war. But others tuned out for a different reason. Americans who vehemently rejected the war increasingly looked beyond conventional channels altogether – irked by the timidity and tendentiousness of what the networks and newspapers of record had to say about what the US was doing in Vietnam, and dismayed by how little these outlets had to offer about what American military power was doing *to* Vietnam. As Christian Appy notes in his oral history of the war, 'No subject was more strikingly inaccessible than the experience of ordinary Vietnamese on all sides' (Appy, 2003, 239). Seeking to redress this deficit, hundreds of alternative papers sprang up, using sources such as the Liberation News Service and Underground Press Syndicate to offer a radical slant on what was occurring in Vietnam.

The late 1960s and early 1970s thus saw deepening skepticism towards 'mainstream media' on the left and right alike. Radicals excoriated the media as part of the imperialist war machine, meekly replicating ruling-class lies about US involvement in Vietnam. On the right, populist attacks on the 'liberal media' spearheaded by Spiro Agnew and George C. Wallace mounted in ways that sound highly familiar today – Wallace protesting that the 1968 election would reveal that 'average Americans' were 'sick and tired of these over-educated, ivory-tower folks with pointed heads looking down their noses at us, and the left-wing liberal press writing editorials and guidelines' (Frankel, 1969, E1).

An 'uncensored war'?

According to political scientist John Mueller, rising American fatalities provide the best correlative for declining rates of popular support for the Vietnam War. As casualties rose by a factor of ten, public support dropped by 15 percentage points. In other words, when casualties rose from 1,000 to 10,000 public support plummeted by 15 per cent (Mueller, 1973, 42–61). That a similar pattern had been evident during the Korean War might have given pause to critics who insisted that television had made the war in Vietnam unwinnable and would prohibit victory in every future conflict unless radical steps were taken to curb its dangerous power. Americans' dissatisfaction with Korea – a war that claimed 36,516 US fatalities, wounded or killed in excess of 3 million Koreans and Chinese, and decimated a peninsula that remained partitioned at the war's end much as it had been at the beginning – suggests that neither the absence of television images nor the imposition of military censorship guarantees domestic support for a protracted military venture of uncertain necessity and questionable outcome.

But the Korean War's unpopularity wasn't the most salient fact that analysts recalled when extracting lessons from Vietnam for future conflicts. Remembering only the relative lack of press criticism of Korea, their attention fixed on the issue of military censorship: imposed in Korea, absent in Vietnam. Working on the flawed assumption that an 'uncensored war' had proven unwinnable for that precise reason, the US military establishment determined not to repeat this mistake again. By 1974, the newly retired General Westmoreland had already come to think that 'there should have been press censorship' (Ayres, 1974, 50).

Vietnam's unique status as America's sole 'uncensored war' implies that reporters, photographers, and camera crews were at liberty to go wherever they pleased, film whatever they chose and write whatever they liked – with precisely no interference from the military or anyone else. The impression is highly misleading. And though numerous other myths about the media's role in Vietnam have been skewered, the degree to which US military and civilian officials attempted to shape the reporting of this war remains underappreciated. Only according to a restrictive definition of censorship – the slashing of a blue pencil through unprintable text or prohibited images – was Vietnam 'uncensored.' While the US military may not have demanded to see journalists' copy prior to transmission, American officers along with civilian propagandists took inordinate efforts to spin a favorable narrative about US 'pacification' efforts, providing positive images and a euphemistic vernacular with which to soften the war's most troubling aspects. In this regard, Vietnam appears as much a precursor of things to come than an unrepeated anomaly.

Far from being completely free agents, reporters in South Vietnam were subject to restriction by both the Saigon regime and the US military. Since the Democratic Republic of Vietnam was ostensibly a sovereign state, however flimsy the pretense of autonomy, the US military couldn't formally insist on reviewing all material written by American journalists without publicly overstepping a mark they were keen to maintain. Controlling the press was Saigon's prerogative – one that President Ngo Dinh Diem exercised capriciously and often, before his CIA-assisted assassination in 1963. In the early 1960s, reporters who wrote articles criticizing him were regularly expelled from the country. 'Mercenary publications peddling propaganda harmful to the national cause' as Saigon saw it, like *Newsweek*, were banned. Journalists who wished to transmit negative copy had to leave the country to do so, effectively exiling themselves before the regime did (*The New York Times*, 1962, 9; *The New York Times*, 1963, 20).

As thousands more US ground troops were committed and the press corps correspondingly expanded, relations between reporters and the leadership of MACV grew increasingly tetchy. This hostility was far less pervasive lower down the chain of command, however. Several journalists formed close relationships with junior officers, whose complaints about the war's mismanagement they frequently shared, not least when MACV intervened to place a buffer between reporters in the field and their disgruntled military informants. In March 1965, correspondents complained that they were no longer admitted to the Danang air base unless an escort officer was present, and that these escorts effectively impeded journalists' ability to do their job. 'This is the first war in American history in which newsmen are being barred from the battle area – in this case air strikes, air bases and the fleet – to talk freely to the men involved,' one reporter complained. Some expressed a preference for formal military review of copy if it meant that they would have access to 'see and cover all aspects of the war as was done in World War II' (*The New York Times*, 1965, 4). Then journalists would at least know what they couldn't report.

In response to this brouhaha, the Johnson administration stepped up its PR campaign, sending more public information officers to staff the United States Information Agency's expanding operation in South Vietnam, and trumpeting a new policy of 'Maximum Candor' (Langguth, 1965, 3; Hammond, 1998, 19–30). But candor's outer boundary didn't extend very far. Later in 1965 'voluntary' guidelines were enacted by US news media at the military's behest. Widely seen as a step towards more formal censorship, this development followed an incident in which UPI and CBS broadcast word of the despatch of two units from Saigon to Ducco, where heavy fighting was going on, in a breach of protocol that the military claimed could have 'assisted the Vietcong.' To guard against such an eventuality, the military insisted that media organizations withhold details of troop movements and reports on the size and type of units involved in ongoing fighting, until such information was officially cleared. Figures of those killed or wounded in operations would not be issued; instead MACV would describe day-to-day casualties as either light, moderate or heavy. 'If reporters attempted to circumvent the rules,' notes Army historian William Hammond, 'MACV would have the right to exclude offenders from official briefings and facilities, and to deny them the right to accompany the troops in the field' (1998, 53). News organizations concurred. They were no keener to lose access than they were to appear a threat to operational security.

Press patience was increasingly tried, however, by the palpable lack of realism that suffused official briefings in South Vietnam, for what 'maximum candor' meant in practice was unrelenting optimism. At the daily encounters that became known as the 'Five O'Clock Follies,' official briefers bombarded reporters with endless statistics, charts and maps that showed how well the United States and its allies were doing: how many 'enemy kills' had been racked up, where the overall 'body count' stood, how many 'search and destroy' operations had been successfully accomplished, and which areas of the countryside had been 'cleared' of VC. But briefers often seemed under-prepared and less knowledgable of conditions outside Saigon than the more mobile journalists. As skepticism mounted, reporters came to mistrust official statistics as massively exaggerated 'WEGs' – 'wild-eyed guesses' (Mohr, 1965, 2).

The easily mocked 'follies' quickly entered journalistic lore, memorably captured by Michael Herr who wrote in *Dispatches* that the briefings were intended to 'do the same thing to your perception of the war that flares did to your night vision' (1978, 122). Perhaps the glare of these show-and-tell peformances explains why reporters didn't do more to challenge the meaningfulness of official statistics until Tet revealed how dimly the 'light at the end of the tunnel' flickered. Until that point, the press may have quibbled with the numbers but had done little to query whether the 'kill-ratio' of 'their' losses to 'ours' – a metric that purported to demonstrate unquestionable success, since VC fatalities were always higher than those of the US and ARVN – provided any credible indication of who was actually *winning*. As an index of progress, the body count assumed not only that corpses had been correctly identified as enemy dead (which was often not the case), but also that the North and NLF could not indefinitely sustain far higher casualty rates. This assumption proved quite mistaken. When Tet exposed this numbers racket as a sham, disillusionment ensued, and a 'credibility gap' yawned.

US public information officers didn't just run numbers in Vietnam. They doctored language too, devising an anodyne vocabulary for military operations: 'words that had no currency as words,' periodically amended as certain terms acquired less felicitous connotations. Thus a military directive 'Let's Say It Right' prohibited the phrase 'kill ratio,' which sounded a little too blood-thirsty, and substituted 'search-and clear' missions for 'search-and-destroy' (*The New York Times*, 1970, 167). Preferred terminology came and went, but what remained constant from one year to the next was a stubborn refusal to acknowledge US military mistakes, setbacks or defeats. As Michael Herr noted:

> Nothing so horrible ever happened upcountry that it was beyond language fix and press relations ... You'd either meet an optimism that no violence could unconvince, or a cynicism that would eat itself empty every day and then turn, hungry and malignant, on whatever it could for a bite, friendly or hostile, it didn't matter. Those men called dead Vietnamese 'believers,' a lost American platoon was a 'black eye,' they talked as though killing a man was nothing more than depriving him of his vigor. (1978, 40–1)

With a major United States Information Agency (USIA) operation supporting the war effort, the machinery of official optimism was as cumbersome as it was ceaseless. No one felt its weight more oppressively than reporters for military newspapers and the Armed Forces' Radio and Television Service (AFRTS) in Vietnam, for whom this was most emphatically a *censored* war. If the commercial civilian media were never technically censored, the channels by which US troops themselves learnt about the war beyond their immediate purview – and the world beyond Vietnam – were stringently controlled.

This control took different forms, from barring publications popular with GIs such as the tabloid *Overseas Weekly* from circulation in Vietnam (after it broke the story of one commanding officer's activities with the far right John Birch Society) to attacks on the *Stars and Stripes* (Pearson and Anderson, 1967, B11). Since the Pacific edition was produced in Tokyo – with the oxymoronic masthead motto 'an authorized unofficial publication' – it fell under suspicion in MACV as dangerously *unauthorized*. Since copy from *Stripes'* reporters in Vietnam was sent directly to Tokyo without censorship by the military command's office of information (MACOI), it was the one place that GIs could 'sometimes read about the shooting, bleeding, bombing, gassing, dying and killing.' Incensed by *Stars and Stripes'* deviation from the official 'clean war' line, MACV undertook a campaign of harassment against the military's own flagship publication, one army colonel going so far as to dub it the *Hanoi Herald* (Mitgang, 1970, 28). The brass, announced *Stars and Stripes'* disgruntled Saigon office bureau chief, wanted it to be 'a pap sheet in which they could air their views and prevent even a hint that all was not wine and roses on the war front.'

In 1969 and 1970, several internal investigations were conducted into allegations of censorship which by then had reached the US Senate. MACV roundly defended itself each time. Unit newspapers and magazines were instruments of 'command information' similar to corporate 'house organs,' and hence legitimately employed to build communal esprit: 'checked for policy and propriety but not really censored at all' (Sterba, 1970a, 1). In the name of sustaining morale – an endlessly elastic category – a huge array of information was withheld from GIs. Breaking this story in 1969, the *Washington Post* reported that the Pentagon's information czar John C. Broger daily flagged 'sensitive' wire service stories that he didn't want to see aired on AFRTS, and that his deputies enacted these 'censorship policies with apparent relish.' When one 27-year-old specialist, a broadcaster for AFRTS with seven years' experience as manager of a civilian radio station, announced on air that he and his colleagues were not 'free to tell the truth' he was hastily court-martialled on spurious charges and then sent upcountry as a chaplain's assistant (Sterba, 1970a, 1).

Military and civilian information officers were unabashed in announcing that their job wasn't keeping troops informed but 'making the military look good' – with a view much more to Stateside audiences than those in the field. Above all, commanding officers wanted to preserve their own reputations, hoping to return home from an unpopular war with their personal image untarnished. 'The fact that we lost a battle is sort of immaterial. I mean, it happens in battle, and anyway, we don't like to publicize it,' one military information officer burbled, explaining in January 1970 'why it is that in the hundreds of issues of newspapers, magazines, brochures and yearbooks and the thousands of feet of movie film and radio tape prepared by "information" units throughout South Vietnam, the Americans have never been reported losing a battle' (Sterba, 1970b, 167).

MACV justified its reticence in part on the grounds that troops might send depressing news home if they found it in their military newspapers – as though their first-hand experience yielded nothing but uplifting developments. Moreover, as Robert Hodierne pointed out in long exposé of military censorship in the *New York Times Magazine* in April 1970, a grunt's 'mother in Des Moines, Iowa, will probably know more about the whole fight' than her son in combat (Hodierne, 1970, SM115). As it was, soldiers faced an impossible struggle to keep informed on the larger progress of the war beyond what they could see with their own eyes. Hodierne noted:

> In Vietnam, a GI can get news of the war and the world in several mostly unsatisfactory ways. He can subscribe to papers from home – any papers, from the most obscene, radical, left-wing underground ones to the most right-wing. These are often weeks late ... But the Vietnam coverage of most Stateside papers, in which the war has moved well off Page 1, does not satisfy the demand of a GI in the war zone. For war news, he must turn to military sources. (Ibid.)

But military sources contained very little war news, and even less that was credible. MACOI's official policy was to deny that US forces used CS gas, napalm, or snipers, just as it denied that there were problems with military discipline, morale and a soaring epidemic of heroin use. Such stories presented a 'highly negative view of the United States fighting man,' and it was the 'grease pencil warriors'' job to cast grunts in the most angelic light possible. Hence MACOI's preoccupation with 'pacification' – the 'other war.' 'There is a concerted effort to play down the fighting and play up the loving,' Hodierne scathingly observed. 'Unit publications and public-relations releases are crowded with cuddly orphans, lovable nuns, sparkling new wells, big new schools and grimacing urchins being given shots by kindly medics. It is hard to find someone killing anyone anywhere.' The issue of *Army Reporter* for the week February 10–16, 1970, a week in which 100 US service personnel died, contained no mention of a single soldier being killed (Hodierne, 1970, SM115).

Military and civilian information officers strove simultaneously to make Vietnam look more tranquil to civilians in the States and America look less tumultuous to soldiers in Vietnam. MACOI not only obfuscated the big picture of the war, they also curtailed grunts' access to what was then being called the 'war at home:' the domestic ferment generated by opposition to the war together with a more expansive rebellion against 'the system' as a whole. Military leaders in Vietnam feared that news of domestic radicalization would fuel GI's anti-war sentiment, exacerbating tension between ranks and races. Tellingly, MACOI was particularly touchy about the April 1968 assassination of Dr Martin Luther King Jr: an event that triggered uprisings in cities from Newark to Detroit and which also, according to Michael Herr, intruded on the war in Vietnam in a way 'no outside event had ever done,' prompting 'a number of small, scattered riots, one or two stabbings, all of it denied officially' (Herr, 1978, 129). Clearly, news of King's murder couldn't be silenced altogether, and wasn't. Nevertheless, Lt. Col. Harold Meyer refused to sanction an interracial GIs' radio panel discussion on King's murder, doing so on the most inflammatory grounds when he told AFRTS managers, 'I don't want you to put those niggers on the air' (Anderson, 1969, D17).

'You are on pretty shaky ground when you can't tell your troops the truth about the war for fear they wouldn't fight it if you did,' concluded Hodierne. Since GIs knew better than anyone that the war wasn't all cuddly orphans, pacified peasants, and happy, well-scrubbed marines, they simply gave up on military newspapers – producing underground newsletters of their own. A policy justified in the name of sustaining morale had quite the opposite effect, exacerbating the chasm of mistrust between officers and men that was one of the Vietnam War's most striking features.

Off-the-record wars: the Falklands and Grenada

While Americans replayed the Vietnam War in popular culture during the first Reagan presidency – getting to win this time, as the tagline for *Rambo* had it – the British military determined to win *their* next campaign by ensuring that it was not a television war. This was quite a feat for 1982. Or it would have been, had the theater of hostilities not been the Falkland Islands, and had these islands lain anywhere other than some 8,000 miles from Britain in the South Atlantic – not adjacent to the Shetlands as many Britons imagined on learning in April 1982 that Argentina had reclaimed territory it called las Malvinas. As media scholar Derrik Mercer notes, 'hardly ever have circumstances been more propitious for a censor than they were for the British in the Falklands' (Mercer, Mungham and Williams, 1987, 39). For much of its duration, this 74-day campaign wasn't a *pictorial* war, let alone a TV war, with some still photographs taking longer to reach London than had William Howard Russell's report of the Charge of the Light Brigade in 1854 (ibid., 39). In the words of photographer Martin Cleaver, 'It wasn't a news war, it's as simple as that. It was in the wrong place' (quoted by Morrison and Tumber, 1988, 1).

The clash between British and Argentinian forces was an anachronistic conflict: a war fought without the full benefits of late twentieth-century communications technology over the fruits of nineteenth-century imperialism, with Argentina laying physical claim to islands over which Westminster was determined to maintain British sovereignty (Adams, 1986). It would be easy to imagine that such an anomalous episode could not possibly yield any usable lessons for future conflicts. Yet the MOD's media policy in the Falklands became a model for how journalists could be 'embedded' with and minded by the military, how copy could be 'reviewed' and pooled that resurfaced in Grenada, Panama and then in the 1990–1 Gulf conflict.

So, what exactly did the MOD do that the Pentagon found so persuasive? The essence of the plan was simple: permit only a handful of journalists to accompany the sea-borne forces into battle; ensure that reporters were never without a military minder, and that they relied exclusively on military communications equipment to transmit copy back home.

Several factors aided the military in putting this plan into action, not least the speed with which a 'Task Force' was mustered for despatch to the South Atlantic. Since Argentina's invasion of the islands on April 2 apparently caught the British defense establishment off-guard, a flotilla of warships – and the accompanying team of war correspondents – had to be assembled at a few hours' notice. Preparations for reclaiming the Falklands accelerated at breakneck speed but also with an air of unreality. Many journalists assumed that an impressive display of British naval might would scare off the 'Argies' without any need for battle: the nineteenth-century art of gunboat diplomacy resurrected. Thinking they were merely sending off reporters on a brief 'boating holiday' (as the BBC television news editor put it), editors selected expendable personnel haphazardly. Many duly packed little more than a toothbrush and change of underwear (Harris, 1983, 22; Morrison and Tumber, 1988, 5–7).

While the fleet was readied for departure, Fleet Street editors lobbied

10 Downing Street to allow more than the initial allocation of ten journalists to accompany the Task Force. Neither Thatcher nor the armed
services were innately well disposed towards the press, and limitations of
space on-board offered a compelling rationale for restricting the press
pool to a minimum. 'For every war correspondent carried a Marine or
Para had to be left behind,' noted one officer. In the gathering whirl of
jingoism, few doubted that an extra soldier would do more to hasten the
Falklands' liberation than an additional 'pencil warrior' (Le Bailly, 1983,
197). Under pressure, however, Thatcher's press secretary, Bernard
Ingham (himself a former journalist) relented somewhat, finally allowing
29 British journalists to set sail. Of these, five represented the BBC and
ITN, with one Reuters correspondent on board to serve the international
media. All were men. If 'a warship in action has no room for a journalist,'
as Winston Churchill insisted during World War I, it certainly had no
space for a *female* reporter.

The official position throughout was that no censorship was practiced.
But states and their militaries are typically loathe to announce themselves
censors, and as two reporters observed at the time, the system used
looked 'remarkably like it' (Low and Bishop, 1982). On 7 April, Sir
Frank Cooper (Permanent Under Secretary of State at the MOD) laid
down guidelines for editors as to what they could not cover, while officers and crews were briefed on what was discussable with their journalist
shipmates. Eight topics were deemed inadmissible: speculation about
possible future action; plans for operations; operational capabilities and
readiness of individual units; details about military techniques and
tactics; logistical information; intelligence about Argentine forces;
equipment capabilities and defects; and communications (Harris, 1983,
26).

As in Vietnam, it wasn't the specifics of these regulations that troubled media organizations. Wartime typically produces broad consensus
between news professionals and the state that reporting restrictions to
preserve military security are entirely appropriate. So it was during the
Falklands conflict – as later in the Gulf. The problem was rather that the
MOD's arrangements seemed motivated less by a desire to protect
soldiers' safety than to safeguard the military's good reputation, eliciting
from the media what one minder termed a '1940 propaganda job'
(Cockerell, 1988, 270). In other words, the press was there to cheerlead,
whipping up support for a war only questionably in the 'national interest'
but on which Prime Minister Thatcher's Conservative Party had pinned
its hopes of electoral success in the 1983 General Election. Media resentment over blatantly political manipulation reached its peak on April 25,

when Thatcher timed her announcement that British troops had landed on South Georgia – 'Rejoice! Rejoice!' – purposely to coincide with ITN's 10pm news broadcast (Glasgow University Media Group, 1985).

The ship-bound arrangements also generated much antagonism, with several reporters feeling that the state's expectations of compliance *exceeded* those of World War II, in which matters of 'tone' had been left to editorial judgement and only matters of fact were subject to excision by the censors (Bishop, 1982, 6). During the Falklands campaign, the 29 journalists with the Task Force were wholly dependent on the minders appointed by the MOD to transmit their images and stories, the latter enjoyed every advantage in sitting on stories they found displeasing. Reporters quickly concluded that minders obliged those who produced rousing color pieces, cheering 'our boys' into action, while those who adopted a more dispassionate or critical tone found their stories delayed for days in transit or referred to the MOD in London for further 'fact checking.' In this way, bad news turned into old news, and hence no news at all.

Not surprisingly, the minders exhibited great prickliness over the writing up of British losses, particularly those incurred when Argentine forces sank the *Sir Galahad* (Morrison and Tumber, 1988, 57). They were little keener to see British naval decisions dissected either, such as the controversial sinking of the *General Belgrano*. Meanwhile, allegations that British troops had bayoneted Argentinian prisoners on Goose Green found no public circulation until after the war, when journalists also ventured stories about the Falkland islanders' less than gracious attitude towards their liberators – though whether MOD pressure or self-censorship kept these stories from seeing the light of day earlier remains a moot point (Morrison and Tumber, 1988, 115–22).

After the war ended, the sharpest criticism arose over why the Falklands War had not been adequately televised and whether it could have been had Thatcher's Cabinet shown greater determination to make it so. When this contentious issue was raised by the House of Commons Defence Select Committee in its postwar hearings on the MOD's handling of the media, both the BBC and ITV insisted that the essential problem was a failure of will rather than technological incapacity. 'I have no doubt at all that if the Government had said, "Call in the best brains in the British electronic industry," and locked them up in a hotel for a weekend and said, "Now ... let's hack this problem," they would have found a solution,' BBC Assistant Director-General Alan Protheroe told the Select Committee. 'The problem was that it was too low a priority' (quoted by Morrison and Tumber, 1988, 164).

It certainly seems that for at least *part* of the journey to the South

Atlantic black-and-white footage could have been screened on television, transmitted via the British military satellite, SKYNET, from the larger naval vessels with the Task Force. But the Navy was reluctant to relinquish so much of its system's bandwidth, arguing that color pictures would have exceeded its capabilities altogether (Morrison and Tumber, 1988, 164–6). Once the flotilla sailed beyond South Georgia, use of SKYNET would also have required a ship to be stationed permanently in the satellite's footprint, diverting resources to what was evidently not regarded as an essential task. During the military hostilities on the Falklands Islands themselves, pictures could have been transmitted from land-based terminals via the American DISCUS satellite had Washington obliged, but responses to informal soundings of the Pentagon apparently dissuaded the MOD from pursuing the matter further (Morrison and Tumber, 1988, 167; Harris, 1983, 58).

In the absence of such initiatives, the television correspondents Brian Hanrahan and Mike Nicholson found themselves reduced virtually to the role of radio correspondents. Piecing together stories from their print colleagues' copy, the two television reporters had to be winched from the *Hermes* to an auxiliary ship, the *Olmeda*, which was equipped with the secure satellite phone system, Marisat, through which they could relay their voice reports (Harris, 1983, 33). Film *was* shot, but as it couldn't be beamed homewards by satellite, video reports had to be shuttled by helicopter or ship to Ascension island for onward journey by plane.

It was a cumbersome process, though precisely how slow seems to have varied considerably, depending on the sense of urgency attached to getting the footage back. Since transmission took anywhere from nine to 21 days to reach London, where it was reviewed again by the MOD, it was almost like the Dead Sea scrolls, according to ITN editor David Nicholas: of historical interest, but hardly the topical stuff of news (Harris, 1983, 56). 'Good news' images invariably made the homeward journey much faster than anything that might dampen popular enthusiasm for the war. Thus Tom Smith's shot of villagers offering a Marine a cup of tea ('Cuppa for a Brave Para,' as it was captioned in the *Sunday Mirror*) arrived much more expeditiously than explicit depictions of battle, such as Martin Cleaver's image of the *Antelope* exploding (Morrison and Tumber, 1988, 181–3; Taylor, 1991, 92–6).

As far as the government's critics were concerned, these discrepancies attested the MOD's wilful interference with the war's visual representation. Ultimately, the postwar Committee of Enquiry refused to adjudicate between the state and broadcasters on the issue of deliberate obstructiveness. Its bland verdict noted that a motive for dishonesty

Illustration 3.2   An official 'good news' image of Sergeant Major Laurie Ashbridge of 3 Parachute Regiment enjoying a cup of tea in San Carlos, shortly after the British Landings there

Source: Ministry of Defence Collection/Imperial War Museum.

wasn't proof that the government had in fact abused the media for political gain (Morrison and Tumber, 1988, 164). But in defending themselves against the broadcasters' charges, military, government and civil service representatives were remarkably candid in acknowledging their antipathy towards television.

If they proved nothing else, the Committee hearings demonstrated the potency of Vietnam-inspired convictions about television news as an irritant and impediment to victory. Sir Frank Cooper, MOD Under Secretary of State, was adamant that news footage of combat, had it existed, would have required MOD adjudication on grounds of 'taste and tone' (Harris, 1983, 59–60). John Nott, Minister of Defence when the crisis began, was equally certain that television's impact in wartime was necessarily negative. 'I do not think that television would have made our operations any easier to conduct and, after all, we were trying to win a war,' he informed the Select Committee, even as he insisted that the government had 'intended that television should go and there were technical obstacles we could not overcome' (Morrison and Tumber, 1988, 170). For their part, senior officers who appeared before the Committee testified that 'unpleasant scenes' would have been 'singularly debilitating to our wives and our families,' as Brigadier Tony Wilson put it, and hence an unconscionable sap to military morale (Harris, 1983, 64). However the evidence-givers dressed up their distaste for television, the specter of Vietnam loomed large. As Thatcher's press secretary Bernard Ingham made clear in his memoirs, the animus against television derived largely from that war and the effect televised footage was believed to have had – even if nobody quite said so directly (Ingham, 1991, 297).

From the military's perspective, the Falklands was a successful if not seamless 'information war.' Although the BBC was assailed for having divulged details of the planned landing at Goose Green prematurely, news coverage in general offered exactly the truncated perspective that the government and MOD intended. As US network news teams soon discovered, it simply wasn't possible to reach the Falklands by independent means. This meant that American TV coverage was every bit as visually impaired as in Britain – a 'file footage war' consisting 'mainly of stand-up reports from London and Buenos Aires, artists' renderings of battle scenes and, while the British fleet was still wending its seemingly merry way toward the Falklands, British-supplied footage of sailors training, cleaning up or playing cards below decks.' Anticipating a trope that would become ubiquitous during the Gulf War of 1991, Tom Shales of the *Washington Post* noted that the radically distanced, apparently bloodless conflict being played out in the South Atlantic looked 'almost like a video game, with so many graphs and maps and little blip-ships on the screen, and so little real evidence of combat' (Shales, 1982, D10).

Reporters who attempted to get around the MOD by covering the war from Buenos Aires, itself 1,000 miles from the embattled islands, fared no better since the Argentinians were every bit as eager to control the representational field as their British foes. Just as Thatcher and the Tory tabloids railed against the despicable Argies, so the Argentinian regime attempted to stir vengeful passions against the blood-thirsty British. Battle footage was also signally absent from Argentine television, while journalists whose reports 'produced panic' or 'contradicted the credibility of official reports' were threatened with jail. Both sides were reluctant to acknowledge naval losses, leading to a flurry of speculation about whether or not particular vessels had been damaged or sunk (Hornblower, 1982, A19).

For civil libertarians, the Falklands War represented a signal defeat for freedom of information. Precisely for that reason, it struck the military as a great success – not just in Britain but also in the United States, where the defense community sought to learn from and emulate the MOD's victory over the media. The key to securing 'favorable objectivity,' as one US naval officer oxymoronically noted in May 1983, lay in excluding hostile correspondents from the battle zone or debarring reporters altogether (Lt Cdr Arthur Humphries, quoted by MacArthur, 1993, 138–40). Total exclusion was, at any rate, the operative principle tested by the US military in the 1983 invasion of Grenada: an operation launched variously in the name of protecting American medical students in the aftermath of a coup that had toppled the tiny island's People's Revolutionary Government; of pre-empting an imminent takeover of the island by Cuban forces; or at the invitation of the Organization of Eastern Caribbean States.

During the launch of 'Operation Urgent Fury' journalists were debarred from the scene altogether. While the press pack cooled its heels on neighboring Barbados, the DOD supplied videotape footage that backed up one of the administration's chief stated reasons for the invasion, showing large caches of arms said to have been stored by the Cubans (*The New York Times*, 1983, 7). Under mounting criticism by day three of this blackout, the DOD permitted a pool of 15 journalists to visit Grenada for the afternoon, on the understanding that this excursion would end with the handpicked reporters, none from a national paper, returning to Barbados at night (Farrell, 1983, A13). After a further three days, the DOD announced that 'all legitimate reporters and photographers' were now allowed to 'see for themselves.' The 'usual camp followers and gypsies' had been sifted out, announced Michael Burch, the Pentagon's Assistant Secretary-designate for Public Affairs (Hunter, 1983, A12).

As Burch's contemptuous tone suggests, disdain for the media saturated official justifications for shutting the media out while US forces invaded a state with which America was not at war. (Arthur Schlesinger Jr, hardly a radical critic of US foreign policy, noted that Operation Urgent Fury wasn't so much a war as a 'sneak attack on a pathetic island of 110,000 people with no army, no navy or air force' (quoted by Lorde, 1984, 178).) Initially, military and civilian spokesmen claimed that reporters had to be debarred from accompanying US forces ashore as their safety couldn't be guaranteed. Later, however, Deputy Secretary of State Kenneth Dam amended this claim, proposing that journalists had been excluded not for their *own* protection but rather to guarantee 'the safety of the people on the island, the Americans on the island, and of the military forces' – without making clear exactly how reporters' presence would have endangered any of those constituencies (Hunter, 1983, A12). Dam's remark confirmed what was already evident: that protecting reporters was hardly the military's first priority. On the day of the invasion, a group of journalists who attempted to reach the embattled island on a hired speedboat found themselves under fire from a US navy fighter pilot, and beat a hasty retreat. When they protested these draconian tactics, the operation's commander in chief gleefully conjured the alternative denouement had the boat not reversed course. 'We would have blown your ass right out of the water,' Admiral Joseph Metcalf told journalists (quoted by Sweeney, 2006, 155). In similar vein, an anonymous senior DOD official sarcastically noted that a 'commando-type' operation of this sort did not lend itself to 'the tender loving care and feeding of the press' (Gailey, 1983, A1).

Hostility towards the media extended beyond these instances of personal vitriol. Another reason why press representatives couldn't be permitted to accompany the invading troops was that they weren't entrusted with – and in military eyes *couldn't* be trusted with – advance warning of the operation. General Vessey thus justified the news blackout on 'need for surprise' grounds, though word of the impending invasion had already been broadcast throughout the Caribbean. Had operational security been a more plausible rationalization, news organizations might well have assented to a temporary embargo. But they didn't like being lied to so flagrantly, and took umbrage not only at the military's flimsy justifications but also at the fact that, mere hours before the launch of 'Urgent Fury,' White House spokesmen Larry Speakes denied as 'preposterous' rumors of a planned invasion. (Speakes later claimed that he hadn't been in the loop either: a revelation that underscored the increasingly aggressive attitude in Reagan's administration towards guarding against possible leaks.)

Just as their British counterparts had the previous year, US media organizations made vigorous representations against reporting restrictions once victory had been declared. Jerry Friedheim, executive vice president of the American Newspaper Publishers Association, called the restrictions 'unprecedented and intolerable' (Farrell, 1983, A13). But other professional associations adopted a more strategic approach in lodging their complaints to the White House. Thus the Society of Professional Journalists, Sigma Delta Chi, wrote to Reagan to protest: 'The result of your Administration's news management is that the American people have received a steady diet of rumors that conjure up images undoubtedly less favourable to the United States Government than the reality' (Friendly, 1983, A16). In other words, the press would have liked to boost support for the invasion – but had been denied the opportunity by an embargo that forced news organizations to rely on ham radio operators in Grenada and, worse yet, on the Cuban state network, Radio Havana.

Based on Sigma Delta Chi's ingratiating approach to the White House, one might imagine that many Americans had registered dissent over the invasion of Grenada as the various official rationales unraveled. Some of the supposedly endangered medical students denied that they had been in jeopardy. Meanwhile, the administration's assertion that Cuban forces had been poised to take over Grenada – a scenario conjured by Reagan on October 27 – proved equally unfounded. Claims that the island was swarming with thousands of Cuban soldiers were hastily pared down. Within days, the military had reduced their estimate to 1,000 'well-trained' Cubans, whose elusiveness was attributed to the fact that several hundred were 'impersonating construction workers.' On interrogation, however, they appeared to be the genuine article: actual construction workers erroneously detained as military prisoners (S. Taylor, 1983, 20).

Yet despite the administration's tendentious cover stories, public protest in the United States was muted almost to the point of non-existence. Opinion polls conducted in October and November 1983 registered consistent majority support for the operation. An ABC News/*Washington Post* poll in October 1983 found 69 per cent of respondents satisfied that Reagan's stated reasons for the invasion were 'good enough,' other polls finding similar levels of credence in the claims that US citizens were endangered and that the Cubans and Russians were 'promoting turmoil' (ABC News/*Washington Post*, 1983). Polling organizations also found that, on balance, more respondents agreed with the administration's reporting restrictions than did not. A *Los Angeles Times* poll conducted in November 1983, for example, found 52 per cent of those questioned in approval of the government's handling of the press, as opposed to 41 per cent who disapproved (*Los Angeles Times*, 1983). Similarly, Roper Report 84-1 (conducted in December 1983) found that just 19 per cent of respondents believed the press should have been 'in on the invasion from the start' (Roper Organization, 1983).

Such findings, together with analagous polling data in Britain, suggested that British and American citizens were less ardent in defense of the public's 'right to know' than were segments of the press in arguing against state restrictions. Shortly after the Falklands War, the BBC's Alan Protheroe wrote in *The Listener* that, 'Vietnam demonstrated that the public expects, requires, indeed demands information and pictures, and that such material needs to be distributed throughout the world.' Yet Britons and Americans weren't telling pollsters of this great hunger for knowledge in overwhelming numbers. Instead, many seemed to endorse the reasons offered by civilian and military officials for withholding information and curbing reporters' access. As many news organizations well recognized, public trust in the media had ebbed while faith in the military was resurgent.

Some journalists and editors noted this diminution of popular confidence with chagrin. Others sought to exploit society's 'remilitarization' by positioning themselves avowedly and vocally on the side of 'our boys,' jettisoning any pretence to objectivity along the way. 'When one's nation is at war, reporting becomes an extension of the war effort,' opined Max Hastings, self-consciously echoing his war correspondent father's dictum from World War II. 'Objectivity only comes back into fashion when the black-out comes down' (quoted by Williams, 1992, 156). Since the scene of battle lay at a remove of some 8,000 miles, Britons hardly needed to black out their windows at night. But the press nevertheless encouraged a participatory war culture that harkened back to World War II, when Britons had been entreated to 'dig for victory,' 'make do and mend,' and 'keep mum (she's not so dumb).'

The Sun took the lead by offering readers avenues for more personal involvement with an otherwise remote campaign. Since most Britons didn't know where the Falkland Islands were, let alone feel any personal animus against Argentinian head of state General Galtieri, the first task was to encourage a wave of national 'Argy-bashing' with headlines like 'Stick It Up Your Junta' and 'Up Yours Galtieri,' alongside a campaign against imported Argentinian corned beef, or 'bully beef' as it was punningly dubbed. Urging its readers to 'Say Knickers to Argentina!' the paper launched a line of embroidered 'nautical naughties' so that women whose husbands or boyfriends had sailed with the Task Force could proudly sport the name of their loved one's vessel – a novel form of what the paper called 'undie-cover warfare.' *Sun* readers were also invited to 'Sponsor a Sidewinder,' another gambit redolent of World War II, when airmen had scribbled grafitti not only on their planes' cockpits but on the missiles themselves (Morrison and Tumber, 1988, 35–8; Harris, 1983, 38–55).

In depressed post-industrial Britain – with one adult in ten unemployed and Thatcher adamant that there was 'no such thing as society' only 'individual men and women' – such campaigns offered a form of community and reassertion of national greatness that resonated with many Britons. The idea that war might be reported from a position of detachment, including from the vantage-point of the other side, found precious little favor in this hyper-patriotic climate. The tabloids roundly abused the BBC for referring to 'British forces' rather than the first person plural '*our* troops,' echoing the government's claim that the

Corporation had been 'almost treasonable' in daring to question MOD statistics (Howard, 1982). British journalists who reported from Buenos Aires met an even more furious response from a press relishing its vigilante role as border guard of patriotic expression. To be present in Argentina was to reveal oneself a traitor – or so the tabloids maintained, demonstrating an absolute refusal to countenance war's multi-sidedness that resurfaced again in 1991 when journalists stationed themselves in Baghdad.

What the Falklands and Grenada campaigns revealed, then, was not only a more intolerant attitude towards press freedom on the part of the state, but a similar intolerance on the part of some news outlets and their consumers. With objectivity shaken off as an outmoded relic, the tabloids revelled in xenophobia, cheering for 'our boys' and hurrahing the death of enemy troops: hence *The Sun*'s notorious 'Gotcha' headline in response to the sinking of Argentinian warship, the *General Belgrano*. But if the Falklands War foreshadowed things to come, it's also worth noting that those most responsible for producing this hyperbolic reportage weren't the pool reporters working under MOD direction. Rather, the tone was set by editors and leader writers back in London, amplifying the register established by Thatcher and her war Cabinet. Despite the state's chronic anxiety over televised images, it was *print* media that mattered most, at least where cultivation of warmindedness went.

Operation Desert Storm: the 'first real television war'

To the British and US militaries, the Falklands War and Grenada invasion demonstrated that military operations in the television age remained a feasible proposition – but only if cameras were kept as far from the action as possible. The odds against being able to keep television crews at bay in future conflicts seemed discouraging, however. Campaigns couldn't perpetually be fought on small islands remote from the routes of commercial transportation. And as communications equipment became more affordable and compact reporters looked ever less susceptible to military control. Moreover, the US news media had kicked up such a fuss after being debarred from Grenada that the White House undertook to assemble a special press pool that would accompany American forces into action during any future operation. A motley collection of favored reporters, mustered at a couple of hours' notice, had duly sat out the 1989 invasion of Panama waiting to be briefed while dimly apprehending explosions in Panama City at a safe remove.

If the strategists' dream of total journalistic exclusion hadn't altogether expired by the end of the 1980s, it was certainly under severe strain. Iraq's invasion of Kuwait in August 1990, and the Washington-led response to it, would force military planners to adjust to new circumstances: war in the age of satellite communication, covered by an international press corps of unprecedented size – some of whom were located in Iraq itself. Not since World War II had such a large multinational force been deployed as the half-million-strong coalition that massed in the Saudi Arabian desert in the fall of 1990. And never had such a vast agglomeration of journalists gathered as the 1,600 or so media personnel who flocked to Dharan as 'Operation Desert Shield' took shape, thronging the United States Armed Forces Joint Information Bureau (JIB). At its height in 1968, the press pack in Vietnam had numbered some 637 reporters (Atkinson, 1994, 159; Rid, 2007, 56). Managing the media en masse, when journalists now also came equipped with their own laptops, camcorders, digital satellite phones and portable (if still tremendously bulky) satellite uplinks represented a daunting proposition for the military.

But whatever else had changed, the stubborn belief that the media were a menace far more liable to do harm than good on the battlefield remained intact. 'Today's officer corps carries as part of its cultural baggage a loathing for the press ... Like racism, anti-Semitism, and all forms of bigotry, it is irrational but nonetheless real,' wrote Bernard Trainor in 1990 (quoted by Rid, 2007, 61). Several of the Gulf War's architects, most prominently Norman Schwarzkopf, were well known scourges of the press, steeped in animosity a quarter-century old. In many ways, then, the first post-Cold War hot war was conducted in the shadow of Vietnam. When President Bush ringingly declared that US troops would not be asked 'to fight with one hand tied behind their back' – an explicit allusion to Reagan – he sounded a warning note that neither Congress nor the press would place limits on military power, as they allegedly had in Vietnam (quoted by Taylor, 1992, 4). But Bush's attempt to 'kick the Vietnam syndrome' was met by Saddam Hussein's equal and opposite conviction that Americans' intolerance of casualties remained firmly entrenched. After all, the 'successful' operations of the 1980s in Grenada and Panama had hardly been *wars* by any conventional definition. If, as the US military appeared to believe, success was contingent on keeping the press at bay and pictures of human harm off the TV screen, then the preconditions for US victory were far from assured in the Gulf.

During the months of 'Desert Shield' (from August to December 1990) Hussein looked to exploit Iraq's putative advantages in the war for public opinion by making the country accessible to western journalists. In particular, the Iraqi regime courted CNN, which first achieved global pre-eminence through its vivid reporting from Baghdad in the months prior to, and then during, the Coalition airwar launched on January 17, 1991. Ted Turner's Atlanta-based network was given the exclusive right to lease a four-wire military communications link to the outside world for a $15,000 weekly fee (Simpson, 1991b, 281–2; Arnett, 1995, 364). When the bombing began, Hussein also permitted the BBC's John Simpson, ITN's Brent Sadler and various other correspondents to join CNN's Peter Arnett.

Television crews' presence in Iraq ensured that the Coalition's commanders could not achieve a hermetically sealed 'information environment' of the kind the MOD had sought in the Falklands and the DOD replicated in Grenada. But the uncontrollability of reporters in Baghdad only reinforced military determination to maintain a tight grip over the gigantic press pack in Dharan by whatever means lay at the Coalition's disposal. Despite technological advances, these means were not insignificant – based on a two-tier system that divided the unruly mob into an elite who would, at least in theory, witness combat action first hand from within 'media reporting teams' alongside the frontline troops, while the majority merely heard about the latest developments through daily briefings at the Coalition's Saudi headquarters.

Naturally, this hierarchical arrangement engendered heated controversy within the ranks of the press. In the early weeks of Desert Storm, the main bone of contention was the composition of the media reporting teams (MRTs). Only British, French and US reporters were to enjoy this privilege, on the grounds that their national forces comprised the largest contingents within the Coalition. Other nationals were shut out of this arrangement altogether, as were representatives of smaller or more critical publications from the three favored nations. Since membership appeared to be a perk dispensed to well-disposed reporters, critics of this patronage system concluded that the teams' primary function was to provide positive copy for Coalition forces – a role that would be enforced by the military public affairs officers watching over them (Fialka, 1991, 34). To join a MRT, journalists were required to sign a set of guidelines, ceding their right to conduct off-the-record interviews with military personnel, agreeing to submit copy for 'security review' and consenting to remain with, and obey, their military escorts at all times (MacArthur, 1993, 19).

'Never in American history has this country been faced with as large a commitment of manpower and equipment with as little opportunity for the press to report,' lamented America's major television networks in a collective letter of complaint to Bush (quoted by MacArthur, 1993, 10). Their lobbying efforts, however, were principally directed towards increasing the size of the MRTs – membership of which, despite the tangle of restrictions surrounding what could be reported, they treated as a privilege, albeit one that should be their natural prerogative. The major networks signally failed to join a legal action pursued by a clutch of liberal publications against the Pentagon's ban on what they called 'ambush' interviews with troops and on photographic depictions of soldiers in 'agony or severe shock' (MacArthur, 1993, 34). In short, the major media organizations were prepared to criticize the state – but only up to a point, and not on the more substantive question of what the DOD restrictions aimed to do.

Once the war began, the desirability of membership in a media reporting team quickly appeared questionable. Although the military insisted

Illustration 3.3   'So … what stories did you cover in the war daddy?' by Paul Szep

Source: *Boston Globe*/Ohio State University Billy Ireland Cartoon Library and Museum.

that the system was designed in the exclusive interests of preserving operational security and to prevent journalists from 'overwhelming the battlefield,' as Pete Williams put it, on the ground things looked very different. After the war, journalists were swift to identify a multitude of ways in which their work had been hampered and, to all intents and purposes, censored. As during the Falklands War, the system of review and transmission of copy was capricious, unpredictable and often tardy. The *Washington Post*'s Michael Getler bemoaned a system of 'censorship by delay' (Getler, 1991, D1). Since journalists weren't authorized to use their own satellite phones to transmit material, minders could sit on objectionable reports or refer them upwards for further review, rendering these perishable products 'hopelessly stale' by the time they were belatedly cleared for publication (Browne, 1991, 227). Reports often took two or three days in transit with videotaped stories relayed, in old-fashioned hand-to-hand style, by way of what reporters dubbed the 'pony express.'

The dilatory pace of transmission exacerbated journalists' concern that their reports were subjected to scrutiny of a different kind than that implied by the formal name for the process, 'security review.' Despite Pete Williams' insistence that 'we're not trying to muzzle the press or keep them from saying bad things about the operation,' this seemed to be exactly what many of the public affairs officers had in mind (Kurtz, 1991, A20). As during the Falklands campaign, the screening process appeared calculated, above all, to protect – and preferably *enhance* – the military's good reputation. Why else would minders take issue at an adjective like 'giddy' to describe a pilot on return from a bombing mission, preferring 'proud' in lieu? And since this was a war in which euphemism was the order of the day, Malcolm Browne found his reference to 'fighter-bombers' amended to plain 'fighters' – as though the aircraft in question weren't involved in aerial bombardment but in something more straightforwardly heroic, 'fighting.'

Fighting was, in fact, in rather short supply during this war, if fighting connotes a two-sided contest between approximately matched foes. After the long build-up of forces, the airwar designed to knock out Iraq's strategic communications centers and military installations lasted some 38 days. Once air power had done its work, Coalition forces bulldozed their way through Iraqi lines into Kuwait, burying many alive, it was later revealed (Sharkey, 1991, 147–8). After much hype about Hussein's crack Republican Guard, the elite of a military reputed to be the world's fourth largest, Iraqi troops put up less than concerted resistance to the Coalition's advance after five weeks of intense bombardment. But precisely how one-sided this conflict was, and the tactics employed to secure rapid victory, remained imperceptible through the military's sand-storm while the ground war lasted. The BBC's Martin Bell complained that frontline footage shot by his crew was returned untransmitted. Although this tape didn't violate the groundrules by showing Coalition casualties, it did contain images of dead bodies. The most harrowing photograph of the conflict, showing the charred head of an Iraqi soldier peeping from the burnt-out shell of his tank, didn't appear until March 3 in London's *Observer*, by which time a cease-fire had been signed.

The brevity of the ground war – a mere 100 hours – meant that the pooling system barely had time to be put to the test in combat conditions before the Coalition declared victory. During that brief interlude, many journalists found themselves far from any discernible action, a phenomenon so prevalent that ABC network vice president Walter Porges termed it 'censorship by lack of access' (Fialka, 1991, 6). 'Lost' in the desert or stationed with units who remained in the rear of the main drive into Kuwait, these ostensibly privileged reporters were scarcely 'lapping up the cream of the breaking news' as they'd been led to expect (Browne, 1991, 227). Moreover, the Pentagon declared a total news blackout on all details of the ground assault for the duration, even temporarily suspending its own daily briefings.

Together, these evasions suggested that the media-management arrangements served primarily to satisfy emotional rather than informational needs, including the military's eagerness to burnish its image and civilians' desire for 'connection' with their uniformed brethren in arms. From this perspective, the beauty of the pooling system, amplified by the more thorough-going embedding arrangements instigated in 2003, was that it turned reporters into characters in a highly self-referential martial drama. The fact of being embedded itself became 'the story,' narrated by television journalists decked out in brand new fatigues, surrounded by men in uniform against an exotic desert backdrop. That they had rather little actual news to relate was hardly the point. *Being there* was what mattered, with television reporters glamorized by a paramilitary status suggestive of mortal danger and the frisson of heroism that came from standing shoulder to shoulder with active duty forces as they went into battle.

In many ways, though, center stage in this media war wasn't at the front – or somewhere close to it – but back at the Joint Information Bureau in Riyadh. For it was there at the daily press briefings that the visual and verbal register of the conflict was established. Even before Malcolm Browne found himself upbraided for referring to 'fighter-bombers,' it was already apparent that obfuscation was the order of the day. The military's linguistic scruples weren't unique to the Gulf War. Public affairs officers in Vietnam had also been keen that journalists would 'Say It Right.' But the lengths to which Coalition commanders went to excise any allusion to killing as fundamental to war was nevertheless remarkable. Thus civilian casualties became 'collateral damage' – a term that not only obliterated the humanness of what or who had been damaged, but stressed the unintentional and purely incidental fact of this 'wastage' having occurred. Similarly, General Norman Schwarzkopf and Charles Horner preferred to talk of 'degrading the enemy's capabilities' rather than bombing, and were as resolutely opposed to any discussion of casualty statistics as they were to acknowledging bodily harm. 'I'm anti-body count,' Schwarzkopf declared. 'Body counts mean nothing, absolutely nothing' (quoted by Sharkey, 1991, 147).

Since the Gulf War was intended to extirpate all vestigial traces of Vietnam, the 'Chuck and Norm Show' was held at 6pm to avoid overtones of the infamous Five O'Clock Follies. In contrast to the latter, the Gulf War performances were slick televised events organized around the screening of DOD-approved video footage filmed from the nose cone of missiles as they locked onto their targets. It was this imagery – grainy black-and-white images that showed objects in the center of the crosshairs being neatly detonated – that immediately defined the Gulf War. The videotapes served to corroborate the impression of an entirely new kind of conflict, fought with 'smart' weapons that unerringly hit their targets. Re-broadcast on news programs around the world, the war appeared as a morality play pitting the high-precision 'Patriots' against the Iraqis' murderous 'Scuds' (Norris, 1994). Just as the war overnight turned certain television reporters into matinee idols, like CBS's Arthur Kent (the so-called 'Scud Stud'), it also transformed the Patriot anti-missile missile into a revered US national icon.

Dazzled by this display of hi-tech weaponry and anesthetized by the military's sense-dulling language, many journalists failed to probe the veracity of what they were told the tapes showed. Only after the war ended was it revealed that Schwarzkopf and Powell's boast that Coalition airstrikes had been '80 per cent effective' in the opening days of the air war did not mean that 80 per cent of bombs had successfully 'degraded' their intended targets. Rather, a 'successful' sortie was simply one in which bombs had detonated – somewhere (Taylor, 1992, 66). The US military also acknowledged in March 1991 that, although briefings extolled the Patriots' 'pinpoint accuracy,' the vast majority of bombs rained on Iraq had been conventional explosives, with conventional levels of inaccuracy. Of 88,500 tons of missiles dropped, only 5,620 tons were precision-guided. A total of 70 per cent had missed their targets (Taylor, 1992, 220). The nightly presentations had thus been thoroughly tendentious – the briefers' slipperiness left unchecked by journalists who 'didn't know a tank from a turd,' as Retired Army Colonel David Hackworth (a correspondent during the Gulf War) pungently put it (Hackworth, 1992, 187).

According to critics on the left, this wasn't war as typically mediated and sanitized, but a radical new departure: an attempt to represent military power as an instrument that could be (and was) implemented with all the finesse of a surgical scalpel, 'taking out' rotten material with minimal damage to the surrounding tissue. If blood looked very red on the television screen, then war must be made to appear bloodless. And so it was. Staged and choreographed specially for the cameras, the Gulf War was the first *real* 'television war', commentators such as Douglas Kellner and Bruce Cumings have proposed (Cumings, 1992, 103; Kellner, 1992). Sanitized beyond all recognition, it didn't seem to be a *war* at all. Pentagon video footage merged seamlessly with computer-generated simulations, each appearing as real, unreal or 'hyperreal' as the other – an indecipherability that prompted French poststructuralist Jean Baudrillard's (in)famous claim that the Gulf War would not, and latterly had not, in fact happened. Mesmerized by television's eerily disembodied images, how would one ever know what or whether this war really was (Baudrillard, 1995; Der Derian, 1992, 173–202)?

That the Pentagon had such far-reaching goals in mind begs the question why more journalists didn't absent themselves from the official system and strike out independently? The experiences of those who did choose to become 'unilaterals,' as they were called, provide several clues towards an answer. In both its political climate and topography, Iraq was less than hospitable to free-range foreign journalists, as attested by the fate of Farzad Bazhoft, an Iranian reporter for the London *Observer*, hanged by Iraq in March 1990 as a spy. Inadvertently straying into Iraq along an intensely militarized border hardly seemed wise. Nor was navigating the Saudi desert easily done. Should journalists stray into Iraq, the chances that they would be arrested, or worse, were increased by the habit many adopted of cultivating a 'rufty-tufty' para-military look, which ranged from adopting Marine-style buzzcuts to covering jeeps with camouflage netting and purloining genuine Coalition uniforms (Fialka, 1991, 45–53; Bishop, 1993, 111–14).

A more common problem for unilaterals, though, was hostility from Coalition forces and Military Police. Since the Saudi government had decreed that any unescorted journalist found within 100 miles of the war zone faced arrest and deportation, the best reporters could expect was 'having their credentials removed' – a phrase that 'always carried an unpleasant implication of amputation, or worse,' noted a wry Patrick Bishop (1993, 111–12). David Hackworth, America's most decorated living veteran and a unilateral during the Gulf War, reported having 'more guns pointed at me by Americans and Saudis who were into controlling the press than in all my years of actual combat' (Getler, 1991, D1). Other journalists complained of having been beaten up and temporarily detained in field jails (Browne, 1991, 227).

If these unpropitious circumstances weren't enough to deter reporters from going unilateral, there was an additional question about what kind of stories they would be able to report from a position of detachment. Troops were firmly instructed not to talk to these reporters. And even if they did, some newspaper readers made clear their own opposition to journalists who presumed to buck the system. The editor of *The Independent*, whose experienced correspondent Robert Fisk was Britain's most high-profile unilateral, received aggrieved letters from readers after publication of Fisk's reports on confusion amongst British forces in the desert (MacArthur, 1991, 113–14). 'Patriotism does not and should not mean telling lies on behalf of the government of the day,' insisted *The Independent*'s editor, recalling the despatches of William Howard Russell which had been commended precisely for exposing military incompetence in the Crimea (ibid., 114–15). But many others took a far less libertarian view, insisting that the measure of patriotism in this war was strict abidance by military rules.

The animus directed towards the unilaterals was as nothing, however, compared with the vilification experienced by reporters in Iraq itself. Their position was indisputably more contentious since they worked under the direct control of the Iraqi Ministry of Information, which obviously sought to present an alternative understanding of events leading up to and during the war. Once the Coalition's bombing campaign began, Iraqi media minders strove to undermine the DOD's image of infrastructure painstakingly 'degraded,' exposing western journalists to the full scale of human destruction while preventing them from filming strategic targets successfully destroyed (Thomson, 1992, 234). Thus, on January 23, the international press pack in Baghdad was taken to the site of what was clearly labeled in English and Arabic as a 'Baby Milk Factory,' which the Coalition claimed was a military installation, duplicitously disguised as a harmless civilian facility. More harrowingly, they also witnessed the devastation of a shelter in the Al Amiriya district on February 13. This building too, according to the Pentagon, was a military command center, in which Saddam had cynically located civilians (Arnett, 1995, 396–401; Taylor, 1992, 187–218). After two precision-guided bombs smashed through its roof, hundreds of Iraqi civilians died agonising deaths as their 'shelter became their destroyer, an oven' (Thomson, 1992, 235).

As Iraqi censorship was lifted, western television crews filmed scenes of charred human remains being removed from the ravaged building. CNN broke the story; the BBC and ITN quickly following. The footage was revelatory, as grief-stricken survivors unwrapped bundles of molten human flesh for the cameras. As BBC2's *Newsnight* presenter Jeremy Paxman put it: 'Until today it had seemed such an uncannily sanitised war: clever bombs that wrecked real estate but somehow appeared to leave people unscathed' (quoted by Taylor, 1992, 208–9). Yet while the BBC's footage was unprecedented for the Gulf conflict, it was neverthe-less broadcast only in expurgated form – not because the Coalition media managers exercised control over footage from Baghdad but because considerations of 'taste and tone' dictated editorial discretion. 'Many of the pictures coming from Baghdad of burned civilian bodies are consid-ered too dreadful to show you,' anchor Michael Buerk warned BBC viewers (quoted by Taylor, 1992, 191).

Despite these scruples, the Amiriyah episode earned the BBC the tag 'Baghdad Broadcasting Corporation' from Conservative MPs and news-papers which deemed *any* coverage of Iraqi civilian casualties tanta-mount to treason. The BBC was once again denounced as an 'enemy within,' as the *Sun* put it, echoing Churchill's wartime utterance to the same effect. Other editors drew more explicit parallels with World War II, likening the decision to screen such footage to the BBC having reported effects of Allied raids on Dresden and Berlin (Thomson, 1992, 238–9). As in the Falklands conflict, print journalists often proved the state's firm ally in disciplining other news organizations whose patriotic credentials they called into question. Similarly in the United States, CNN's fiercest critics included outraged press columnists and rival networks only too eager to affirm Pennsylvania Congressman Lawrence Coughlin's charge that Peter Arnett was the 'Joseph Goebbels of Saddam Hussein's Hitler-like regime' (Arnett, 1995, 420).

Senior British and US military personnel also did not disguise their belief that reporters had no business being in Iraq. General Sir Peter de la Billière, commander of the British forces, insisted that reporters in Iraq were 'mouthpieces for the enemy, whose aim was to destroy and kill our own servicemen' (1995, 65). His implicit conviction that journalism's function was an adjutant to military power found wide adherence amongst civilians. Viewed in this way, attention to the suffering of an enemy population served only to sap popular will to continue prosecuting the airwar with due vigor, and hence represented an obstacle to victory. For de la Billière, reporters had no obligation to report war from a position of detachment, and indeed wartime offered no neutral ground that journalists might occupy. Either one got on side or one aided the enemy.

Kicking the syndrome?

The vast majority of news organizations did indeed get on side for the duration. After the war, however, the mood abruptly shifted. As *Harper's* publisher John MacArthur pointed out, it was 'difficult to find anyone who didn't, at least officially, count Desert Storm as a devastating and immoral victory for military censorship and a crushing defeat for the press and the First Amendment' (1993, 8). When Defense Department spokesman Pete Williams crowed that the pools 'gave the American people the best war coverage they ever had,' critics took this as corroboration that television had simply become 'Pentavision' for the duration (ibid., 16). But while scholars lamented that in this most intensively mediated of wars, 'the more you watched the stupider you got,' many British and US citizens took a rather different view (Cumings, 1992, 117; Morgan, Lewis and Jhally, 1992, 216–33). Polls consistently found overwhelming public approval of the military's press handling arrangements. If anything, civilians tended to believe the military ought to exercise *greater* control over the media (Oliver, Mares and Cantor, 1993).

When Bush jubilantly proclaimed 'By God, we've finally kicked the Vietnam Syndrome,' his assertion celebrated this public embrace of military values. Yet such triumphalism begged nagging questions. After all, if the Gulf War proved that the United States could now fight wars without fear of collapsing public support, why such acute sensitivity to the images being broadcast from Baghdad by CNN and the BBC? The ferocity of de la Billière's insistence that reporting from the 'enemy side' directly aided the Coalition's foes suggested that he for one remained convinced of civilian 'casualty shyness' – as though the sight of Iraqi victims would generate instanteous and overwhelming public pressure to halt the war. That the British commander was not alone in this anxiety was underscored by civilian leaders' similar response to footage shot during the ground war of the so-called 'Highway of Death': film showing cindered Iraqi corpses caught in a procession of vehicles on the main highway out of Kuwait by Allied bombardment.

Illustration 3.4 British official war artist, John Keane, captures a US soldier recording a fatality in the Kuwaiti desert – an image rarely seen on television or in print during the Gulf War

Source: The Gulf War 1990–1 Collection/ Imperial War Museum.

Pondering why Bush had called a halt to the ground war after just 100 hours when 'regime change' in Iraq had appeared an implicit Coalition war aim, critics questioned whether the president had taken fright at the putative impact of these visceral images on public opinion (Simpson, 1991b, 7). There were, of course, other explanations for the precipitate halt to the war. Kuwait had been liberated and hence the main objective achieved. If Saddam Hussein were toppled, what form of international authority would govern Iraq, with what broader consequences for Middle Eastern stability? These geostrategic calculations may well have underpinned the White House decision, but they did not convince Norman Schwarzkopf. He later complained that 'Washington was ready to overreact, as usual, to the slightest ripple in public opinion' – though as political scientist John Mueller points out, if the administration did wobble, it did so reflexively as American civilians hadn't yet seen the alarming images viewed by President Bush (Mueller, 1994, 122–3, 134–6; Gowing, 1994, 13–14).

Had Americans really overcome their 'Vietnam syndrome'? In private, Bush didn't seem so sure. Popular reponses to televized conflicts later in the 1990s would merely compound leaders' doubt about images of suffering and their motive force.

Chapter 4

Other People's Wars:
Interventions in Real Time

The 'CNN effect' emerges

In February 1991, as the Gulf War entered its second month, media pundits in the United States noted a new affliction that seemed to be immobilizing Americans en masse. Across the country, millions of people were so transfixed by CNN's round-the-clock war coverage that they refused to leave their living rooms, loathe to miss any breaking developments. The 'coach potato' of yore had been transformed into a 'scud spud' (Penley and Ross, 1991). As a result, consumer spending had nose-dived and the tourism industry was suffering. *The New York Times* quoted a young nanny from Washington, DC, whose symptoms were typical. 'When the war first started I didn't want to leave the television set, let alone travel,' Bridgid McDonnell confessed. Only after some weeks, as the real-time war lost its initial novelty, was she able to wean herself off the addiction. For this syndrome the *Times* had a name, the 'CNN effect' – a phrase that quickly caught on, dominating much discussion of media power in the 1990s (Mydans, 1991).

The term's meanings soon multiplied as CNN's global audience expanded and as the Cable News Network played – or appeared to play – a determinative role in successive post-Cold War interventions in Kurdistan, the Former Yugoslavia, Somalia, and Rwanda. For some commentators, the 'CNN effect' described the capacity of images of human suffering, delivered in real time, to mobilize outrage worldwide, forcing national governments and international agencies to ameliorate humanitarian crises or take up arms on behalf of beleaguered underdogs in 'other people's wars.' By way of evidence, such analysts cited pictures of starving infants as the catalyst for 'Operation Restore Hope' in Somalia in 1992; images of Rwandan refugees pouring into Kigali as the impetus behind a massive relief effort in 1994; and coverage of atrocities perpetrated by the Belgrade regime against Kosovar Albanians as the tinder that ignited NATO's 1999 bombing campaign to indict Serbian 'ethnic cleansing.' Hailing television's potential to animate moral consciousness, one author summarized the 'CNN effect' as 'media attention causing improvements in the human condition' (Marx, 2008).

But not everyone was convinced that real-time television was indeed revolutionizing norms of sovereign statehood. Skeptics included advocates of multilateral intervention to deter, halt, and punish grave violations of human rights who noted that while images of human anguish provoke strong public feelings, thus pressuring states and non-governmental agencies (NGOs) to 'do something,' CNN and its counterparts aren't effective at sustaining these impulses. The self-same viewers who press for immediate humanitarian interventions aren't always prepared to shoulder their longer-term costs. 'Operation Restore Hope' seemed to prove the point. As soon as CNN aired images of US casualties in the Somali capital, Mogadishu – gruesome footage of the bodies of four Rangers being dragged through the streets by their assailants (an episode that inspired Ridley Scott's *Black Hawk Down*) – public outrage was agitated once again, this time working to undermine support for the mission. In the words of one US congressman, 'pictures of starving children, not policy objectives, got us into Somalia in 1992. Pictures of US casualties, not the completion of our objectives, led us to exit Somalia' (quoted by Minnear, Scott and Weiss, 1996, 46). For some analysts, this fickleness typifies the 'CNN effect:' a push-me-pull-me phenomenon better understood as insistent but changeable pressure on government officials to act precipitately rather than as a force for humanitarianism per se.

Other critics approached the issue from a different perspective. Foreign policy realists – those who maintain that a hard-headed calculation of national interest should dictate policy rather than idealistic do-gooding – lamented the emergent power of CNN to skew policy-makers' priorities. George F. Kennan, realism's eminence grise and architect of US Cold War containment strategy, made a signal statement to this effect in an op-ed piece published in *The New York Times* in September 1993. Pointing to the expense and inefficacy of an operation that couldn't possibly address what he considered the fundamental reason for Somalis' starvation, namely the absence of a functioning central government, Kennan took aim at television for engendering uncritical support for this ill-conceived venture. Television's cardinal sin, in Kennan's eyes, was to kindle an 'emotional reaction' – sentimentality that could only impede the formulation of sagacious policy. '[I]f American policy from here on out ... is to be controlled by popular emotional impulses, and particularly ones provoked by the commercial television industry' he concluded, 'then there is no place – not only for myself, but for what have traditionally been regarded as the responsible deliberative organs of our government' (Kennan, 1993a, A25).

Television, in short, was usurping the prerogative of policy-makers to organize national priorities, formulate appropriate courses of action, and judiciously weigh ends against means. As 'Operation Restore Hope' ran aground, many in the Clinton administration adopted Kennan's position, blaming the media for what had turned into an ill-starred debacle. 'American foreign policy is increasingly driven by where CNN points its cameras,' lamented national security adviser, Anthony Lake (Summers, 1993).

Such debates, narrowly cast, may now seem rather anachronistic. Twenty years on, CNN is no longer in the ascendant, having lost its status as the sole 'global' news provider, challenged first by the rise of BBC World and then by other regional satellite stations with an increasingly global audience for their on-air and on-line content. In recent times, more buzz has been generated by the notion of an 'Al Jazeera effect' and hypotheses about a 'YouTube effect' which some media commentators anticipate will be yet more powerful, since people with video-capable cell phones are everywhere while CNN's cameras are found only in some very particular places, some of the time (Seib, 2008). We might conclude, then, that innovations in communications technology invariably generate wildly mixed reactions. Where some hail the potential of new media as progressive forces of change, others mourn the erosion of quality that has accompanied the proliferation of content and instantaneity of exchange. Policy-makers, in particular, have tended to greet each new technological development as a harbinger of their own diminished authority, with power trickling from executive hands into the grip of impassioned but ill-informed masses.

The 'CNN effect' debate thus takes its place in a long succession of moral panics over media effects, from the printing press to the motion picture and, more recently, the internet and new social media. Disagreements over the moralizing or debasing ramifications of real-time television can also be understood as the product of a particularly fluid post-Cold War moment. Following the dissolution of the Soviet Union in 1991, America's 50-year confrontation with global communism was at an end – and with it the organizing framework for US grand strategy. Policy-makers, scholars, and opinion-formers struggled to predict the shape of things to come, arguing over whether the 'New World Order' proclaimed by President George H. W. Bush in 1991 was simply code for an imperial

Pax Americana or whether, with ideological gridlock at an end, the UN would now be able to discharge its peacekeeping and protective functions in earnest, ushering in a new age of global humanitarianism. It was within this broader climate of uncertain expectancy that disputes over the potency of real-time television first unfolded, intertwined with contending interpretations of 'globalization' as a force of divisive fragmentation or homogenizing integration – or both at once, as James Rosenau, coiner of the ungainly term 'fragmegration,' proposed (Rosenau, 1997).

But to historicize the 'CNN effect' debate is not to deny that the issues clustered under that umbrella merit ongoing attention. At stake are questions of agenda-setting and agency necessarily at play in any consideration of when and how media influence policy formation. To consider the impact of real-time television is also to contemplate the motive force of moving images and the constitution of 'the public' or, as some commentators propose, a latent 'global civil society' mobilized by technologies that enable widely dispersed individuals to appreciate their shared humanity: an epiphany effected by witnessing bodies in pain and deepened when such images are relayed instantaneously (J. Keane, 1996, 172–3, 182–3).

In exploring the relationship between policy-makers, publics and pictures this chapter addresses themes intrinsic to the study of media and war. But it also tables a fresh set of issues by inquiring into the circumstances under which 'other people's wars' receive 'our' attention. When and why do certain far-off crises attract attention, and sometimes armed intervention, while others fail to achieve visibility? For while enthusiasts heralded CNN's 'lamp-lighting' role in illuminating distant suffering and in creating a world where 'once again there are no "Others,"' skeptics noticed a striking corollary (Giddens, 1990, 175). Global television channels, national networks, and local stations alike – in North America and much of Europe – were markedly *reducing* the range of foreign stories they offered in the 1990s, a trend that has intensified in the early years of the new millennium (Pedelty, 1995, 189; Douglas, 2006). Although talk of a 'CNN effect' has subsided since then, the shrinking of foreign news budgets has continued apace, calling television's humanitarian credentials into serious doubt and posing difficult questions about why some wars seem so easily overlooked while others monopolize the limited television bandwidth available for war reportage. Contrary to received wisdom, war does *not* sell – at least not uniformly and indefinitely. Some wars have only a limited shelf-life. Others, 'stealth conflicts' as Virgil Hawkins terms them, hover so far below the media radar as never to appear for remote spectators' inspection at all (Hawkins, 2002).

Considering the cases

Before examining specific cases in which the 'CNN effect' is thought to have played a consequential part, it's worth pausing to distinguish the many hypothesized effects attributed to CNN – often itself a loose descriptor for television news in general or real-time imagery more specifically (Gilboa, 2005). As communications scholar Steven Livingston has noted, much literature on the topic is 'disjointed and conceptually vague:' a deficiency he set out to remedy by offering a typology of effects that various analysts have imputed to television news (Livingston, 2007a, xiv).

Livingston offers a tripartite categorization. Proponents of the strongest CNN effect discern an *'agenda-setting manifestation,'* whereby media 'entice leaders to engage in distant conflicts or crises, even those lacking a clear rationale of national interest' (2007a, xv). This corresponds to the view espoused by George Kennan but also, in a more congratulatory vein, by journalists who embrace a rights-advocacy role and point to their own success in nudging political leaders away from self-interested calculations of Realpolitik to a more compassionate international politics of rescue. A second tranche of opinion postulates what Livingston terms an *'impediment manifestation.'* In other words, media coverage at times 'undermines public and elite support for an *extant* operation,' typically by stressing casualties incurred in militarized operations. Third, Livingston identifies an *'accelerant manifestation,'* whereby rolling news coverage is held to quicken the tempo of decision-making in crisis situations. 'In the process, the rapid-response rush to meet the demands of global media bypasses intelligence agencies, counselors, and the more deliberative elements of governance' (2007a, xv). While different analysts tend to accentuate one or other of these claims, Livingston's three propositions aren't mutually exclusive. It's possible, after all, that real-time media coverage may generate different effects in distinct situations or in successive phases of an evolving crisis. The question then becomes one of determining the circumstances that give rise to stronger or weaker effects – an evaluation of variables that several scholars have attempted (Robinson, 2002; Mermin, 1999; Jakobsen, 1996).

Helpful though Livingston's schema is, it doesn't exhaust the menu of options. His focus is exclusively on the policy process. But other issues are also at stake in the CNN debate, most immediately *how* policymakers come to feel whatever ripples television coverage produces. Many accounts of the 'CNN effect' in action locate real-time television's affective center of gravity in public responses to moving representations of human suffering. This agitated constituency then pushes policy-makers to respond with all due speed to urgent humanitarian crises. Or so the theory goes. But this scenario begs several questions. How exactly do state officials experience this pressure? Are they deluged with letters and phone calls (or, more recently, with emails, texts or tweets)? Do they consult opinion polls that register overwhelming favor for activist responses? Or do political leaders simply intuit public responses, imagining that graphic images necessarily prompt impassioned reactions (Kull and Ramsay, 2000)?

In this debate, as in other discussions of media effects, 'the public' is the most elusive category: an agglomerated mass to which propulsive force is easily ascribed but empirically verified with greater difficulty. Some scholars thus refer to '*perceived* public opinion' to underscore the flimsy evidence from which policy-makers – and the media – are apt to extrapolate popular responses to news stories and images (Nacos, Shapiro, and Isernia, 2000, 4–5). Taking issue with the assertion of civil society theorists who see global media as facilitating an activist transnational public that policy elites can no longer ignore, Robert Entman argues that the public's growing power has been exaggerated.

> The media reify and promote the power of a putative 'public opinion' that, because it bears only imperfect resemblance to actual public sentiments and interests, does not necessarily augment the public's representation in foreign policymaking. Rather, by raising the salience of alleged public feelings as depicted by the news, this process further increases the media's influence. (Entman, 2000, 12)

CNN's emergence as a globe-spanning network represented a qualitatively new development: a purveyor of news boasting, by the mid-1990s, some 65 million subscribers in '209 countries and territories' (Parker, 1995, 440). In the past television news, whether funded by the state or by private commercial interests, had been an exclusive *national* enterprise. Capitalizing on the rapid spread of cable and satellite communications technology in the 1990s, CNN appeared poised to break the possessive grip of nationhood over broadcasting, offering its vast international audience news that could claim to be 'from nowhere.' Territorial boundaries need no longer mark the outer limit of viewers' interest and sympathies. That, at any rate, was the implied promise of 'global television.'

But CNN's transcontinental reach wasn't its sole claim to uniqueness. Implicitly, if not more explicitly, proponents of the 'CNN effect' have attached particular weight to the transmission of live imagery from sites of suffering. For several commentators, instantaneity greatly augments the power of pictures to stir viewers. It makes a difference to know that, however many thousands of miles away, this starving child's agony is of the moment; that, *right now*, this group of refugees is miserably encamped on a snowy mountain, even as the privileged viewer cosily watches TV or sits down to dinner. Conceived in this way, real-time transmission is a force multiplier of guilt by activating an uncomfortable awareness of the disparities separating 'here' from 'there' – a chasm bridged in no time at all by satellite technology that has effaced the long-standing equation of distance with delay, and of physical remoteness with emotional detachment. This sense of here-and-nowness may also encourage viewers to believe that swift action on their part – or their government's – may indeed save lives perilously close to extinction.

For some analysts, it's precisely this global consciousness-raising capacity that marks out CNN and its subsequent competitors from media of the past, whether the 22-minute newscast scheduled at precise but infrequent intervals during the day or the still news photograph that, however visceral, nevertheless necessarily represented only the residue of a moment past. Thus sociologist Martin Shaw proposes that whereas in previous eras 'people responded to local or national events and to epochal world conflicts which – once or twice in a lifetime – engulfed national societies,' today they are 'faced with a constant stream of wars, each of which is represented to us and demands, in a sense, our response' (1996, 2). But while Shaw celebrates television's role in activating a sense of global citizenship, others lament what they discern as 'compassion fatigue' occasioned by sensationalist media's excessive tugging of heartstrings. In the view of Susan Moeller, individuals *can't* respond to ceaseless demands for empathy – a finite resource – as over-exposure dulls the power of images to shock (Moeller, 1999).

Whatever one makes of them or believes others make of them, pictures are not, of course, the sole commodity purveyed by CNN. The latter's most consequential innovation arguably wasn't instantaneous satellite transmission of far-off events but the introduction of rolling 24-hour coverage. In the past, news was governed by immovable deadlines. Newspapers 'went to bed' at a fixed hour in order to roll off the printing presses for timely delivery, just as news broadcasts, occupying prescribed slots, were carefully pre-scripted to meet their allocation of airtime. Very rarely did an epoch-making event like John F. Kennedy's assassination disrupt regular scheduling. For at least some scholars, it's the *ceaselessness* of reporting in the age of dedicated news channels that endows CNN – and its later rivals – with their real power to rattle policy-makers, forcing them to respond on the hoof to breaking developments.

At the same time, media sociologists and some disenchanted professionals have also noted the way in which rolling news has tended to stretch content more thinly, supplanting reporters as informed authorities with a constant parade of talking-head 'experts.' Forced to be endlessly available for on-camera performance, television reporters can no longer do the real stuff of journalism: cultivating contacts, deepening their local knowledge, and triangulating multiple different points of view. What we understand by news has thus been radically altered by the arrival of 24/7 coverage – the most far-reaching result being, in at least some critics' eyes, a decline in the depth of coverage offered to viewers.

There are, then, multiple vantage points from which to probe the 'CNN effect.' Often overlooked by scholars focused on the shifting balance of power between media and policy elites, the consequences of real-time news coverage for its *subjects* – as opposed to its subscribers – also merits critical scrutiny. Whatever CNN and its ilk may have done to shake up policy-making in Whitehall, on Capitol Hill, the Quai d'Orsay or at the UN, its presence surely also alters material circumstances on the ground wherever a local crisis is transformed into a global media spectacle. Perhaps the most profound 'CNN effect' is that experienced by the often voiceless individuals whose privations become the stuff of real-time reportage. As many humanitarian agencies agree, the presence of cameras is neither neutral nor innocent. If CNN shifts policy priorities, it can also impact the work of relief agencies – where they go and what they do – since, like everyone else in an acutely image-conscious age, they're keen to exploit media power to raise money and consciousness alike.

The Kurdish crisis: 'Operation Provide Comfort' (1991)

Several commentators propose that the first post-Cold War humanitarian intervention, 'Operation Provide Comfort,' or 'Operation Haven' as it was termed in Britain, best fulfils the definition of a media-defined global crisis (Gowing, 1991; Shaw, 1996; Strobel, 1997). In the view of ABC's Deborah Amos, the media response to Kurdish refugees' plight marks 'a moment when the power of television journalism was at its height' (quoted by Seib, 1997, 39). From April 6 to July 24, 1991, a multinational force of British, American, French and Turkish troops helped construct camps and provide relief and protection to millions of Iraqi Kurdish refugees who had fled their homes, heading for the Turkish border. This exodus came in the wake of a failed uprising by Kurds who had attempted to seize control of the Kurdish area of northern Iraq after the Gulf War in 1991. Taking advantage of Saddam Hussein's defeat and the demoralized condition of the Iraqi military, Kurdish rebels temporarily gained control over several northern towns and cities, encouraged by US radio broadcasts and clandestine CIA aid. It wasn't long, however, before the Iraqi regime sent fighter-bombers into action to reverse and punish this rebellion and another uprising, staged in southern Iraq by Shiites similarly inspired by what they believed were US promises of assistance if they completed the work of toppling Saddam begun by the Coalition (Shaw, 1996, 22–3; Taylor, 1997, 172–9).

Though it claimed more lives, the Iraqi state's repression of the Shiite revolt went largely unreported by western television reporters who lacked access to southern Iraq. Kurdistan, by contrast, could easily be reached through Turkey, allowing camera crews to film the Kurdish refugees' predicament (Shaw, 1996, 80–3). In contrast to the Shiite rebels, whose uprising was pejoratively framed in terms of Muslim fundamentalism, the Kurds were presented as more purely blameless victims of a brutal regime: 2 million people in extremis, lacking food and shelter, huddled in flimsy encampments on snowy mountainsides where they were liable to be strafed by their state's aircraft. According to Martin Shaw's analysis of British television coverage of the crisis, reporters went beyond merely showing Kurdish suffering to direct advocacy of intervention on the Kurds' behalf. To this end, they emphasized the moral responsibility incurred by western leaders who had surreptitiously instigated these rebellions only to abandon the rebels once Baghdad responded with force. '[T]elevision was putting world leaders on the spot,' notes Shaw, 'linking them directly to the visible plight of the miserable refugees, putting the victims' accusations against the powerful' (1996, 87–97).

Over the course of a month, Washington and Westminster both came to adopt a more assertive posture. On March 3, 1991, Norman Schwarzkopf warned Iraq that Coalition aircraft would shoot down Iraqi military planes flying over the country – a threat which solidified into action on March 20, when a US plane shot down an Iraqi fighter-bomber. One month later, on April 5, the UN Security Council passed Resolution 688, calling on Iraq to end repression, and the following day 'Operation Provide Comfort' began, combining the establishment of refugee 'safe havens' in northern Iraq with the implementation of a No Fly Zone above the 36th Parallel. British Prime Minister John Major, who had initially abjured any responsibility for the rebellion – 'I don't recall asking the Kurds to mount this particular insurrection' – retracted (quoted by Shaw, 1996, 89). As late as April 3, President Bush was still insisting that, despite 'a sense of grief for the innocents that are being killed brutally,' the Coalition was 'not there to intervene' (quoted by Robinson, 2002, 64). Yet within days, a ground force of British, American, French, and Turkish forces had entered northern Iraq to begin the work of securing Kurdish refugees, while relief supplies were dropped by airlift (Minear, Scott and Weiss, 1996, 51).

With this sudden turn-around of elite orientation under pressure, the Kurdish crisis appears a classic case of television-led intervention. BBC diplomatic correspondent Nik Gowing, whose writings generally question the power of real-time TV to shift policy in substantive ways, treats Operation Haven as an exception. John Major himself, playing up to his Pooterish image of beleaguered little man with shirt-tails tucked into his underpants, confirmed as much in an interview with Gowing. He had been moved, he said, by footage of the Kurdish refugees 'as he was putting his socks on in his flat,' and had, against diplomatic advice, devised the safe havens scheme 'on the back of an envelope' flying to an EC summit in Luxembourg (Gowing, 1994, 38). In this scenario, Major presents himself as the personification of outraged British opinion – a counter-establishment force for moral activism, rushing in 'where pinstripes fear to tread' (Bell, 1995, 137–8).

However, Major's account of his response to televised suffering omits much that might explain why the apparent power of the media in this instance was not replicated in other humanitarian crises of the 1990s, including those heavily televised. As Shaw acknowledges, the Kurdish crisis was exceptional in that responsibility could be easily attached to western leaders, particularly Bush and Major, who had encouraged Iraqi dissidence during and immediately after the Gulf War. BBC and ITN reporters did not have to spell out Britain's and the United States' obligation to help the Kurds directly (though they sometimes did). By interviewing refugees who made the linkage between their rebellion and the West's desire to end Saddam's rule, journalists implicitly urged intervention. Washington-based reporters were more forceful in stressing Bush's responsibility to the Kurds (Shaw, 1996, 156). What produced results, then, was less the pictures themselves than the taint of bad faith that surrounded the Coalition's treatment of Iraqi rebels. By instituting the safe havens, British and US leaders recouped moral capital while also shoring up the international basis for using airpower to police postwar Iraq. The safe haven policy also served to allay the fears of Coalition partner Turkey about the impact of 2 million refugees seeking access to Turkish Kurdistan (Robinson, 2002, 64–6; Strobel, 1997, 130). Television coverage of other humanitarian crises did not animate the same sense of bad faith, nor did geopolitical considerations push so heavily in favor of intervention.

Furthermore, as Minear, Scott and Weiss note, there were 'domestic political factors' at work in Major's about-turn. 'Sources close to the decisionmaking process noted that Prime Minister John Major feared criticism for inaction from his predecessor Margaret Thatcher, who had taken it upon herself to meet with Kurdish refugee leaders in an effort to goad her government to act' (1996, 51). While Thatcher went on to make similar protestations of solidarity with the Bosnians, which Major largely ignored, it should be remembered that in April 1991, Major had occupied Number 10 Downing Street for just five months. He had assumed the premiership, moreover, in a bitter Conservative Party leadership contest following Thatcher's deposition, in which he presented himself as the moderate 'unity' candidate capable of healing the Tories' self-inflicted wounds. The following April, Major had yet to be elected Prime Minister by the British public – his premiership resting solely on the selection of the Conservative parliamentary membership. Still anxious to appease both wings of his party, he was therefore particularly vulnerable to pressure from his predecessor, not least if her views seemed to chime with those of the public. Neither of these factors remained such powerful incentives to action when Major faced conflict in Former Yugoslavia. For 'CNN effect' skeptics, then, the Kurdish case suggests that alliance politics and domestic electoral concerns were far more influential than television pressure (Robinson, 2002; Miller, 2007).

Somalia: 'Operation Restore Hope' (1992–3)

In the early 1990s, while European attention was focused on Former Yugoslavia, starvation decimated east African populations in Somalia and southern Sudan. In both cases, drought leading to crop failure was not the sole cause of food scarcity. Famines are rarely straightforward 'natural disasters' but rather the product of precarious political situations, in which some groups – by dint of being closer to power and better armed – monopolize resources at the expense of others. Civil conflict played a critical role in denying food to thousands of Sudanese and Somalis in the early 1990s. One of these famines received overwhelming media coverage and was the subject of a US-led UN intervention. The other, in Sudan, was at best intermittently covered, although it claimed a greater number of lives (Livingston, 1996; Neuman, 1996, 229).

For some time, relief workers and western state aid officials feared that Somalia's famine might go similarly neglected. In July 1992, UN Secretary General Boutros Boutros Ghali created a stir by announcing that Somalia was the victim of a highly publicized 'rich man's war' in Yugoslavia (cited in Minear, Scott, and Weiss, 1996, 54). Contrary to received wisdom, however, western media did not 'discover' starvation in Somalia and bring it to the attention of hitherto ignorant distant governments. The sudden mass descent of news crews into Mogadishu in the fall of 1992 may have fueled an impression that CNN was acting as both the intelligence service and moral tutor of western governments, but the impression is seriously misleading.

In reality, US media began to take an interest in Somalia after American officials and aid organizations encouraged them to do so, and only after an estimated 300,000 to 500,000 Somalis had died of starvation by mid-summer 1992 (Livingston and Eachus, 1995, 417). Political communication scholars Steven Livingston and Todd Eachus argue convincingly that personnel within Washington's specialized relief agencies worked to put Somalia at the top of the policy-making agenda, attempting to direct media attention to the story, partly as a means of overcoming bureaucratic obstacles and military resistance within Bush's administration to a large-scale humanitarian intervention (1995, 418). According to Andrew Natsios of the Office of Foreign Disaster Assistance, initial efforts to this end were notably unsuccessful, as had been Red Cross press briefings and tours for journalists the previous autumn (Gassman, 1995, 155). Scant media attention was paid to a US Congressional Hunger Caucus at which Natsios testified and to 'sparsely attended media briefings on Somalia in January and February 1992' (Natsios, 1996, 159). Gradually, however, Natsios's attempts to frame the Somali famine as 'the worst humanitarian crisis in the world today' – in the words of his testimony – began to take effect. Livingston and Eachus report 50 usages of similar phraseology by the media over the next few months (1995, 424).

Arguably, though, a more conventional piece of diplomatic traffic impelled a decisive shift towards militarized intervention: a telegram from the US ambassador to Kenya, graphically describing his visit to Somali refugee camps along Kenya's border (Strobel, 1997, 132). The so-called 'day in hell' cable was brought to President Bush's attention by national security adviser Brent Scowcroft, himself an opponent of military involvement. However, the dispatch apparently stirred presidential memories of a trip George and Barbara Bush had made to a CARE shelter in Sudan during the Sahelian famine of the mid-1980s. Bush claimed that what he'd witnessed there 'clearly affected his decision to send troops into Somalia' (Natsios, 1996, 161, 168). Only later did he attribute his resolve to watching televised images of 'those starving kids ... in quest for a little pitiful cup of rice' (Feaver and Gelpi, 1999).

As Bush's different versions of what moved him to launch 'Operation Restore Hope' suggest, researchers face a problem in trying to establish or disprove a 'CNN effect' through anecdotal evidence of this kind. Not only is memory – like television – fickle and selective, policy-makers are liable to offer self-serving accounts of their own humanitarian sensibilities when it suits them, just as, at other times, they prefer to deny any susceptibility to moving images. Although Bush may indeed have been moved by the telegram and the pictures, complex motivations were also in play. Stung by Clinton's charges during the 1992 presidential election campaign that the current incumbent was doing too little about starvation in Somalia, Bush 'had some personal wish to leave office a humanitarian' (Minear, Scott and Weiss, 1996, 54; Neuman, 1996, 229). Strikingly, he chose not to respond to southern Sudan's famine, despite his moving visit there the previous decade, but instead preferred a militarized operation in Somalia. In his critics' eyes this was a move calculated to rekindle memories of victory in the Gulf War, allowing the departing 'Foreign Policy President' to exit in a 'blaze of glory' that would push aside charges that he had neglected to act in Bosnia (Rather, 1995, 33; Dowden, 1995, 94–5; Mayall, 1996, 111). Intervening in Somalia promised to be a 'low-cost' operation that would recoup presidential prestige 'without any great danger of body bags coming home,' or so Secretary of State Lawrence Eagleburger advised (quoted by Minear, Scott and Weiss, 1996, 55). How US forces subsequently disengaged was a less carefully weighed issue, since Bush's successor would be the one left to fathom an exit strategy.

That the Somali intervention was conceived in many ways as a PR stunt is further suggested by the manner of the US Navy SEALs' dramatic arrival in Mogadishu during the pre-dawn hours of December 9, 1992. According to Thomas Keenan, the US military's Somalia strategy was

from the start ... oriented toward the production of images ... conceptualized, practiced and evaluated – by all parties – strictly in terms of the publicity value of the images and headlines it might produce. Comprehensive media coverage has not just changed the conduct of military operations – images and publicity have become military operations themselves, and the military outcome cannot easily be distinguished from the images of that operation. (Keenan, 1994, 142–3)

Thus when the Navy SEALs arrived in anticipated darkness on the beach at Mogadishu they were met by around 600 members of the international press corps, including anchors from the four US networks. Military commanders might complain that the unseemly media scrum created the wrong effect – that television lights dazzled the troops in their night vision goggles – but in fact US officials had invited cameramen to attend the seals' 'taking' of Somalia. According to one British journalist who was present, from the moment of the televized landing he knew 'that Somalia would become a disaster for the United States ... To invade Somalia as if it were a military objective and treat all Somalis as potential enemies was worse than a mistake. It was to lead to catastrophe' (Dowden, 1995, 93).

Staging the landing was easy. Providing the international media circus with an ongoing stream of positive images of the US/UN humanitarian forces delivering the Somalis from one another, and delivering assistance to those most in need, proved more difficult. US military commanders

Illustration 4.1 US Special Forces land on the beach of Mogadishu under cover of darkness, 1992

Source: AP/Wide World Photos.

found themselves in the midst of fighting between armed Somali factions – and against foreigners' intrusive presence – in a state where government had apparently broken down. 'Mission creep' soon set in as the objectives of the US-led UN operation incrementally widened. The initial food-delivery mandate of the United Task Force (UNITAF) mission gave way to UNOSOM II (UN Operation in Somalia), charged with disarming warring Somali militia, hunting down General Mohammed Farrah Aidid, and restoring order and authority, not merely hope. In the words of Frank Stech, '"mission-creep" became "mission gallop" as larger numbers of nations sent UN forces which tried to satisfy increasingly conflicting objectives' – nation-building, food security, peace enforcement, and peacekeeping. After Aidid's forces killed a number of UN/Pakistani troops in retaliation for an attack on their radio station, the UN placed a bounty on Aidid. 'What had been professional became personal. As one senior US officer observed, "manhood was on the line"' (Stech, 1994, 266).

As the situation spiraled out of control, so a process of narrative drift occurred. The story now was less one of US forces saving innocent victims of famine than an inconclusive manhunt that had 'got personal,' and in which journalists as well as UN blue berets and scores of Somalis were being killed. During the summer and autumn of 1993, security deteriorated to the point where US forces were no longer able to guarantee the safety of the diminished number of western reporters still in Somalia. In July, three journalists were beaten to death by Somalis after 60 people were killed in a US helicopter attack on an Aidid stronghold (Lyman, 1995, 126). Other media personnel found themselves under assault from the US military. In an incident in September 1993, three photographers and reporters reported having stun grenades lobbed at them to keep them away from the scene of a military operation (Keenan, 1994, 156).

This was the violent backdrop against which the notorious images of a dead US Ranger being dragged through the streets of Mogadishu were projected on October 4, 1993, after Aidid's forces shot down two Black Hawk helicopters, triggering a sustained clash of arms that left 19 US soldiers dead together with several hundred (possibly as many as 1,500) Somali militiamen and civilians (Strobel, 1997, 176; Dauber, 2001). In many accounts, the gruesome images broadcast on US network news of what would become known as the Battle of Mogadishu put paid to 'Operation Restore Hope,' whipping up such a furious public animus against ongoing involvement in Somalia that Clinton was obliged to pull out US troops forthwith. The White House apparently received thousands of enraged calls (Minear, Scott and Weiss, 1996, 55). Clinton himself was reported to be 'very angry,' calling this the 'worst day of my life'

(Gowing, 1994, 67). National security adviser Anthony Lake corroborated the salience of the images. '[T]he pictures helped make us recognize that the military situation in Mogadishu had deteriorated in a way that we had not frankly recognized,' Lake averred, seeming to prove a point made with increasing frequency that CNN was supplanting the CIA as policy-makers' most up-to-date source of intelligence (quoted by Gowing, 1994, 67). An announcement of withdrawal swiftly followed.

So, does Somalia provide the paradigmatic case of the 'CNN effect'? After US news networks aired images of Iraqis dragging the mutilated bodies of four American contractors round the streets of Fallujah in 2004, numerous commentators cast back 11 years to the images from Mogadishu that, most agreed, had caused the Clinton administration to withdraw (Timms, 2004). Several caveats are required, however. First, it should be noted that the footage itself – wrenching though it undoubtedly was – did not derive any of its impact from being delivered in real time. By October 1993, the international press pack had dwindled from its peak of 600 to a mere six to eight individuals, none of them American. The images that served to emblematize humanitarianism undone were, in fact, shot by a Somali driver, bequeathed a Hi-8 camcorder by the departing Reuters crew for whom he now acted as a stringer. His shots of the US Ranger were relayed by CNN and quickly rebroadcast by other channels, but they were not simultaneous with the events themselves (Pilkington, 1993).

Second, it has been suggested that the Clinton administration, contra Lake's claim to have been caught unawares by the footage, had actually been considering scaling down and then abandoning the Somali operation for some time. The dire news from Mogadishu, paradoxically, provided the pretext to make this public announcement. Even then, as Gowing points out, Clinton resisted the temptation to make an instant withdrawal, initially strengthening the US presence while announcing that the operation would terminate on March 31, 1994. Public pressure to withdraw was perhaps not insurmountable after all. Certainly, one study conducted at the University of Maryland found that most sentiment in favor of a precipitate withdrawal stemmed from Americans' perception that Somalis *wanted* US troops to leave. Asked whether they would continue to support the operation if that were not in fact the case, 54 per cent of poll respondents responded positively (Kull and Ramsay, 1994a).

For some commentators, then, Somalia offers stronger evidence of policy-makers' failure to lead than of television's irrepressible influence. 'Had the Clinton administration chosen ... to galvanize public opposition to Somali warlord Mohamed Farrah Aidid,' conclude political scientists

Peter Feaver and Christopher Gelpi, 'our research shows that Americans would have tolerated an expanded effort to catch and punish him' (Feaver and Gelpi, 1999). But Clinton had no interest in indefinitely sustaining an operation that had spilled so far beyond its initial parameters, and so the operation was brought to an end. Thereafter, tighter limits were set on the circumstances in which the US would intervene overseas, a policy statement enshrined in Presidential Decision Directive No. 25. The Somalia debacle served to reinforce the post-Vietnam conviction that Americans are intensely 'casualty shy.' Resting on inconclusive or unconvincing evidence, this belief nevertheless had profound consequences for future crises in Bosnia, Rwanda and Kosovo, heightening presidential reluctance to act and orienting Pentagon plans towards the goal of zero-casualty military operations (Gelpi, Feaver, and Reifler, 2009, 45; Jakobsen, 2000, 136).

The wars in Former Yugoslavia (1991–5)

The series of wars that accompanied the dissolution of the Federal Republic of Yugoslavia in the 1990s did not lack media attention. Former BBC correspondent Martin Bell goes so far as to propose that 'No other war – not even the Gulf War, which took on the character of a made-for-television CNN special event – has been fought so much in public, under the eye of the camera' as the conflict in Bosnia-Herzegovina between Bosnian government forces and Bosnian-Serbs supported by Belgrade (1995, 137). For Bell and a number of other television and print reporters, such as the *Guardian*'s Maggie O'Kane, the Bosnian cause was one which demanded an reappraisal of sterile formulations of balance. The Bosnians' abandonment by the so-called international community demanded a new 'journalism of attachment,' which went beyond the straightforward replication of contending truth-claims to an evaluation of where justice lay and advocacy of principled intervention of behalf of wronged parties.

Some scholars see impassioned reportage from Bosnia as compelling evidence of the 'CNN effect' in action, with key shifts in EU, US, NATO and UN policy brought about by reporters' attention to human rights violations perpetrated by Bosnian Serbs. To substantiate the point, they invoke a number of graphically rendered incidents that attracted sustained headline attention, such as images of emaciated prisoners at Omarska and Trnopolje in August 1992, the bombing of a Sarajevo market on February 5, 1994, and a photograph carried on the front page of the *Washington Post*, showing a Muslim woman who had hanged herself following a Serb assault.

But not all commentators concur with this estimation of media power. Indeed, for those minded to debunk the 'CNN effect' Former Yugoslavia offers the clearest illustration of the *absence* of any causative link between media images of human suffering and decisive intervention to alleviate it. For Piers Robinson, Yugoslovia demonstrates that a 'strong CNN effect' operates only when policy-makers are undecided or divided over their course of action, as US policy-makers remained until well into 1995, when airpower was used against Bosnian Serb positions for the first time (Robinson, 2002). Minear, Scott and Weis go further, seeing the Balkan wars of the 1990s as a case of 'blanket coverage, selective action' (1996, 57). Similarly, CBS anchor Dan Rather, addressing George Kennan's *New York Times* op-ed on the disruptive power of the media, retorted that if the former national security adviser were right, 'there would be US marines on the ramparts of Sarajevo right now, defending the Bosnian Muslims' (Rather, 1993). In short, media advocacy was no match for official obduracy.

In the judgement of several international relations scholars, a determination to avoid committing ground troops to halt aggression in Former Yugoslavia was western leaders' overriding policy objective. They certainly showed no commitment to preserving Bosnia, an ethnically heterogeneous polity, in the face of violent initiatives by Serbian and Croatian forces to create ethnically pure states and cantons where a federal republic, inhabited by people of different ethnic and religious backgrounds, had previously existed. According to James Gow, western governments managed to steer a more or less straight path of avoidance: a 'triumph of the lack of will' in his ironic formulation (1997).

Determined to set clear limits on their commitment, key members of the Security Council ensured that UN resolutions did no more than authorize the dispatch of a spineless 'protection force' (UNPROFOR) whose mission was restricted to providing safe passage for supplies of food and medicine in areas cut off by fighting. UNPROFOR was not, then, a peace-enforcement or peacekeeping force – a point underscored by the fact that its soldiers weren't permitted to return fire if the beleaguered areas under its ostensible protection came under attack. It wasn't until 1995, after Bosnian Serb nationalists took UNPROFOR personnel hostage and two supposedly 'safe areas' fell to Serbian forces, that the UN finally authorized airstrikes against the assailants, having failed to follow through on earlier threats to employ punitive air power (Robinson, 2002, 75). Only after the ethnic partition of Bosnia had been irrevocably achieved by Serbian force did President Clinton agree to commit 25,000 US ground troops to police a peace agreement based on the country's ethnic cantonment. Bosnia's break-up, to which Clinton had earlier professed his aversion, was thus to be overseen by US forces whom the president had refused to deploy in defense of a multiethnic Bosnia.

Despite persistent journalistic attention to the plight of besieged Bosnian towns, western policy-makers rarely appeared to experience irresistible pressure to act. These occasions suggest that intermittently the media could dent politicians' resolve, but the resultant actions were largely at the level of tactics, not strategy. As Minear, Scott and Weiss elucidate:

> Security Council Resolution 770 of 1992 supported humanitarian aid. Subsequent US aid-drops of aid, emergency medical evacuations from Sarajevo by the UK, and even NATO's protection measures for the Bosnian capital were all responses to well-televised predicaments. In retrospect, these actions appear to have been exercises in damage control in response to public exposure of governmental impotence instead of key elements in established or evolving policy. (1996, 57–8)

Indeed, Douglas Hurd (UK Foreign Secretary for much of the period) made a boast of *not* being deflected from his government's preferred path. In September 1993, he loudly announced that Her Majesty's Government would not be propelled into military intervention 'simply because of day-to-day pressure from the media' (quoted in ibid., 58).

On what occasions, then, did news apparently prompt policy adjustments? Gowing suggests that the first occasion came in the wake of US and British press and television reports on Serbian concentration camps at Omarska and Trnopolje in August 1992 (1994, 40–5). Images of emaciated Bosnian prisoners, shockingly redolent of photographs of Holocaust survivors, put the treatment of prisoners on the policy-makers' agenda, together with the wider practices of 'ethnic cleansing' that underlay the Serbs' forced round-ups and slaughter of Bosnian men (ibid.). Some controversy exists as to whether western leaders already knew of these camps thanks to the UN High Commissioner for Refugees. But if they were aware, these policy-makers hadn't acted decisively in advance of reporters' exposés (Gutman, 1993, xiii; Gowing, 1994, 43–5). Thereafter, at the London UN/EU Conference on Yugoslavia in late August, the Serbian death camps were a major issue, and a commitment was extracted from Bosnian Serb leader Radovan Karadžić to close them.

Arguably, then, the media *did* have an impact on this occasion, albeit not such a decisive one as Pulitzer prize-winning reporter Roy Gutman, who first revealed the camps, had hoped (Gutman, 1993, xxxii).

A similar argument could be made concerning UN Resolution 819 of April 1993, which authorized the creation of 'safe areas' in besieged Bosnian towns – Srebrenica, Zepa, and later Gorazde – around which Bosnian Serb forces had almost completed their task of 'ethnic cleansing.' This tactical shift has been attributed largely to television footage from Srebrenica shot by cameraman Tony Birtley, who had smuggled himself into the town, coupled with the defiance of the UN's General Philippe Morillon, who pledged personally to save Srebrenica whatever Headquarters in New York might advise to the contrary. According to Gowing, Birtley's footage so moved the non-permanent members of the UN Security Council that they pushed through the safe area plan in the teeth of permanent member opposition (1994, 49). However, whether the safe areas did in fact protect Bosnians, in the absence of any UN mandate to UNPROFOR to target their assailants, or were conducive to a just longer-term settlement – since they did nothing to reverse the ethnic cleansing of surrounding areas – looks highly doubtful (ibid., 54).

In 1994, a more forceful approach was espoused, after some vacillations, by NATO and Clinton. Airstrikes against the Bosnian Serbs were threatened and later actually enacted on some occasions. This stiffening of resolve was also apparently the result of television footage which depicted the gruesome consequences of a mortar attack on a Sarajevo market in February 1994. 'Bodies ripped apart, a chaotic scramble to rescue badly wounded victims, cries of agony, wrenching grief,' wrote one print journalist of the TV pictures. 'All that was missing was the stench of death' (Matthews, 1994). In Martin Bell's opinion, coverage of this episode generated a shift in policy, though he concedes that:

> The timing may also have had something to do with it. A new take-charge commander, Lieutenant-General Sir Michael Rose, was on the scene. The UN was fulfilling its mandate for the first time in months, and had embarked on a policy of threatening force against the Serbs ... but the TV images certainly made a difference. Among other effects, they brought about a change of policy by the British and Canadian governments about the use of airpower. (1995, 143–4)

Gowing argues a more limited-effects case. Although purportedly 'outraged' at the televised scenes of carnage, Clinton in fact reacted tentatively at first, holding an inconclusive impromptu Oval Office meeting.

The real pressure for airstrikes came from the French government, Gowing claims, which had been agitating for them for some time (1994, 70–2). The combination of diplomatic and media pressure explains why these images, not earlier atrocities, prompted action. Even then, Clinton apparently continued to waver after the decision had been taken but before Serbian positions had actually been bombed.

Clinton's ultimate decision to make good on the long-threatened use of air power came the following year, coupled with an 'end-game strategy' to invigorate UNPROFOR, re-commit to the protection of Gorazde, and impose a territorial settlement on the warring parties. This move came in July 1995, after the supposedly 'safe area' of Srebrenica fell to Bosnian Serb forces, leaving both the UNPROFOR mission and NATO looking hopelessly unequal to the task of protecting Bosnian lives. Graphic television reports detailed the massacre of 8,000 inhabitants and outpouring of refugees from the beleaguered town, while editorials and columnists on both sides of the Atlantic urged policy-makers to grasp the nettle. The situation was 'the worst mess we have seen in Europe since the end of World War II,' conceded Assistant Secretary of State Richard Holbrooke on ABC's *Nightline* (quoted by Robinson, 2002, 76). In Robinson's judgement, 'empathy framed' news coverage was particularly influential at this juncture as US policy-makers were divided over their next steps, some favoring Anthony Lake's 'end-game' proposal while others continued to hesitate. With Clinton also under mounting pressure from the French government to toughen his stance and NATO credibility on the line, news media may have helped tip the balance without being the sole determinative force (Robinson, 2002, 76–86).

The most incontrovertible cases of instant response to manipulative imagery are those where the resultant action was most obviously designed for television consumption – not a shift in policy so much as a 'pseudo event' calculated to give the appearance of compassionate action. A striking instance of this phenomenon occurred in August 1993, when the BBC showcased the predicament of a five-year-old Bosnian girl with shrapnel wounds to her spine. Overnight, 'little Irma' became a media darling, as various tabloids competed to evacuate her from Bosnia and bring her to London for specialist medical treatment (Gowing, 1994, 80–2). However, they were outstripped by the British government, which itself organized a military airlift for the injured infant and 40 other Sarajevan casualties. The desire to be seen to be doing something – making an Instant Response to Media Attention, as UN Commander Brigadier Hayes punned – proved overwhelming: a low-cost way to appear responsive to suffering without actually taking decisive steps to address its causes (Bell, 1995, 143). Shrugging off accusations of cynicism, Douglas Hurd claimed that the government had realized that just 'because you can't help everybody doesn't mean you shouldn't help somebody' (quoted by Gowing, 1994, 81).

The Yugoslav case thus provides considerable support for the view that television is fickle in its attention, selectively singling out certain pitiable individuals or groups while neglecting to offer viewers an interpretive framework that would make sense of violence in Former Yugoslavia. Western television news largely failed to explain what role external powers had played in enabling the Balkan wars (by lending impetus to the federal republic's dissolution), just as they neglected to examine how, or whether, they might also contribute to a just peace in the region. In the eyes of some liberal internationalists, television – so recently hailed as an agent of global civil society – had failed to perforate the armor of national interest, or as Michael Ignatieff put it, television reportage had not 'pierce[d] the carapace of self-absorption and estrangement that separates us from the moral worlds of others' (1998, 29). Others, though, insisted that television had succeeded only too well in jolting distant publics into a stunned awareness of bloodletting in Former Yugoslavia. Richard Holbrooke contended that gruesome images had contributed to Americans' *disinclination* to commit ground forces to Bosnia, fearing submersion in an inescapable quagmire as 'ancient tribal hatreds' – a dominant interpretive frame for the wars – cycled on endlessly (Kincaid, 1995).

Was Holbrooke's assessment correct, or was there an element of disingenuousness to his claim? One might retort, as did skeptics over an alleged 'CNN effect' in Somalia, that political leadership involves explaining and building consensus for difficult policy choices. US public support for intervention in Bosnia had in fact grown steadily over the period from 1992 to 1995, propose political scientists Peter Feaver and Christopher Gelpi – critics of the notion of American 'casualty shyness.' When political leaders cited a lack of public will for intervention, it was often cover for their *own* reluctance to act – another indication of the latitude for maneuver that policy elites enjoy, even as they insist their choices are constrained by inflammatory media images and their citizens' oscillations between engagement and detachment.

Rwanda (1994)

Media responsibility for inspiring the massive relief operation to assist refugees who fled Rwanda in the wake of 1994's genocide has been less discussed than the other cases reviewed here, though television's impact on inter-governmental and NGO policy was, argue Minear, Scott and Weiss, 'more important and direct than elsewhere' (1996, 62–3).

However, many commentators – including journalists themselves – point out that praise for the media in alerting far-off audiences to Rwanda's plight is scarcely warranted. After all, most television networks missed the 'big story' in Rwanda: the genocide of approximately 800,000 Tutsis and moderate Hutu by the *interahamwe* militia (Thompson, 2007). Although a handful of journalists, including Anne Chaon of Agence France-Presse and the BBC's Mark Doyle, reported on this mass slaughter while it was in progress, television crews arrived en masse only once the killing was over and a vast crush of refugees was pouring out of the country, including thousands of individuals who had actively participated in the genocide (Chaon, 2007; Doyle, 2007). This crucial point was overlooked by some journalists who confused the mainly Tutsi victims of the genocide with the mainly Hutu refugees in the camps, seeing simply an undifferentiated mass of 'victims.' Many refugees, however, had fled fearing retribution for their participation in the killing from the Rwandan Patriotic Front – a Tutsi exile movement that had returned to Rwanda from Uganda following the assassination of President Habyarimana.

How do we account for media inattentiveness to Rwanda's genocide? ITN correspondent Lindsey Hilsum notes that Rwanda was off the beaten track for Nairobi-based east Africa correspondents, of whom there were in any case very few. During the 1980s, this small land-locked country had been regarded as 'boring – a place where farmers farmed and the government governed' (1995, 148). That this anodyne description was palpably not true of Rwanda in the early 1990s should have been obvious, given the clear preparations for mass killing that were in train (as Chapter 1 explains). If nothing else, a massacre in Burundi in October 1993 ought to have alerted reporters to a turbulent situation in Central Africa. But this too was ignored (Lorch, 1995, 102).

In self-defense, journalists would doubtless point to several logistical and organizational obstacles confronting them. Nairobi-based correspondents are expected to cover a huge geographical news-beat. Since they can't be everywhere at once, their attention is likely to be directed to those locations where they can gain fairly easy access, thanks to cooperative authorities and available transport. For many of the same reasons that Sudan's famine was underreported – poor transport coupled with government visa restrictions – so too was the initial stage of Rwanda's genocide (Livingston, 1996, 68–89).

Volatile Rwanda was also extremely unsafe. American journalist Donatella Lorch, who arrived shortly after Habyarimana's death, painted a vivid picture of dangers confronting those reporters who attempted to describe the genocidal killing that followed:

> In April 1994, six days after the plane crash, I entered Kigali in a Red Cross medical convoy driving in from Burundi. With the airports closed, it was the only way in. The roads were clogged with fleeing refugees, but the terror started on the outskirts of the city. At each checkpoint, drunken, armed men threatened us, banging grenades on our windows, demanding money and passports. There was no law, no sense than anyone was in command. Bodies lay everywhere. Several truckloads of frenzied screaming men waving machetes and screwdrivers drove by. At night, screams followed by automatic gunfire could be heard from the churches in Kigali. (Lorch, 1995, 104)

In such circumstances journalists couldn't expect, and didn't always receive, exemption from harm by dint of their professional status. Lorch relates that some colleagues encountered organizational resistance from their US-based editors to covering this assignment (1995, 101). These editors weren't alone in putting protection of their staff ahead of other priorities. Most strikingly, the UN's minimal presence in Rwanda was withdrawn when the genocide began. The agency evacuated its western staffers to safety, leaving Rwandan personnel to fend for themselves (de Waal, 1994, 29; Hilsum, 1995, 158–9). Initially, then, Rwanda seemed a case of media attention calibrated not to the magnitude of the killing but to the level of (un)interest it was arousing in distant capitals.

While the *interahamwe* set to work in Rwanda, a concurrent 'good news' story was being played out on the African continent's southern tip. On May 10, 1994, Nelson Mandela was inaugurated as president of the new 'multiracial' South Africa, and it was this story – the exultant climax of a decades' long struggle against apartheid – that gripped western media attention. Some news outlets apparently felt unable to cover both stories simultaneously. Pierre Gassman, head of media at the Geneva headquarters of the International Red Cross, recounts his visit to CNN's Atlanta offices in early April 1994 to discuss the network's coverage of 'under-reported conflicts:'

> I tried to persuade its assignments editor to cover Rwanda immediately. Yes, of course, they said, they knew about Rwanda, but all their available crews and satellite uplinks were in South Africa. The editors

also expressed doubt about the possibility of showing two African topics at the same time as this might confuse their audience. (Gassman, 1995, 157)

The latter remark offers little encouragement to those who see the 'global media' as agents of enlightened humanitarian awareness, revealing not only CNN's parochialism and its limited capacity to be everywhere at once, but also its dim view of an audience liable to be perplexed by simultaneous good and bad news emanating from Africa. This confusion would presumably arise from the unexpectedness of the good news – Mandela's inauguration against a backdrop of less interracial tension than some anticipated – in a continent where bad news is considered normative: typically framed in terms of acts of God (such as drought) and acts of men endlessly repeating the same cycle of 'ancient tribal hatreds.' As Fergal Keane, then BBC Southern Africa correspondent, pointed out, 'African news is generally only big news when it involves lots of dead bodies' (F. Keane, 1996, 7). Rwanda duly claimed the spotlight only after there were indisputably 'lots of dead bodies' and once the international press corps departed South Africa, parachuting into Rwanda on its return journey north (Lorch, 1995, 104). Live satellite broadcasting facilities weren't established in the refugee-swollen border town of Kigali until late May (Minear, Scott and Weiss, 1996, 64).

If the media can be criticized for their dilatory pace, so too can states and inter-governmental agencies. The gathering of world leaders in Johannesburg to fete Mandela's inauguration might have provided an opportunity to coordinate a multinational intervention force. But in Andrew Natsios's words, 'American efforts to recruit African troops were lethargic' (1996, 162). The Clinton administration was particularly recalcitrant, suffering (one former official suggests) from 'Vietnam and Somalia syndrome' – namely, a 'fear of losing', which had been given tangible expression in Presidential Decision Directive No. 25 (Shattuck, 1996, 173). When Washington did later contribute to a UN relief effort, it was aimed purely at helping refugees, now beset by an outbreak of cholera in Goma, where a makeshift refugee city had formed. If television added an impetus to 'do something,' it would be hard to argue that the compressed response time often imputed to rolling 24-hour television news produced an instant response in this case.

The more pertinent issue concerning television's impact on the situation in Rwanda is not whether it provoked intervention but how news media framing of events – and reporters' very presence in such droves from late May until well into the summer of 1994 – shaped humanitarian operations on the ground. For aid workers, journalists could be a considerable nuisance. The 500 media people clustered in Goma in late July 1994, Hilsum noted, 'added to the chaos of clogged roads. They inflated the costs of hiring a car or an interpreter. Nurses resuscitating children with cholera found themselves tripping over tripods and cameramen looking for a better angle' (Hilsum, 2007, 167). Relief workers complained that the media presence encouraged duplication of efforts among the myriad agencies at work in the refugee camps. Since the cameras *were* in attendance, they could scarcely be ignored. Moreover, aid agency press officers recognized that the media could be useful. Every organization wanted to raise its own profile – to be captured on film performing the most telegenic acts of relief that would prompt viewers to make donations. The result was predicable. '[O]nly a limited number of agencies were prepared to work in the sanitation sector ... a situation that contrasted starkly with the number of agencies working in the higher-profile activities, such as establishing cholera treatment centres and centres for unaccompanied children' (Minear, Scott and Weiss, 1996, 66). NGOs, anxious to capitalize on the public awareness afforded them by television, colluded in the projection of stereotypical images of 'suffering Africa,' even if that meant contravening their own codes of conduct relating to non-exploitative use of images (Benthall, 1993, 182–3).

Other distortions also arose from the media's framing of Rwanda as a 'refugee crisis' rather than a 'genocide and its aftermath' story. NGOs and the subsequent UN operation concentrated their efforts on those who had left Rwanda, neglecting to aid the internally displaced or to assist the new RPF regime in restoring stability (Lorch, 1995, 105–6; Minear, Scott and Weiss, 1996, 66). As the UN and NGOs made little attempt to understand who the refugees were and why they had fled, the camps became, in the words of a *Médecins sans Frontières* official, 'humanitarian havens' for the killers (quoted by F. Keane, 1996, 186). To facilitate food distribution and bring order to the massive camps around Goma, aid workers permitted the social structures of Hutu Rwanda to be reconstituted inside the camps (de Waal, 1994, 25). Consequently, these temporary settlements fell under effective *interahamwe* control. Militia members encouraged Hutu refugees to remain in the camps semi-permanently, inciting fears of a retaliatory genocide that would be unleashed by the newly installed RPF government should the refugees attempt to return home.

According to Joel Boutroue, head of the UNHCR delegation in Goma, the most significant impact of CNN was its power to magnetize attention.

Where CNN goes, even if it's following agency reporters or competitors, others cluster. 'Each one acts as an alibi for the other,' notes Italian reporter Furio Colombo (1995, 86). And where camera crews converge, relief agencies will also congregate. As a result, Boutroue observed, dozens of NGOs that the UNHCR 'didn't want' arrived on the scene – all eager to be seen doing good, yet often ill-prepared or positively disruptive in their camera-oriented efforts (quoted by Hilsum, 2007, 176). CNN does not, of course, bear sole responsibility for this NGO swarming effect. However, the chaotic situation in Goma attests the degree to which cameras don't simply capture human action but do a good deal to shape behavior. No matter how well meaning journalists may be, their presence tends to obstruct the alleviation of suffering and obscure its underlying causes.

Focusing on urgent needs, while sometimes frustrating their relief, television news rarely invites us to ponder the agencies and phenomena that contribute to human discord and distress, processes in which 'we' – the far off and well off – are inextricably enmeshed. Many reporters, especially for television news, settled on the easy explanation that Rwanda's troubles arose from primordial 'tribalism.' Reporters invariably failed to discuss the plummeting price of coffee on the world market as a source of strife in Rwanda – poverty aggravated by the EEC's insistence that the stricken country submit to a World Bank/IMF structural adjustment program of fiscal austerity. In the words of anthropologist Johan Pottier, economic collapse 'sentenced many poor [Rwandans] to unprecedented levels of despair, making them vulnerable to manipulation by politicians in search of extreme solutions to their country's (and their own) growing insecurity' (Pottier, 2002, 21). That Rwanda's problems were more economic than ethnic – hence more susceptible to long-term resolution through debt forgiveness than short-term relief – was not an issue western media cared to broach, for that would be to acknowledge that 'their' problems are, at least in part, of 'our' making.

'Global media' reconsidered

Since the early 1990s, when talk of the ascendant power of global media to shape foreign policy was all the rage, more than one academic has termed the 'CNN effect' a 'myth' (Mermin, 1999; Robinson, 2002). The scholarly consensus, shared by several journalists who've written extensively on the topic, is that television news rarely, if ever, *drives* policy, though it can generate pressure to choreograph hasty 'pseudo responses' and may sometimes reshuffle priorities. The idea that televized images instantly produce (or destroy) popular resolve, commanding not only attention but action, seems naively simplistic. Presented in this way, bold assertions of the 'CNN effect' recall outmoded 'hypodermic' theories of media effects and magical modes of thinking about pictures as independent agents of world-shaking epiphanies that similarly characterized much discussion of Vietnam war imagery. The belief that a single image might 'change the world' itself replicates a central assumption of episodic news-framing: the idea that history moves in unpredictable fits and starts, and that capricious acts of fate can be reversed or redeemed by equally fateful actions of men and women.

To express skepticism about the 'CNN effect' is not to deny that news images provoke emotional reactions. Pictures evidently can and do move those who look at them, informing perceptions of present-day events and serving as the flash-cards by which we recall past happenings (Sontag, 2003). But pictures aren't endowed with irresistible powers of compulsion nor with incontestable meanings. Like all texts, they're open to multiple, sometimes incompatible, interpretations. And as the foregoing case studies suggest, they're at most one component in play during any set of policy deliberations, in which the desire to alleviate human distress is typically subordinate to budgetary, electoral, and geostrategic considerations.

Those who attribute to CNN a lamp-lighting role in dispelling the darkness that shrouds much human misery invest the network with more autonomy and greater ubiquity than it merits. Camera crews do not, after all, restlessly prowl the world in search of unnoticed pockets of abjection to record. If they did, European, Japanese and North American news consumers would have heard more of a civil war in Angola that killed an estimated 3 per cent of the country's entire population in the 1990s or of a conflict in the Democratic Republic of the Congo that, according to the International Rescue Committee, claimed approximately 3.9 million lives between 1998 and 2004, with 1 million killed in the year 2000 alone (Mamdani, 2009a, 20). As UN Secretary General Boutros Boutros Ghali complained in 1993, at the height of the Bosnian war, 'When one crisis is in the spotlight, other equally serious situations are left in the dark.' More people were killed in one day in Luanda during Angola's civil war than in months in Sarajevo. Yet TV hardly blinked, Boutros Ghali noted, before ticking off other forgotten conflicts on a list that included Afghanistan, Armenia and Azerbaijan, Myanmar, and Tajikistan (Cox News Service, 1993). Commercial media clearly aren't, and can't be expected to act as, a humanitarian early warning system – or even a belated chronicler of mass death.

Illustration 4.2   Matt's cartoon, printed in 2001 shortly before the launch of Operation Infinite Justice, underscores the role of CNN in determining which events require serious attention

'Don't panic until
you see CNN'

Source: *The Daily Telegraph*.

The fact that so many conflicts in the global South pass unreported by media headquartered in the North challenges the idea that a simple ethnocentric rule of thumb determines newsworthiness. In media scholar Jaap van Ginneken's reckoning, '10,000 deaths on another continent equal 1000 in another country equal 100 deaths in an outpost equal ten deaths in the centre of the capital equal one celebrity' (1998, 24). But as the Angolan and Congolese cases attest, numbers of corpses alone don't suffice to magnetize outside media attention. Given an 'almost complete media-blackout' of sub-Saharan Africa, how many residents of the wealthy G7 states would appreciate that, in the post-Cold War world, around 90 per cent of conflict-related deaths have occurred there (Hawkins, 2002, 229)?

So, what does set the news agenda? Why is a media searchlight shone on some wars but not others? While it's easy to imagine that journalists 'are where the news is' – that news somehow presents itself for inspection ready-made – 'news is where journalists are,' insists Martin Bell (1995, 59). How, then, are decisions reached about when a distant crisis warrants the dispatch of a crew whose presence will stamp that situation as 'news'? One pithy response would be that journalists often go where the elite sources on whom they depend for cues, leads, and information suggest they should be, as was the case in Somalia in 1992. In the phrase of John Zaller and Dennis Chiu, media remain 'government's little helper,' though today's primary agenda-setters need not necessarily be state officials (Zaller and Chiu, 2000). By dint of persistent lobbying, charitable organizations and advocacy groups can sometimes lure reporters to sites of humanitarian catastrophe, but as NGO press agents commonly point out, their persuasive task is ever harder.

As news organizations' budgets and viewers' attention-spans both contract, so each successive crisis must outdo the last in severity in order to establish its newsworthiness. This scarcity environment creates pressure to inflate projections of likely casualties and to employ a heightened language of moral abhorrence – for example, labeling violence as 'genocide,' a legal definition that mandates intervention – that might not be warranted by a strict definitional reckoning. One activist organization especially successful in galvanizing media attention, the Save Darfur Coalition, has been critiqued for both terminological elasticity and statistical sloppiness, grossly exaggerating numbers killed in western Sudan in the attempt to mobilize an outside military intervention (Mamdani, 2009a and b).

Editorial judgements are based on a multitude of different factors, of which the most self-conscious deliberations involve a crude financial bottom-line. Since news organizations operate on fixed budgets and must (if they're commercial outlets) generate advertising revenue, which means keeping ratings high – and thus holding audience attention – editors necessarily have to weigh how costly it will be to cover a distant conflict against anticipated viewer interest.

Wars in faraway strife-torn places are an expensive proposition. Few of them can be covered simultaneously or for very long. Moreover, irrespective of utopian claims about media's constitutive role in producing a global cosmopolitan consciousness, editors generally conceive their viewers' interests to be narrowly bounded – still very much rooted in local and national attachments. Criteria such as 'proximity' and 'relevance' structure news judgements, and though people close at hand may also be marginalized by mainstream news, notions of who and what is proximate nevertheless remain closely correlated to physical distance (Shoemaker and Reese, 1996, 110–12; Shaw, 1996, 9). Think how often a remote conflict or disaster becomes headline news when one or more of 'us' is imperiled by it: students stumbling into a war zone; tourists swept up in a tsunami; aid workers kidnapped by rebels. By domesticating foreign news, this framing device also insinuates that 'our' lives merit greater concern, naturalizing the presumed lack of interest in others' conflicts and a hierarchical valuation of human life (Gassman, 1995, 149).

The persistence of parochialism in the age of globe-spanning media means that stories ostensibly about 'other people's wars' are often narrated as stories primarily about 'us' and 'our' interventions. Thus the news may be about what our troops or relief workers are doing to bring order and succor to benighted places, or it may focus on the person of the reporter him- or herself. As Girardet notes, the rise of celebrity journalism has fueled a tendency for stories to be framed around, and *about*, the star (1996, 60). Where news editors anticipate a lack of interest among their viewers, the reporter-personality serves as a fulcrum of audience identification and empathy. Anthropologist Ulf Hannerz observes:

> In the contemporary cultural market place, some news correspondents become commodities in their own right. Their reporting is imbued with their own personal authority, and in the end the places they go, and the events they report on, may be marked as more important by their presence. They are the people you can trust to give you trouble. (1996, 122)

And yet the phenomenon of 'parachute journalism' – reporters dropping into trouble zones for a signature report from Goma or a whistle-stop tour of Kurdistan – also signals the misplaced trust vested in these eye-witness authorities. After all, they're barely on the ground long enough to develop an appreciation of local conditions, other than the supplement that sensory perception adds to second-hand background knowledge. Issues of causation, rarely at the forefront of television news, recede even further as complex struggles are molded into crude pre-shaped templates: natural disasters, tribal bloodletting, ancient hatreds, ethnic violence, or virulent nationalism. 'Intervention,' meanwhile, is often represented as implicitly virtuous, equated with selfless acts of rescue and rarely subjected to scrutiny as to either its motives or methods. 'Humanitarianism, it seems, is its own justification,' proposes Alex de Waal (1994, 21).

But more than simply being its *own* justification, 'humanitarianism' came in the 1990s to license all manner of practices that might have otherwise appeared questionable, if not outright illegal. Indeed, with hindsight what appears most distinctive about that decade was not the emergence of global media or the pervasive spread of real-time television but rather the discourse of humanitarianism that legitimated, enabled, and valorized interventions in settings such as Iraq, Former Yugoslavia, Somalia, Rwanda, and Haiti.

This is not to say that human rights had been wholly absent from great power rhetorical politics hitherto. The Carter presidency was especially given to strident attacks on Soviet human rights abuses within its own borders and beyond: from the Kremlin's treatment of dissidents to its anti-Semitic oppression of Soviet Jewry and the Red Army's brutal occupation of Afghanistan (Smith, 1994, 239–65). Ronald Reagan subsequently took up the anti-communist cudgel of human rights, inflicting it (as the next chapter shows) with the language of anti-terrorism. But no matter how vehement their attacks on human rights abuses, these administrations did not elevate humanitarianism into an international right of intervention. On the contrary, Reagan's initiatives in support of 'freedom fighters' – often themselves no great respecters of human rights, like UNITA in Angola and the Nicaraguan Contras – were conducted by proxy. Even as it deplored human rights abuses in those states, Washington didn't make a public case for sending US troops into Nicaragua to topple the Sandinista government or into Angola to depose the Marxist regime in Luanda.

Over the course of the 1990s, however, leaders of western states and the multilateral agencies under their control came to enunciate a new doctrine that moved beyond 'humanitarian intervention' in situations like Kurdistan and Somalia to a concept of 'humanitarian war' – an oxymoronic formulation much in evidence during NATO's 78-day bombing campaign over Kosovo from March to June 1999 (Hammond and Herman, 2000). Op-ed columns celebrated NATO's action in 'bombing against barbarism,' even as the same air power that purported to halt Serbian ethnic cleansing of Kosovar Albanians created its own refugee crisis, and its own civilian fatalities. Supported by liberal internationalists, western leaders denounced notions of sovereign inviolability as an outmoded precept of the old international system of states. Sovereignty, long considered the protective container of national self-determination, was now denounced as the legalistic shield behind which tyrants like Milosevic and Saddam Hussein slaughtered innocents – a cover to be torn aside by the rights-minded 'international community' and its armed enforcers (Feher, 2000, 1–30).

With sovereignty toppled from its position of primacy, military force was rhetorically elevated as a civilizing instrument. Airpower, in particular, found new favor as the 'humanitarian' weapon of choice, liberally applied not only to Kosovo but to 'degrade' Iraq's weapons of mass destruction capability in the 1990s. As some skeptics noted, whereas in the past liberal internationalists had tended to campaign for peace, now they were often at the forefront of those clamoring for military interventions – a phenomenon that reached its apogee with the Save Darfur movement, whose call to arms was 'Out of Iraq and into Darfur' (Mamdani, 2009a, 70).

As this last example suggests, there's greater continuity between the international politics of the 1990s and those of the post-9/11 era than often imagined. Many commentators greeted the attacks of September 11 as a world-shattering rupture, just as they have since hailed new digital media as effecting another revolution in global communications and consciousness. Where globalization in the 1990s was often celebrated as an agent of earth 'flattening' integration, a decade later it had come to be seen as more productive of fragmentation and *illiberal* Islamic transnationalisms. Viewed in another light, however, there's no decisive break between a pre-September 2001 'before' and a radically altered 'after.' Assailing principles of sovereign inviolability in the name of human rights, western leaders in the 1990s cemented the normative foundation for the next decade's 'war on terror.' And in reconfiguring the rules of the game, these leaders enjoyed much support from scholars, columnists, and opinion-formers who relished the prospect of a new era of 'virtuous war.'

Chapter 5

Wars on Terror

Over the past 30 years no topic related to media coverage of violence has attracted greater attention, generated more verbiage or aroused fiercer controversy than the reporting of terrorism. Long before the 'twin towers' fell on September 11, 2001, terrorism was already a highly charged issue. Thereafter, Washington's Global War on Terror – combining military operations in Iraq, Afghanistan, the Philippines and elsewhere with a worldwide campaign for 'hearts and minds' – reignited long-standing debates about what terrorists want, how they go about getting it, who the *real* terrorists are, and what position media organizations should adopt towards attention-seeking insurgents or approval-hungry administrations.

In one sense, this clamor might appear disproportionate to the phenomenon itself. Terrorism, understood as a tactic calculated to generate fear with politically efficacious results, kills far fewer people (approximately 7,000 per annum over the last 35 years) than either conventional war or a whole array of maladies – from traffic accidents to AIDS, gun crime to malnutrition (Jackson, 2005, 5). But in another sense, it's entirely to be expected that this form of violence should occasion prolonged and impassioned debate. After all, nothing about terrorism is universally accepted, including its very definition. Even a seemingly straightforward declarative assertion like the one just made about annual terrorist-related casualties is open to question. How does one compute such a figure? Whose violence is included and whose excluded from the calculus? Does the total incorporate deaths inflicted by the uniformed militaries of states whose violence may also aim to put civilians in a state of behavior-altering fear? Or does it refer solely to the victims of non-state actors? If so, on what grounds would one make such a distinction, and on what intellectual basis?

Since terrorism is entangled in a thicket of definitional, ethical and ideological binds, some analysts would jettison it altogether. For them, this 'essentially contested term' can't be retrieved from politicization as a neutral term. 'Terrorism' – a word which requires the skeptical swaddling of scare quotes – can only be critiqued for the ideological work it performs as a term of abuse (Hocking, 1992, 86). Pinned onto political actors whose recourse to violence the name-caller considers illegitimate, it serves not to describe but to stigmatize, since few words offer a more open-ended invitation to vitriol than 'terrorist.'

This view, however, is clearly not the one that prevails among political elites, many of whom (whether in Western Europe, North America, Israel, Russia or China) regard terrorism as a particularly reprehensible form of violence: one which can be succinctly defined and that properly animates moral revulsion. From this perspective, terrorism is illegitimate violence, perpetrated by non-state actors who launch attacks on innocent civilians without warning or only the most minimal of notice. Where regular militaries fight in the open, targeting those in uniform, terrorists emerge from the shadows to shatter peacetime life, offering no immunity to women or children, the infirm or the aged. By these lights, Al Qaeda's attacks on September 11, 2001 represent the quintessential terrorist atrocity: civilian aircraft hijacked and turned into weapons of war, hurtling through cloudless skies to slam into the pre-eminent symbol of US economic might, killing some 3,000 civilians in the process.

Understanding why the media loom so large in discussions of terrorism begins with an appreciation that policy-makers, strategists and pundits have long understood terrorism as a strategy in which gaining *publicity* is the perpetrators' pre-eminent concern. The argument runs as follows. Terrorism is a weapon of the weak, adopted by aggrieved groups that want to up-end the existing status quo but can't do so by waging conventional war. After all, states alone enjoy the privilege of declaring war – other recourses to armed struggle are, by definition, illegal. Faced with opponents who possess impressive military arsenals terrorists seek to maximize their comparative advantages. Unconstrained by the laws of war they pinpoint resonant symbolic targets, selected with a view to generating the maximum dramatic impact. The aim of such attacks is, as the term suggests, to terrorize: to generate widespread, chronic fear in the hope that panicked populations will pressurize their leaders to capitulate to the group's demands. Terrorism is thus an *indirect* strategy (Stohl, 1990, 93). As RAND corporation analyst Brian Jenkins remarked in the 1980s, 'terrorists want a lot of people watching, not a lot of people dead' (Jenkins, 1988, 253). In other words, the immediate *physical* targets of violence are less consequential than the message – or messages – transmitted by the fact of the attack: violence that, while terrorizing some, may also win fresh adherents among other onlookers.

If terrorism is to succeed, then, it requires the media to act as its amplifier. People will only be mobilized or immobilized by the catalytic impact of violence if they're aware that particular targets have been hit. Without publicity, remarked ABC anchor Ted Koppel, terrorist actions would resemble the 'philosopher's hypothetical tree falling in the forest': an occurrence that, unwitnessed, never demonstrably happened at all (quoted by Clawson, 1990, 242). For terrorists to terrorize, it's not enough that by-standers in the vicinity know an attack took place. Widespread media attention alone ensures that the terrorists' axe swinging in the forest is sufficiently audible to produce the desired effect – recognition that the existing order of things has become too fragile, and hence too costly, to sustain.

While conventional warfare can be waged with or without reporters present, terrorism makes media coverage a fundamental requirement. This interpretation of how terrorism functions has deep historical roots, as we'll see. It also has a corollary in the notion of a 'symbiotic' relationship between terrorists and the media. In other words, terrorists crave media attention and the media supply it, in thrall to these disruptive agenda-senders whose camera-ready spectaculars boost circulation figures and drive up audience numbers. Hijackings, hostage-takings, bombings and assassinations are too dramatic and sensational – too perfectly concordant with what constitutes news in western media culture – to be ignored. Whether they approve of the political ends in question or not, news organizations can't resist covering terrorists, the 'super entertainers of our time,' and cover them exhaustively (Laqueur, 1977, 223). Wittingly or otherwise, they become terrorism's most powerful accomplice. Not only do the media gratify these 'event promoters'' hunger for headlines, they also constitute a vector by which the 'contagion effect' spreads, encouraging copycat atrocities while simultaneously raising the bar for future spectaculars to pass muster as newsworthy (Paletz and Boiney, 1992; Schmid and de Graaf, 1982, 117–42).

It bears stressing that the existence of a productive synergy between media and terrorist organizations is an interpretation of what terrorism strives to do and how it succeeds, not an incontrovertible fact. Critics point out that the relentless demonization of terrorists by news media and in popular culture works entirely to the advantage of states, legitimizing repressive tactics that might otherwise appear much more questionable. But their contention that it surely matters what *kind* of publicity terrorists receive hasn't dented the received wisdom. And so long as terrorists are perceived as pathological attention-seekers then curbing media coverage will continue to be a central component of counterterrorist strategy, as it has been for the past 80 years.

'Hearts and minds': the prehistory of terrorism

Precisely when terrorism first emerged on the world stage is, needless to say, a moot point. Some scholars identify the Muslim assassins of the twelfth and thirteenth centuries or the Jewish Zealots of the first century as the prototype – a lineage disputed by those who see the targeted assassination of particular individuals as the very antithesis of terrorism, 'the random murder of innocent people' (Walzer, 1992, 198). Like Michael Walzer, many commentators locate the origins of terrorism *proper* in the post-World War II era, taking 1968 to mark the dawn of a new era, inaugurated by the hijacking of an El Al airliner by the Popular Front for the Liberation of Palestine (Schmid and de Graaf, 1982, 16).

A spate of 'terrorist spectaculars' soon followed, whether aimed at drawing attention to the plight of stateless Palestinians or angled towards national liberation struggles in countries still colonized by European powers. As protest against America's war in Vietnam escalated, the late 1960s and early 1970s were an era of global radicalization and mass revolt. National separatists, like the Basque independence movement *Euskadi Ta Askatasuna* (ETA) and the Irish Republican Army (IRA), together with self-styled' 'urban guerrilla' groups, such as Italy's Brigate Rosse, Germany's Baader-Meinhof organization, America's Weather Underground and the Symbionese Liberation Army adopted tactics of bombing, kidnapping, or assassination. An 'age of terror' had apparently been born. In the opinion of Gérard Chaliand, it had been spawned 'almost exclusively' by new developments in transport and communications technologies that enabled bodies, images, and information to travel the world at unprecedented speeds (Chaliand, 1987, 13).

What this origins story misses, however, is an appreciation that terrorist scares were a recurrent feature of the twentieth century. Cast back to Manhattan in the early 1900s – an increasingly crowded island, with new construction and newly arrived immigrants everywhere apparent, and fresh forms of popular entertainment like the nickelodeon theaters showing short silent films coupled with sundry live acts. Among the disparate topics showcased on celluloid anarchist terrorism enjoyed a special niche. D. W. Griffith's *The Voice of the Violin* of 1909 exemplifies this moralizing genre at its most overwrought. As the title hints, this 16-minute-long black-and-white melodrama is about music – but only tangentially. Its plot pivots around a humble violin teacher who, spurned by an attractive and handsomely well-off female pupil, falls prey to the machinations of an anarchist group who recruit him to their cause. Consumed by hatred for her capitalist fat-cat father, the violinist is an easy mark for these class warriors who soon assign him the role of bomb-carrying assassin. At the 11th hour, however, he's assailed by a clarifying pang of conscience and refuses to go through with the attack. Heroically saving the day, he also wins the hand of the girl.

Watched 100 years later (courtesy of YouTube) the film might seem nothing but an idiosyncratic historical oddity. However, *The Voice of the Violin* signifies something noteworthy about the social construction of terrorism as a threat and the longevity of popular culture's fascination with the thrillingly dangerous (yet invariably thwarted) figure of the terrorist. Where today's stereotypical 'jihadi' is a bearded and be-scarfed Arab, a century ago this demonic character was a swarthy eastern European, often physiognomically coded Jewish. A ragtag bunch of exaggerated immigrant types, D. W. Griffith's anarchists lurk on the shadowy fringes of polite society, constantly on the lookout for vulnerable naifs to recruit and for opportunities to rend the fabric of bourgeois life.

The Voice of the Violin appeared in the aftermath of 1908's 'anarchist scare' – a panic occasioned by several 'outrages,' including the murder of a Denver priest by an Italian immigrant and the attempted killing of a Chicago police chief by a Russian Jew, allegedly tied to anarchist circles (Porton, 2005, 53). Such irruptions, taken in the larger context of turbulence in Russia after its 1905 revolution, caused ruling classes everywhere to recoil in horror, menaced by the specter of bomb-wielding anarchists. D. W. Griffith obviously shared these intimations of dread – a dread that wasn't simply (or perhaps even primarily) *political* in the narrow sense. With heavy-handed emphasis, *The Voice of the Violin* assails anarchists for their impoverished ideas and dastardly deeds. But, not at all subliminally, Griffith's melodrama also licensed xenophobia, depicting immigrants as a threat to the purity and well-being of the body politic, in much the same way that a *San Francisco Chronicle* editorial of 1908 had castigated anarchists with their 'damnable doctrines' as 'worthless as rats and far more dangerous' (quoted by Porton, 2005, 53).

Then as now the language of terrorism flexibly accommodated multiple social discontents. Indictments of terrorism often carried a racialized sting, the physical danger posed by 'propaganda of the deed' seemingly less potent than the dread of noxious ideas and unassimilable persons, whether European immigrants in turn-of-the-century New York or radical Islamists 100 years later. Terrorism as a tactic generally appeared less menacing than particular *persons* deemed terrorist: a point underscored by Griffith's own oeuvre. Six years after *The Voice of the Violin*, he delivered *The Birth of a Nation*, one of the first narrative features in cinema history and one of the most notorious. As that film makes clear, Griffith patently had no objection to sub-state violence that, through kidnapping, bombing, and murder, aimed to terrorize a whole population. By any other name, the Ku Klux Klan was a terrorist organization – a point Martin Luther King made explicit in the 1960s, as others had before him. In Griffith's eyes, however, anarchists terrorized; the Klan purified. As this disparity suggests, the elastic discourse of terrorism constitutes a form of social discipline, working to normalize certain forms of violence while pathologizing others.

After World War I, fears of specifically *anarchist* terrorism subsided. With Irish republicans deploying guerrilla tactics in their campaign for independence from British rule, terrorism acquired different shadings. As characterized by British newspapers, the terrorist was now a Fenian who sprang ambushes for British troops and members of the Royal Irish Constabulary or its auxiliaries. He terrorized the local population into providing Republican irregulars with shelter and food with threats – often realized – of lethal retribution against those who collaborated with the British authorities. And though he shrank from open battle, he nevertheless wooed public attention with uncommon zeal. 'Nothing,' opined the Secretary of State for War in August 1919, 'would annoy the Irish so much as the conviction that they were not absorbing the minds of the people of Great Britain' (quoted by Carruthers, 1996, 104).

The Irish Republican movement, as adversaries perceived it, was as drawn to propaganda of the word as of the deed. From the latter decades of the nineteenth century onwards, republicans had courted opinion – in Ireland, Britain, the United States and beyond – with prolix verbosity. Different Republican groups all produced their own publications and acts of violence were invariably justified in newsletters, pamphlets, posters, and impassioned public oratory. Republican funerals, in particular, became occasions for open defiance of British authority and rededication to the cause of Irish independence. 'They think that they have pacified Ireland,' Patrick Pearse railed over the coffin of Jeremiah O'Donovan Rossa (founder of the Irish Republican Brotherhood, popularly known as the Fenians). 'They think that they have purchased half of us and intimidated the other half. They think that they have foreseen everything … but the fools, the fools, the fools! – they have left us our Fenian dead, and while Ireland holds these graves, Ireland unfree shall never be at peace.' As Pearse's oratory suggests, martyrdom – infused with specifically Catholic connotations of sacrificial suffering and redemption – formed a dominant motif in the Republican imaginary. British officials recognized the value of martyrs to their adversaries but couldn't refrain from supplying more Fenian dead, responding to the 1916 Easter Rising with the imprisonments and executions that Republican leaders seemed positively to invite.

In the ensuing War of Irish Independence (1919–21), both sides fought not only for control of territory but over perceptions of where legitimacy lay in this bloody struggle over Irish sovereignty. The IRA engaged in 'wordy warfare' angled towards winning recruits in Ireland and well-placed sympathizers in the United States, Britain, and its far-flung empire, where other subjugated populations were also adopting overtly nationalist programs. In the realm of persuasive communication, Sinn Féin (the IRA's political wing) was aided by literary talents, including *Riddle of the Sands'* author Erskine Childers. Its *Irish Bulletin* reached audiences around the world and drew their attention to the brutality of British tactics in Ireland, which included the application of martial law over large parts of the country, stringent censorship, and (most controversially) the wholesale application of internment without trial of persons suspected of aiding the IRA. From an early twenty-first-century vantage point, much of this sounds eerily familiar: 'terrorist suspects' rounded up and imprisoned; the rule of law suspended and replaced with 'military courts of enquiry' – a quasi-judicial system extended to Ireland's civilian population as a whole with the 'Restoration of Order in Ireland Act,' passed by the Westminster Parliament in August 1920 (Townshend, 1975).

In the days before the phrase 'winning hearts and minds' had been coined, the notion itself nevertheless existed – albeit in somewhat rudimentary form. The British state launched a concerted attempt to justify its draconian tactics, drawing attention to the IRA's campaign of terror against British troops and loyalists alike, raising the specter of a campaign of 'ethnic cleansing' against Ireland's Protestant community. In August 1920, a Propaganda Department was established at Dublin Castle (the seat of British authority in Ireland), which vainly attempted to hold the Unionist line. Among other opinion-influencing activities, it sought to place 'unmarked' articles in British and overseas newspapers, stigmatizing the IRA and legitimizing the use of harsh counterterrorism measures against a lawless foe – an attempt to 'inspire' favorable press stories, or more crudely pay for their placement, redolent of the activities of the Lincoln Group in planting stories in the Iraqi press 90 years later. Despite their proliferation, however, these efforts lacked the moral force and rhetorical eloquence of the Republican case. Throughout the war of 1919–21, as in later counterinsurgency campaigns, the British state's efforts at self-justification struggled to surmount the surplus violence its armed forces, paramilitary auxiliaries and constabulary employed in quelling nationalist revolt (Townshend, 1983; Boyce, 1972).

Anyone who claims that terrorism is always counterproductive, destined to inexorable defeat, needs to reckon with the IRA's success in this campaign. Admittedly, the Republican army did not achieve a complete victory. Ireland's six northeasterly counties were omitted from the independent Irish Free State founded in 1922, and remained under the authority of the British Crown – triggering successive waves of Republican violence over the decades since then. But unorthodox guerrilla tactics succeeded in rendering large parts of the Irish countryside ungovernable. As British repression catalyzed further resistance, which in turn provoked retaliatory state violence, Westminster lost the will to continue. With the Pope himself intervening to urge moderation, the cost of clinging on to an unruly territory increasingly outweighed the benefits of retaining the whole island of Ireland within the British Empire. Was the game worth the candle? By July 1921, Lloyd George's government had decided not, and negotiated a compromise that established an Irish Free State as a Dominion of the British Empire.

Few anti-imperial movements subsequently achieved such impressive results, or with such speed. But certain patterns were already clear from this early showdown between imperial forces and their challengers. Indeed, sociologist Philip Schlesinger proposes that the key techniques of British counterterrorist strategy all crystallized during the Irish War of Independence (Schlesinger, 1991, 66–91). In terms of their media component, these included currying favor with a national and international press corps, whose reliance on official handouts was cultivated, alongside a concerted attempt to delegitimize the enemy by exaggerating atrocities and stressing the 'cowardliness' of terrorist tactics. At the same time, more heavy-handed legislative moves severely constrained press freedom in the contested territory itself. Numerous printing presses were seized in Ireland between 1919 and 1921. The British Cabinet even debated outlawing images of Éamonn de Valera, considering his picture to be seditious in its own right – as though the likeness itself would stir Irish newspaper readers into spontaneous revolt.

Throughout the middle decades of the twentieth century terrorism remained a term primarily applied to nationalist organizations that took up arms against European or US imperialism. After World War II, conditions were propitious for many such movements to strike against a corroded imperial order. The war had not only weakened European metropoles' grip over their colonies but provided millions of young colonial subjects with military training, experience, and esprit – whether as conscripts in European armies or as members of anti-Japanese resistance forces, also trained and equipped by the Allies (Chaliand and Blin, 2007, 208–17).

For the United States, the first postwar brush with what Washington termed terrorism began in 1946, when the Communist Party of the Philippines Hukbalahap military wing (first formed to fight the Japanese occupation in 1942) launched a campaign against the postwar leaders Truman's administration had installed after the collapse of Japan. While attempting to quell this insurgency, US policy-makers also began to cast an anxious eye further across the Pacific to Indochina. There another guerrilla army that the western allies had assisted during the war in harry-ing the Japanese had regrouped to fend off the reassertion of colonial rule: a 'vacuum' left by the French into which US advisers soon stepped (Young, 1991). By 1954, defeated in Vietnam, France also faced concerted and armed resistance to its rule in north Africa, with Algeria's Front de Libération Nationale (FLN) waging a guerrilla campaign against French settlers and French rule alike.

Meanwhile, the British confronted terrorism from Zionist organiza-tions, Irgun Zvai Leumi and Lohamei Herut Israel (or the Stern Gang) in Palestine between 1944 and 1948, when the State of Israel was created after Westminster turned the vexed Mandate question over to the UN. In rapid succession, British colonial authorities declared an Emergency in Malaya in 1948, as the Malayan Communist Party's armed wing, the Malayan Races' Liberation Army, sought to wrest the peninsula from British control, and another in Kenya (1952–60), where the colonial state battled the Land and Freedom movement more commonly known as Mau Mau. Concurrent with these campaigns, another violent confrontation was under way in Cyprus, as the National Organization of Cypriot Fighters (EOKA) sought to unite the island with Greece, in the face of opposition from both the British colonial state and the island's Turkish population (Carruthers, 1995).

These organizations employed a variety of different methods: rural guerrilla warfare; targeted assassinations, bombings and other 'outrages' in urban areas; labor protests and general strikes. To different degrees, they also sought to mobilize global opinion, as had the IRA, but in a world that included new courts of appeal, namely the United Nations General Assembly together with a more mobile and expansive interna-tional press corps. While some, such as Kenya's Mau Mau, fought local-ized struggles over land and allegiance, others self-consciously wooed international sympathy. According to Menachem Begin, through sensa-tional acts like the bombing of the King David Hotel, Irgun aimed to make Palestine a 'glass house' into which the world would look 'with ever increasing interest' – an interest combining support for the Zionist cause with condemnation of the repressive tactics employed by British forces (Begin, 1977, 68). A decade later, Algeria's FLN similarly strove to internationalize their battle against French colonialism, seeking to expose (and provoke) French brutality while simultaneously impressing 'world opinion' with the moral case for independence (Connelly, 2002).

Irrespective of the particular tactics anti-imperialist fighters employed, state authorities tended to regard publicity as their opponents' primary objective in every case. Colonial personnel and their metropolitan peers often regarded nationalist violence not so much as a *means* to an end but as the essential purpose of terrorism – a depoliticization that deflected attention from fundamental issues of sovereignty and redirected it to the realm of sociopathology.

Yet having trivialized their challengers in this way, the incumbents of power almost invariably regarded themselves as laboring at a distinct disadvantage – a self-conception also espoused by more recent counterinsurgents. Thus Malaya's disgruntled High Commissioner Sir Henry Gurney noted, with reference to a string of attacks on rubber plantations: 'The BBC is the worst offender in creating the impression that life in Malaya (as in Palestine) consists of a series of incidents. The aim of the grenade thrower is to hit the headlines, and our press and broadcasting do the job for him to his complete satisfaction' (quoted by Carruthers, 1995, 90). Moreover, through their undaunted persistence, insurgents might come to acquire not just attention but an aura of heroism. 'Men who were at the start no more than a band of thugs preying on the law-abiding members of a community,' noted colonial official Sir Thomas Lloyd, 'may attract to themselves some of the glamour of national heroes' – no longer terrorists but freedom fighters (quoted by Carruthers, 1996, 105).

If time was on the terrorists' side in these asymmetric wars of attrition, so too were the media, or so colonial officials believed. This partiality didn't necessarily derive from overt sympathy for nationalist aspirations but from journalistic notions of newsworthiness that favored the short-lived terrorist 'spectacular' – the assassination in a crowded city street, the blowing up of a hotel or ambush of a patrol – over the tedious, frustrating work of counterinsurgency soldiering: endless house-to-house searches and sweeps through the countryside to clear urban and rural areas of insurgents and those who sustained them.

How, then, to regain the initiative? Colonial states took language to be fundamental to perceptions of legitimacy, understanding that what one called one's enemy mattered, and that there was nothing worse an opponent could be called than 'terrorist.' Efforts at agenda-setting thus began with questions of nomenclature. In Palestine, military press releases self-consciously referred to Zionist militants as 'terrorists' until the latter bombed the Tel Aviv Goldsmith Officers' Club in March 1947, at which point British officers rejected that descriptor – on the grounds that it was no longer possible to distinguish between 'passive onlookers and active armed members of the Jewish population' (quoted by Carruthers, 1996, 115). In Malaya, the term 'bandits' was abandoned in favor of 'communist terrorists': a phrase that conjoined the contemporary political lexicon's two most contaminating pejoratives.

Although they often failed to appreciate it, colonial officials generally enjoyed the privilege of establishing the semantic terms of engagement – in the metropole and beyond. The British press, for example, routinely described Mau Mau, EOKA, the MRLA and Irgun as terrorist organizations, as did reporters at a greater geographical remove. Thus *The New York Times* opened its first substantive report on the newly declared state of Emergency in Kenya in September 1952 as follows: 'The fears of the spread of terrorism in British East Africa have been revived by the attack last night of a gange [sic] of Negroes, said to be adherents of the Mau Mau secret society' (*The New York Times*, 1952, 2). The *Washington Post* went a step further, referring to Mau Mau as a 'white-hating secret society' that had 'sworn to liquidate Kenya's British rulers' (*Washington Post*, 1952, 3). If Mau Mau were indeed a 'white-hating society' its activities gave little such indication. When the Emergency ended in 1960, British security forces and their local allies had killed over 10,500 Mau Mau fighters, while European civilian deaths amounted to just 32 (Corfield, 1960).

As these overtly racialized depictions of anti-imperial movements suggest, colonial states enjoyed another entrenched (but to them largely invisible) advantage over their opponents in the international battle over legitimacy. In projecting colonial counterinsurgency campaigns as confrontations between 'decency' and 'savagery,' they tapped into a deeply rooted racial imaginary – to productive effect. As presented by British and French officials, their armed forces represented civilization, the rule of law, progress and modernity while their indigenous opponents threatened to plunge colonial subjects back into the primordial darkness of tribal anarchy, or worse (Lonsdale, 1990).

French opinion-formers in Algeria conjured the fearful prospect of an Islamic crescent curving through North Africa to pierce Europe's exposed southern flank. Their British counterparts in Kenya meanwhile cultivated a vision of sub-Saharan Africa rent between the forces of darkness and light to great effect. They raised the specter of a global race war at a time when the United States was not only fearful that colonies lost to colonialism would swiftly be incorporated within the 'slave world' of communism but also experiencing an upsurge of civil rights militancy at home which left some wondering whether the fundamental global schism wasn't so much between left and right as between black and white. To kindle such fearful responses, British officials developed a vigorous clandestine trade in Mau Mau atrocity photographs. The most horrific, showing heavily bandaged bodies of infants subjected to panga attacks, were kept in reserve when newspaper editors or foreign visitors to Kenya showed signs of deviation from the preferred line and needed a shot in the arm. Then the file was 'shown at great discretion to persons who it is thought would benefit by seeing them,' the British government's Director of Information Services delicately noted (quoted by Carruthers, 1995, 168).

Imagining itself outflanked by publicity-seeking insurgents, the colonial state enjoyed numerous advantages. It developed elaborate mechanisms of press management in the colonies to complement those of the metropole, and it also typically controlled reporters' physical access to the most fiercely contested areas. Emergency powers included sweeping curbs on 'seditious' local newspapers – powers the French in Algeria exercised so liberally that by 1957 no independent Arabic-language paper remained in circulation (Connelly, 2002, 29). And, despite grumbles to the contrary from military governors who took any murmur of criticism as an intolerable personal affront, imperial regimes also enjoyed considerable loyalty from metropolitan media.

As in other 'limited wars,' news organizations routinely stressed that they did *not* regard themselves as impartial between the state and its challengers, even if they reserved the right to criticize particular tactics that appeared less than helpful. Thus, for example, when the BBC's Director-General affirmed the Corporation's right to broadcast an interview with EOKA's alleged 'terrorist mastermind' in 1955, he did so not with reference to abstract principles of free speech, or to the BBC's Charter obligation to political impartiality; rather by stressing how thoroughly *partial* the interview had been. The televised exchange between Archbishop Makarios and journalist Woodrow Wyatt had been 'a fair and interesting exposure of a shifty rascal,' the Director-General insisted to a disgruntled government (Grisewood, 1968, 191). Given enough rope, in other words, the gunmen would always hang themselves.

But the colonial state's greatest advantage – its vastly superior firepower – could also constitute its gravest disadvantage. Colonial counterinsurgency campaigns were, in every instance, ferociously contested and unmistakably lopsided. No matter how hard London or Paris insisted that terrorists responded to the language of force alone, that their lack of respect for the civilian immunities of conventional warfare demanded a response in kind, the most brutal tactics nevertheless raised eyebrows. When the upholders of civilization adopted torture as a systematic feature of prisoners' treatment (as the French did in Algeria), defended the practice of beheading insurgents (as the British did in Malaya) or incarcerated one third of all adult males (as with Kenya's Kikuyu population), it was hard to maintain the dominant interpretive frame intact. Charges that the colonial state was the *real* agent of terror began to look more credible – even to supporters of the status quo.

Journalists, kept at a discrete remove, might remain largely oblivious to the area bombing of free-fire zones in the jungles of Malaya and forested highlands of Kenya, or to the French military's systematic massacres of Muslim villagers in Algeria. But it was hard to keep enormous networks of barbed-wire encampments secret, and since counterinsurgency's most punitive measures also often purported to be ventures in 're-education,' colonial officials didn't necessarily attempt to debar reporters. So it was that a furor erupted in the House of Commons over the lethal mistreatment of eleven Kikuyu prisoners beaten to death by guards at Hola camp in March 1959 for refusing to work. This episode, initially whitewashed by ham-fisted officials who tried to attribute the fatalities to 'infected water,' provoked unprecedented condemnation of carceral conditions in Kenya. That the outcry was led by Enoch Powell, the Member of Parliament later infamous for his anti-immigrant 'rivers of blood' rhetoric, underscores the crisis of imperial confidence occasioned by what British newspapers dubbed the 'Hola massacre.' No longer was any and every measure undertaken in the name of counter-terrorism permissible. Or as Powell put it: 'We cannot say, "We will have African standards in Africa, Asian standards in Asia and perhaps British standards here at home"' (quoted by Carruthers, 1995, 267).

Causes célèbres like Hola curdled metropolitan opinion. Yet they surely came as no surprise to the inhabitants of contested territories, whose everyday experience of counterinsurgency methods was of brutality. Collective punishments, additional taxes, mandatory labor service, forcible relocation, food denial, and conscription into loyalist militias were standard procedures – this despite the fact that winning the 'hearts and minds' of subject populations was the plinth on which counterinsurgency success avowedly rested.

In the 1940s and 1950s, European commanders in the field trumpeted the benevolent acts designed to impress local populations with the virtues of the existing political order – or one tentatively modified in the direction of self-rule. The phrase 'winning hearts and minds' first emerged in Malaya, where High Commissioner, Field Marshal Sir Gerald Templer claimed a disputed paternity over counterinsurgency's reigning cliché. But how did one go about winning a heart or capturing a mind? Colonial authorities devised numerous routes to their desired destination, with the development of communication technologies one important vehicle. Even as they clamped down on local printing presses, colonial states cultivated new media with which to impress on colonial subjects the desirability of gradual evolution towards self-rule under European stewardship and, correspondingly, the need to stand up against the terrorists in their midst. In Malaya, British colonial officials devised a film strip, *The Adventures of Yaacob*, closely modeled on the Tarzan films, starring an 'anti-bandit' hero (Carruthers, 1995, 94–5). Elsewhere radio was the preferred medium. And everywhere indigenous populations found themselves

Illustration 5.1   'Masai Natives Holding Their Initial Newspaper' ran the caption to this photograph taken in Kenya, 1955

Source: Bettmann Collection/Corbis.

bombarded with millions of leaflets, often in cartoon-strip form, exhorting them to join the government side and denounce the terrorists.

If media programs constituted the 'minds' part of the strategy, 'hearts' were ostensibly targeted by a colonial propaganda of the deed that sought to win people over by providing them with stability, social services, and practical reasons to favor the existing status quo over anything that might supplant it. But while this may sound shrewd enough in theory, how such projects were enacted in practice often constituted another form of violence. Thus the 'model villages' of Malaya and Algeria – billed as secure spaces for rural populations to practice local democracy, receive healthcare, and education free from the menace of terrorists – looked very much like concentration camps to the untrained eye. Surrounded by barbed wire, with watch towers and armed guards poised to shoot curfew violators, they gave every appearance of being designed to lock villagers in as much as to keep terrorists out (Purcell, 1954). As indeed they were – a point some military officers made unapologetically. 'Call me a fascist if you like,' one French colonel serving in Algeria told *Le Monde*: 'but we must make the population docile and manageable; everybody's acts must be controlled.' For their part, though, critics of a policy that saw no less than 2 million Algerians forcibly 'regrouped' – one quarter of the non-European population – didn't hesitate to speak bluntly either. Raphael Lemkin, the American architect of the UN Convention on the Prevention and Punishment of the Crime of Genocide, unabashedly announced the French to be in violation of this statute (Connelly, 2002, 89).

In the 1950s, European officers recurrently complained that reporters ignored their positive achievements in embattled colonies. Attuned to sensational, disruptive events – terrorist attacks most specifically – they ignored the less dramatic 'good news' of peace and progress. As we've already seen, this complaint resurfaced in Vietnam in the 1960s, where the 'Viet Cong' were also routinely labeled terrorist, and where US officers similarly rued the lack of journalistic attention to the vaunted success of 'pacification.' The 1980s saw yet another reiteration of the charge. Attempting to redress the deficit, British press officers began escorting journalists on tours to impress them with Northern Ireland's growing prosperity and peacefulness (Miller, 1994). More recently, the charge that good news is systematically marginalized has again been heard from British and US officers in Iraq and Afghanistan, frustrated that their successes in restoring order and winning friends do not receive the same media play as the insurgents' victories in spreading disorder.

Military complaints about western news values strike an uncanny chord with those of anti-war activists who have long drawn attention to the way in which reports of violence systematically displace 'peace news.' But the fundamental fault here is less with the media than with the practices of counterinsurgency themselves. For while public affairs officers speak (not softly) of what they're doing to secure hearts and minds, the big stick of enforcement remains highly visible – at least to those on its receiving end, though seemingly not to those wielding it. In short, what's hailed as evidence of success rarely resembles either peace or progress to those whose hearts and minds form the bulls-eye of these violent struggles over authority.

Reagan, Thatcher and the 1980s' 'war on terrorism'

When President Bush declared a Global War on Terror in the fall of 2001 he invoked various historical precedents, the heroism of World War II's 'greatest generation' most stirringly, but paid little attention to any previous 'war on terrorism.' Such campaigns have recurred with surprising regularity, each one presenting itself as, in effect, the first – as though the demonstrable lack of success of previous campaigns might dampen public enthusiasm for rejoining the battle. *The New York Times* reported its first 'war on terrorism' in 1881, as the Russian and German governments simultaneously clamped down on anarchist assassins. Woodrow Wilson, announcing US entry into World War I, pledged war on German 'terrorism on land and sea' (*The New York Times*, 1917, 1). But George Bush had a more proximate model to hand. For in 1981, when George Bush Sr was vice president, Ronald Reagan had girded America for a global campaign of extirpation also flagged as a 'war on terrorism.'

It was to be expected that Reagan would devote part of his first inaugural address to excoriating terrorism. On January 20, 1981, just hours before the inauguration, 52 men and women who had spent the previous 444 days as hostages in the US Embassy in Teheran were finally released. Iran's gesture seemed one final indignity to the outgoing president, whose many attempts to negotiate the hostages' release or strategize their military rescue had all ended in failure. Carter's apparent impotence in the hostage crisis, coupled with resurgent Soviet expansionism in the third world, emblematized by the Red Army's invasion of Afghanistan in December 1979, gave Reagan ample opportunity to present himself as a man of decisive action – in stark contrast to his ineffectual predecessor. Where Carter had spoken of national malaise, Reagan promised Americans a regenerative new dawn. And where Carter had admonished citizens to trim their aspirations and expenditures to more modest proportions, Reagan announced that Americans were 'too great' to limit themselves to 'small dreams.' Along with the scourge of high taxes, big government and inflation, the 40th US president pledged to slay the hydra-headed monster of terrorism.

Reagan's first administration is remembered less for its 'war on terror' than its blistering attacks on the 'evil empire' of communism and rapid build-up of tactical nuclear weapons in Western Europe. For Reagan, however, the fight against international terrorism wasn't a distraction from competition with the Soviets; it was integral to waging Cold War. According to Reagan's advisers, the 'terror network' stretching from Southern Africa to Central America, Belfast to Beirut, could be traced all the way back to the Kremlin (Sterling, 1981). To thwart terrorism's local manifestations was thus to stymie Soviet aspirations to world hegemony: a geopolitical orientation that located counterterrorism and its corollary, assistance to 'freedom fighters,' at the heart of the Reagan doctrine.

The elision of communism and terrorism in turn ensured that the 'symbiosis' between the latter and the media received fresh attention, resulting in a plethora of symposiums, reports, and investigations into the subject during the 1980s. Questions about media coverage of terrorism were, of course, already being asked before Reagan's inauguration. With 'America held hostage' by militant Iranian students following the Islamic revolution of 1979, news organizations' handling of terrorism was a divisive issue – as was White House handling of the press. Critics attacked Carter for his so-called 'Rose Garden strategy' of making frequent, if not daily, appearances on the White House lawn to update the Washington press corps on new developments in Teheran. This unwavering focus on the hostages' predicament played straight into their captors' hands, presidential detractors claimed. Carter's fixation, intended to signal solidarity with the beleaguered Embassy employees, instead drew attention to the terrorists' demands, most notably that Washington surrender the exiled Shah, admitted into the US to receive medical treatment after fleeing revolutionary Iran. In effect, the Rose Garden strategy made Carter as much a captive of the Iranian debacle as the hostages themselves, awaiting 'the horror of that evening news guillotine dropping every evening,' as his vice president, Walter Mondale, later put it (quoted by Schlesinger, 1995, 250). While the president was unable to escape a trap largely of his own making, the hostages' ordeal was correspondingly prolonged by his haplessness, critics claimed.

This damning verdict was widely accepted, though the implicit claims it rests on are open to question. Could Carter in fact have remained mute in the face of such a situation? Had he tried to minimize the crisis by maintaining a strictly 'business as usual' air, the press would doubtless have excoriated him for callous neglect of the captive Americans. US newspapers and television networks hardly adopted a policy of avoidance towards events in Teheran, and it seems unlikely that they would have turned a blind eye had their president done so (Wallach, 1991, 88).

But skeptical caveats of this kind received little airplay in the voluminous 1980s disquisitions on terrorism and the media. After all, Carter had allegedly committed the cardinal sin of counterterrorism by ensuring that the hostage-takers received a daily supply of the commodity they most craved: publicity. Whatever else was up for discussion during the Reagan–Thatcher years, this long-standing *idée fixe* was barely challenged. Instead, debate focused on 'how-to' strategies that would assist news-media in their avowed determination not to provide terrorists with attention – since *any* attention, no matter how negatively coded or overtly hostile, was held to gratify their desire for the spotlight. Accordingly, any step that deprived terrorists of publicity – their oxygen, as Margaret Thatcher famously asserted in 1985 – would hasten the day when terrorists beat a woebegone retreat.

In Reagan's war on terrorism discussion turned from the long-term winning of hearts and minds to short-lived 'terrorist spectaculars' – dramatic episodes in which journalists often appeared to be more *participants* than observers, with broadcast television news the worst offender (Schmid and de Graaf, 1982, 142). In the eyes of counterterrorism experts, journalists' errors were multiple, and sometimes life-threatening. In crisis situations, they tied up lines of communication with the hostage-takers that could more productively be used by security agents trying to broker a release (Wardlaw, 1989, 79). On some occasions they acceded to terrorist pressure to publicize their demands, becoming a conduit for political propaganda. And invariably their emotional framing of hijackings and hostage-takings as heart-rending dramas of familial severance put undue pressure on officials to act precipitately towards a resolution, when a patient waiting-game stood more chance of producing a felicitous outcome than a hastily mounted rescue operation.

Charges of media irresponsibility reached a head during the 17-day hijacking of TWA 847 by Lebanese gunmen in June 1985. Critics lambasted the excessive coverage networks devoted to this incident: almost 500 reports, totaling some 12 hours of news-time (Schlesinger, 1995, 251). Worse yet was the 'deferential' treatment broadcast news provided Nabih Berri, head of the Shiite Amal group. Berri, said to have received PR counsel from American media studies graduates, was interviewed several times by the US networks. To the chagrin of the White

House, they treated him 'like a political leader, virtually no differently than the President of the United States.' On one occasion, ABC anchor David Hartman even concluded an interview by asking Berri whether he had 'Any final words to President Regan this morning?' This was the last straw. 'When TV reporters interview kidnappers ... it risks international outlaws seem[ing] like responsible personalities,' Reagan's Secretary of State Al Haig complained. 'Television should avoid being used that way' (quoted by Nacos, 1994, 66–7).

Haig's words constituted a warning that journalists should shape up or face government curbs. To underscore the message, Reagan appointed a Task Force on Terrorism under Vice President Bush. In the capital, the air was thick with talk of 'enforced "voluntary" guidelines:' an oxymoronic conceit evocative of World War II, when censorship was also voluntary – under pain of prosecution if editors didn't clear sensitive stories with state censors in advance.

News organizations bristled. But their willingness to parry government barbs only extended so far. The charge of aiding and abetting terrorism was not one to be shrugged off lightly – especially when US citizens came under attack in a series of episodes in, and related to, the Middle East, including the hijacking of the *Achille Lauro* in October 1985, grenade assaults on El Al passengers at Rome and Vienna airports on December 27, and another TWA hijacking in April 1986. Three days later, a disco frequented by US soldiers in Berlin was blown up, leading to three fatalities (one Turkish woman and two US servicemen) and over 200 casualties (Dobkin, 1992, 18–19). With US officials claiming to have intercepted messages between Libya and East German agents, animosity towards terrorists in general and Libya's Colonel Muammar Qaddafi in particular hardened. Reagan's decision to bomb Tripoli and Benghazi on April 15 met overwhelming public and media support in the United States.

Many US poll respondents weren't convinced that this retaliatory raid would halt Libya's sponsorship of terrorism. But they approved it in any case – one indication that wars on terrorism often privilege the gestural over the practical, satisfying domestic desires for vengeance without excessive concern either for international legality or strategic wisdom. *Action* was what mattered, with Secretary of State George Shultz soliloquizing that Americans could not 'allow themselves to become the Hamlet of nations, worrying endlessly over whether and how to respond' (quoted by Dobkin, 1992, 99). In this febrile climate, US news organizations busily set to work scripting their own internal guidelines for restraint in covering terrorism, thus saving Bush's Task Force the necessity of doing so for them.

In matters both rhetorical and logistical, Reagan possessed no more ardent ally than Margaret Thatcher. In April 1986, when other NATO members refused to lend assistance – 'Euro-wimps' in Lord Carrington's phraseology – Thatcher authorized the US Air Force to make use of RAF bases for their bombing raid on Libya. In return, the British Prime Minister sought reciprocal assistance in her own 'war on terrorism,' urging Washington to cooperate in the extradition of suspected IRA members – assistance that many pro-Irish Republican lawmakers were loathe to tender, though ultimately did.

Marked by a recrudescence of IRA activity and increasing violence on the part of loyalist paramilitaries determined that Ulster remain within the Union, the 1980s saw relations between British broadcasters and the government rapidly deteriorate. Thatcher was adamant that terrorists must be deprived of the 'oxygen of publicity' – a remark she first made with reference to the TWA hijacking. At a packed meeting of the American Bar Association at the Royal Albert Hall in July 1985, she expressed distaste for censorship ('In our societies we do not believe in constraining the media') before musing, 'ought we not to ask the media to agree among themselves to a voluntary code of conduct, under which they would not say or show anything which could assist the terrorists' morale or their cause while the hijack lasted?' (quoted by Terrell and Ross, 1991, 92).

A series of programs made both by the BBC and independent networks caused rising ire in Thatcher's Cabinet at a time when the deregulation of British broadcasting had already embittered relations between Downing Street and the television industry. As in the United States, televised appearances with terrorists formed the sorest point in this vexed relationship. Very few interviews had in fact been broadcast on British television, thanks in no small measure to the 1974 Prevention of Terrorism (Temporary Provisions) Act, which appeared to prohibit televised appearances by making it a criminal offense not to pass to the authorities any information about terrorist whereabouts or activities. Since filmed interviews required a pre-arranged rendezvous with the subject, their legality was called into question (Article 19, 1989, 14–15). The law's very ambiguity encouraged broadcasters' caution. Thus the BBC interviewed IRA members once in 1972 and again in 1974, then not at all until 1977. In the same period ITN interviewed Daniel O'Connell, an IRA leader, twice (Schlesinger, Murdock and Elliott, 1983, 125).

On those few occasions when the BBC did air interviews, it remained adamant – as in the 1950s – that such events were confrontations framed specifically to *delegitimize* those who employed violence. Lord Hill (then

Chairman of the BBC's board of governors) duly reassured Home
Secretary Reginald Maudling in November 1971:

> the BBC and its staff abhor the terrorism of the IRA and report their
> campaign of murder with revulsion … [A]s between the government
> and the opposition, as between the two communities in Northern
> Ireland, the BBC has a duty to be impartial no less than in the rest of
> the United Kingdom. But as between the British Army and the
> gunmen the BBC is not and cannot be impartial. (Hill, 1974, 209)

Thatcher remained unconvinced. Despite complex rules within the BBC
for 'referring upwards' any potential interview to the highest managerial
levels – a stipulation that engendered considerable reluctance to tackle the
'Troubles' when so much bureaucratic trouble ensued – those few
program-makers who chose to do so met a furious governmental response
(Curtis, 1984, 173–96; Schlesinger, 1987, 205–43). Thatcher's animus had
deeply personal roots. Her close friend, Conservative Party Northern
Ireland spokesman Airey Neave, had been assassinated by the Irish
National Liberation Army in 1979 – in the wake of which the BBC tested
the Prevention of Terrorism Act's *de facto* ban by interviewing an INLA
representative. With hindsight, the wisdom of this move looked all the
more questionable when the IRA assassinated Lord Mountbatten the
following year: an act that seemed to confirm 'contagion' theories of television as the stimulus to copycat acts of terrorism aimed at upping the ante.

Certainly, one television program after another upped the stakes in the
war between broadcasters and government. In 1979, Thatcher was report-
edly driven 'scatty with rage' by a BBC *Panorama* team's filming of an
IRA roadblock at Carrickmore – footage that was never broadcast. Yet
more incendiary was a 1985 documentary in the BBC *Real Lives* series,
entitled 'At the Edge of the Union,' which offered a dual portrait of Sinn
Féin's Martin McGuiness and Democratic Unionist Party leader Gregory
Campell. According to BBC Governor Daphne Park, it was a 'Hitler
loved dogs' program. Ten months after the IRA's Brighton hotel bombing had left five dead, including one Conservative MP, Thatcher was
adamant that the documentary should not be shown (Milne, 1988, 190).
Home Secretary Leon Brittan duly wrote to the Corporation urging that
they drop it. Reiterating Thatcher's 'oxygen of publicity' phraseology, he
insisted that even 'if the programme and any surrounding material were,
as a whole, to present terrorist organizations in a wholly unfavourable
light, I would still ask you not to permit it to be broadcast' (quoted by
Leapman, 1987, 304).

Under severe pressure, the BBC's Board of Governors acceded to this demand. For his part, the Director-General affirmed the Corporation's right to explain 'the views and motives of those who avow terrorist activity,' reiterating that the BBC had not 'and will not provide unchallenged opportunities for the advocacy of terrorism' (Milne, 1988, 194). This left it to current affairs and news personnel, joined by their ITN colleagues, to stage a one-day strike in protest against their own management as well as Thatcher's Cabinet – a display of labor militancy that hardly endeared the BBC to Number Ten. Since the broadcasters refused to curb themselves, the government would do so for them. Brittan's letter foreshadowed what was to come. If the mere fact of appearing on television conferred legitimacy on terrorists, then new ways would have to be found to turn this glamorizing medium into something more stigmatizing.

Thatcher's attempt to do so culminated in 1988's Broadcasting Ban – one of the oddest and most sweeping legislative moves against press freedom ever enacted by a British government, in or out of wartime. Until it was revoked in 1994, the ban kept representatives of 11 proscribed Republican and Loyalist organizations, or those whose views could be construed as soliciting support for them, from '*direct*' broadcast on British television and radio. Introducing the Ban in the House of Commons in October 1988, Home Secretary Douglas Hurd justified it with reference to the 'widespread offense to viewers and listeners' caused by terrorists' broadcast appearances: a point broadcasters disputed, since interviews had been so infrequent and not, they protested, an occasion of profound public protest (Henderson, Miller and Reilly, 1990, 43). Hurd was adamant that the ban was neither a form of censorship nor of censure towards broadcasters. 'This is not a restriction on reporting,' he insisted before the House of Commons. 'It is a restriction on direct appearances by those who use or support violence' (House of Commons Debates 138, October 19, 1988, c. 885).

If not a 'restriction on reporting,' then what was the Ban? Its precise remit appeared a matter of some mystery, to the government as well as the broadcasters. But what it apparently meant was that representatives of the proscribed organizations could no longer be interviewed *live* on radio or television – or not if their statements appeared to constitute a solicitation of support for terrorism. This did not mean that such individuals were debarred from appearing altogether, though the government may have hoped that broadcasters would now be so cautious as to avoid any such appearances. But this was not to be. Sinn Féin was, after all, a legal political party in Northern Ireland, if also the political wing of the IRA. It was hard to conceive that lawfully elected politicians with seats in the House

Illustration 5.2   Nicholas Garland points to the counter-productivity of the broadcasting ban

Source: N. Garland/*The Independent* (10/20/1988).

of Commons (albeit seats they refused on principle to occupy) could be banned altogether from appearing on British television. And indeed they were not altogether banned. They could be, and were, still *seen* on television – but as voiceless talking heads whose words were either lip-synched by actors or subtitled on the screen. In this way, their views were not 'directly' broadcast.

Was this what Thatcher had intended? It was hard to know. Certainly, the sight of Sinn Féin leaders like Gerry Adams appearing subtitled on BBC or ITN news elicited a good deal of ridicule of the Ban and its architects. Several commentators wondered whether this muffling maneuver hadn't done more harm than good, allowing proscribed organizations to depict themselves as victims of a repressive gagging order. But condemnation was far from unanimous within the ranks of the British press. On the contrary, the Conservative press leapt to discipline unruly broadcasters. In 1985, the *Sunday Times* had played an inflammatory role in the *Real Lives* furor, encouraging Thatcher to extend her 'oxygen of publicity' postulate to any televised appearance of an IRA leader. Similarly in 1988, Conservative editors and columnists not only endorsed the Ban but urged that it be toughened up further to suture the lip-synch loophole. This was war, and as Thatcher put it, 'To beat off your enemy in a war you have to suspend some of your civil liberties for a time' (quoted by Article

19, 1989, 25). As in wartime past, segments of the press appeared more eager to wage war on one another than to mount a concerted defense of the principle of free speech – 'not a popular cause,' noted *The Wall Street Journal*, even (or especially) among reporters (Kull, 1985, 17).

But the larger question remains: do counterterrorist campaigns in fact constitute a state of war? If so, what restraints on civil liberties are necessary and proportionate to the threat posed by terrorism? In declared states of war such questions are inevitably matters for political negotiation. There's no diagnostic guidebook that establishes which liberties might be curtailed and for how long in wartime – only greater or lesser degrees of public willingness to abbreviate civil liberties so long as doing so seems likely to hasten victory.

In practice, the Reagan–Thatcher 'war on terrorism' wavered back and forth between treating terrorism as war – understood as a condition in which ordinary jurisprudence didn't apply, rights were trammeled, and the gloves were off – and as criminal behavior that could be, and should be, pursued in civil courts. But the latter approach proved exceedingly vexing. In the United States, press criticism mounted over Reagan's failure to produce convictions, or even to produce suspects in court. During his first term, Reagan had liked to warn terrorists, 'You can run, but you can't hide.' However, as Stephen Engelberg noted in *The New York Times* in 1989 at the tail end of Reagan's second term, 'the perpetrators of international terrorism have proved adept at both running and hiding.' Only one individual accused of terrorism, Fawaz Yunis, had been brought to the United States to stand trial – this despite Reagan's authorization of US intelligence agents to seize suspects overseas and bring them back to America. 'Almost anything short of torture can be implemented,' Engelberg added, 'provided nothing is done that "shocks the conscience of the court," as determined by the Supreme Court' (Engelberg, 1989, E3).

The war on terrorism had taken a subterranean turn. Below the media radar, the CIA had been licensed to seize suspects, extract self-incriminating evidence, and spirit these prisoners into American jails. Reagan's supporters could, and did, invoke Thatcher's gloves-off logic to justify moves of such dubious legality. But his administration had done more than abridge civil liberties. It had violated international law and flouted Congressional resolutions with breathtaking chutzpah. As the Iran-Contra revelations of 1986 made clear, a vast chasm separated the high moral plateau on which Reagan's rhetorical war was waged from the murky clandestine realm in which it was actually prosecuted. To secure the release of hostages held by the Lebanese Shiite organization

Hezbollah, Reagan's inner circle had done considerably more than just negotiate with Iran: a state high on its own list of terrorist sponsors and the subject of an international arms embargo. Via Israeli intermediaries, his key advisers had sold arms to Teheran. They then funneled a share of the profits to Nicaraguan 'freedom fighters' – a circuitous route necessitated by the Boland Amendment, a series of Congressional prohibitions against federal aid to the Contras, 'terrorists' by any other name.

While Reagan continued to protest his ignorance of these arms-for-hostages dealings, 14 administration officials were later charged with crimes, and 11 convicted, including then Secretary of Defense, Casper Weinberger. For a brief moment, 'Irangate' threatened to terminate several political careers and to discredit a highly politicized concept. But in fact it did neither. Just as George H. W. Bush offered pardons to all 11 convicted officials at the end of his presidency, so his son would issue a reprieve to the 'war on terror' at the start of his. Ironically, America's new primary foes – Osama bin Laden, Al Qaeda and the Taliban regime in Afghanistan – had been beneficiaries of the estimated $3 billion in US aid and equipment channeled to the anti-Soviet Mujahedin during the Reagan era. In intelligence-world parlance, the attacks of 9/11 represented 'blowback' on a stupendous scale (Johnson, 2000; Mamdani, 2005, 119–77).

The Global War on Terror, v. 2.0

In packaging the Global War on Terror (GWOT), Bush and his advisers studiously avoided mentioning its antecedents in favor of more affirmative conflicts from which the United States had emerged triumphant. Parallels with World War II lent the luster of a morally unambiguous conflict – America's last unquestionably popular war. But since this was a battle of potentially indefinite duration, as implied in the codenames 'Operation Infinite Justice' and 'Operation Enduring Freedom' for the military dimensions of the GWOT, it also had overtones of the 50-year Cold War. Indeed, administration officials and supportive opinion-formers developed this parallel by casting the 'war on terror' as an epoch-making struggle against 'Islamofascism' – a dangerous, militant ideology on the march worldwide, preying on the disadvantaged and deluded, just as communism had in the late 1940s and 1950s. Even as they raised the fearful specter of terror, the GWOT's architects gestured towards a decisive conclusion: either unconditional surrender or outright collapse.

Critics were quick to ask how exactly one waged war on a *tactic* and who the enemy was in such an open-ended, rhetorically imprecise conflict: an individual (Osama bin Laden); an organization (Al Qaeda); an idea (Islamism or 'Islamofascism'); or an entire religion (Islam)? Since 2001, numerous scholars have deconstructed the discursive war on terror and the politics of fear on which it relies (Giroux, 2006; Altheide, 2006; Jackson, 2005). Rather than reprise that literature, the aim here is to *historicize* this most recent war on terror with a view to questioning the orthodox wisdom that has underpinned each successive campaign to deny terrorists oxygen while capturing the hearts and minds of waverers. This task seems all the more necessary given the frequency with which commentators on the right and left alike claim that new media have swept all before them, rendering the pre-digital era obsolescent, whether to the advantage of terrorists or the state. Defenders of the status quo fret that the internet has provided terrorists with a vast ethereal recruitment arena: a 'new Afghanistan,' in the words of New York Police Commissioner Raymond Kelly (presumably conjuring Afghanistan as Al Qaeda's lost safe haven, not as a zone of lawlessness which the US-led coalition has failed to bring under control). But with equal conviction, some critics on the left see digital culture as trapping atomized individuals in an airless bell-jar of fear, just where the neo-liberal state wants them – too trans-fixed by the spectacle of terror to do anything but shop (Giroux, 2006, 12).

As viewed by the US/NATO defense community, the twenty-first-century world has been transformed by digital media that exponentially enhance terrorist networks' ability to recruit adherents and inculcate a 'jihadi' worldview among widely dispersed individuals. Thanks to social-networking media like chat-rooms, discussion boards, and blogs, new radicalized communities coalesce on-line, reaffirming and heightening one another's anti-western convictions. Where terrorists of the past aimed at capturing the headlines, today's insurgents see the internet as a path to pursue terrorism by other means. *Actual* violence may thus decrease, while virtual activism proliferates at a rate counterterrorist agencies can barely follow (Winn and Zakem, 2009).

In US counterinsurgency circles, '*influence warfare*' has become the new buzzword (Forest and Honkus, 2009, 1). With the web facilitating patterns of nodal connection favored by terrorist cells, the 'conceptual battle-space' is simultaneously nowhere and everywhere – an every-where that includes the West. 'Al-Qa'ida prizes geek jihadis as much as would-be suicide bombers and gunmen,' noted an Associated Press story of March 2008. These tech-savvy recruits produce 'sophisticated web documentaries and multimedia products aimed at Muslim audiences in the United States, Britain and other western countries.' And these Islamist ideologues, opinion-formers warn, are more likely to be at work in a basement near you than in the foothills of Tora Bora (Forest and Honkus, 2009, 15).

The prognoses of contemporary terrorism experts often convey a familiar sense of beleaguered disadvantage – usually latent but sometimes quite explicit. Thus, for example, NATO General Secretary Jaap de Hoop Scheffer noted ruefully that, lacking an ability to gather video from the field and without a prominent web presence, his organization languished in the digital 'stone age.' That terrorists no longer require mainstream terrestrial or cable channels to ensure the trees they fell don't topple unseen in the forest is, by now, a well-worn lament. Who needs CNN, the BBC, or NBC when you can directly upload to your own website footage of prisoner beheadings or IED attacks – images far more gruesome than western news media would in any case consent to broadcast? In the ostensibly lawless virtual 'Afghanistan,' states can't censor such posts on grounds of 'taste and tone' or prevent their migration from esoteric Arabic-language sites to frequently visited blogs (Johnson and Kaye, 2006, 316). Thus, during the week of May 11 – 17, 2004, the terms 'Nick,' 'Berg,' 'beheading' and 'video' were among the top ten words searched on Lycos. Those conducting such searches didn't lack for hits, with popular sites such as andrewsullivan.com providing links.

It seems likely that the vast majority of Americans who seek out such material are far less likely to be radicalized by it than to find their anti-Islamist animus confirmed or their pruriently voyeuristic impulses gratified. Not surprisingly, however, US national security agencies tend to adopt a less sanguine attitude. According to their interpretation of the predicament, states, their militaries, and multilateral forces are not only less technologically sophisticated than their terrorist foes but more scrupulous. 'They' can lie; 'we' can't. Insurgents can 'make exorbitant promises and point out government shortcomings, many caused or aggravated by the insurgency,' observes the recent US Army Marine Corps' *Counterinsurgency Field Manual*, while counterinsurgents 'must stick to the truth and make sure that words are backed up by deeds' (2007, 1–13).

But what states *can* do, according to contemporary US strategists, is join the battle more aggressively. Since 'Al-Qaeda and other terrorists' center of gravity lies in the information domain,' noted Dell Dailey (head of the State Department's counterterrorism operations) 'it is there that we must engage it' (cited by Forest and Honkus, 2009, 2). A whole array of new coinages, acronyms, and conceptual paradigms has arisen to capture the unique dimensions of twenty-first-century counterterrorism. 'Influence warfare' is now the name of the game, and 'non-kinetic operations' are what this form of disembodied combat requires: a term more hip and less sinister than its antecedent, 'psyops.' As Defense Secretary Robert Gates made clear, the targets of influence included US citizens as well as potential allies and putative enemies worldwide: 'Success will be less a matter of imposing one's will and more a function of shaping behavior – of friends, adversaries, and most importantly, the people in between' (quoted by Hoffman, 2009, viii).

Obscured by a flurry of new buzzwords, Bush era 'influence warfare' was in practice less novel than the terminology surrounding it. On closer inspection, many of its techniques look decidedly familiar. If the first necessity of the GWOT was to win US citizens' consent to a campaign of open-ended scope and duration, the language of terror itself served a vital strategic function. Bush's declaration of war, while invoking the remembered moral clarity of the 'good war,' also resembled President Truman's pitch to a conflict-weary nation in 1947 that it must remobilize for a fresh global struggle. Launching what came to be known as the Truman Doctrine – in a Congressional address that needed to 'scare hell' out of the American people, in the phraseology of Republican senator Arthur Vandenberg – 'terrorism' was also an operative category. Greece, Truman warned, was threatened by 'the terrorist activities of several thousand armed men, led by Communists.' A stark choice lay ahead between 'alternative ways of life,' the President forecast: one based on majority rule, the other 'based upon the will of a minority forcibly imposed upon the majority,' reliant on 'terror and oppression, a controlled press and radio, fixed elections and the suppression of personal freedoms' (Truman, 1947, 322–3).

Conceiving the Cold War as an ideological battle for the 'minds of men,' Washington developed a bureaucracy centered in the capital but with outposts around the world dedicated to winning friends and influencing people: the United States Information Agency (USIA). In 2001, Washington required a new apparatus for 'influence warfare,' having hastily disbanded the USIA once its Cold War nemesis collapsed (Cull, 2008). But it quickly ran into trouble, both jurisdictional and ethical.

When journalists publicized the clandestine existence of an Office of Strategic Influence in the Department of Defense in February 2002, they roundly denounced its embrace of 'strategic deception' as beyond the pale of acceptable governmental action. Recognizing the desirability of a less covert approach to shaping the informational environment, the administration then established a State Department under secretary for public diplomacy (Brown, 2003, 92). Later that year, Bush also launched an Office of Global Communications to 'coordinate strategic communications overseas that integrate the President's themes while truthfully depicting America and Administration policies.' 'Global Communications,' its archived website explains, 'helps our government inform audiences about positive news stories, Iraqi children, the women of Afghanistan, the President's HIV/AIDS initiative and Millennium Challenge Account, and freedom in Iraq. Other efforts include telling the stories of torture and brutality in Saddam's Iraq and updates on the liberation of the Iraqi people' (Bush, 2003).

Drawing on Cold War precedents, the Bush administration also established new channels of communication, targeting the heartland of this battle for influence which, while notionally everywhere and nowhere in particular, in practice lies squarely in the Middle East. Keen to counter the rising influence of Al Jazeera, the US government unveiled Al Hurra (The Free One), a DC-based satellite television channel, broadcasting in Arabic and operated by a non-profit corporation, Middle East Broadcasting Networks, Inc. (MBN), 'financed by the American people through the US Congress' (Al Hurra, 2010). At the same time, VOA broadcasts to the Middle East were also stepped up, while Radio Liberty began broadcasting in Dari and Pashto to Afghani audiences (Brown, 2003, 93).

Despite insistent claims regarding new media's unique qualities, historical precedents are plainly discernible in these Bush-era efforts. Indeed, history itself became newly fashionable among military strategists. The pendulum having swung back from the short-term 'terrorist spectacular' as the key source of concern to the long, slow courtship of hearts and minds, Templer – 'Tiger of Malaya' – reappeared as the GWOT's man of the moment. As the RAND's principal terrorist expert Bruce Hoffman pointed out, it was Templer who 50 years earlier had presciently warned: 'The shooting side of the business is only 25% of the trouble and the other 75% lies in getting the people ... behind us' (Hoffman, 2009, viii).

This rediscovery of counterinsurgency theory makes it no surprise that an Oxford D. Phil. thesis written by Lt Colonel John A. Nagl on 'counterinsurgency lessons from Malaya and Vietnam' should have become required reading for US officers in Iraq (Nagl, 2005). Or that General David Petraeus, architect of Iraq's 'surge' who told his commanders that 'sixty percent of the battle was to be for and about information,' would provide cover puff for the new *Counterinsurgency Field Manual,* written in part by Nagl (Arraf, 2009). (A book 'on the bedside table of the president,

204 The Media at War

vice president, secretary of defense, 21 of 25 members of the Senate Armed Forces Committee' deserves 'a place on your beside too,' Petraeus prompts prospective customers from the dustjacket.) Sure enough, the updated *Field Manual* contains dozens of entries under 'information,' 'information environment,' 'information operations,' and 'propaganda,' with such familiar advice as 'Consider word choices carefully,' and 'Publicize insurgent violence and use of terror to discredit the insurgency' (US Army Marine Corps, 2007, 5–11). What it doesn't point out, however, is that the famously irascible Templer, on departure from Malaya in 1954, threatened to 'shoot the bastard who says that this Emergency is over' – just as he later seemed keen to throttle anyone who used that 'bloody phrase' hearts and minds (Cloake, 1985, 2).

Hearts, minds, and other vital organs: the persistent failure of counterinsurgency

When the Bush era ended, the Global War on Terror also came to a precipitate full stop. At any rate, President Barack Obama hastily retired that overburdened phrase, insisting that the preferred term would henceforth be 'overseas contingency operations' (Government Press Releases, 2009). Yet with a downsized US military presence in Iraq set to continue well into the second decade of the twenty-first century and an even less conclusive war in Afghanistan still ongoing, the brevity implied by this euphemism appears misplaced. In many ways, the phenomena constitutive of Bush's war on terror continue unabated – if under new management and nomenclature.

To date, the battle for Muslim hearts and minds has been singularly unsuccessful. Rather than revisiting the Malayan emergency, the Bush and Blair administrations might have done better to rediscover the counterinsurgency prosecuted by American soldiers against Filipino insurgents at the dawn of the twentieth century. A speculative article from the *Washington Post* in August 1899, written at the start of what was to be a long, vicious and divisive campaign might have given pause. The editorial opinion forcefully advanced was that 'the war will be popular, indeed overwhelmingly popular, with the people of the nation if it shall be prosecuted vigorously and speedily ended.' However, President McKinley was correspondingly warned that

If there shall be bungling management of the war, needless sacrifice of life and treasure, and the insurgents permitted to continue it after the coming winter campaign, the war will be unpopular with all classes, and the administration under which it was inaugurated can't escape the retributive blow of popular resentment. (*Washington Post*, 1899, 6)

One year later, *The New York Times* lamented that Filipinos 'as a people ... hate the Americans,' having 'not yet been impressed with the fact that the Americans honestly have their welfare at heart' (*The New York Times*, 1900, 6). But the islanders could surely be forgiven for failing to appreciate American beneficence in the midst of a campaign that saw the wholesale scorching of land, razing of villages and torture of captured insurgent suspects, most controversially with a technique then known as the 'water cure,' now dubbed 'waterboarding.' As explained by *The Hartford Courant*, 'this method of punishment consist[ed] of pouring water down the throats of men until they would swell up, and becoming frightened, would tell what they might know' (*The Hartford Courant*, 1902, 1).

Over the next two years, atrocities continued to shadow US press discussion of the campaign to pacify the Philippines. The insurgency's durability was ascribed to the 'terrorism' of a ferocious armed minority, whose ruthless coercion cowed a population otherwise well-disposed towards their American benefactors. As complaints about US troops' excesses mounted, Governor Taft insisted that 'never had a war been conducted in which more compassion, more restraint and more generosity had been exhibited than in connection with the American officers in the Philippines' (*The Atlanta Constitution*, 1902a, 1). Instances of maltreatment were explained, and dismissed, with reference to the enemy's savagery. 'One of the traits of Filipinos is cruelty,' Taft blithely asserted when called to account in February 1902. Torture, the subject of several investigations and courts-martial later that year, was justified in ways now thoroughly familiar. Condemned in principle, it was sometimes rationalized as a retaliatory surfeit of emotion after American soldiers' bodies had been mutilated by insurgents. At other times, officers insisted that the 'war cure' wasn't in fact torture at all, at worst a temporary unpleasantness. 'Water Cure Is Not So Bad,' trilled a headline in *The Atlanta Constitution* in May 1902 – 'no worse in its effects than the native vino' (*The Atlanta Constitution*, 1902b, 10). Just as intoxication loosened inhibitions, so the sensation of drowning dissolved uncooperative insurgents' tongue-tied obduracy. What the water cured, then, was silence: a fail-safe way of procuring intelligence unreachable by other means. *In vino veritas*, as the classical adage had it.

Illustration 5.3   *Life* illustrates the 'water cure'

Source: *Life* (5/22/1902).

Understanding Filipino insurgency as a 'crime against civilization' and convinced of their own rectitude, American policy-makers and officers struggled to comprehend the islanders' animosity towards them – in much the same way that more recent US administrations have expressed bafflement as to why 'they' hate 'us,' unless animated by envy or resentment. Why, it is repeatedly asked, are the recipients of American largesse so incapable of perceiving their redeemers' benevolence?

Turning the question around, we might ask why Americans often experience such difficulty in understanding how their actions strike others. Why does a strategic community avowedly so sensitive to the 'information environment' seem so tone deaf to the chorus of alienation and protest occasioned by its actions? In part, the answer surely owes something to Americans' resistance to seeing themselves through others' eyes. One telling example of this refusal can be seen in the failure of Al Jazeera's English-language station (launched in 2006) to find US cable and satellite providers willing to carry it. As a result, a station that boasts 130 million viewers in over 100 countries can be seen in just two small regional markets in the US: Toledo, Ohio, and Burlington, Vermont (NPR, 2009).

Another answer lies in the structure of counterinsurgency warfare itself, and the gap between its humane self-image and its quotidian practices. It would seem that Templer's 'bloody phrase' has continued to bamboozle students of COIN, who believe not only that 'hearts and minds' were indeed won in Malaya but that their capture provides the key to success – a template that can surely be replicated elsewhere. This conviction, however, relies on an imperial optic with all the same blindspots and evasions of the 1950s. Thus Templer is celebrated for his psychological insight without a corresponding appreciation that British forces prevailed in Malaya by wholesale relocation of the rural population, extensive deportation of the colony's ethnic Chinese population, and by promising to leave by a set date – on which power would be ceded to a postcolonial Malay ruling class at the expense of an ethnic Chinese population that had formed the majority in pre-Emergency Malaya and Singapore. This promise was duly fulfilled, but not before British officials had also determined that the shortest route to hearts and minds lay through the wallet, paying insurgents to surrender and cooperate: an expedient recently revived in Iraq's 'Awakening Councils' of paid-off Sunni insurgents.

Should these inducements fail, nothing was believed to impress a 'fence-sitting' population like the demonstration effect of aerial bombardment. In Malaya, the jungle was 'neutralized' (another of Templer's famous adages) with the aid of 1000-pound and then 4000-pound bombs. This was to be expected – despite all the talk of winning 'hearts and minds.' Airpower had formed a staple of British imperial policing since the 1920s, when unruly fedayeen in Palestine, Iraq and the Sudan became the guinea pigs for this marvelously inexpensive new disciplinary technology. 'Tribesmen,' the Chief of Air Staff, Lord Trenchart informed a mildly skeptical House of Commons in 1930, 'have no objection to being killed' (Omissi, 1990). Historical antecedents like this offer a salutary reminder that excess violence inheres in the very project of unmaking and remaking colonized societies by force.

Theories of terrorism as pathologically oriented towards publicity – *any* publicity, at *any* cost, and no matter how negative – are constitutive of counterinsurgency's self-defeating predicament. So long as terrorism remains shallowly understood, strategists will keep seeking to defeat it through a combination of oxygen-denial, cash payments, and optimistic news-stories – punctuated by the demonstration effect of overwhelming force when the indigenous population's desired level of gratitude falls short. And so long as western policy-elites and opinion-formers continue to write themselves out of the history of postcolonial societies' development, they'll persist in thinking that the larger 'battle for Muslim opinion' can be won by supplying positive images of western society that undermine skewed perceptions, alleviate a misplaced sense of grievance, and propel peoples mired in tradition along the digital highway towards enlightened modernity (Salt, 2008). In short, until policy-makers, militaries, the media and their publics ask of politically motivated violence, 'publicity *to what end*?,' wars on terror will continually flounder.

Chapter 6

War in the Digital Age: Afghanistan and Iraq

A digital revolution?

The 1990s began with much heated discussion over the rise of CNN and the power of real-time television. By the decade's end technological anxieties had migrated elsewhere. Television no longer appeared the key locus of communicative power – networked computers did. Cyberspace had become so crucial for storing and sharing data that potential threats to this invisible domain occasioned widespread panic. As Y2K loomed, the air was thick with talk of a 'millennium bug' poised to cripple networks as a result of computers' inability to make the transition from a year abbreviated as 99 into one ending 00. Unless corrective action were taken, many feared that systems would break down when the old ascending numbers assumption became invalid. Networks would crash; banking and financial transactions would snarl up; traffic lights would cease working; hospital equipment would malfunction ... As we know, these apocalyptic scenarios did not come to pass. With hindsight they seem absurdly far-fetched. But they also provide a reminder of how quickly computers transformed almost every aspect of life in industrialized societies and of how much anxiety surrounded technological change at the dawn of the digital age.

Consider how rapidly this communications revolution occurred. In 1983, the year of 'Operation Urgent Fury' in Grenada – also, coincidentally, the year in which Motorola developed the first mobile phone – personal computers were objects owned by a tiny, technologically sophisticated avant-garde, sufficiently well-off to afford these cumbersome devices and curious enough to learn how to use them. 'Computing' remained tinged with a rarefied aura of science: a technically specialized pursuit generally conducted in isolation, like any number of predominantly male hobbies. The idea that computers might *talk* to one another still seemed a scenario of science fiction, which yielded numerous dire warnings about how readily security systems might be compromised. In the popular 1983 Hollywood movie *War Games*, an adolescent computer whiz who has hacked into the Pentagon computer that controls the US nuclear arsenal inadvertently triggers the countdown to World War III when he responds to the machine's devious invitation to play what purports to be a war game with Russia. The film in turn prompted Congressional hearings on and legislation aimed at regulating a 'teenaged technology' (Schulte, 2008).

At the time, few American teenagers and even fewer Europeans actually owned personal computers. Many people had never actually seen or handled one. Two decades later, not only had personal computers, along with cell phones, digital cameras and camcorders, become near ubiquitous in homes across western Europe and North America, they had also become much more compact and lightweight. No longer occupying a sizable table-top and a good deal of floor-space below, as did the first generation of personal computers, laptops had been reduced to a few pounds in weight, while desktops were significantly sleeker and cheaper. Computers also performed far more functions than they had just a few years earlier. Gone were the days when this bulky electronic box of tricks served primarily to store or process data. Now they doubled as play-stations for electronic games, viewing and listening devices for music and movies, and as camera, phone, stereo, and instant mail or messaging system rolled into one. Within ten years of its initial debut in 1990, the world wide web had become a vast and variegated realm in which individuals could seek and swap text, graphics, and video clips; shop for consumer goods or potential partners; pursue private peccadilloes or publicize coruscating opinions. All this could be done at relatively low cost and increasing speed as fiber optic cables facilitated the rapid transmission of compressed digitized information.

The web was seemingly whatever the individual user wished it to be. Like previous technological innovations, the internet generated wild predictions of unprecedented individual emancipation on the one hand, or ruinous social disintegration on the other. Information libertarians thus hailed its democratizing potential to provide 'global citizens' with access to a vast cornucopia of news and views from around the world, untouched by government censors or corporate media filters. Freed from old constraints of distance, immobility and nationality, web-users would form virtual networks with the power to foster progressive change worldwide. Others, however, foresaw a gloomier future of radical atomization and social decay as isolated individuals retreated ever further from face-to-face community into personalized worlds-of-one, where fantasy, hedonism, and consumerism would reign supreme.

To date, the world has neither been transformed nor disintegrated in the ways these utopian and dystopian projections anticipated. Indeed, 'the world' has not yet been thoroughly enmeshed by the web. Despite its seemingly unstoppable growth, the internet is currently accessible to just one quarter of the globe's population. In many parts of the developing world, cell phones and satellite television have penetrated significantly further. So, when we note that the channels through which a growing number of individuals worldwide receive news, find entertainment and maintain contact with others have indisputably altered, we should also recall that this is far from universally true – just as we should recall that many of these changes aren't effected by the internet per se.

Television broadcasting has undergone multiple transformations of its own. Satellite networks headquartered in regions outside the US and Europe have eroded the erstwhile global dominance of CNN and BBC World. Nowhere has this challenge to Anglo-American broadcasting hegemony been more pronounced than in the Middle East. Since its founding in 1996, the Qatar-based network Al Jazeera has developed a significant international audience for its on-air and on-line news content. With a hard-hitting style at odds with the state-controlled channels typical of the region, the network's rapid growth has catalyzed the emergence of numerous Arabic-language competitors, including Abu Dhabi TV, LBC (Lebanon Broadcasting Corporation), Arab News Network, and the Dubai-based Al-Arabiya – a proliferation sometimes dubbed the 'Al Jazeera effect.' By 2005, some 150 Arabic satellite television channels were on the air (Seib, 2005, 605).

Meanwhile, the miniaturization of digital communications technologies has also facilitated live reporting from inaccessible places under inhospitable conditions. During the Gulf War of 1991, satellite uplinks still literally weighed a ton: bulky dishes that required transportation by truck. A decade later, as Washington launched a war against Afghanistan, the latest video satellite phone, nicknamed 'Talking Head,' weighed 5kg and was little bulkier than a thick laptop. Together with its satellite communications terminals, the phone cost approximately $16,000: beyond the reach of independent freelancers but well within the means of news corporations. Musing on this latest innovation, Margaret Engel, director of the 'Newseum' in Arlington, VA, anticipated the day when everybody could 'be their own reporter and camera crew' and 'the power of the censor [would] fall away' (*The Economist*, 2001, 75–6).

Engel's prognosis points to the rise of amateur journalism facilitated by new digital media. While major news organizations, TV networks and newspapers alike, have shifted much of their content on-line, blogging (a new phenomenon of the early 2000s) allows anyone with internet access the opportunity to post reflections on current events, to document personal experiences and share photos or video footage with a potentially global audience. Sometimes referred to as 'citizen journalism,' blogging has polarized critical judgement. Some commentators have greeted the exponential growth of the 'blogosphere' as part of a regrettable trend whereby uninformed ranting has supplanted professional information-sharing; hence journalist Randal Rothenberg's dismissive verdict that blogging is 'little more than hype dished out largely by the unemployable to the aimless' (quoted by Johnson and Kaye, 2006, 320). Others, however, have welcomed the peer-to-peer interaction that conventional news media did not hitherto permit, along with a more avowedly opinionated style of writing that generally makes no pretence to objectivity and detachment – old-school journalistic values that obscure the 'situatedness' of all reporting. From this perspective, the complaint that blogging is all opinion profoundly misses the point.

This democratization of information-sharing extends beyond civilian society to the ranks of the military. Watch any film or TV show about the US military in Iraq – from Deborah Scranton's documentary *The War Tapes* (2006) to Paul Haggis's *In the Valley of Elah* (2007), Brian de Palma's *Redacted* (2007) or the HBO series *Generation Kill* (2008) – and you'll see soldiers taking pictures or making movies about their tours of duty. This conceit isn't just a self-reflexive artistic device. In recent years, the Pentagon has struggled to catch up with and outpace the proliferation of digital technologies that, whatever their battlefield uses, have also turned soldiers into their own docu-dramatists, pundits, commentators, and activists – complicating the 'information environment' in ways the top brass often find decidedly unhelpful.

Issues of control have acquired new urgency as political and military leaders have felt their ability to constrain the flow of information wane, the 'censor's power falling away.' And yet, as we've seen repeatedly before, ruling elites typically imagine themselves laboring at decided disadvantage against enemies construed as both more sophisticated in their grasp of persuasive communication and more ruthless in their application of deadly force. In other words, we would be wise to treat policymakers' complaints of powerlessness with some caution.

If the most striking feature of the digital revolution has been the rise of the internet and associated new social media, other signal changes in the communications landscape have been far more congenial to the status quo. Most obviously, the contraction of media ownership into the hands of a small number of moguls who preside over vast multimedia empires – a phenomenon set in motion by the deregulation policies of Reagan and Thatcher in the 1980s – has led to a predictable shrinkage and homogenization of content. As smaller newspapers, radio stations, and television affiliates have been swallowed up or bankrupted by giant corporations, the 'mainstream' has expanded in width while the parameters of expression have narrowed.

Meanwhile, the pervasive spread of corporate imperatives to cut bottom lines and increase profitability has encouraged the growth of cheap formats, like talk shows and 'reality' TV, at the expense of costly programming such as news and current affairs. Over the course of the 1990s, commercial television and radio in the United States increasingly became an arena for histrionic performance. And yet while partisanship seemed to be all the rage, with television and radio personalities giving loud and often intolerant expression to their political views, watchdog organizations grew more active in exposing perceived 'liberal bias' in the

Illustration 6.1   Cox and Forkum decry the 'liberal media' in a cartoon riffing on Defense Secretary Donald Rumsfeld's widely repeated remark that 'you go to war with the army you have – not the army you might want or wish to have at a later time'

Source: www.CoxAndForkum.com.

mainstream media. Whatever space for dissent existed at the margins was squeezed ever further in the aftermath of 9/11 – an event that gave the White House unparalleled sway over news-making.

Although the communications environment may never have looked harder for political leaders to control without resorting to the kind of heavy-handed intrusions for which Beijing is regularly excoriated in the West, the ideological climate of America after September 11, 2001 was uncommonly conducive to waging retaliatory war. Rarely, in fact, has it been easier for a president to rally support than it was for George W. Bush in October 2001. But popular consent of this kind doesn't necessarily persist, as the ongoing wars in Afghanistan and Iraq have made very evident. Nor was domestic consent matched beyond US borders, making one of the most pronounced aspects of these wars the stark discrepancy between how they've been represented to American audiences and how others – particularly in the Muslim world – have understood the meaning and morality of these ventures.

Afghanistan: long war, short attention span

When President George W. Bush declared the start of hostilities against Afghanistan on October 7, 2001, after the Taliban leadership refused to hand over Osama bin Laden and other Al Qaeda leaders as Washington had demanded two weeks earlier, American public outrage over 9/11 remained at a high pitch of emotional intensity. That same day, the first airstrikes of what was initially referred to as 'Operation Infinite Justice' began, launched from British and US ships and submarines. 'On my orders, the United States military has begun strikes against the al Qaeda terrorist training camps and military installations of the Taliban regime in Afghanistan,' Bush announced. 'These carefully targeted actions are designed to disrupt the uses of Afghanistan as a terrorist base of operations and to attack the military capability of the Taliban regime,' he continued, signalling what was to be a key theme in the White House narrative of this campaign: the precision use of air power (CNN, 2001a).

As was to be expected, the 'rally round the flag' effect that typically greets any declaration of war was heightened at a time when the stars and stripes was already a focal point of national mourning, with many TV news anchors prominently sporting patriotic lapel pins. Bush had begun preparing the US public for war against Afghanistan within days of 9/11, announcing on CNN on September 17 that:

we're going to find those evildoers, those barbaric people who attacked our country and we're going to hold them accountable and we're going to hold the people who house them accountable. The people who think they can provide them safe havens will be held accountable. The people who feed them will be held accountable. And the Taliban must take my statement seriously. (CNN, 2001b)

That the assault on Afghanistan was a vital front in the 'war on terror' was taken as given on US network news – not just uncritically accepted but positively lauded. Thus CNN editorialized on October 7 that Bush was 'not letting up on the quest for justice' (quoted by Jasperson and El-Kikhia, 2003, 117). Both responding to and channeling public expressions of pain, anger and puzzlement, news media framed the 9/11 story in ways that underscored the monstrous outrage perpetrated against America but simultaneously stressed national resolution to punish whoever was responsible and protect citizens against further attacks. NBC gave its coverage the tagline 'America Strikes Back,' an allusion to the *Star Wars* trilogy, while Fox News ran the banner 'America United.' For their part, print media adopted similar framing devices. Until the end of 2001, *The New York Times* ran a special daily section entitled 'A Nation Challenged,' which not only reported the latest counterterrorist developments but printed individual 'portraits in grief' devoted to each one of the victims of 9/11 (Kaplan, 2003).

With the US on a state of high alert against an enemy that could be anywhere and everywhere, official secrecy reached unprecedented levels of stringency, even as the USA PATRIOT Act permitted extensive eavesdropping on private communication. Free speech was no longer rhetorically valorized as a marker of America's liberal constitution but recast as a weakness waiting to be exploited by unscrupulous terrorists. 'People have to watch what they say and watch what they do,' warned White House press secretary Ari Fleischer, before erasing this remark from the record in an Orwellian gesture redolent of *1984* (Hess and Kalb, 2003, 99).

In search of supremacy over the information realm, the White House and Pentagon determined to keep journalists far from the scene of operations: a move that generated complaints that press arrangements were more akin to the total embargo imposed during the 1983 invasion of Grenada than the restrictions of the 1991 Gulf War. On the whole, though, US media organizations were far more circumspect in agreeing to the new ground rules than they had been during those previous conflicts. It wasn't hard to see why. As Victoria Clarke, Assistant

Secretary of Defense for Public Affairs, frequently reminded the press, polling data showed that a majority of Americans thought the media disclosed too much information, and (by implication) ought to be more tightly controlled (O'Brien, 2002, 16; Hess and Kalb, 2003, 101). This point was vividly underscored by a live performance on *The Tonight Show with Jay Leno* in mid-November 2001, when comedian Dennis Miller got the studio audience to begin a chant: 'We don't want to know!' 'It's not for us,' Miller explained, with reference to the public's vaunted 'right to know.' 'It's for you and your cocktail chatter at parties in DC. Leave our boys alone over there' (Kulman, Newman and Mazzetti, 2001, 44).

This testy public mood facilitated the administration's restrictive approach. So too did the unorthodox military tactics adopted in Afghanistan. As Defense Secretary Donald Rumsfeld reiterated, this was necessarily an 'unconventional war' waged against an unorthodox enemy that did 'not have armies, navies, and air forces.' Avoiding an armed confrontation of ground forces, this campaign would 'exploit American advantages in technology with unmanned drones and precision weapons' and, as Peter J. Boyer noted in *The New Yorker*, 'would come as close as a Western nation can come to answering terrorism in kind – with a full deployment of Special Forces, operating "behind the wire."' Fighting on the ground, to the extent that there would be actual *combat*, would be done by these special operatives in conjunction with indigenous Afghan militias. Should they encounter fierce resistance they would call in air support (Boyer, 2003). In the first instance, however, the campaign was largely aerial, with US and British forces launching missile strikes from bombers, carrier-based fighters, and cruise missiles launched from British and American ships and submarines.

A war of this kind – fought by clandestine operatives and from on high – didn't lend itself to up-close media coverage. The idea that journalists might temporarily join military units, as pool reporters had during the Gulf War, was initially rejected outright by Clarke and Rumsfeld. To allow reporters to 'embed' with Special Forces was to risk diluting their specialness to the point of operational nullity. What was the value of such agents (some of whom were under CIA control) if everyone, including the enemy, knew about their operational procedures and day-to-day routines? The need to preserve the cover of these shadow warriors seemed unarguable, although the Pentagon did later backtrack and allow a few favored reporters, such as *Newsweek*'s Donatella Lorch, to embed – but only when there was little for them to see. As Lorch later remarked of her week with a Special Forces A-Team, 'it would have been a lot nicer if I had been there when the A-Team was doing some fighting, but I got there when they were already in Mazar[-i-Sharif]' (Rid, 2007, 106). It didn't take long, however, before journalists frustrated by their enforced dependence on the DOD for authorized footage began making their own way into the country, reprising the role of the 'unilaterals' during the 1991 Gulf War. As had been the case then, going it alone wasn't necessarily easy as reporters confronted a daunting battery of technological, topographical, and political obstacles. Writing in *The New Republic*'s October 29, 2001 issue, Elizabeth Rubin conjured the scene among the mob of media workers thronging Islamabad in search of visas, leads, and tips:

> We exchanged anxious stories we'd heard from journalists inside Afghanistan – malaria, dysentery, lice, crabs, hepatitis, typhoid, astro-nomical expenses for vehicles, four to five days on mountain passes made for goats with rock-climbing shoes, sleeping on mud floors, ten to a room, no water, no electricity. 'And there's no war!' said one American photographer. 'And no stories,' said another. We heard about TV crews encouraging the Northern Alliance, by whom most foreign media are protected, to fire off artillery for the cameras. (2001, 25)

As Rubin's cameo suggests, foreign journalists found Afghanistan a peculiarly off-putting environment. Where was this evanescent war grounded? Its locus appeared as elusive as the hunt for Osama bin Laden – a manhunt, seemingly *the* big story in Afghanistan, that quickly ran aground in the abandoned caves of Tora Bora. What else to report? The so-called Northern Alliance, a fighting force cobbled together by the US and British military architects of what was soon rebranded Operation Enduring Freedom – in deference to Muslim complaints that God alone could deliver 'infinite justice' – was a motley assemblage of haphazardly armed, diversely motivated Afghans who presented a less than appealing face to many western journalists. The latter found themselves dependent on local forces, but often considered the Northern Alliance far from dependable. By November 2001, journalists were filing stories of having been beaten up, robbed and imprisoned by Afghan soldiers – sometimes with US military collusion.

Narrative disorientation as to where and how to find 'the story' was compounded by forbidding mountainous terrain, lack of telecommunica-tions infrastructure, and journalists' equally non-existent linguistic capacity in Afghanistan's main languages. These impediments left the

media heavily reliant on local minders for assistance in a land some west-
erners located at a temporal remove of several centuries. Many clearly
found this relationship unsettling – infantilizing and precarious if not also
financially exploitative, for journalists were quick to complain that, in
this war, everyone was on the make. While they held sway there, Taliban
forces were rumored to be charging western journalists $2,000 per person
to tour the southern city of Kandahar, where they could witness destruction caused by US airstrikes. Drivers, meanwhile, exacted exorbitant
sums for transportation, while rudimentary accommodations in the Tora
Bora mountains came at the price of $200 a night. Since this informal
black market forced reporters to carry around large amounts of cash, they
became what one journalist dubbed 'walking ATMs' – a lucrative target
for robbers and kidnappers. Such fears weren't idle. By the end of
November 2001, eight journalists of different nationalities had been
killed and a Canadian freelancer kidnapped. These grim events quickly
made Afghanistan the deadliest place in the world to practice journalism,
according to the New York-based Committee to Protect Journalists.
Strikingly, in November 2001 the country was also more lethal for the
media than for the US military, none of whose lives had yet been claimed
(Peterson, 2001b, 1).

This statistical imbalance did not persist indefinitely, of course. But
the dangers confronting reporters didn't abate with the Taliban's ouster.
After the first spate of killings and kidnappings, the BBC and a number of
US organizations opted to pull out rather than further imperil the lives of
their personnel. At the start of December 2001, the *Guardian* reported
that the Taliban had placed a $50,000 bounty on the head of western jour-
nalists, while Walter Cronkite, the eminence grise of US network news,
declared Afghanistan 'the most dangerous [situation] that correspondents
have ever put themselves in in modern times' (Campbell, 2001, 2).

As quickly as it had descended in October, the western press pack
dispersed and left in December, briefly returning in mid-2002 when an
assembly of national power-brokers, the *loya jirga*, met to choose new
Afghan leaders. The consequence of this exodus was predictable: a rapid
decline in coverage of the war in Afghanistan by print and broadcast
news media, once again dependent on official briefings supplemented by
reports from local stringers. Before long, Afghanistan was being referred
to, *when* it was referred to, as the 'forgotten war.' This neglect became all
the more pronounced after the start of Operation Iraqi Freedom in March
2003. Whereas in January 2002 US network news had together aired a
monthly total of 106 minutes on Afghanistan, the comparable figure a
year later was 11 minutes. In March 2003, it was a scant 60 seconds

(Robertson, 2003, 24). By 2005, only two US news organizations had full-time reporters in Kabul, *Newsweek* and the *Washington Post*. Nightly broadcast news coverage amounted to 147 minutes for the entire year (Hart, 2005, 12; Ricchiardi, 2006, 48–55). Explaining this fall-off, foreign news editors cited truncated domestic attention spans and shrinking budgets in a faltering economy. Afghanistan, it seemed, had been a notoriously expensive splurge back in 2001. Resources being in short supply, the obvious choice was to concentrate on Iraq, a story several editors regarded as essentially the same but bigger and fresher: ousting the 'bad guys' followed by a protracted effort at nation-building (Robertson, 2003).

Despite the press's chaotic retreat in December 2001, Afghanistan soon became stamped as a *victory*, at least by US media. The prematurity of this verdict should have been (and was) obvious to those observing the tenuous grip of Afghanistan's new, US-backed rulers over the country as a whole. But the same unquestioning embrace of Operation Enduring Freedom that muted criticism of DOD reporting restrictions also impeded American journalists' willingness to ask searching questions about how, and how well, this war was being conducted. As one reporter mused retrospectively in 2003, the media were in a position akin to 'reporting on the home football team, the hometown fans and hometown football team headed for the Super Bowl, and that's perhaps understandable. You don't want – nobody, I think, wants – to splash cold water on this sort of mood' (Hess and Kalb, 2003, 100). And none did.

Drawing on experience from Kosovo, the Bush administration also enjoyed signal success in wrapping the war in Afghanistan in the discursive drapery of human rights. In mid-November, concerned that reporters on the ground were placing too much credence in Taliban statements and setting insufficient store by the Pentagon's, Victoria Clarke and her British counterpart Alistair Campbell established new 'Coalition Information Centers' in Islamabad, London, and Washington. One of the Clarke–Campbell partnership's key aims was to encourage the media to adhere to approved 'messages of the day,' and one of their earliest (and largest) successes was the 'women campaign' (Rid, 2007, 103–4). With contributors ranging from Condoleezza Rice to Cherie Blair and Laura Bush, Operation Enduring Freedom was pitched as a campaign to emancipate women and girls from oppression by the Taliban (Cloud, 2004; Dubriwny, 2005; Shepherd, 2006). Judged by this yardstick, the operation was a success, or so at least the White House presented it. Afghan women had been liberated from their burkas. For the first time in years, girls could attend schools – schools which US troops would rebuild.

Confronted with this insistent message, liberal critics found themselves in a bind. Opposition to the war could readily be depicted as injurious to the cause of women's rights, a cause they had no wish to hamper. Few commentators noted that the *loya jirga* convened under US auspices in June 2002 included not a single woman, or drew attention to the parlous human rights record of the Northern Alliance. Even fewer questioned the politics of Bush's claim to be rescuing Muslim 'women of cover' (Abu-Lughod, 2002).

Stories about Afghan women tended to be congratulatory tales of emancipation and beautification. But one aspect of the official narrative did come under mounting scrutiny: namely, the issue of civilian casualties of airstrikes. In the opening phase of Operation Enduring Freedom, American and British military commanders and political leaders stressed that airpower was employed with humanitarian objectives firmly in mind, referencing the food parcels that were being dropped over remote areas of Afghanistan. DOD briefings also painstakingly detailed the astonishing precision of missiles used to 'take out' terrorist hideouts in Afghanistan – give or take the odd 'error.' When journalists began reporting the use of daisy cutter bombs, however, it was clear that US airpower in Afghanistan could also be an extremely blunt weapon.

Despite the name's suggestion of floral delicacy, the daisy cutter weighs 15,000 pounds, measures 17 feet in length and five feet in diameter – about the same size as a Volkswagen Beetle – and obliterates everything within a 600-yard radius. Precision targeting is scarcely the point of such a weapon. Rather, it is intended to 'psychologically unhinge the enemy': to encourage terrorized soldiers to surrender before unquestionably superior military power. But this psychological effect doesn't happen without massive physical destruction – a point that descriptions of this weapon's utility to psyops tends to overlook. In an irregular war, with no clear spatial separation between insurgents and civilians, and hence no discrete battle-space, use of a 15,000 pound bomb will necessarily generate civilian casualties. Some humans aren't reduced to 'gibbering wrecks,' in the words of Robert Hewson (editor of *Jane's Air Launched Weapons*), without others being reduced to nothing at all (Williams, 2001).

No issue reveals the divergence between US media and other news organizations' coverage of Afghanistan more starkly than that of civilian casualties of air power. Initial reports of the daisy cutter's use already suggested a divergence of attitude that would deepen over time. Most US press stories on November 6, 2001 introduced this Pentagon-confirmed detail in a casually matter-of-fact way to underscore the allies' seriousness

Illustration 6.2 US Department of Defense leaflet, dropped early in the war in Afghanistan, encourages Taliban fighters to surrender by illustrating the devastating destructive power of American bombs.

Source: Library of Congress.

of purpose in 'smoking out' Al Qaeda terrorists from their mountain hideaways. While the bomb's colossal destructive power was routinely mentioned, its enormity attracted no negative commentary. After all, the daisy cutter's intended target was Osama bin Laden and his henchmen. That being so, some headlines and op-eds were positively congratulatory in tone. 'Give war a chance,' urged *The New York Times*' liberal columnist, Maureen Dowd, arguing that these bombs could no more be relied on to 'get the rat' unassisted than could the feckless Northern Alliance, whose fighters 'smoke and complain more than they fight.' Daisy cutters were all well and good, but ground troops would also be required (Dowd, 2001, 23).

In Britain, the news elicited a more varied response. Several papers greeted this confirmation of the airwar's escalation in gleefully vengeful tones akin. 'Pulverized by the Daisy Cutter,' ran the *Daily Mail*'s November 7 headline, suggesting that whatever was rained down on the terrorists couldn't do enough damage (Williams, 2001, 16). But since the 'war on terror' enjoyed less unanimity of sentiment in Britain than in the US, it was also predictable that some op-ed columns would sound a cautionary note. The *Guardian*'s Seamus Milne duly warned that the 'new appetite for intervention [would] only increase the likelihood of anti-western terror' (Milne, 2001).

Whether caused by daisy cutters or other types of missiles dropped from manned aircraft or unmanned drones, civilian casualties became a central focus of reporting from Afghanistan in most countries other than the United States. In the early stages of Operation Enduring Freedom, major US news outlets were often extremely reluctant to tackle the issue at all – including organizations such as National Public Radio (NPR) and CNN, regarded as 'liberal media' by right-wing critics. It's particularly telling, then, that CNN's senior management insisted that when news stories reported civilian fatalities in Afghanistan these deaths be relativized by a 'balancing' reference to those killed on 9/11 (Bamford, 2001, 20). 'We must redouble our efforts to make sure we do not seem to be reporting from [the Taliban's] vantage or perspective,' cautioned CNN chief Walter Isaacson in a staff memo. 'We must talk about how the Taliban are using civilian shields and how [they] have harbored terrorists responsible for killing close to 5,000 innocent people' (Kulman, Newman and Mazzetti, 2001, 44). In other words, Afghan civilians killed by airstrikes couldn't be seen as blameless victims. To draw attention to their suffering was thus to peddle Taliban propaganda. Body counts were what *they* did, and of course the Taliban would exaggerate egregiously. 'It seems too perverse to focus too much on the casualties and hardships in Afghanistan,' Isaacson declared, making explicit the primacy of American suffering that colored much US reporting after 9/11 (Nimmo, 2002).

In the United States, few wanted to hear about Afghan civilian casualties in late 2001. CNN's injunction against covering this issue was soon matched by Fox News (Rutenberg, 2001b, C1). Reporters who did file such stories often found themselves furiously rebuked by listeners, readers, and viewers. In the period of more intense journalistic concentration on Afghanistan, from October 2001 to March 2003, one study found that while more than 800 US press stories on casualties focused on reporters who had been killed there, fewer than 40 reports detailed Afghan civilians' deaths (Rentschler, 2004, 303). Meanwhile, protest in the Islamic world against Operation Enduring Freedom was dismissed by CNN as 'loud and noisy, but controlled' – a gestural display of Muslim volatility, full of sound and fury that need not be taken too seriously (CNN, 2001c).

But the rising casualties couldn't be willed away. Although the US military maintained the stance adopted during the 1991 Gulf War – that it no longer 'did' body counts – several organizations, such as Human Rights Watch and iCasualties.org, have sought to document and verify civilian casualties, using the internet both to compile and publicize data. Journalists of other nationalities have also devoted sustained attention to the issue of civilian casualties, particularly in countries such as the UK and Germany where participation in the 'war on terror' occasioned more public dissent than in the US. Asked at a panel discussion in February 2002 why Americans journalists hadn't pursued the casualty question more rigorously, Tom Squitieri of *USA Today* cited the extreme difficulty of verifying civilian deaths and ascertaining precise figures and the superior scrupulousness of US news media, with 'higher reporting standards than foreign media' – a defensive jab that seems to obscure other reasons why American journalists exhibited less interest in documenting this war's casualties (Fleeson, 2002, 18).

The starkest discrepancy, however, wasn't between US and European news organizations but between western media, broadly defined, and Al Jazeera, which in 2001 claimed an audience of some 35 million Arabic-speakers (Hickey, 2002, 40). Soon after 9/11, Al Jazeera attracted American attention, and a good deal of opprobrium, for running bin Laden's taped messages – messages that National Security Advisor Condoleezza Rice requested US networks not to air without prior official approval on the improbable grounds that they could contain coded messages to Al Qaeda operatives (Krimsky, 2002, 57). In the editorial judgement of the *New York Daily News*, this made the network 'one of the most potent weapons in the Islamic Axis arsenal' (quoted by Quinn and Walters, 2004, 59). From Al Jazeera's perspective, though, giving airtime to bin Laden was perfectly reasonable, quite in keeping with the network's motto, 'The Opinion and the Other Opinion.' Following Al Qaeda's attacks on the World Trade Center and Pentagon, bin Laden was undoubtedly a major protagonist in international affairs whose utterances required airtime, as did those of Bush administration officials. Responding to the charge that Al Jazeera was, in effect, the 'bid Laden Channel,' Dana Suyyagh, a former employee, crisply observed: 'Maybe. But that would make us Bush's mouthpiece as well. He gets more airtime, actually' (quoted by Tatham, 2006, 193).

In October 2001, Al Jazeera was the sole international media organization represented in Kabul, having established an office there in 1999. As US airstrikes began, the Taliban government ordered western journalists out. Al Jazeera, however, was permitted to remain, and was thus uniquely positioned to document the bombing. Immediately, its cameramen were in the streets of Kabul, filming scenes of rubble-strewn streets and interviewing residents whose homes had been destroyed – footage the network sold to CNN (Jasperson and El-Kikhia, 2003, 115). Posted to Al Jazeera's website, this material – the only extant visual depiction of what was going on in Kabul – attracted millions of hits.

When Al Jazeera's own building was destroyed by two 500-pound US bombs on November 12, as Kabul fell to the Northern Alliance, skeptics doubted the American military claim that this hit was unintentional. Al Jazeera personnel were adamant that the coordinates of its office were well known to American authorities (Zednick, 2002, 45). Moreover, Washington had made little secret of its disdain for Al Jazeera, with Vice President Dick Cheney and Secretary of State Colin Powell both pressuring the emir of Qatar to 'muzzle' the channel. Writing in the *New York Times Magazine*, Fouad Ajami (a Johns Hopkins professor and prominent supporter of the war) lamented the network's tendentious and inflammatory coverage. 'In its rough outlines, the message of Al Jazeera is similar to that of the Taliban: there is a huge technological imbalance between the antagonists, but the foreign power will nonetheless come to grief.' His point was clear. Representing the twin menace of Osama (the network's 'star') and the Taliban combined and amplified, Al Jazeera wasn't just a mouthpiece for the enemy, it *was* the enemy – a 'dangerous force' which 'should be treated as such.' It stood to reason, Ajami noted, that 'the problem of Al Jazeera's role in the current crisis is one that the White House has been trying to solve' (Ajami, 2001). Given that the station's Kabul office had been bombed just days earlier, Ajami's essay read as an extended justification, though his lengthy cover story nowhere mentioned an airstrike that the Pentagon represented as accidental.

Ajami was right that Al Jazeera didn't scruple to point out the technological imbalance between the Taliban and the US-led coalition military. In like fashion, it had consistently depicted the Second Intifada between Palestinians and the Israeli Defense Force as a battle between mismatched contestants – the former resisting the 'terrorism' of the latter. Similarly, after March 2003, Al Jazeera would refer not to 'Operation Iraqi Freedom' but the 'War On Iraq:' a preposition no American network would ever have contemplated. To detractors, these news frames underscore the network's irremediable institutional bias, itself expressive of deep-seated anti-Americanism and anti-Semitism. In the eyes of Al Jazeera's news managers, however, depicting these stark imbalances and drawing attention to the illicit character of US aggression against Iraq, or Israeli brutality towards Palestinians, is not a manifestation of bias so much as a statement of the self-evident (Iskandar and El-Nawawy, 2004).

Al Jazeera correspondents are equally adamant that to cover a war requires unflinching treatment of its casualties on both sides – a position that further fueled American charges of sensationalism against a network seen as fanning the flames of fanaticism on the 'Arab street.' In the words of editor-in-chief Ibrahim Hilal, 'We have to show that there are people killed in this war.' This commitment to showing 'the horror of the bombing campaign, the blown-out brains, the blood spattered pavements, the screaming infants, and the corpses' was evident in Afghanistan in 2001. It would become yet clearer in Iraq in March 2003 (Seib, 2005, 602).

Operation Iraqi Freedom: the 'soda straw war'

Despite US news organizations' hesitance to broach difficult questions in Afghanistan, the Pentagon was evidently less than satisfied with both media performance and its own handling of the press. The Pentagon's initial refusal to permit reporters anywhere near the scene of military operations had encouraged the emergence of what it disparagingly referred to as 'four-wheel-drive' or 'cowboy' journalism: wandering gonzos who were liable to reproduce exaggerated claims about civilian casualties without the corrective influence of American troops to curb their credulity. For the US military, Afghanistan offered a cautionary example of what happened when the opponent achieved a 'first-strike' capability in setting the casualty agenda. Captain Terry McCreary (Chairman of the Joint Chiefs of Staff's special assistant for public affairs) described his frustration with this situation in Afghanistan: 'You'd raid a camp, there wouldn't be any press with you, you do an operation, you leave, the enemy comes back, the press come in, and everybody tells them you murdered innocent people, you slaughtered them, and that becomes a story for the next 48 hours until you can fix it' (quoted by Rid, 2007, 107).

What to do? For McCreary the answer was clear:

> the only way you can counter deception was to have the truth told first. The only way to do that is have an independent truth-teller tell it first. The only way to have an independent teller tell it first, is to have them with us. And the only way to have them with us was to embed. (Rid, 2007, 108)

Embedding, as the Pentagon called it, duly became the preferred strategy in Iraq to ensure that no retrospective 'fixing' was required. The story would be fixed from the very outset – by 'independent truth tellers' telling things from a perspective entirely dependent on the US military.

By 2006, the claim that Operation Iraqi Freedom had been inadequately planned had become a standard complaint, voiced by those who favored the March 2003 invasion and anti-war critics alike (Ricks, 2006). But in one domain it was hard to argue that pre-war planning had been dilatory or half-hearted. The campaign to manage the 'information environment' – to package this operation with all the pyrotechnic panache of a new Hollywood blockbuster – consumed considerable time, attention and money in Washington, with the White House establishing a new Office of Global Communications to coordinate the war's hi-tech, multimedia presentation in a way that would appeal to the diminished attention span of the digital-age citizen-consumer (Boyer, 2003). In the estimation of *The Nation*'s Carol Brightman, the Bush administration coordinated 'a wartime media campaign as audacious as any ever attempted' (Brightman, 2003, 5). This initiative offered journalists positive inducements to get on side, while hinting that those who strayed off-message could expect more than a cold shoulder. When Defense Secretary Donald Rumsfeld delivered his first briefing of the war in front of an image of a little girl in pigtails captioned 'Don't kill her Daddy with careless words,' the point was as clear it was emotionally manipulative (Purdum and Rutenberg, 2003).

The inaugural outing of the war's commander, General Tommy Franks on March 22, 2003, day three of Operation Iraqi Freedom, was calculated to produce a differently impressive effect. Appearing at centcom's Coalition Media Center outside Doha, Qatar, Franks was 'surrounded by a thirty-eight-foot map of the world, digital clocks displaying the time in the war zone and in Washington, and an array of plasma video screens projecting battlefield images,' noted *The New Yorker*'s Peter J. Boyer. But though the general 'seemed to be at the very epicentre of the global war on terrorism,' he was in fact 'standing on a

Illustration 6.3   General Tommy Franks appears on a specially constructed media briefing stage at the Coalition Media Center, Camp As Sayliyah, Doha, Qatar, 2003

Source: Richard Lewis/AP/Wide World Photos.

briefing stage, finished just days before the war (at a cost of $250,000), that had been devised by a Hollywood set designer to look like the hub of decision and, by implication, of news.' As Boyer sardonically noted, 'actual news emanated from the Coalition Media Center only by mistake, however, when someone strayed from the script' (Boyer, 2003).

Indeed, Franks would make just two further appearances during the March–May phase of Operation Iraqi Freedom (Knight, 2003). The main source of 'big picture' briefings was the Pentagon, which together with the new Office of Global Communications had crafted a presentational style aimed to merge seamlessly with news programs' amalgam of complex animations, film footage, archival stills, split screens, scrolling headlines and music (Brockus, 2009, 32). These briefings were held daily at the Pentagon, presided over by an ebullient Defense Secretary, accompanied by the chairman of the Joint Chiefs of Staff, General Richard Myers. But the mode of news delivery that generated most excitement, and controversy, in the early days of Operation Iraqi Freedom was that provided by the 'embeds' – reporters ensconced within particular military units.

Hailed by the Pentagon as a revolutionary innovation in wartime press policy, the scheme permitted more than 600 journalists to be embedded with the US Army, Air Force, Navy and Marines for periods ranging from a few days to several weeks, with a further 128 journalists joining the British forces. As a laudatory 2004 RAND report put it, reporters 'travelled with the soldiers in their units, saw what the soldiers saw, and were under fire when troops were' (Paul and Kim, 2004, xiii). Unlike the 1991 Gulf War, when many members of the media reporting teams found themselves immobilized in the rear echelon, the Pentagon promised that far more embeds would receive frontline access to Operation Iraqi Freedom. And while reporters would have to agree to certain basic ground rules regarding the use of communications equipment and sensitive material they could not report, they would nevertheless be empowered to transmit their own copy and images using personal digital satellite phones (Paul and Kim, 2004, 28). This represented a signal difference from 1991, when all text and footage was subjected to 'security review' before onward transmission via military channels. In 2003, media outlets retained exclusive proprietorship over their reporters' output.

In other ways too the embed scheme struck many large news organizations as a distinct improvement on its predecessor. During the earlier war against Iraq, membership of media reporting teams with American forces had been restricted to US nationals, with slots monopolized by the biggest media players. This time, however, there were to be reporters of many nationalities and both sexes, with 67 women among the initial participants (Rid, 2007, 112). The Pentagon made a point of publicizing that the embed program encompassed some 100 foreign outlets, including the Russian news agency Itar-Tass and Al Jazeera, though the latter's embeds quickly disengaged, citing obstructionism from US officers who refused to brief them because theirs was a 'station with a reputation' (Katovsky and Carlson, 2003, 182). The scheme further differed from its 1991 progenitor by including a greater variety of media outlets, including cable channel MTV, and popular magazines such as *Rolling Stone*, *People*, and *Men's Health*. This more expansive approach reflected the Pentagon's appreciation that many people – the 'accidentally attentive public' – don't regularly read newspapers or watch television news, but receive information through feature-led 'soft news' formats such as talk shows and lifestyle magazines (Purdum and Rutenberg, 2003; Baum, 2003).

Given their institutional affiliations, many of the embeds weren't *news* reporters in the conventional sense, and they certainly weren't well-seasoned foreign or defense correspondents. Since at least some of them would accompany frontline combat forces, the embed scheme also entailed a brief stint at 'media boot camp' for the journalistic enlistees (Lindner, 2009, 22–3). This experience itself became a choice pre-war story – whether narrated in the thrilled tones of the new uniformed initiate, delighted with the paraphernalia of the warrior class, or given a more gothic treatment that emphasized the macabre preparations for gas attacks that Saddam was expected to unleash (Ayres, 2005).

Some reporters opted to 'disembed' as a result of their boot camp experiences, raising questions about the unreasonable peril that frontline reporting posed to untrained civilians. *The New Yorker*'s Hampton Sides took flight after one officer told him 'We want you there to document the gas and the other stuff Saddam has in his arsenal. If he has it, or, God forbid, uses it, the world's not going to believe the US Army. But they'll believe you' (Sides, 2003a). Sides was not alone in choosing to forego this demonstration effect. However, to reassure journalists that they were more than simply pit canaries and to underscore the embedding scheme's virtues, the military offered an array of other positive explanations. The Pentagon, its boosters claimed, had scaled a steep learning curve after the unsatisfactory early days of Operation Enduring Freedom, prompted to adopt this 'gutsy,' 'risky' strategy by the DOD's great innovator, Donald Rumsfeld. 'I doubt that in a conflict of this type there's ever been the degree of free press coverage as you are witnessing in this instance,' he boasted (Purdum and Rutenberg, 2003).

For the US military, this up-close coverage had a number of attractions. For one, it would furnish a visual and verbal record of martial endeavor signally lacking from the Gulf War of 1991. In the opinion of Michael Kelly of the *Atlantic Monthly*, 'There was a real sense after the last gulf war that witness had been lost ... The people in the military care about that history a great deal, because it is their history. I think that was the primal motivating impulse here' (Carr, 2003). That embedded reporters would also be able to disprove spurious claims about 'collateral damage' represented another plus. As Deputy Assistant Secretary of Defense for Media Relations Bryan Whitman explained it: 'We realized early on that our adversary was a practiced liar. What better way to mitigate the lies and deception of Saddam Hussein than by having trained, objective observers out there in the field?' (Carr, 2003). Furthermore, he added, the US public 'deserved to see exactly how well trained their military forces were, how dedicated and professional' (Purdum and Rutenberg, 2003).

This arresting statement – that Americans *deserved* to admire their troops' professionalism – hinted at the most substantial critique of embedded journalism. Namely, that its intention was to bring reporters' and soldiers' perspectives into complete alignment. As a result, civilian audiences in the US would also apprehend the war through the military's sights: a spectatorial position that would enhance popular support for the invasion and occupation of Iraq. After all, the viewpoint of soldiers under fire is hardly conducive to critical reflection on the war's politics. Survival is the sole preoccupation. When the dominant trope of reporting is that of deadly threat – of troops facing sniper fire, explosions, and rocket attacks – the invading forces necessarily appear not as aggressors, themselves inflicting harm, but as beleaguered *victims*. Questions about the legitimacy of Operation Iraqi Freedom simply couldn't be broached from this perspective, since embedded reporting allowed no critical space for the coalition military to be understood as anything other than an imperilled force of liberation.

How could journalists, themselves coming under fire alongside their units, possibly *not* identify with the uniformed men and women on whom their protection depended? 'Nothing creates empathy like a three-hundred mile ride inside a Bradley Fighting vehicle,' noted one caustic observer, while a jauntier UPI correspondent put a more positive gloss on this enforced intimacy: 'Reporters love troops. Put us with those eighteen-year-old kids and we just turn to jelly' (Boyer, 2003; Katovsky and Carlson, 2003, xiii). It stood to reason that journalists would replicate their minders' point of view, unselfconsciously adopting a first person plural mode of address. As one embed later recalled: 'When a unit was fired on, the story said "We were fired upon," instead of: unit X was fired upon. In battle the journalist hoped for the victory of his unit because his own life and safety relied on it' (Brockus, 2009, 34). Some reporters, like *The Boston Globe*'s Scott Bernard Nelson, further acknowledged that they'd helped soldiers scope out targets when they found themselves under sniper attack, becoming active participants in combat, not its detached chroniclers (Nelson, 2003).

Other journalists insisted that, despite the undoubted proximity and dependence by media personnel on the military, they nevertheless maintained their professional objectivity. Thus Ted Koppel of ABC proudly declared: 'I am an American citizen, and I love these young men and women for what they are doing. But that doesn't mean that as a journalist I can't maintain my objectivity.' What could objectivity mean in such circumstances, however? Even allowing for the narrowly mechanistic way in which objectivity has been construed in the American journalistic profession – as balance within a narrow spectrum of elite opinion – embedded reporting ruled out the familiar practice of juxtaposing every 'he said' with a 'she said.' As the *National Reporter*'s George C. Wilson explained, being embedded was like being the second dog on a dogsled team: 'You see and hear a lot of the dog directly in front of you, and you see what is passing by on the left and right, but you cannot get out of the traces to explore intriguing sights you pass, without losing your spot on the moving team' (quoted by Lindner, 2009, 23). In short, there was only one story they were positioned to tell: that of American men and women at war. No other human subjects fell within the reporter's field of vision or access to interview.

That Koppel saw no contradiction between an avowed love for his state's military and professional objectivity alerts us to the way in which patriotic partisanship is often taken as an unproblematic given of wartime reporting – an attachment seemingly so natural as not to constitute any form of bias at all. And indeed so it was with much American embedded journalism. Many reporters adopted a congratulatory stance towards the uniformed personnel involved in Operation Iraqi Freedom, documenting their privations, fears, courage, and commitment in endlessly updated detail but with an unchanging focus of subject and sympathy.

Live transmission amplified these effects of embedding. Viewers watched televised reports from Iraq with the fearful thrill of knowing that if 'anything bad' were to happen – should an IED explode or a sniper take aim at the passing American convoy – the reporter would capture and relay it in real time, or might even become a casualty him- or herself. This 'in-the-moment' quality was constantly underscored by studio-bound news anchors, who not only drew viewers' attention to the live-and-exclusive character of what they were seeing but also frequently interacted with embedded reporters via satellite phone. These dialogs underscored the novelty of the embedding arrangement, conveying a frisson of danger that implied a purely reactive character to coalition military action while conferring on the viewer a sense of special privilege: that of vicarious presence (Brockus, 2009).

Immediacy seemed to confirm embeds' unrivalled authority as firsthand witnesses: the war's simultaneous interpreters for distant civilians. Yet it was often precisely this live connection with the studio anchor that gave the embed something to do, masking the fact that they generally had little hard news to convey. *Chatting*, rather than reporting, was the essential function of the embedded television reporter. After all, what they saw of the campaign's progress was extremely restricted, as was their access to wider sources. Ted Koppel admitted as much in conversation with ABC anchor Peter Jennings when he acknowledged: 'we get much of our news either when we chat with you or when we listen ... to the BBC on shortwave on the hour' (Boyer, 2003).

Rather than doing what war correspondents are commonly imagined to do – providing history's first rough draft – the embeds served primarily as conductors of energy between the battlefield and civilian society. Yet reportage that purported to provide unexpurgated exposure of war in all its nerve-jolting immediacy in fact conveyed a truncated version of one particular point of view, minimizing common elements of combat experience such as incapacitating fear, unrestrained violence and post-traumatic stress. If the embeds didn't ignore 'dark stories' altogether, their somber shades were reserved almost exclusively for coalition forces' privations – not those of Iraqi civilians (Lindner, 2009, 45).

While some commentators questioned the politics of embedding, others aired more aesthetic or commercial concerns as to whether it made for 'good television' (Lewis *et al.*, 2006; Miller, 2004). Writing in *The New York Times*, Charles McGrath complained that 'within a week or so, the television coverage of the invasion had become so confusing, so repetitive – so boring for the most part – that it was almost as burdensome to turn it on as it was not.' The footage, such as long tracking shots of the desert as seen from atop a moving tank, wasn't nearly as compelling as the fact that it was broadcast live from Iraq's moving frontline. This thrill quickly wore off, yet no matter how visually tedious or uninformative, such material was broadcast simply because it could be – and because, in an era when liveness is considered a key attribute of good TV, the images' immediacy promised to redeem all other deficiencies (Brockus, 2009, 30–1).

Was the Pentagon privately hoping that American viewers' attention deficit disorder would kick in after the initial excitement of 'shock and awe' had dulled? Or did Operation Iraqi Freedom's planners expect that it would be over so quickly that there wouldn't be time for home front audiences either to lose interest or start asking pointed questions about why Iraqis weren't greeting their liberators with overwhelming displays of appreciation? It certainly appears that the US military was taken aback by the sporadically fierce resistance coalition forces met on their route to Baghdad, worrying that embedded reporters might accentuate sudden mood-swings, from premature proclamations of victory to equally unwarranted projections of disaster or intimations of a quagmire in the making.

Intensive efforts were thus undertaken by Pentagon spokespersons to allay the 'week-two wobble,' when the offensive began to stall after its dynamic opening thrust. At the same time, troubling news surfaced of a British plane being shot down by a Patriot missile, a 'friendly fire' incident that killed all aboard, and of a fragging episode in the 101st Airborne Division in central Kuwait (Boyer, 2003). Briefly, it seemed that the great advantage to the military of embedded reporting – its blinkered perspective – might become a liability. Just as reporters had been charged with misrepresenting the Tet offensive in 1968 by focusing exclusively on the disorder immediately visible to them, not the larger strategic picture, so DOD personnel feared that embeds might do something similar in April 2003. By relating that their units were getting 'bogged down,' meeting sustained resistance, or exhibiting signs of indiscipline, panicked reporters threatened to generate public opposition to a putatively long war – not the 'cakewalk' Americans had been led to expect (Paul and Kim, 2004, 55).

However, this quiver was soon stilled. On April 1, the televised rescue of Army private Jessica Lynch by Special Operations forces, after she had been held under guard in an Iraqi hospital, gave Centcom a 'tipping point in the message war' – a staged captivity drama that would later attract much skeptical commentary (Boyer, 2003; McAlister, 2003). On April 9, footage of Iraqis pulling down a statue of Saddam Hussein in Baghdad's Firdos Square provided a striking bookend to the campaign: an image that, at least in much US media framing, crystallized Operation Iraqi Freedom's success in toppling a tyrannous regime (Tatham, 2006, 136–40). By the third week of April, many embeds had returned home again. Once Bush had declared victory on May 2, 2003, the 'Iraq War' began to be spoken of as a discrete event in the past tense.

Looking back on the six weeks of Operation Iraqi Freedom, many analysts announced themselves well pleased with how embedding had worked: a 'win–win–win proposition' for military, media, and public alike enthused a Brookings Institution report (Paul and Kim, 2004, 110). Military commentators conceded that such micro-focused journalism produced a 'soda-straw view of the world' (James DeFrank, quoted by Rid, 2007, 152). But they also stressed a penetrative reach that compensated for the narrow aperture, enabling what Bryan Whitman called 'extremely deep, rich coverage.' In an age when networked media users routinely trolled on-line for nuggets of information, assembling their worldview in magpie fashion from multiple sources, this bricolage approach to war reporting was satisfyingly up-to-the-minute. As Vincent Morris of the *New York Post* put it: 'This war is whatever piece of dirt you are sitting on. I'm working with a helicopter unit, so if you were only reading me, you'd think the whole war was about helicopters.' But presumably no media-savvy American would be foolish enough to make such a myopic mistake (Carr, 2003). Moreover, if the individual slices of reality offered by embeds didn't quite add up to a complete pie, the Pentagon briefings supplied that 360-degree overview.

In expressing satisfaction with their bold experiment, Department of Defense officials also cited polling evidence that demonstrated US public enthusiasm for embedded journalism. A widely cited Pew Research Center report found 80 per cent of respondents considered embedded reports 'fair and objective' (Jurkowitz, 2003). As we've seen before, the idea that war might be represented as a multifaceted phenomenon eliciting diverse and conflicted human responses on all sides is typically a minority position in wartime. When their country is at war, many citizens apparently expect – or even demand – that war stories are presented exclusively from their own side's point of view. Moreover, in the name of 'supporting the troops' breathing room for critical reflection on the war's larger ambitions or its human consequences is tightly compressed, as though discussion itself were a form of wartime sabotage. This stifling of dissent – from the bottom up as well as the top down – was particularly evident in 2003, with *causes célèbres* such as the consumer boycott of best-selling country band, the Dixie Chicks, for having expressed opposition to the war and regret that Bush hailed from their own state of Texas. To demonstrate outrage, fans gathered to deposit their CDs for crushing by bulldozers, and one Colorado radio station sacked two disc jockeys who continued to play the Texan group's music (CNN, 2003).

An intolerance of pluralism was also evident in the US military's practices on the ground in Iraq, for while Whitman claimed that the 'big picture' would emerge when individuals pieced together multiple sources, one piece still remained signally absent: Iraqi subjects. When the coalition's 'shock and awe' bombing campaign began, its ground-level impact was reported by a handful of foreign journalists then under the control of the Iraqi Ministry of Information, which was eager to expose these journalists to bomb damage but made for an unreliable intermediary between reporters and civilians (Garrels, 2004). Once Saddam Hussein's regime collapsed, these Baghdad-based reporters were joined by an influx of other so-called unilaterals – that is, journalists who were not formally embedded with coalition forces but also had to agree to a set of Pentagon ground rules and wear a badge with the word 'unilateral' emblazoned in red letters (Lindner, 2009, 24). Of the 2,200 reporters in Iraq in March/April 2003, some 1,400 belonged to this category (Haigh *et al.*, 2006, 140). As several subsequently attested, they encountered considerable hostility from the US military, which turned the term unilateral into a pejorative laden with the taint of treachery.

In military eyes, to step outside the embedded arrangement was to declare one's opposition to Operation Iraqi Freedom and thus to invite rough treatment. Writing in the on-line journal *Slate* on May 1, 2003, Jack Shafter noted that 'unilaterals were often treated as pests with no right to the battlefield.' In the southern cities of Basra, Umm Qasr, Nasiriyah and Safwan they were prevented from reporting altogether. Tension reached a head on March 23, 2003 with the death of ITN journalist Terry Lloyd and two colleagues, who were shot by US military personnel – or accidentally caught in crossfire, depending on which version of the story one credited – despite their vehicle being plastered with 'TV' in large taped letters (Gopsill, 2004, 253–4). Equally controversial was the April 8 bombing of Al Jazeera's Baghdad office building, which killed Tareq Ayyoub, a Jordanian reporter. Although the strike was justified by American briefers as self-defensive, US troops having allegedly come under sustained fire from the building, this account was rejected by Al Jazeera editor-in-chief Ibrahim Hilal (Iskandar and El-Nawawy, 2004, 325). If Iraq quickly displaced Afghanistan as the world's most lethal reporting destination, the source of danger didn't appear restricted to Baathist fedayeen or Shiite militias.

Meanwhile, as the campaign to pacify Iraq lengthened, in tandem with an intensification of violence in Afghanistan, reports began to surface that the Pentagon was using a private PR company, the Rendon Group, to vet applicants to the embed program in place in both countries (Bamford, 2005). Their background checks included sampling journalists' past stories to ascertain whether their outlook was basically well disposed towards the military. *Stars and Stripes* reported that two of its reporters who had fallen out of favour were debarred from Afghanistan after such background checks, while the fear of being negatively profiled blunted others' critical edge. Although the Pentagon denied that profiling had served this restrictive/coercive function, it did cancel the Rendon Group's contract in September 2009 (*The New York Times*, 2009). But the vetting program itself suggests an extraordinary degree of official sensitivity to negative coverage, coupled with a lack of confidence that embedding would work its own positive spin on journalists' appreciation of the twin wars in Iraq and Afghanistan.

Unauthorized images: caskets, prisoners and corpses

The Bush administration's eagerness to mold attitudes towards the wars in Iraq and Afghanistan – both domestic opinion and foreigners' increasingly hostile perceptions of US military action – assumed numerous guises, overt and more clandestine. The same Rendon Group that was engaged to run background checks on journalists had also assisted the Pentagon in attempting to tamp down the civilian casualties issue in Afghanistan, monitoring international news coverage and convening focus groups to help the administration hone its message delivery (Strobel and Landay, 2001). In 2002, the Pentagon awarded Rendon another contract, this time focused predominantly on Al Jazeera: to provide daily digests of its output, identify individual journalists' biases and trace their 'specific relationships and sponsors' – in other words, to insinuate espionage connections. News of such activities periodically surfaced in the US press without decisively calling a halt to practices that were not, after all, unprecedented. John Rendon had also been active in assisting the exiled Kuwaiti royal family craft its PR message in 1990, later taking personal credit for supplying the small US flags that Kuwaitis waved at the advancing coalition forces (Bamford, 2005).

The most controversial, and certainly most explicit, of the Bush administration's efforts to contain wartime image-making was the ban on photography of caskets containing the corpses of US military personnel killed in Afghanistan and Iraq. In March 2003, the Pentagon reiterated a policy intermittently observed hitherto that dated from the 1991 Gulf War. 'There will be no arrival ceremonies for, or media coverage of, deceased military personnel returning to or departing from Ramstein air base or Dover base, to include interim stops,' announced a DOD directive, referencing bases in Germany and Delaware which serve as the main facilities through which US soldiers' bodies return. The ban initially went so far as to prohibit families of the deceased from attending the arrivals altogether – an injunction lifted in May 2004, while keeping the ban on photography in place. Defending the policy, Senator John Warner (R-Va), chairman of the Senate Armed Services Committee, told the *Washington Post* that it was necessary to 'preserve the most important priority, and that's the privacy of the families' (Penrod, 2004, 7).

Such scruples had not prevailed in previous US wars, however. On the contrary, pictures of coffins swathed in the stars and stripes have formed a recurrent motif of approved wartime iconography. One signal break-through in the OWI's strategy of greater visual realism during World War II was licensing news-magazines to publish precisely such images after FDR's initial reticence was replaced by a new emphasis on 'grimness.' *Life* duly featured on its July 5, 1943 cover a photograph of six service-men bearing aloft a flag-draped coffin (Brewer, 2009, 122). Rather than triggering twitchy anti-war sentiment, such images potentially served to regenerate civic commitment to the war effort.

So ran the OWI's logic in 1943 – but not that of the Bush administration some 60 years later. In 2003, the Pentagon seemed as inured to the putatively recuperative impact of such images as it was unmindful of military families' varied responses to grief, even as the President rhetori-cally urged Americans to accept further fatalities in pursuit of a victory that would redeem earlier losses. Faced with this ban, some bereaved relatives made it clear that they valued privacy less highly than formal acknowledgement of losses that merited a place in the headlines, and hence in public consciousness. Others hoped that wider awareness of the wars' casualties might stir opposition to a cause they didn't believe warranted such sacrifices. And some military families, irrespective of their views on the war, simply asserted a right to witness and record their loved ones' caskets being removed from transport planes at Dover Air Force Base (*Time*, May 3, 2004, 28–9).

The Pentagon's prohibition on photography was challenged in various settings. Critics attacked what they saw as a politically motivated policy to 'conceal the true costs of the war' – eliminating the presumptive 'Dover effect' (namely, declining public approval for a war as coffins return). The sensitivity issue was just a smokescreen. Since the DOD's own website displayed images of coffins containing the corpses of soldiers killed in Korea and Vietnam, and since President Bush himself had used images of coffins of 9/11 victims in campaign ads, the principle of respect for privacy seemed entirely elastic in its official application

(*Quill*, 2004, 7). However, an amendment that would have overturned the ban in the US Senate was voted down by a margin of 54–39 on June 21, 2003. Consequently it wasn't until the following April that the DOD prohibition encountered a frontal assault from two unlikely sources: the employee of an American defense contractor, and the US Air Force.

On Sunday, April 18, 2004, *The Seattle Times* published a large front-page photograph depicting several flag-covered coffins inside a transport plane at Kuwait International Airport under the headline 'The Somber Task of Honoring the Fallen.' It had been taken by Tami Silicio, a civilian cargo worker employed by Maytag Aircraft in Kuwait – employed, that is, until April 21 when she was fired for having disregarded 'government and company rules,' along with her co-worker spouse (*Quill*, 2004, 6). Explaining her motives, Silicio insisted that she had no political objective in mind. Rather, she'd been struck by how reverently military personnel 'work with the fallen heroes.' As a mother who had lost a child herself, she hoped her pictures might bring comfort to families who would be reassured to see the dignity and grace with which their loved ones were handled. She had sent her photographs to a friend in her hometown of Seattle, who then passed them on to their local newspaper. By a curious coincidence, on the same day that Maytag fired Silicio and her husband, an anti-government secrecy activist and curator of www.the-memoryhole.org, Russ Kick, received a CD from the Air Force in response to his Freedom of Information Act request for all photographs showing caskets of US military personnel at Dover taken since February 2003. Some 288 of the images depicted war fatalities, which Kick immediately posted on his website (Penrod, 2004; Smolkin, 2004).

Although its photographic line in the sand had been breached by the Air Force, the Pentagon insisted that the ban still remained in place. This position was maintained until Bush's successor, Barack Obama, ordered a review that led to its lifting in April 2009, albeit with caveats concerning battlefield photographs of US casualties, though the American press scarcely needed to be told to treat such images with extreme caution (Chase, 2009).

But despite the high degree of compliance the Bush administration elicited from media organizations in constraining public perceptions of these wars, a story that broke one week after Tami Silicio was fired underscored the fragility of official control over image-making. Just as Silicio's evocative image was an amateur shot, captured with a digital camera she happened to carry around, so too were the photographs that stunned audiences when they aired on CBS's *Sixty Minutes* on April 28 – pictures taken not by professional photojournalists but by US soldiers and

Military Police (MPs). What they showed were prisoners at Abu Ghraib in Iraq being abused by their American guards. The photographs depicted Iraqi men in an array of different postures of abjection, all thoroughly degrading: posed in sexually humiliating scenarios; chained to beds; hooded with what appeared to be electrodes dangling from them; naked but for women's underwear over their heads; snarled at by dogs as they cowered against filthy prison walls. Some shots also featured their American tormentors, apparently enjoying the degradation ceremonies over which they presided – grinning and giving the thumbs' up, as though larking for the camera on a casual outing. That some of these gleefully sadistic MPs were women also occasioned much comment, not only for the unexpectedness of female participation but because it seemed calculated to humiliate Arab sensibilities yet further.

Responding to these images, several US commentators anticipated that their publication would mark a turning point in the war. Seymour Hersh, the investigative journalist who had exposed My Lai and published a long essay in *The New Yorker* on Abu Ghraib two days after the CBS revelations, proposed that Bush would no longer be able to command popular support in the US for a campaign that, one year along, appeared to be going so badly (*Charlie Rose Show*, 2004; Hersh, 2004). And no one had any doubt that the images would inflame anti-American sentiment throughout the Middle East and beyond – a fear the administration took sufficiently seriously that President Bush himself appeared on two Arab television networks (one sponsored by the US government) to explain that these repugnant pictures did not 'represent America.'

Undoubtedly, the Abu Ghraib photographs further tarnished America's already sullied image in the Muslim world. But despite the immediate furor in the US, these images did not make the Iraq war unsustainable in the way Hersh and others predicted. That the outcry proved rather shortlived and far from unanimous offers another illustration of the point that pictures – even of a kind that might appear to have only one irrefutable meaning – are susceptible to multiple interpretations, and hence have a more diffuse political impact than often posited. Not all Americans looking at the Abu Ghraib photographs saw the same thing. Even those who were aghast at the treatment of prisoners these photos depicted couldn't agree whether this degradation represented torture or, less damagingly, 'abuse.' Few seemed to express particular alarm over the fact that at least one of the images showed a female guard cheerily giving the thumbs up next to an Iraqi male corpse, crudely wrapped in plastic sheeting and packed with ice. The possibility that this prisoner had been beaten to death suggested torture at its lethally unmistakable.

Whatever else could be depicted as merely 'harsh treatment,' a corpse clearly signalled that abuse had overstepped its authorized limits. Killing a detainee is, after all, murder – not mistreatment. With the photographs themselves the center of attention, comparatively little media attention focused on the Pentagon's admission on May 3, 2003 that it was currently investigating 25 prisoner deaths in custody.

One reason why the gravest implication of the Abu Ghraib story went under-attended was that many of those looking at the pictures were far less interested in their degraded Iraqi subjects than in the *Americans* in the frame: the leering MPs and the picture-takers. Without the pictures, it was widely agreed, there would have been no scandal. (One appalled MP triggered the uproar by handing a CD to the Army's Criminal Investigation Division – some of these images later being aired by CBS (Hersh, 2004).) With the photographs in public circulation, the state of Iraq's prisons could no longer be kept under wraps. CBS's revelation begged questions as to why the guards had photographed themselves, and what kind of informal distribution such images enjoyed among military personnel. Were these pictures a kind of macabre collectors' card swapped for pleasure? Was photography itself a form of torture – a force multiplier of abuse – that could be used to heighten the shame and humiliation of prisoners so depicted (Eisenman, 2007, 35)? Or were the images, as some of the arraigned MPs later averred, taken to attest abuses with a view to later exposing them (Carruthers, 2007)?

For other commentators, the central issue raised by the pictures wasn't the provenance and purpose of photography in Abu Ghraib, but rather what the actions depicted amounted to, who (if anyone) had authorized them, and what the appropriate punishment was for the perpetrators. Were these MPs just a 'few bad apples,' as Rumsfeld insisted, or had the rot spread down from the top, with these horrifying practices authorized at the apex of the Pentagon and US judicial system? These debates would rumble on for several years, through various official investigations and murmurings that a new incumbent in the White House might initiate criminal proceedings against those, like Donald Rumsfeld and Attorney General Alberto Gonzalez, who had indeed authorized 'enhanced interrogation techniques,' sanctioning the infliction of pain up to any point short of death itself (Danner, 2004).

In May 2004, however, many prominent opinion-formers were adamant that the pictures didn't depict prisoner abuse, let alone torture. Instead, endorsing the '*Animal House* on the night watch' theory, popular radio hosts like Rush Limbaugh (whose show commands a weekly audience of 20 million), stressed that these were just pictures of frustrated and stressed-out guards blowing steam and having a little fun. Really, what the pictures showed was nothing worse than the kind of thing that routinely went on in frat houses across US campuses. Fox News's Bill O'Reilly, meanwhile, invited his viewers to considered whether, in placing Abu Ghraib on its front page on 26 of the previous 28 days, the *Los Angeles Times* hadn't 'declared war on the Bush administration' (Ricchiardi and Cirillo, 2004).

What, then, did the Abu Ghraib scandal reveal of media power in the twenty-first century? Attempting to play one of few trump cards available to the Pentagon in April 2004, Rumsfeld insisted that it showed how far behind the curve investigative journalism had fallen. His department had been onto this story before any reporters sniffed it out, with military investigations already in train weeks before the media got hold of the story (Ricchiardi and Cirillo, 2004, 22). But the Defense Secretary's claims, while they touched a raw journalistic nerve, also smacked of disingenuousness. US newspapers and international wire services *had* reported allegations of prisoner abuses – and of escalating sexual assault within the US military – before CBS aired the infamous photographs on April 28 (Shanker, 2004; Tyson, 2004). Associated Press filed a story on mistreatment at three detention centers, including Abu Ghraib, as early as November 1, 2003. That print and television journalists hadn't subsequently pursued these leads more aggressively suggests several things, including an amount of trepidation over stories that could be viewed as adopting an empathic viewpoint towards Iraqis or Afghans. In other words, news organizations were wary of courting exactly the kind of slur Fox News issued when O'Reilly labelled prisoner abuse a purely partisan weapon. It required some determination, under these circumstances, to pursue a story about the torture of prisoners presumed to be 'terrorist suspects,' even if (as the military later acknowledged) many Iraqi men ended up at Abu Ghraib entirely arbitrarily, the vast majority later released without charge.

But even if reporters *were* minded to pursue this story, as CBS ultimately did, they encountered a severe problem of access. For obvious reasons, prisons aren't locales into which anyone can wander at will. To investigate rumors first hand would have required military authorization, and this was signally lacking. CBS's debut story on Abu Ghraib was delayed by two weeks, its producer Molly Mapes later claimed, by the Army's tardiness in finding someone senior enough, and sufficiently well informed, to comment on the allegations (*Charlie Rose Show*, 2004). As it was, the Abu Ghraib story showed that both television networks and 'slow' print outlets did in fact continue to undertake serious investigative journalism. New media, notably the on-line political journal Salon.com, followed up with Freedom of Information requests – as Russ Kick had earlier done with the coffin images – to secure the release of more photographs, many of which had been withheld by the Pentagon as yet more shocking to public sensibilities. Salon.com posted what they elicited on their website in February 2006. Despite promising a radically different approach to his predecessor, Barack Obama preserved this restrictive approach once he became president in January 2009, continuing to argue that further photographic disclosures would imperil US security.

For the administration, what the Abu Ghraib story most powerfully revealed wasn't the erosion of investigative journalism, but rather the dangers posed by non-professional image-makers – most particularly by soldiers themselves. This wasn't what the new 'network-centric' information warfare was meant to be all about. In the much vaunted Revolution in Military Affairs of the new millennium, soldiers had been reconceived as players on a digitized battlefield whose precise grid coordinates could be constantly tracked by GPS technology, and who would apprehend their surroundings with the aid of helmet-mounted cameras – sci-fi's 'cyborg soldier' made flesh (Der Derian, 2001). That men and women in uniform would be transformed into war's independent documentarians and photojournalists had seemingly not been foreseen by the military; or if this possibility had been mooted, it certainly hadn't been forestalled.

In early twentieth-century wars, military personnel were explicitly debarred from carrying cameras into battle. Britain and France in World War I both treated possession of a camera at the front as a capital offense – a draconian response to a somewhat unlikely scenario, given the paucity of cameras as everyday possessions and their lack of portability as stowaway items (Moeller, 1989). By the early years of the twenty-first century, however, very few soldiers didn't possess a digital camera. The most mundane, and perhaps most plausible, explanation as to why the Abu Ghraib MPs took the pictures that led 11 of them to receive prison sentences themselves, is that their snapping was purely reflexive. Taking digital photos, downloading them, and sharing them by email or on disk has become such ubiquitous behavior as to require no premeditated thought whatsoever. Picture-taking is just what you *do* – in the same way that grinning and making thumbs up signs is how you behave if someone is pointing a camera at you. So, at any rate, some of the guards protested in documentary films made about prisoner abuse, such as Rory Kennedy's *Ghosts of Abu Ghraib*, Alex Gibney's *Taxi to the Dark Side* and Errol Morris's *Standard Operating Procedure* (Carruthers, 2007).

This 'democratization' of image-making signals the photojournalist's diminished authority as creator of war's licensed portraiture. As *Washington Post Magazine* picture editor Keith W. Jenkins remarked, with reference to both Abu Ghraib and Silicio: 'With the technology now, the amateur photographer is as capable as a professional journalist, and is operating with the same tools: digital camera, laptop and an Internet connection' (Simon, 2004). Echoing Jenkins, other commentators similarly mooted in May 2004 that the circulation of digital images – casually shot and carelessly, if not more deliberately, circulated via email or posted on-line – could no longer be controlled by civil and military authorities, for better or worse.

New media, new rules

Photography, observed Susan Sontag in 2003, is a medium uniquely subject to anti-professional prejudice:

> For the photography of atrocity, people want the weight of witnessing without the taint of artistry, which is equated with insincerity or mere contrivance. Pictures of hellish events seem more authentic when they don't have the look that comes from being 'properly' lighted and composed. (Sontag, 2003, 26–7)

With the rise of blogging, a phenomenon that coincided with the early years of the war in Iraq, one might argue something similar about journalism in the digital age. The reigning values of professional 'objectivity' – detachment, balance, neutrality – have arguably been swept aside in favor of on-line posts that are avowedly opinionated, impassioned and argumentative.

Although blogs are often discussed in dichotomized terms, as 'Other' to traditional formats they threaten to supplant, their forms vary considerably. Far from constituting a realm apart, the 'blogosphere' exists in close connection with older media. Several popular bloggers are professional reporters, such as CNN's Kevin Sites, *Time* freelancer Joshua Kucera, and former AP reporter Christopher Allbritton, author of the blog 'Back to Iraq 2.0' (Wall, 2006a, 296). In many other cases bloggers' relationship with traditional journalism is simultaneously antagonistic and parasitic. While vituperating against MSM (mainstream media), conservative bloggers routinely dispute the perceived shortcomings, biases, and reportorial lapses of print or television news. They may regard themselves as offering a corrective, but nevertheless exist in symbiosis with the very sources they routinely scorch. As InstaPundit's Glenn Reynolds points out: 'If you don't read the paper, you don't get mad at the paper' (Kaye and Johnson, 2004, 296).

No shortage of Americans was maddened by press coverage of the war in 2003. One survey conducted in April/May found that blog aficionados were overwhelmingly well-educated, high-earning, professional white men, many of them disgruntled with what they regarded as 'liberal bias' in media too generously disposed towards 'Islamic terrorism,' too quick to demonize US soldiers, and constantly on the lookout for signs that the war was going badly (Kaye and Johnson, 2004, 292–4). Conservative bloggers were quick to excoriate manifestations of these attitudes among mainstream media personnel. In February 2005, they demonstrated their formidable power to shape professional careers when their lobbying efforts forced the resignation of CNN's chief news executive Eason Jordan. The latter had made remarks at an ostensibly off-the-record session at the World Economic Forum to the effect that journalists killed in Iraq had been deliberately targeted, and so should not be regarded as 'collateral damage.' Although Jordan hastened to add that he didn't mean reporters had been purposely shot by US forces, the firestorm occasioned by his comment was fanned by bloggers, who established a website, Easongate.com, to mobilize public outrage against the CNN executive. Within a week this campaign had succeeded in its campaign to force Eason out (Allan, 2006, 115–9).

But right-wing disgruntlement was not the only variety of dissatisfaction that propelled people to seek out alternative on-line accounts of the war in Iraq. Where conservatives attacked 'liberal bias,' many liberals in turn regarded corporate media as dominated by the administration's preferred perspective – one centered on US forces whose actions and larger purposes in Iraq were framed in the most ennobling terms. Those eager to apprehend the quality of day-to-day life in wartime Iraq from the vantage point of its civilians turned to blogs for a citizen's-eye perspective almost completely lacking from commercial US news reports. In the early months of 'Operation Iraqi Freedom' two such blogspots attracted much discussion, as word spread from other blogs, email, on-line discussion groups, and print media reports: 'Where is Raed?,' pseudonymously posted by Salam Pax, and 'Baghdad Burning,' authored by a young woman styling herself Riverbend.

Where political comment blogs beg the question 'but is it *news*?', these more intimate posts raise different issues about credibility and provenance. Neither author was, after all, setting themselves up as a superior

breed of journalist. But introspective on-line diaries of this kind nevertheless depend on trust. For most readers, at any rate, the value of such blogs
rests on their claim to first-hand authenticity. Certainly in a culture that
privileges personal disclosure but lacks tolerance for revelations that
prove either wholly or partly fictionalized, it mattered to many American
readers that Salam Pax was 'for real,' not a retired librarian in Oklahoma
with a good knowledge of Baghdad's topography and a gift for empathic
invention. It wasn't long, then, before an intensive search was underway
to unmask who lay behind the pseudonym. Anonymity, while it may have
protected the Baghdad blogger from retribution, didn't satisfy those eager
to know his true identity, especially as rumors proliferated that the blog
might be an elaborate hoax, the work of Iraqi officials, or even part of a
CIA disinformation scheme (Allan, 2004, 360). Soon Salam Pax was
revealed as a gay, 29-year old architect. As this 'outing' suggests, in an age
of electronic invention where identities can readily be fabricated,
discarded, and refashioned on-line – and anonymity may be the enabling
condition of candor – the desire for epistemological certainty persists.

With one sub-set of bloggers, however, this problem of indeterminate
identity is less pervasive: namely, 'milbloggers' who are active-duty
service personnel and whose chronicles of military life unmistakably
emanate from embattled zones. In tandem with the rise of so-called citizen journalism, blogging has become increasingly popular with soldiers
serving in Iraq and Afghanistan and correspondingly unpopular with
their superior officers, stuggling to cope with the challenges new media
present to old ways of controlling information. When the war in Iraq
began blogging was still sufficiently novel that the DOD had 'no specific
guidelines on blogging per se.' So long as soldiers blogged in their own
time and on their own laptops the practice was initially tolerated (Simon,
2004). But as this new form of public–private self-expression spread
from a few dozen to over 1,000 on-line soldier-diarists whose blogs were
collectively aggregated under the umbrella of Milblogging.com – and
latterly under the commercial aegis of Military Advantage, an organization claiming a 30 million-strong membership base – the US military
gradually abandoned its laissez-faire approach (Wall, 2009, 37).

In at least some regards, social networking media appealed to military
leaders. Technologies that allowed personnel deployed overseas to
communicate readily and cheaply with friends and family back home –
via email, instant-messaging, blogging, and Skype – had a positive
impact on morale. Being in easy and instant touch with the 'outside
world' decreased feelings of alienation and homesickness, providing an
outlet to vent steam over the frustrations and privations of life in a

warzone (Chenelly, 2005). For many in the military, the emergent 'blogosphere' provided a welcome alternative forum to the much mistrusted conventional media. Soldiers who felt that the 'jihad-loving mainstream media' (as one milblogger put it) failed to show the true face of war, while disparaging the US missions in Iraq and Afghanistan, had a chance to redress the balance (Oshry, 2007). Blogging offered not just a way to connect with a pre-existing social circle but to give a disparate readership an alternative 'boots on the ground' perspective on combat. Blogs could contain language unfit to print, just as video-sharing sites could be used to post images that would never make it onto the sanitized pages of *The New York Times* or network news. In expanding the range of visual and verbal registers for events in Afghanistan and Iraq, bloggers also served to remind civilians (albeit ones inclined to seek out such reminders) that these wars were indeed still going on – a fact that many American civilians seemed all too inclined to forget. With their gallows humor, candor and grit, bloggers were the 'best PR the military has' proposed Matthew Burden, editor of the printed anthology, *The Blog of War* (Oshry, 2007).

But if some bloggers were the war on terror's best salesmen, others were arguably its worst. At any rate, from a command perspective it seemed less than ideal that some soldiers were also using blogs to *protest* the war, challenging both the purposes of Operation Iraqi Freedom as well as its practical consequences – for Iraq and America alike. If the majority of military blogs, or milblogs as the 1,000 or more such sites had collectively come to be known by 2005, were supportive of the missions in Iraq and Afghanistan, several others expressed emphatic opposition. Disgruntled soldiers now enjoyed an unprecedented outlet to condemn day-to-day conditions and the operations they were compelled to undertake; to expose declining morale within the ranks and the military's increasingly heavy-handed maneuvers to retain personnel who wanted out (the policy known as 'stop loss'). No previous generation had enjoyed such a platform. Soldiers' anti-war papers in Vietnam typically circulated only within military circles. In earlier wars, letters home had also been subject to formal censorship, blocking out material considered both sensitive to operational security and injurious to the military's reputation. But for young servicemen and women who'd grown up in the Web 2.0 age, formal oversight of private communications seemed almost impossible to conceive. Meanwhile, for officers too old to have grown up with instant-messaging and Facebook, clamping down on social media appeared almost as difficult to execute – as unpopular an expedient as it was technically challenging.

Yet however much resistance curbs on individual internet use would generate, the American military was evidently troubled both about operational security and, to a yet greater degree, its own good image – as were the DOD's British and Australian counterparts, which made similar efforts to clamp down on soldiers blogging (Wall, 2009, 40). While OPSEC was commonly announced as the reason for restrictions, concerns over military PR also seemed to underlie the increasingly restrictive official approach. Not surprisingly, the top brass didn't always agree that gritty depictions of everyday soldiering posted by bloggers – including those who expressed support for the cause and relish for the business of war – were actually serving its best interests. In August 2005, the US army introduced regulations requiring soldiers to inform their commanding officer if they planned to start a blog, further tightening the rules in 2007 such that bloggers were obliged to receive express permission from their CO before uploading any fresh material (Waterman, 2005; Baldor, 2007; Weiss, 2007). Justified in the name of preserving operational security from web-savvy jihadis on the lookout for clues as to US military vulnerabilities, this clampdown met a predictable outcry from milbloggers and their civilian allies. But it wasn't long before the rules produced one of their intended effects. The number of military blogs dropped off. Those who continued posting did so either under the wire or under increased surveillance, disregard for which could (and did) lead to the imposition of fines and demotions in rank, as well as orders to shut down offending sites.

Shortly after promulgating these new guidelines in May 2007, the Pentagon further announced that military personnel would no longer enjoy free access to sites such as YouTube, MySpace, and 11 other popular social networking sites, stating that heavy traffic was overburdening the network (Badkhen, 2007). Henceforth, active duty personnel could use such sites only at privately run internet cafés in Iraq or wherever they were stationed. In particular, the military had become troubled by soldiers' postings to on-line bulletin board NowThat'sFuckedUp.com, a pornographic site to which soldiers' gained access by posting graphic war images – their form of 'payment' since they couldn't use credit cards. Likewise, video uploads to YouTube had become a source of concern, some showing, in wrenching detail, the aftermath of IED attacks, the (mis)treatment of prisoners, and other images falling into the category known as 'body horror.' Stills and footage of this kind stood in stark contrast to more antiseptic representations of war supplied by other media. And while those who took, posted, and viewed the images no doubt had multiple uses for them, the DOD evidently feared that such material could only jeopardize US objectives – a goad to Islamic militants' recruitment drives, to worldwide anti-Americanism, and domestic anti-war activism alike (Andén-Papadopoulos, 2009; Tait, 2008).

This desire for a cleaner military self-image did not sit happily with those eager to present war at its dirtiest, who found their access to new media suddenly jeopardized. Nor did it help alleviate rank and file dissatisfaction that, one week before announcing its clampdown in May 2007, the DOD had unveiled its own YouTube channel, MNFIRAQ (Multi-National Force – Iraq). With the stated goal of giving 'viewers around the world a "boots on the ground" perspective of Operation Iraqi Freedom from those who are fighting it,' MNFIRAQ hosted a series of short clips shot by US forces. In contrast to the material that individual military users had been posting on YouTube, these films avoided profanity, eschewed 'overly graphic, disturbing or offensive content,' and made a point of showcasing positive interactions between American soldiers and Iraqi civilians, while also depicting the day-to-day work of occupation soldiering: 'terrorist' round-ups, street patrols and house-to-house searches (Christensen, 2008, 155–75).

MNFIRAQ represents one Defense Department attempt to appropriate new media – part of the US government's broader offensive to wage information war, or (as official-speak would have it) to enhance the state's 'public diplomacy' capabilities in an increasingly networked world. Recognizing the potency of social media applications, the American military has sought to develop its own internal version of MySpace predominantly aimed at junior officers who can network with one another, share advice, and maintain blogs, all in a password-protected, secure 'MilSpace.' In 2008, blogging became a required part of the graduate-level military curriculum at Fort Leavenworth, Kansas (Axe, 2008). The following September, *The New York Times* reported that, whatever restrictions ordinary soldiers face, General Ray Odierno, commander of US forces in Iraq, is on Facebook, while chairman of the Joint Chiefs of Staff Admiral Mike Mullen has a YouTube channel and posts regular Twitter updates (Dao, 2009).

While developing its own new media profile, the DOD has also undertaken aggressive measures to cultivate civilian bloggers who post on military affairs. The Pentagon's head of new media operations attends major blogging and technology conferences, while Central Command's Electronic Media Engagement Team scrutinizes the 'milblogosphere,' supplying well-disposed authors with press releases, facilitating interviews with military personnel, and arranging for particularly favored bloggers to embed with US forces. The same team also posts responses to blogs on Iraq and Afghanistan with which it takes issue (Wall, 2009, 37–9; McLeary, 2008). In short, just as some newspapers have sought to harness the popularity of certain bloggers by inviting them to post regularly on their websites, and commercial publishing houses have capitalized on the phenomenon by printing the work of Salam Pax, Riverbend and milblogger Colby Buzzell, so the US government has attempted to coopt a medium it clearly recognizes as a key weapon of the digital age.

Unpopular war revisited

The longer-term significance of the wars in Iraq and Afghanistan for media scholars awaits retrospective judgement. But in at least one sense it could be argued that both were lost some time ago – in terms of US administration efforts to garner public support in America and beyond. In many parts of the world, the legitimacy of these wars was questioned from the outset. This was true not just in the Middle East and Muslim-majority countries such as Indonesia and Malaysia, but also in states dismissive of Washington's avowed objectives in waging war in Iraq and Afghanistan (Noor, 2004; Wijadi, 2004). By 2009, the Pew Global Attitudes Project found that in just five states surveyed did 50 per cent or more of respondents favor the ongoing presence of US and NATO troops in Afghanistan, with support well below 20 per cent in several countries, including Egypt, China, Russia, Turkey, and Argentina (Pew Global Attitudes Project, 2009).

Other than in Pakistan, popular disapproval of the US-led wars has, not surprisingly, been especially intense in the Middle East. With the war in Iraq, the United States signally 'lost' Arab hearts and minds, proposes Steve Tatham (who served as a press officer at the Maritime Press Information Centre in Bahrain). Of course, one might counter that Washington had long since ceased to enjoy this allegiance as a result of its long-standing alliance with Israel, support for some of the region's most authoritarian regimes, while simultaneously trumpeting 'democratization,' and the punitive sanctions regime imposed on Iraq after the 1991 war. Arabs, and Muslims more broadly, were further alienated by wars in Afghanistan and Iraq in which civilian lives were seemingly held cheap and Islamic sensibilities routinely affronted in the everyday course of occupation soldiering – with women searched by male soldiers at checkpoints, homes broken into, mosques and Korans desecrated, and thousands of Iraqis and Afghans swept off into indefinite detention, often on extremely flimsy grounds.

In the eyes of many Muslims, these were wars of aggression, resulting in illegal occupations. If these military enterprises were lost causes from the start, however, it didn't help that Washington was so quick to demonize Arab media, treating them, in effect, as enemy agents. Just a few years earlier, American neo-conservatives had hailed Al Jazeera as a democratizing challenge to the enforced obsequiousness of Arab state broadcasting. Now Donald Rumsfeld castigated its reporting as 'vicious, inaccurate and inexcusable,' while his second-in-command Paul Wolfowitz charged the network with 'inciting violence' and 'endangering lives of American troops' in Iraq. Bush even took time in his 2004 state of the union address to brand the network's coverage of the Iraq war as 'hateful propaganda' (quoted by Powers and Gilboa, 2007, 61).

It was easier to stamp such networks 'anti-American' than to reckon with *why* Arab media so thoroughly resisted Washington's preferred narrative of its actions in Iraq and Afghanistan. Yet this dismissal of a different worldview as expressive of nothing more than cultural prejudice – whether born of envy, resentment, or conspiricism – scarcely assisted Washington's stated objective of wooing Muslim sentiment. Indeed, characterizing Al Jazeera as little more than Al Qaeda's PR wing could not help but make matters worse. The calculated snub of excluding Arab media representatives from press briefings in which coalition military plans were outlined in March 2003 unmistakably announced that Arab journalists weren't trusted to preserve operational security (Tatham, 2006, 106–8; 115–6). Ironically, it was the hyperpatriotic Fox News correspondent Geraldo Rivera who proved least trustworthy with confidential military intelligence when, live on-camera, he drew a map of his unit's location in the sand – a piece of theatricality that ensured his prompt de-accreditation and eviction from Iraq (Potter, 2002). Nor was it lost on Al Jazeera that the very people constantly lecturing them on bias had effectively made stars and stripes lapel pins mandatory for US newscasters in the months after 9/11 (Tatham, 2006, 198). If Dan Rather could insist there was no contradiction between patriotism and objectivity, why could Americans not accept Al Jazeera's contention that an Arab perspective – untethered to any particular national affiliation – was entirely compatible with journalistic professionalism?

Over time, wars that had initially found majority support in the United States became unpopular there too. Since 2006, opinion polls in America have regularly found disapproval of the war in Iraq hovering around 60 per cent: a significant drop, given that Operation Iraqi Freedom began with approval ratings that registered between 70 and 77 per cent for some months. By the end of 2009, even though a majority of Americans considered Bush's influx of troops in 2007 (the so-called 'surge') to have been a success, they still maintained that the war itself had been a mistake (CNN/Opinion Research Corporation, 2009a).

With regard to Afghanistan, the picture is a less consistent and data more sparse, reflecting that war's intermittent disappearances from the public radar. When Obama announced the commitment of 30,000 additional troops in December 2009, a CNN poll showed public approval for the war running at just 46 per cent (CNN/Opinion Research Corporation Poll, 2009b). And while polling organizations tallied support for Obama's troop increase at between 51 and 62 per cent, about the same percentage of respondents did not believe it would yield success. Asked about the most likely outcome of the war, only 29 per cent expressed confidence in a victory, with 57 per cent expecting a stalemate and 12 per cent anticipating defeat (ibid).

Despite the dwindling popularity of the campaigns in Iraq and Afghanistan, few scholars have thus far pondered the relationship between declining American public support and the wars' mediated representation – a connection so insistently probed during and after the Vietnam War. Conservative ideologues may insist that 'liberal' media wilfully downplayed progress in Iraq, determined to see America lose the war in order to vindicate their knee-jerk opposition to any undertaking of President Bush. But such partisan claims aside, the oppositional media thesis has found few takers. Indeed, for some commentators, the most telling attitudinal aspect of these wars hasn't been the fall-off of popular support, rather its surprising *persistence*. After all, since the 1970s Americans' vaunted 'casualty shyness' has been an article of faith so profoundly entrenched as to make the very prospect of a prolonged military campaign unthinkable: an *idée fixe* reinforced by wavering commitment to Operation Restore Hope in Somalia after just a few US servicemen's lives were lost. Based on their reading of Iraq war polling data, political scientists Christopher Gelpi, Peter Feaver and Jason Reifler propose that the American public is actually better regarded as 'defeat phobic' than casualty averse. In other words, so long as people believe that a war's projected benefits will outweigh its costs and retain confidence in a successful outcome they will continue to support the endeavor, irrespective of rising casualties (Gelpi, Feaver and Reifler, 2009, 236–7).

While Americans may have proven more willing to tolerate casualties than anticipated, a majority nevertheless had come to believe the war in Iraq a mistake by 2006. More gradually, a similar level of disenchantment with the operation in Afghanistan emerged. Yet little analysis has been devoted to the particular *way* in which these wars have been unpopular in the United States. Opposition has not found expression in massive street protests, like those that greeted the invasion of Iraq in London and elsewhere, but in more passive dissatisfaction that doesn't necessarily (or even primarily) spring from principle so much as an impatience to be done with benighted countries and their ungrateful populations.

Those drawn to a political critique of the wars, and hence minded to seek out graphic images, detailed body counts, witness testimony, and informed commentary certainly enjoy readier access to such material than in the pre-digital age. New social media also undoubtedly carry the potential to facilitate grassroots activism, on-line and off. And indeed anti-war organizations have made creative use of the internet to mobilize opposition. But beyond the self-selecting audience for these electronic resources and campaigns, the wars in Iraq and Afghanistan have been relatively easy to ignore. Not supporting the wars and not paying them much attention have been common responses among American civilians. Tuning out hasn't been difficult, given the diminishing attention paid to Iraq and Afghanistan by television news and the light imprint on popular culture made by these wars. Hollywood's few forays onto contemporary military terrain – features such as *Home of the Brave*, *The Valley of Elah*, *Lions for Lambs* – have performed poorly at the box office, while offering more lamentations for the state of American democracy than for the fate of Iraqis and Afghans (Carruthers, 2008b).

Since dwindling numbers of Americans regularly watch television news or go to the movies in any case, one might further argue that the fragmentation of hitherto national publics into ever more niche-oriented splinters makes it ever easier for individuals to tune out particular news stories that don't pique their interest. The 'irony of technology in a globalized world,' posits American cultural critic Susan J. Douglas, is a 'narcissism bias' – a preoccupation with matters personal not political, local not global (Douglas, 2006).

Hence even a story as putatively damaging to US public attitudes towards the war in Iraq as the Abu Ghraib revelations appeared a relatively brief blip on the US public radar. Within months, a majority of Americans asked by pollsters to identify what Abu Ghraib signified could not do so correctly. An Associated Press poll in May 2009 found that 20 per cent of those questioned believed torture 'often justified' and 32 per cent 'sometimes justified' – this in a context where the number who consider 'waterboarding' to constitute torture has steadily *decreased* (Associated Press/Gfk, 2009). In July 2009, *The Economist* reported that most US citizens deem torture acceptable in certain circumstances, noting the 'surprising' result that 'Americans are more willing to tolerate the use of torture than are Chinese' (economist.com, 2009). Anyone familiar with US culture might find this rather less of a surprise, however. Popular dramas – most notably FOX network's *24* – provide every encouragement to believe that torture is not only permissible but the *only* efficacious way to extract timely intelligence (Prince, 2009, 238–48). Television news has also contributed to minimizing the blunt force of torture. The military trial of Specialist Charles Graner, chief among the accused of Abu Ghraib, was almost entirely absent from US television news in January 2005, eclipsed by a more compelling abuse of military uniform: Prince Harry's appearance at a 'native and colonial' fancy dress party in Afrika Corps regalia. As *The New York Times*' columnist Frank Rich pointed out, 'If a story isn't on TV in America, it doesn't exist in our culture' (Rich, 2005, A1).

Despite public qualms over their escalating costs, the wars in Iraq and Afghanistan haven't galvanized the kind of anti-war protest generated by Vietnam – a radical movement fueled (at least in part) by a far-reaching critique of imperialism and social injustice. But there is one point of similarity that unites all three: their continuation long after a majority of Americans ceased supporting them. The Vietnam War lasted for five years after opinion turned decisively against it in 1968. Under the guise of 'Vietnamization,' Nixon not only continued a palpably unpopular war but escalated it into Laos and Cambodia, even as press attention drifted away. By then the narrative had been fixed that America was 'on the way out.' Something similar has happened in Iraq and Afghanistan. As popular commitment ebbed and media attention turned elsewhere, so the 2007 'surge' increased US troop levels while the message was that this strategy would secure America's hasty exit and the war's 'Iraqization.' Likewise, Obama's 2010 injection of troops into Afghanistan aimed at shoring up indigenous security forces' capacity to 'clear and hold' territory regained from the Taliban.

Perhaps scholars have been reluctant to ponder these issues because they threaten to expose a stark contradiction between liberal political theory and practice. While leaders are undoubtedly preoccupied with public opinion – and, as we've seen, take inordinate efforts to monitor and manipulate it in congenial ways – they're not so overwhelming concerned with negative opinion in wartime as to abandon unpopular ventures. Blair, Bush, and Obama in turn have all confronted publics who, in the main, opposed wars they were determined to fight. Yet they forged ahead regardless, whether banking on future success or too fearful of immediate failure to retrench. Where, then, does the persistence of unpopular war leave democratic notions of the 'fourth estate' and popular accountability?

Conclusion: After War, More War

Postwar reconstruction

War never ends when the shooting stops. On the contrary, struggles in the realm of representation tend to intensify once combat, that great amplifier of noise and dampener of debate, has come to an end. When the dust clears, strenuous battles over interpretation begin in earnest. Justifications for going to war are held up to scrutiny and sometimes found wanting. Journalists wring their hands, recriminating against those who lied to them and swearing never again to be so credulous, while cultural producers – film-makers, artists, writers, curators – shape the raw material of war into a source of inspiration or warning. Wars freshly ended or long since past provide opportunities to celebrate heroism, mourn shared losses, affirm a sense of community forged through sacrifice or to kindle the enduring enmities around which collective identity frequently coalesces.

Since this book began with a consideration of how media enable war in its preparatory phase, it's appropriate to conclude by contemplating how media process wars past and how they are sometimes *compelled* to behave in the wake of defeat. Recognizing the contribution film, radio, television, and print media make in fostering ideologies of aggression, victors often insist on constricting their former foes' arteries of public expression. For peace to prevail, not just physical infrastructure but belief structures must be rebuilt. Thus the conquerors' logic goes. And so it was that in May 1945, the British, French, Soviet and US forces occupying Germany shut down newspapers, assumed control of the airwaves, closed all cinemas that had not been reduced to rubble, embargoed films made during the 12-year *Hitlerzeit* and asserted dominance over postwar cultural and artistic life (Goldstein, 2009, 47). In the British and US occupation zones, new democratic German media were established with a mandate that required them to be simultaneously impartial and in favor of Allied policies of demilitarization and de-Nazification (Gienow-Hecht, 1999).

British and American authorities placed particular faith in *visual* media as the most effective vehicle of moral reorientation, quickly seeing

the value of reopening German cinemas to screen suitably vetted material (Fay, 2008; Goldstein, 2009). Political leaders' wartime anxiety that
images of human destruction would animate pacifistic revulsion found a
postwar corollary in the conviction that Germans would recoil in horror
when exposed to graphic depictions of genocide. To instill the desired
awareness of 'collective guilt' among Germans – too many of whom
were deemed insufficiently cognizant of their personal responsibility for
the Third Reich's atrocities – British and US personnel set out to produce
films documenting the appalling scenes found in the concentration camps
as Allied troops encountered them in the spring of 1945. Their intention
was that all Germans would be made to view these documentary productions, facing penalties, including denial of food rations, should they resist
(Carruthers, 2001).

Not surprisingly, Germans did resist both the compulsory viewing of
such unpalatable material and the occupiers' heavy-handed insistence on
shared culpability. Only in Hollywood movies – like *The Stranger*
(1946), *Verboten* (1958) and *Judgment at Nuremberg* (1961) – did hitherto unreconstructed Nazis flinch in chastened recognition when
confronted with visual proof of their crimes. In real life, by contrast,
German viewers proved quite capable of refusing to accept the veracity of
documentary footage that Allied film-makers strove to present as
irrefutable. Some disgruntled viewers insisted that the stacks of corpses
and skeletal camp survivors were in fact *German* POWs abused by their
captors; hence the films actually attested the barbarity of enemies who
hadn't hesitated to reduce Berlin, Dresden and Hamburg to rubble, yet
now had the gall to insist that Germans alone were guilty of war crimes
(Carruthers, 2001).

In postwar Japan, the US military government that presided over the
country from 1945 to 1952 undertook a reconstructive project yet more
prescriptive than its counterpart in Germany. As historian John Dower
observes, 'The overall censorship operation eventually came to entail
extensive checklists of taboo subjects, and in the best Orwellian manner
these taboos included any public acknowledgment of the existence of
censorship' (1999, 407). Among the prohibited topics, none was more
sensitive than the atomic bombs dropped on Hiroshima and Nagasaki in
August 1945 that had brought the Pacific war to a precipitate halt – a
subject of such delicacy that American journalists were also initially
prohibited from reporting on the effects of radiation sickness and the
firestorms that engulfed the two cities, killing and mutilating thousands of
residents. One Japanese writer later noted, 'We were not allowed to write
about the atomic bomb during the Occupation,' adding (in corroboration

of Dower's point), 'We were not even allowed to say that we were not allowed to write about the atomic bomb' (Sadako Kurihara, quoted by Braw, 1991, 7). More broadly, American officials disallowed any discussion of the country's devastated condition that failed to stress 'Japanese responsibility for the war' (Hirano, 1992, 54).

At the same time, US officials busily encouraged the six main Japanese film studios to produce suitably pro-democratic fare, while debarring from theatrical distribution Hollywood movies that might display America in a less than perfect light. Even a film as innocuous as Frank Capra's paean to the common decency of the American everyman, *Mr Smith Goes to Washington*, was found wanting on account of its depiction of unscrupulous ne'er-do-wells on Capitol Hill (Hirano, 1992, 246). The long list of 'don'ts' – essentially anything that evoked Japan's imperial past or criticized the Supreme Commander of the Allied Powers, General Douglas MacArthur – was supplemented by an equally eclectic set of 'dos'. The latter included an injunction that Japanese films should show men and women publicly kissing. American censors didn't read the prior absence from Japanese screens of public displays of affection as cultural aversion to such indelicacy, but rather as evidence of 'sneakiness' – the national characteristic supposedly responsible for Pearl Harbor, now earmarked for replacement by American-style openness (Hirano, 1992, 155–6).

Attempts to refashion a defeated nation's media from the ground up have not been limited to the age of Total War. In March 2003, the Pentagon unveiled a media plan for post-invasion Iraq: a scheme that anticipated hand-picked, US-trained 'rapid response teams' as the public face of 'a new Iraq (by Iraqis for Iraqis) with hopes for a prosperous, democratic future.' Warming to its theme, this DOD white paper imagined Iraqis' rhapsodic response to their newly de-Baathified media:

It will be as if, after another day of deadly agit-prop, the North Korean people turned off their TVs at night, and turned them on in the morning to find the rich fare of South Korean TV spread before them as their very own.

The white paper went on to envision the elimination of media regarded as unfriendly to US purposes in Iraq, notably Al Jazeera, in tandem with the creation of new television channels oriented towards the preoccupations of US media, with Hollywood gossip taking pride of place over hard news (National Security Archive, 2007a).

The Pentagon took concrete steps to implement this scheme. Shortly before the launch of Operation Iraqi Freedom, the DOD awarded a no-bid $15 million contract to Scientific Applications International Corps (SAIC), a San Diego-based defense contractor with no prior media experience but a wealth of Washington connections. SAIC's mission was to establish 'Iraqi Free Media.' One month later, Ahmed al-Rikaby (hired as the first Iraqi Media Network television director) made his inaugural broadcast from a tent erected by the US military. But it didn't take long for things to unravel. Several US contractors in charge of the media plan resigned or were sacked, while Iraqi employees went on strike in protest at monthly salaries a fraction of the daily wages enjoyed by American contract workers. Meanwhile, Iraq's new media, plumped on 'good news' items translated clumsily from English into Arabic, struggled to find receptive audiences (National Security Archive, 2007b).

In Iraq, as in postwar Germany and Japan, the contradictions of 'democratization by force' – often invisible to the occupation forces – proved unmistakable to populations expected to embrace these media as expressive of their newly unleashed free will. Yet even as many US forces prepared to leave Iraq, some seven years after the launch of Operation Iraqi Freedom, the Pentagon was stepping up efforts to influence media coverage in (and on) Iraq. Issuing a new bid for 'strategic communication management services' in May 2010, the Department of Defense deemed effective promulgation of Washington's 'core themes and messages ... essential to the success of the new Iraqi government' and to the mission of the remaining US forces (Pincus, 2010). Thus the battle for influence over opinion continues.

Reconstructing memory

Left to their own devices media deal with wars past in multiple ways. Some indecisive conflicts fall quickly from sight and remain long submerged, as did the Korean War soon after ending in stalemate in July 1953, at least from the US perspective. Since then, it has rarely featured as the subject of popular film or television programming, going unmemorialized on the Mall in Washington, DC, until 1995. Similarly, 'small wars' in faraway places – like Britain's string of post-1945 campaigns against anti-imperial forces in Africa and Asia – have provided few resources for a 'usable past'. But these forgotten wars aside, what's most striking about the way in which popular media tend to treat wars past is the dominance of *affirmative* meanings attached to conflict. More often than not, 'guts and glory' trump 'sorrow and pity' in mediated revisionings of historical battles. Even disastrous and divisive wars, like Vietnam, are restaged as putative victories or as tragedies in which everyone suffered without anyone in particular being to blame.

The starkest exception to this generalized claim is World War I, which quickly came to emblematize the squalor and squander of mechanized industrial-age warfare. Stamped as a monumental folly, thoroughly devoid of grandeur, the 'Great War' acquired a bitterly ironic ring. No previous conflict demonstrated the tragedy of war so completely – a judgement shared by cultural producers on both sides of the Atlantic, irrespective of which side their state had fought on. Lewis Milestone's *All Quiet on the Western Front* (1930), based on Erich Maria Remarque's 1929 novel, remains the best-known cinematic representation of World War I. But it wasn't the first, nor was it the biggest popular success at the time (Kelly, 1997). Abel Gance's *J'accuse* (1919), sometimes regarded as the 'first great cry of protest in cinema', attracted a conservatively estimated audience of 1 to 2 million in Europe and North America. It was followed by even more successful films, including Pabst's *Westfront 1918* (1930) and Renoir's *La Grande Illusion* (1937) (Winter, 1995, 137–8; Sorlin, 1991, 24–7). The somber commemorative tradition did not come to an end with World War II, even though the latter's outbreak proved that to remember was not to render war unthinkable. Since 1945, successive generations of British school children have studied the 'war poets', Siegfried Sassoon, Wilfred Owen, Edward Thomas, and Robert Graves. Even if they know no other Latin, they would understand the ironic final line of Owen's mordant elegy, 'Dulce et Decorum Est.' Red poppies, no longer produced by the Great War's disabled veterans, continue to be worn each Armistice Day, and annually thousands of visitors to London's Imperial War Museum undergo the 'trench experience.'

If World War I soon came to signify everything brutal, reckless and futile about war, the global conflagration of 1939–45 met just the opposite postwar fate, at least among its victors. Today, World War II serves as the very epitome of the 'good war,' remembered as a time of absolute moral clarity and unity of purpose. Faced with enemies like Hitler and Hirohito, who could possibly have doubted the rectitude of Allied purposes and the evil they confronted? The American public, writes Eric Larson, 'had an excellent cause ... derived from the shared perception of important stakes and vast benefits of eliminating a grave threat to US security and from optimism that the outcome would be a decisive victory and punishment of the Axis powers' (1996, 14). Yet it took time, creative ingenuity and a good deal of willful forgetting to turn 'the worst war in history' into the 'good war' with which we've become so familiar. As the scholar and veteran Paul Fussell points out, this was a 'war without nobility, where women and children were without apology killed or maimed by area bombing and where "liberated" people ... could be treated with utmost contempt' (2004, viii–ix). While it was in progress, many American civilians and soldiers, far from regarding themselves as valiant warriors against German racism and Japanese imperialism, remained confused about the war's larger purposes. As late as March 1944, fewer than 60 per cent of respondents to a Gallup poll agreed that they had 'a clear idea of what the war is about' (Berinsky, 2009, 37).

Recollected as an era of unparalleled national unity, wartime failed to eliminate labor unrest, racism, anti-Semitism or gender discrimination in either Britain or the United States. On the contrary, like any period of accelerated social change, the war produced a good deal of friction between classes, sexes, and races – to say nothing of the animosity that not infrequently arose between allies. Rarely, however, do we recall that strikes, race riots and fist fights (or worse) between soldiers ostensibly on the same side all accompanied the 'good war.' Only in recent years has the internment of Japanese Americans become a standard part of the US history curriculum: seemingly an isolated blot on the good war's otherwise unsullied copybook. To suggest, as Nicholson Baker's 2008 novel *Human Smoke* did, that World War II was as immoral a war as its predecessor is still to invite vehement rebuke from those determined (as Baker puts it) to 'fondle a small, clean, paperweight version of this war' (Baker, 2010).

Even in retrospect, many dimensions of war remain dimly understood – generally not because states prohibit discussion of war's less palatable aspects, but because human scruples construct barriers to clearsightedness. Infrequently do media invite us to scrutinize quotidian realities of wartime, from the willful killing of civilians to desecration of corpses; from looting and black marketeering to the sale – or violent appropriation – of sex that typically flourishes around military encampments. Atrocities and war crimes may become matters of public discussion, but we generally hear far more about those perpetrated by enemy soldiers than our own: stories that serve to reinscribe the boundary between barbarous others and our civilized selves.

Tellingly, lawmakers, opinion-formers and publics often demonstrate greater willingness to tolerate in fictionalized representations what's deemed impermissible in news reporting concurrent with war itself. As we've seen, reporters are commonly obliged to draw a discrete veil over death and injury, or themselves choose to police the boundaries of 'taste and tone' with a vigilance that may surpass any state-imposed restraint.

The mere assertion that corporeal harm is an incontrovertible fact of war can appear near seditious for journalists in wartime, tearing the veil of euphemism that obscures what exactly militaries do and how their actions damage human bodies and minds. It's hard not to be struck by the radical disjuncture between the careful sanitization of news images to excise signs of suffering and the hyperrealism with which popular culture reinstates, or may even reify, bodily harm in its representations of combat. Even as state officials prohibit pictures of coffins, corpses and mangled bodies, popular culture tends to foreground the corporeality of combat. Indeed, the realism of these representations' special effects is often central to their self-promotional pitch. This was certainly the case with publicity for Steven Spielberg's *Saving Private Ryan* (1998), which opens with a stomach-churning 20-minute recreation of the D-day Normandy landings, or more recently with Kathryn Bigelow's Oscar-winning drama, *The Hurt Locker* (2008), set not just in present-day Iraq but largely inside the protective bomb disposal outfit worn by its central protagonist.

To what end, though, do film-makers conjure the spectacle of killing with painstaking verisimilitude? Some make expansive claims on behalf of their creations, insisting that revulsion against war is proportionate to the realism of its depiction. To show war in all its blood-seeped viciousness is to condemn it. Thus Michael Cimino, director of *The Deer Hunter* (1978), has insisted that 'any good picture about war is an anti-war picture' (cited by Christensen, 1987, 152). But *is* it? Not every critic would agree that Cimino's landmark film offers 'any sort of critical take on Vietnam' (Quart, 1990, 166). Instead, some see his celebration of blue collar, small town values as a bid to come to terms with the war without decisively reckoning with what US forces had done in and to Vietnam – as opposed to what the war had done to Americans and America.

Critical opinion similarly cleaves over Oliver Stone's *Platoon* (1987), a production hailed by David Halberstam as the 'first real Viet Nam film,' directed by Hollywood's first 'veteran auteur.' Several commentators regard Stone's gut-wrenching portrait of combat as a powerful anti-war statement, but others vehemently dissent. 'Meticulously aping an atrocity is an atrocity,' proposes film critic Gilbert Adair. '[T]he hyperrealistic depiction of an obscenity cannot avoid being contaminated with that atrocity' (Adair, 1989, 159). To endorse Adair's insight is to reject the automatic equation between visual literalism and pacifism, and to query the very possibility of an anti-war film – or at any rate, an anti-war film that foregrounds the visceral reconstruction of violence. Can one, in fact, show war without valorizing it? 'Take the glamour out of war! I mean how the bloody hell do you do that?' enquired photographer Tim Page of Michael Herr. 'It's like trying to take the glamour out of sex, trying to take the glamour out of the Rolling Stones' (Herr, 1978, 199). Hence Francis Ford Coppola's suggestion that 'to make a film that is truly anti-war, it would not be set anywhere near battlefields or theaters of war, but rather in human situations far from those' (Weschler, 2005).

That combat movies *invariably* provide renewable resources for war-making is a point bluntly made in Anthony Swofford's Gulf War memoir, *Jarhead*, itself later turned into a feature film. In August 1990, waiting in the Saudi Arabian desert to 'get some' in Iraq, Swofford and his platoon of fellow Marines pass the time watching and rewatching Vietnam War films like *Platoon*, *Full Metal Jacket*, and *Apocalypse Now*:

> There is talk that many Vietnam films are antiwar, that the message is war is inhumane and look what happens when you train young American men to fight and kill, they turn their fighting and killing everywhere, they ignore their targets and desecrate the entire country, shooting fully automatic, forgetting they were trained to aim. But actually, Vietnam war films are all pro-war, no matter what the supposed message, what Kubrick or Coppola or Stone intended. Mr and Mrs Johnson in Omaha or San Francisco or Manhattan will watch the films and weep and decide once and for all that war is inhumane and terrible, and they will tell their friends at church and their family this, but Corporal Johnson at Travis Air Force Base and Seaman Johnson at Coronado Naval Station and Spec 4 Johnson at Fort Bragg and Lance Corporal Swofford at Twentynine Palms Marine Corps Base watch the same films and are excited by them, because the magic brutality of the films celebrates the terrible and despicable beauty of their fighting skills (Swofford, 2003, 6–7)

Swofford was hardly the first to note how Hollywood seduced young men into seeing war as the ultimate test of masculine prowess, and combat as the bond of true brotherhood. American grunts in Vietnam, noted Michael Herr, had grown up on celluloid fantasies of wartime hero-ism and camaraderie in which death appeared noble and any wounds less than fatal, bearable. Kids got 'wiped out by seventeen years of movies before coming to Vietnam to get wiped out for good' (1978, 169). Needless to say, the reality of this war starkly diverged from generic screen conventions. 'Vietnam – the Movie' – as characters in Stanley Kubrick's *Full Metal Jacket* (1987) mockingly refer to journalists' efforts to film them – was not a production in which many young

Americans wanted starring roles on closer inspection of the script (Doherty, 1999, 286).

The militarization of everyday life

War cycles into and out of cinematic fashion, but the relationship between Hollywood and the military has arguably never been closer than today, despite the commercial failure of many recent war-themed films. Some media theorists go so far as to talk of a 'military–industrial–media–entertainment' network, offering a digital era update of Dwight Eisenhower's warning against militarization. When he left office in 1961, the outgoing president warned of an 'immense military establishment and a large arms industry' whose 'total influence – economic, political, even spiritual – is felt in every city, every statehouse, every office of the federal government' (quoted by Der Derian, 2001, xx). A half-century later, there's increasing intimacy between the military-industrial establishment and purveyors of popular entertainment. This synergy takes many forms, from set designers working on Pentagon briefing stages (as they did prior to 'Operation Iraqi Freedom') to film industry involvement in devising military training scenarios and the employment of professional animators, scenarists and special effects technicians as 'imagineers' in the tremendously lucrative video game industry: a sector of the US export economy that now outstrips Hollywood's foreign earnings.

While gaming has surged in popularity over the past decade, the habit of cinema-going suffered a precipitous fall-off. In November 2009, the launch of Infinity Ward's game 'Call of Duty: Modern Warfare 2,' fabricated around a terrorist incident at a Russian airport, broke all prior records by earning $550 million from sales in the UK and US in the first five days alone. By contrast, the new *Harry Potter* film and *The Half-Blood Princess*, two Hollywood holiday blockbusters released concurrently, garnered a paltry $394 million worldwide in the equivalent period (Watson, 2009).

The popularity of video games owes much to the excitement of interaction, unlike the more passive pleasures of film spectatorship. In recent years, many political organizations and commercial corporations – from Pepsico to white supremacist groups, the United Nations to McDonald's – have come to appreciate video games as a vehicle to promote particular messages or products. Among them, the US Army has assumed a leading role. In response to a 30-year low in military recruitment in 1999, Congress authorized 'aggressive, innovative' new strategies to encourage enlistment, hiring the advertising agency Leo Burnett to form an Army Marketing Brand Group. One key plank of its campaign was 'America's Army,' a free video game which in its successive incarnations has been downloaded more than 40 million times. According to a 2008 Massachusetts Institute of Technology study, 'the game had more impact on recruits than all other forms of Army advertising combined.' For the first time since the US military became an all-volunteer force in 1973, it met all its recruitment goals in 2009 (Holmes, 2009). While it wouldn't be wise to attribute this achievement to shrewd marketing alone at a time of rapidly rising unemployment, the military's avid espousal of gaming – to the tune of some $32.8 million spent on 'America's Army' alone – remains striking (Saint, 2009).

Video games have long raised questions about players' desensitization to violence. In the eyes of critics, first-person shooter games like 'America's Army' train trigger reflexes without animating awareness of the human and psychological consequences of either taking life or being killed. Since this is a game, the shooter enjoys immunity from death. Whatever happens on-screen, he or she is always at liberty to re-set and start over. And while war games' realism is a key selling point, they're necessarily realistic only up to a point. 'America's Army' carries a T (for Teen) rating because designers are 'very careful on the blood thing,' in the words of one military spokesman (Holmes, 2009). As critics further point out, 'realism' doesn't extend to games envisioning the experience of being profoundly wounded and living with amputations, paraplegia and other debilities that severely restrict action and perception. This is hardly surprising since rapid, precise action is the sine qua non of gaming and, more particularly, since the objective of games like 'America's Army' is to encourage a positive appreciation of military life with a view to boosting enlistment. It stands to reason that, whatever their educative claims, such games accentuate aspects of war that afford a thrilling adrenalin surge – that make it seem cool to the teenage demographic at which they're aimed (Swanson, 2009).

'America's Army' hasn't altogether escaped criticism in the US (Lobe, 2008). But attempts to recruit young teenagers with the enticement of getting to shoot people and blow things up do not elicit the horrified response that greets the phenomenon of child soldiering in Africa or first-person shooter games when roles are reversed as, for example, in Hezbollah's 'Special Force' game, based on actual firefights with Israeli forces. When this game sold out its initial run of 100,000 in the first week it went on sale in Lebanon, Syria, Iran, Bahrain, and the United Arab Emirates in February 2003, it occasioned much fretful discussion in

Europe, North America and beyond about the potential of this game – and others featuring Palestinian fighters – to spawn a new generation of Arab terrorists, tutored by the games in fanatical hatred of Israel (Wiltenburg, 2003). An Australian member of parliament charged that they 'encourage[d] young people to become suicide bombers and to participate in attacks on people from the West,' while *The New York Times*' columnist Thomas Friedman accused the games of turning Islam into a 'death cult' (Souri, 2007, 540).

As media scholar Helga Tawil Souri points out, while US Army spokesmen defend 'America's Army' as teaching 'military values' and 'patriotism' – self-evidently 'good things' – few western critics seem minded to accept that Arab video games could also be defended on instructional grounds (2007, 543). Haj Fouad, of Hezbollah's Central Internet Bureau, explains the games' purpose as 'interest[ing] the players to learn the history of what really happened in the south of Lebanon ... and deliver[ing] a message that man should defend his country and land against the usurpers and occupiers' – patriotism of a different stripe. In a situation where dehumanizing violence is part of everyday lived experience, the games provide Arab children with an opportunity for self-assertion, their advocates claim, bestowing 'digital dignity' that real life constantly undermines (Armstrong, 2005).

Hezbollah and other Islamic manufacturers of video war games aren't alone in attempting to reverse the medium's dominant tropes. Anti-war activists have also developed countercultural uses of gaming and digital video culture. After the invasion of Iraq in 2003, Gonzalo Frasca, a game designer and professor at the University of Copenhagen, launched a game called 'September 12' that challenges players to respond to a terrorist attack. 'You can target any of the buildings in an Arab village and blast them away with your warheads, but when you do, Muslim women weep over their dead children and more terrorists grab guns to defend their homes,' reported the *Guardian*. In this way, 'September 12' underscores the futility of retaliatory violence. A game that can't be won isn't fun to play for any extended period, which is of course precisely the point. 'It exists purely to intrigue you long enough so you poke around and figure out the underlying argument: an op-ed composed not of words but of action' (Thompson, 2006).

Other games, more pedagogical than polemical, have attempted to promote different values and sensibilities among gamers. The United Nations' 'Food Force' teaches awareness of the difficulties of delivering humanitarian assistance, while a team at Carnegie Mellon University in Pittsburgh developed 'Peacemaker,' in which players – assuming the roles of either the Israeli prime minister or Palestinian president – must take actions to resolve the Israel–Palestine crisis. But as developers admit, building 'morally ambiguous worlds' is much harder than creating a standard first-person shooter game, as is attracting and sustaining players' interest in games where winning by zapping things isn't an option (Thompson, 2006).

Without war?

Western culture is marked by a glaring disjuncture. Rhetorically, we elevate peace as humankind's desired normative condition, with war cast as a hateful aberration – 'the worst thing we do'. Yet despite such pieties, it looms increasingly large both in digital culture and as a mode of dispute settlement between peoples and states. War, proposes political scientist Andrew Bacevich, is 'the new normal', as the 'forever wars' in Afghanistan and Iraq drag on indefinitely, and as militarized ways of seeing and thinking burrow ever deeper into imaginary life. Americans, claims Bacevich, have grown numb to the significance of war – sold on a bogus vision of military force as 'precise, discriminating, and humane' – by bellicose leaders and 'a cheerleading media' (Keller, 2010).

Although particular military commitments undoubtedly generate popular discontent, war nevertheless remains a 'force that gives us meaning,' as former *New York Times'* war correspondent Chris Hedges puts it (Hedges, 2003). With war retrospectively cherished as a time of intense collective unity, it may be easy to forget that wartime community draws on the exhilaration of collective enmity, or 'properly directed hatred,' as the Office of War Information termed it. Offered so many inducements by diverse expressive media to *enjoy* war – what it does *for* us and *to* our enemies – we might well conclude that it is not, in fact, 'the worst thing we do' at all but rather a vital fount of social regeneration.

Technologically, we now have the capability to know and see more – with greater immediacy – than ever before. However, that capacity doesn't automatically generate superior understanding of why particular wars occur, whether they might be prevented, and how they could be ended. The current predicament of CIA analysts trying to interpret footage from pilotless drones over-flying Afghanistan and Pakistan offers an exaggerated metaphor for a more generalized condition of information overload and its attendant interpretive deficit. In 2009 alone, these drones collected video intelligence that would take 24 years to watch if viewed continuously. Moreover, the raw imagery itself isn't particularly illuminating.

Illustration C.1   British Cartoonist Jak (Raymond Jackson) presciently imagines US generals, at the end of the war in Vietnam, dreaming up a new venture in Afghanistan

" Well, how about starting a `war with Afghanistan ? "

Source: *The Evening Standard* (1/29/1973).

'Imagine you are tuning in to a football game without all the graphics,' proposes Lucius Stone, whose company supplies the US military with its surveillance technology. 'You don't know what the score is. You don't know what the down is. It's just raw video' – which is why, as one military intelligence analyst puts it, 'You need somebody who's trained and accountable in recognizing that that is a woman, that is a child and that is someone who's carrying a weapon' (Drew, 2010, A1, A3).

No doubt the ability to discriminate would be helpful if one is in the business of detecting threats and pinpointing targets. But yet more helpful, in broader terms, would be sharper analytic tools to help understand *why* someone is carrying a weapon and the conditions under which they might put it down. Conventional media are often not very instructive in generating such insights – but the failure is hardly theirs alone.

Residents of the wealthy industrialized world are surrounded by images of war, the paraphernalia of combat, and by invitations to participate vicariously in its pulse-quickening thrill. Yet many citizens are less than attentive to conflicts as they're actually waged than to attenuated forms of visualization and enactment that assert their referentiality to 'real life' without making war palpable in all its destructive enormity. In practice, we're often intolerant of dissent, disdainful of protest and reluctant to contemplate how our wars appear to those on the other side – or those who refuse to take sides. Wars that 'drag on' become a bore. We don't want to hear or see too much in close-up, often announcing a preference to wait until it's all over for revelations that might only damage morale or 'hurt our troops' while conflict continues.

The moment of deferred revelation seems capable of indefinite postponement, however. New wars break out – a fact of life, a lamentable expression of human nature. Or so it might seem. But as John Mueller reminds us, 'unlike, breathing, eating or sex,' war is 'not something that is somehow required by the human condition.' We've just come to think of it that way.

Bibliography

ABC News/*Washington Post* (1983) Poll USABCWP.90B.R32F, October 28.

Abu-Lughod, L. (2002) 'Do Muslim Women Really Need Saving? Anthropological Reflections on Cultural Relativism and Its Others', *American Anthropologist*, 104, iii, 783–90.

Adair, G. (1989) *Hollywood's Vietnam: From the 'Green Berets' to 'Full Metal Jacket'*, London: Heinemann.

Adam, G. (1995) 'Radio's Peacekeeping in Humanitarian Crises' in Girardet.

Adams, V. (1986) *The Media and the Falklands Campaign*, London: Macmillan.

African Rights (1994) *Rwanda: Death, Despair and Defiance*, London: Macmillan.

Ajami, F. (2001) 'What the Muslim World Is Watching', *New York Times Magazine*, November 18.

Alali, O. and Eke, K. (1991) *Media Coverage of Terrorism: Methods of Diffusion*, Newbury Park, CA: Sage.

Aldgate, A. and Richards, J. (1994) *Britain Can Take It: The British Cinema in the Second World War*, Edinburgh: Edinburgh University Press.

Aldridge, M. and Hewitt, N. (eds) (1994) *Controlling Broadcasting; Access Policy and Practice in North America and Europe*, Manchester: Manchester University Press.

Alexander, Y. and Latter, R. (eds) (1990) *Terrorism and the Media: Dilemmas for Government, Journalists and the Public*, Washington, DC: Brassey's.

Alexander, Y. and O'Day, A. (eds) (1984) *Terrorism in Ireland*, London: Croom Helm.

Alexander, Y. and Picard, R. (eds) (1991) *In the Camera's Eye: News Coverage of Terrorist Events*, Washington, DC: Brassey's.

Alexievich, S. (1992) *Zinky Boys: Soviet Voices from the Afghanistan War*, New York: W. W. Norton.

Al Hurra (2010) *About Us*, http://www.alhurra.com/Sub.aspx?ID=266, date accessed May 20, 2010.

Al-Jadda, S. (2007) 'Does Al-Jazeera Belong in the USA?', *USA Today*, December 19.

Al-Kindi, A. (2004) 'War Against Media in the 2003 Gulf War' in Berenger.

Allan, S. (2004) 'The Culture of Distance: Online Reporting of the Iraq War' in Allan and Zelizer.

Allan, S. (2006) *Online News: Journalism and the Internet*, Maidenhead: Open University Press.

Allan, S. (2009) 'Histories of Citizen Journalism' in Allan and Thorsen.

Allan, S. and Thorsen, E. (2009) *Citizen Journalism: Global Perspectives*, New York: Peter Lang.

Allan, S. and Zelizer, B. (eds) (2004) *Reporting War: Journalism in Wartime*, London: Routledge.

Allen, T. and Seaton, J. (eds) (1999) *The Media of Conflict: War Reporting and Representations of Ethnic Violence*, London: Zed.

Alleyne, M. (1995) *International Power and International Communication*, London: Macmillan.

Alleyne, M. (1997) *News Revolution: Political and Economic Decisions about Global Information*, London: Macmillan.

Alozie, E. (2004) 'African Perspectives on Events Before the 2003 Iraq War' in Berenger.

Alozie, E. (2006) 'Information Warfare: E-mail as an Instrument of Propaganda During the 2002–2003 Iraq Crisis' in Berenger.

Altheide, D. (2006) *Terrorism and the Politics of Fear*, Lanham, MD: AltaMira Press.

Ambrose, S. (2001) 'Preface' in Library of America.

Andén-Papadopoulos, K. (2009) 'Body Horror on the Internet: US Soldiers Recording the War in Iraq and Afghanistan', *Media, Culture and Society*, 31, 6, 921–38.

Anderegg, M. (ed.) (1991) *Inventing Vietnam: the War in Film and Television*, Philadelphia: Temple University Press.

Andersen, R. (2006) *A Century of Media, A Century of War*, New York: Peter Lang.

Anderson, J. (1969) 'Armed Forces Radio-TV Censored', *Washington Post*, October 22.

Ang, I. (1985) *Watching 'Dallas': Soap Opera and the Melodramatic Imagination*, New York: Methuen.

Appy, C. (2003) *Patriots: The Vietnam War Remembered from All Sides*, New York: Viking.

Arendt, H. (1958) *The Origins of Totalitarianism*, Cleveland: Meridian.

Arlen, M. (1982) *The Living Room War*, New York: Penguin.

Armstrong, R. (2005) 'Jihad: Play the Game', *The Independent*, August 17.

Arnett, P. (1992) 'Why I stayed Behind' in Smith.

Arnett, P. (1995) *Live from the Battlefield*, London: Corgi.

Arraf, J. (2009) 'Disappearing Iraq', *Columbia Journalism Review*, September/October, 29–31.

Article 19 (1989) *No Comment: Censorship, Secrecy and the Irish Troubles*, London: Article 19.

Article 19 (1991) *Stop Press: the Gulf War and Censorship*, London: Article 19.

Article 19 (1994) *Forging War: The Media in Serbia, Croatia and Bosnia-Herzegovina*, London: Article 19.

Atkinson, R. (1994) *Crusade. The Untold Story of the Gulf War*. London: HarperCollins.

Associated Press/Gfk (2009) Poll USAP.060209G.R09, May 28–June 1.

Atkinson, R. (2001) 'Special, Not Super', *The Washington Post*, October 4, A31.

Atlanta Constitution, The (1902a) 'Only Savages in Rebellion Against Flag', February 5, 1.

Atlanta Constitution, The (1902b) 'Water Cure Is Not So Bad', May 16, 10.

Atwater, T. (1991) 'Network Evening News Coverage of the TWA Hostage Crisis' in Alali and Eke.

Aubin, S. (1992) 'Bashing the Media: Why the Public Outrage' in Smith.

Aufderheide, P. (2004) 'Big Media and Little Media: The Journalistic Informal Sector during the Invasion of Iraq' in Allan and Zelizer.

Aulich, J. (1992) *Framing the Falklands War: Nationhood, Culture and Identity*, Milton Keynes: Open University Press.

Axe, D. (2008) 'The Military's Internet "Civil War"', *Washington Independent*, May 30.

Axelrod, A. (2009) *Selling the Great War: The Making of American Propaganda*, New York: Palgrave Macmillan.

Ayres, B. (1974) 'Westmoreland Faces Decision on Entering Carolina Politics', *The New York Times*, January 13.

Ayres, C. (2005) *War Reporting for Cowards*, New York: Grove Press.

Azran, T. (2006) 'From Osama Bin-Laden's Mouthpiece to the Darling of the Alternative Media Web Sites: Representation of English.aljazeera.net in the West' in Berenger.

Badkhen, A. (2007) 'Popular Web Sites Now Off-Limits to Troops', *San Francisco Chronicle*, May 15.

Badsey, S. (1983) 'Battle of the Somme: British War Propaganda', *Historical Journal of Film, Radio and Television*, 3, iii, 99–115.

Badsey, S. (1994) 'Modern Military Operations and the Media', Camberley: Strategic & Combat Studies Institute Paper, No. 8.

Bahador, B. (2007) *The CNN Effect in Action*, Basingstoke: Palgrave Macmillan.

Baird, J. (1974) *The Mythical World of Nazi War Propaganda, 1939–45*, Minneapolis: University of Minnesota Press.

Baker, N. (2008) *Human Smoke: The Beginnings of World War II, The End of Civilization*, New York: Simon & Schuster.

Baker, N. (2010) 'Questions for Nicholson Baker', amazon.com http://www.amazon.com/Human-Smoke-Beginnings-World-Civilization/dp/B002RAR3KG/ref=sr_1_5?ie=UTF8&s=books&qid=1276002505&sr=8-5, date accessed June 7, 2010.

Balabanova, E. (2010) 'Media Power During Humanitarian Interventions: Is Eastern Europe Any Different from the West?', *Journal of Peace Research*, 47, i, 71–82.

Baldor, L. (2007) 'Army Warns: Soldiers Will Be Punished For Putting Sensitive Information in Blogs', *Associated Press Archive*, May 2.

Baldouf, S. (2001) 'In Pakistan, War Coverage Is a Booming Business', *Christian Science Monitor*, November 2, 7.

Baldwin, T., McVoy, D. and Steinfield, C. (1996) *Convergence: Integrating Media, Information and Communication*, London: Sage.

Balfour, M. (1979) *Propaganda in War, 1939–45*, London: Routledge, Kegan, Paul.

Bamford, J. (2001) 'Is the Press Up to the Task of Reporting These Stories?' *Nieman Reports*, Winter, 19–22.

Bamford, J. (2005) 'The Man Who Sold the War: Meet John Rendon, Bush's General in the Propaganda War', http://www.rollingstone.com/politics/story/8798997/the_man_who_sold_the_war, date accessed December 14, 2009.

Barber, B. (1996) *Jihad vs McWorld: How Globalism and Tribalism are Reshaping the World*, New York: Ballantine.

Barber, J. (1993) 'The Image of Stalin in Soviet Propaganda and Public Opinion during World War 2' in Garrard and Garrard.

Barnouw, E. (1982) 'The Hiroshima-Nagasaki Footage: A Report', *Historical Journal of Film, Radio and Television*, 2, i, 91–9.

Bartov, O. (1996) *Murder in Our Midst: The Holocaust, Industrial Killing and Representation*, New York: Oxford University Press.

Basinger, J. (1986) *The World War Two Combat Movie: Anatomy of a Genre*, New York: Columbia University Press.

Bass, G. (2008) 'Humanitarian Impulses', *New York Times Magazine*, August 17.

Baudrillard, J. (1995) *The Gulf War Did Not Take Place* Bloomington: Indiana University Press. Translated by Paul Patton.

Baum, M. (2002) 'Sex, Lies, and War: How Soft News Brings Foreign Policy to the Inattentive Public', *American Political Science Review*, 96, i, 91–109.

Baum, M. (2003) *Soft News Goes to War: Public Opinion and American Foreign Policy in the New Media Age*, Princeton, NJ: Princeton University Press.

Beckett, I. (1988) '*Total War*' in McInnes and Sheffield.

Bedway, B. (2007) 'An Erie Tale in Baghdad', *Editor and Publisher*, 140, ii, February, 6–7.

Begin, M. (1977) *The Revolt*, New York: Nash.

Behr, E. (1992) *Anyone Here Been Raped and Speaks English? A Correspondent's Life Behind the Lines*, Harmondsworth: Penguin.

Bell, M. (1995) *In Harm's Way: Reflections of a War Zone Thug*, London: Hamish Hamilton.

Bell, M. (1997) 'TV News: How Far Should We Go?', *British Journalism Review*, 8, i, 6–16.

Bell, M. (1998) 'The Truth is Our Currency', *Press/Politics*, 3, i, 102–9.

Belsey, A. and Chadwick, R. (eds) (1992) *Ethical Issues in Journalism and the Media*, London: Routledge.

Bennett, W. (1990) 'Toward a Theory of Press-State Relations in the United States', *Journal of Communication*, 40, 103–25.

Bennett, W. and Paletz, D. (eds) (1994) *Taken by Storm: The Media, Public Opinion and US Foreign Policy in the Gulf War*, Chicago: University of Chicago Press.

Benthall, J. (1993) *Disasters, Relief and the Media*, London: IB Tauris.

Berenger, R. (ed.) (2004) *Global Media Go to War: Role of News and Entertainment Media during the 2003 Iraq War*, Spokane, WA: Marquette.

Berenger, R. (ed.) (2006) *Cybermedia Go to War: Role of Converging Media During and After the 2003 Iraq War*, Spokane, WA: Marquette.

Berg, R. (1991) 'Losing Vietnam: Covering War in an Age of Technology' in Rowe and Berg.

Bergmeier, H. and Lotz, R. (1997) *Hitler's Airwaves: The Inside Story of Nazi Radio Broadcasting and Propaganda Swing*, New Haven, CT: Yale University Press.

Berinsky, A. (2007) 'Assuming the Costs of War: Events, Elites, and American Public Support for Military Conflict', *Journal of Politics*, 69, iv, 975–97.

Berinsky, A. (2009) *In Time of War: Understanding American Public Opinion from World War II to Iraq*, Chicago: University of Chicago Press.

Berinsky, A. and Druckman, J. (2007) 'Public Opinion Research and Support for the Iraq War', *Public Opinion Quarterly*, 71, i, 126–41.

Berkowitz, D. (1997) *Social Meanings of News: A Text-Reader*, London: Sage.

Bishop, P. (1982) 'Reporting the Falklands', *Index on Censorship*, 11, vi, 6–8.

Bishop, P. (1993) *Famous Victory: The Gulf War*, London: Sinclair-Stevenson.

Bishop, R. (2006) 'The Whole World Is Watching, But So What? A Frame Analysis of Newspaper Coverage of Antiwar Protest' in Nikolaev and Hakanen.

Blake, M. (2005) 'From All Sides: In the Deadly Cauldron of Iraq, Even Arab Media are Being Pushed Off the Story', *Columbia Journalism Review*, March/April, 16–18.

Boccardi, L. (1995) 'Let the Reporters Report' in Girardet.

Boelke, W. (1970) *The Secret Conferences of Dr Goebbels: The Nazi Propaganda War, 1939–43*, New York: E. P. Dutton.

Boettcher, W. and Cobb, M. (2009) '"Don't Let Them Die in Vain": Casualty Frames and Public Tolerance for Escalating Commitment in Iraq', *Journal of Conflict Resolution*, 53, iii, 677–97.

Boggs, C. and Pollard, T. (2007) *The Hollywood War Machine: US Militarism and Popular Culture*, Boulder, CO: Paradigm.

Boltanski, L. (1999) *Distant Suffering: Morality, Media and Politics*, Cambridge: Cambridge University Press.

Bolton, R. (1990) *Death on the Rock and Other Stories*, London: W. H. Allen.

Bond, B. and Roy, I. (eds) (1975) *War and Society: A Yearbook of Military History*, New York: Holmes & Meier.

Bonham-Carter, M. (1989) 'Broadcasting and Terrorism', *Index on Censorship*, 18, ii, 7–8.

Boorstin, D. (1961) *The Image: Or What Happened to the American Dream?*, Harmondsworth: Penguin.

Borden, A. (1993) 'War of Words and Pictures' in Scott and Jones.

Bourdieu, P. (1998) *On Television and Journalism*, London: Pluto Press.

Boyce, D. (1972) *Englishmen and Irish Troubles: British Public Opinion and the Making of Irish Policy, 1918–22*, London: Jonathan Cape.

Boyer, P. (1996) 'Exotic Resonances: Hiroshima in American Memory' in Hogan.

Boyer, P. (2003) 'The New War Machine', *The New Yorker*, June 30, 54–71.

Braestrup, P. (1989) 'An Extreme Case' in Sevy.

Braestrup, P. (1994) *Big Story: How the American Press and Television Reported and Interpreted the Crisis of Tet 1968 in Vietnam and Washington*, Novato, CA: Presidio.

Bramsted, E. (1965) *Goebbels and National Socialist Propaganda, 1925–45*. London: Cresset Press.

Brauman, R. (1993) 'When Suffering Makes a Good Story' in *Médecins sans Frontières*.

Braw, M. (1991) *The Atomic Bomb Suppressed: American Censorship in Occupied Japan*, New York: Armonk.

Breed, W. (1955) 'Social Control in the Newsroom', *Social Forces*, 33, 326–35.

Bremer, L. (1991) 'Terrorism, the Media and the Government' in Matthews.

Brewer, S. (2009) *Why America Fights: Patriotism and War Propaganda from the Philippines to Iraq*, New York: Oxford University Press.

Briggs, A. (1985) *The BBC: The First Fifty Years*, Oxford: Oxford University Press.

Briggs, A. (1995) *The War of Words, 1939–45*, Oxford: Oxford University Press.

Brightman, C. (2003) 'In Bed With the Pentagon', *New Statesman*, March 17, 5–6.

Brockus, S. (2009) 'Coming to You "Live": Exclusive Witnessing and the Battlefield Reporter', *Journal of Communication Inquiry*, 33, i, 27–42.

Brooks, J. (1995) '*Pravda* Goes to War' in Stites.

Brooks, J. (2000) *Thank You, Comrade Stalin!: Soviet Public Culture from Revolution to Cold War*, Princeton: Princeton University Press.

Brothers, C. (1997) *War and Photography: A Cultural History*, London: Routledge.

Brough-Williams, I. (1996) 'War Without End?: The *Bloody Bosnia* Season on Channel Four' in Gow, Paterson and Preston.

Brown, C. (1967) *The Correspondents' War: Journalists in the Spanish-American War*, New York: Charles Scribner's Sons.

Brown, J. (1963) *Techniques of Persuasion: From Propaganda to Brainwashing*, Harmondsworth: Penguin.

Brown, R. (2003) 'Spinning the War: Political Communications, Information Operations and Public Diplomacy in the War on Terrorism' in Thussu and Freedman.

Browne, M. (1991) 'The Military vs The Press', *The New York Times*, March 3, 227.

Brownlow, K. (1979) *The War, the West, and the Wilderness*, London: Secker & Warburg.

Buitenhuis, P. (1989) *The Great War of Words: Literature as Propaganda, 1914–18 and After*, London: Batsford.

Bumiller, E. (2009) 'Defense Secretary's Trip Encounters Snags in Two Theaters', *The New York Times*.

Burns, J. (1996) 'The Media as Impartial Observers or Protagonists: Conflict Reporting or Conflict Encouragement in Former Yugoslavia' in Gow, Paterson and Preston.

Burns, J. H. (2004) *The Gallery*, New York: New York Review of Books.

Buruma, I. (1995) *The Wages of Guilt: Memories of War in Germany and Japan*, London: Vintage.

Bush, G. (2003) *The Office of Global Communications*, http://georgewbush-whitehouse.archives.gov/ogc/aboutogc.html, date accessed May 20, 2010.

Buzzell, C. (2005) *My War: Killing Time in Iraq*, New York: G. P. Putnam's Sons.

Calder, A. (1969) *The People's War: Britain, 1939–45*, London: Panther.

Campbell, D. (1993) *Politics Without Principle: Sovereignty, Ethics and Narratives of the Gulf War*, London: Lynne Reinner.

Campbell, K. (2001) 'Today's War Reporting: It's Digital But Dangerous', *Christian Science Monitor*, December 4, 2.

Caplan, G. (2007) 'Rwanda: Walking the Road to Genocide' in Thompson.

Capozzola, C. (2008) *Uncle Sam Wants You: World War I and the Making of the Modern American Citizen*, New York: Oxford University Press.

Cardel, K. (2006) 'Bloodsport: Thomas Goltz and the Journalist's Diary of War', *Biography*, 29, iv, 584–604.

Carr, D. (2003) 'Reporters' New Battlefield Access Has its Risks as Well as Its Rewards', *The New York Times*, March 31.

Carruthers, S. (1995) *Winning Hearts and Minds: British Governments, the Media and Colonial Counterinsurgency, 1944–60*, London: Leicester University Press.

Carruthers, S. (1996) 'Reporting Terrorism: The British State and the Media, 1919–94' in Stewart and Carruthers.

Carruthers, S. (2001) 'Compulsory Viewing: Concentration Camp Film and German Re-education', *Millennium: Journal of International Studies*, 30, iii, 733–59.

Carruthers, S. (2004) 'Tribalism and Tribulation: Media Constructions of "African Savagery" and "Western Humanitarianism" in the 1990s' in Allan and Zelizer.

Carruthers, S. (2006) 'Say Cheese: Operation Iraqi Freedom on Film', *Cineaste*, Winter, 30–6.

Carruthers, S. (2007) 'Question Time: The Iraq War Revisited', *Cineaste*, Fall, 12–17.

Carruthers, S. (2008a) 'Bodies of Evidence: New Documentaries on Iraq War Veterans', *Cineaste*, Winter, 26–31.

Carruthers, S. (2008b) 'No One's Looking: The Disappearing Audience for War', *Media, War & Conflict*, 1, i, 71–7.

Casey, S. (2001) *Cautious Crusade: Franklin D. Roosevelt, American Public Opinion, and the War against Nazi Germany*, New York: Oxford University Press.

Casey, S. (2008) *Selling the Korean War: Propaganda, Politics and Public Opinion, 1950–1953*, New York: Oxford University Press.

Cassara, C. and Lengel, L. (2004) 'Move Over CNN: Al-Jazeera's View of the World Takes on the West' in Berenger.

Castonguay, J. (2006) 'The Spanish–American War in United States Media Culture' in Slocum.

CBS News/NYT (2003) Poll USCBSNYT.032303.R34, March 22.

Cecil, H. and Liddle, P. (eds) (1996) *Facing Armageddon: The First World War Experienced*, London: Leo Cooper.

Chaliand, G. (1987) *Terrorism: From Popular Struggle to Media Spectacle*, London: Saqi.

Chaliand, G. and Blin, A. (eds) (2007) *The History of Terrorism: From Antiquity to Al Qaeda*, Berkeley: University of California Press.

Chambers, J. (1996) '*All Quiet on the Western Front* (US, 1930): The Antiwar Film and the Image of Modern War' in Chambers and Culbert.

Chambers, J. and Culbert, D. (eds) (1996) *World War II: Film and History*, New York: Oxford University Press.

Chandler, D. (2002) *From Kosovo to Kabul: Human Rights and International Intervention*, London: Pluto Press.

Chaon, A. (2007) 'Who Failed in Rwanda, Journalists or the Media?' in Thompson.

Chapman, J. (1998) *The British At War: Cinema, State and Propaganda, 1939–45*, London: IB Tauris.

Charlie Rose Show (2004) 'Implications of Photographs Inside Prison in Iraq', PBS, May 3.

Chase, R. (2009) 'Media Witness Return of War Casualty at Dover', *Associated Press*, April 6.

Chayes, S. (2003) 'Breaking Ranks', *Columbia Journalism Review*, November/December, 66–7.

Chenelly, J. (2005) 'The Blogs of War: Troops Offer "The Truth" via Web Journals', *Army Times*, March 14.

Chomsky, N. (1989a) *Necessary Illusions: Thought Control in Democratic Societies*, London: Pluto Press.

Chomsky, N. (1989b) *The Culture of Terrorism*, London: Pluto Press.

Chrétien, J.–P. (2007) 'RTLM Propaganda: the Democratic Alibi' in Thompson.

Christensen, C. (2008) 'Uploading Dissonance: *YouTube* and the US Occupation of Iraq', *Media, War and Conflict*, 1, ii, 155–75.

Christensen, T. (1987) *Reel Politics: American Political Movies from 'Birth of a Nation' to 'Platoon'*, Oxford: Blackwell.

Cigar, N. (1995) *Genocide in Bosnia: the Politics of 'Ethnic Cleansing'*, College Station, TX: Texas A&M University Press.

Clark, I. (1997) *Globalization and Fragmentation: International Relations in the Twentieth Century*, Oxford: Oxford University Press.

Clark, M. (1985) 'Vietnam: Representations of Self and War', *Wide Angle*, 7, iv, 4–11

Clawson, P. (1990) 'Why We Need More But Better Coverage of Terrorism', *Orbis*, 27, 701–10.

Cline, R. and Alexander, Y. (1986) *Terrorism as State-Sponsored Covert Warfare*, Fairfax, VA: Hero.

Cloake, J. (1985) *Templer: Tiger of Malaya: The Life of Field Marshal Sir Gerald Templer*, London: Harrap.

Cloud, D. (2004) '"To Veil the Threat of Terror": Afghan Women and the "Clash of Civilizations" in the Imagery of the US War on Terrorism', *Quarterly Journal of Speech*, 90, iii, 285–306.

Clutterbuck, R. (1981) *The Media and Political Violence*, London: Macmillan, 1981.

CNN (2001a) 'President Bush Says Taliban Paying a Price', CNN, October 7, http://archives.cnn.com/2001/US/10/07/ret.bush.transcript/, date accessed June 4, 2010.

CNN (2001b) 'Bush: "There's No Rules"', CNN, September 17, http://archives.cnn.com/2001/US/09/17/gen.bush.transcript/, date accessed June 4, 2010.

CNN (2001c) 'Correspondents Discuss Coverage of War Overseas and at Home', October 13, http://transcripts.cnn.com/TRANSCRIPTS/0110/13/rs.00.html, date accessed June 4, 2010.

CNN (2003) 'Dixie Chicks Singer Apologizes for Bush Comment,' March 14, http://www.cnn.com/2003/SHOWBIZ/Music/03/14/dixie.chicks.apology/, date accessed June 4, 2010.

CNN/Opinion Research Corporation (2009a) Poll USORC.112309.R25, November 13–15.

CNN/Opinion Research Corporation (2009b) Poll USORC.120709.R25, December 2–3.

Cockburn, A. (1991) 'The TV War', *New Statesman and Society*, March 8, 14–15.

Cockerell, M. (1984) *Sources Close to the Prime Minister: Inside the Hidden World of the News Manipulators*, London: Macmillan.

Cockerell, M. (1988) *Live From Number 10: The Inside Story of Prime Ministers and Television*, London: Faber.

Cole, J. (2009) *Engaging the Muslim World*, New York: Palgrave Macmillan.

Collins, R., Hennessey, P. and Walker, D. (1986) *Media, Culture and Society: A Critical Reader*, London: Sage.

Colombo, F. (1995) 'The Media and Operation Restore Hope in Somalia' in Girardet.

Connelly, M. (2002) *A Diplomatic Revolution: Algeria's Fight for Independence and the Origins of the Post-Cold War Era*, New York: Oxford University Press.

Conners, J. (1998) 'Hussein as Enemy: The Persian Gulf War in Political Cartoons', *Press/Politics*, 3, iii, 96–114.

Conway, M. (2007) 'Terrorism and the Making of the "New Middle East": New Media Strategies of Hezbollah and al Qaeda' in Seib.

Cook, D. (2005) *Understanding Jihad*, Berkeley: University of California Press.

Cook, E. (1920) *The Press in Wartime*, London: Macmillan.

Cook, T. (1994) 'Washington Newsbeats and Network News after the Iraq Invasion of Kuwait' in Bennett and Paletz.

Cooper, S. (2006) *Watching the Watchdog: Bloggers as the Fifth Estate*, Spokane, WA: Marquette.

Cooper, S. and Kuypers, J. (2004) 'Embedded Versus Behind-the-Lines Reporting on the 2003 Iraq War' in Berenger.

Cordingley, P. (1996) *In the Eye of the Storm: Commanding the Desert Rats in the Gulf War*, London: Hodder & Stoughton.

Corfield, F. (1960) *Historical Survey of the Origins and Growth of Mau Mau*, London: Her Majesty's Stationery Office.

Cornebise, A. (1993) *Ranks and Columns: Armed Forces Newspapers in American Wars*, Westport, CT: Greenwood Press.

Corner, J, Schlesinger, P. and Silverstone, R. (eds) (1997) *International Media Research: A Critical Survey*, London: Routledge.

Costello, J. (1985) *Love, Sex and War, 1939–45*, London: Pan.

Couldry, N. and Downey, J. (2004) 'War or Peace?: Legitimation, Dissent, and Rhetorical Closure in Press Coverage of the Iraq War Build-Up' in Allan and Zelizer.

Coultass, C. (1984) 'British Feature Films and the Second World War', *Journal of Contemporary History*, 19, i, 7–22.

Cox News Service (1993) 'TV Helps Shape Policy on Bosnia', *Press-Telegram* (Long Beach, CA), May 9.

Crane, A. (2006) '"Embed" Goes For a Spin', *Editor and Publisher*, December, 5–6.

Cripps, T. (1983) 'Racial Ambiguities in American Propaganda Movies' in Short.

Cripps, T. (1997) *Hollywood's High Noon: Moviemaking and Society before Television*, Baltimore: Johns Hopkins University Press.

Crowley, M. (2009) 'COIN Toss: The Cult of Counterinsurgency', *New Republic*, December 30, 8–10.

Cruikshank, C. (1977) *The Fourth Arm: Psychological Warfare 1938–45*, Oxford: Oxford University Press.

Culbert, D. (1983) '*Why We Fight*: Social Engineering for a Democratic Society at War' in Short.

Culbert, D. (1985) 'American Film Policy in the Re-education of Germany after 1945' in Pronay and Wilson.

Culbert, D. (1988) 'Television's Vietnam and Historical Revisionism in the United States,' *Historical Journal of Film, Radio and Television*, 8, iii, 253–67.

Culbert, D. (ed.) (1990) *Film and Propaganda in America: A Documentary History, Vols II & III, World War II*, Westport, CT: Greenwood Press.

Cull, N. (1995) *Propaganda for War: the British Propaganda Campaign against American 'Neutrality' in World War II*, New York: Oxford University Press.

Cull, N. (2008) *The Cold War and the United States Information Agency: American Public Diplomacy, 1945–1989*, New York: Cambridge University Press.

Cumings, B. (1992) *War and Television*, London: Verso.

Cunningham, B. (2003) 'Re-Thinking Objectivity', *Columbia Journalism Review*, July/August, 24–32.

Curran, C. (1990) 'The New Revisionism in Mass Communication Research: A Reappraisal', *European Journal of Communication*, 5, ii–iii, 135–64.

Curran, C. and Porter, V. (1983) *British Cinema History*, London: Weidenfeld & Nicolson.

Curry, R. (1995) 'How Early German Film Stars Helped Sell the War(es)' in Dibbets and Hogenkamp.

Curtis, L. (1984) *Ireland: The Propaganda War: The British Media and the Battle for Hearts and Minds*, London: Pluto Press.

Curtis, L. and Jempson, P. (1993) *Interference on the Airwaves: Ireland, the Media and the Broadcasting Ban*, London: Campaign for Press and Broadcasting Freedom.

Dadge, D. (2006) *The War in Iraq and Why the Media Failed Us*, Westport, CT: Praeger.

Daglish, L. (2004) 'Censoring the Truth about War', *News Media & The Law*, 4.

Dahlgren, P. and Sparks, C. (eds) (1991) *Communication and Citizenship: Journalism and the Public Sphere*, London: Routledge.

Dallaire, R. (2007) 'The Media Dichotomy' in Thompson.

Danner, M. (2004) *Torture and Truth: America, Abu Ghraib, and the War on Terror*, New York: New York Review of Books.

Dao, J. (2009) 'Pentagon Keeps Wary Watch as Troops and Their Superiors Blog', *The New York Times*, September 9.

Dauber, C. (2001) 'The Shots Seen 'Round the World: The Impact of the Images of Mogadishu on American Military Operations', *Rhetoric & Public Affairs*, 4, iv, 653–87.

DeBauche, L. (1997) *Reel Patriotism: The Movies and World War I*, Madison: University of Wisconsin Press.

De la Billière, P. (1995) *Storm Command: A Personal Account of the Gulf War*, London: HarperCollins.

Demm, E. (1993) 'Propaganda and Caricature in the First World War', *Journal of Contemporary History*, 28, 163–92.

Denton, R. (ed.) (1993) *The Media and the Persian Gulf War*, Westport, CT: Praeger.

Déotte, J.-L., *et al.* (eds) (1994) *Visites aux armées: tourismes de guerre (Back to the Front: Tourisms of War)*, Basse-Normandie: FRAC.

Der Derian, J. (1992) *Antidiplomacy: Spies, Terror, Speed and War*, Oxford: Blackwell.

Der Derian, J. (2001) *Virtuous War: Mapping the Military–Industrial–Media–Entertainment Network*, Boulder, CO: Westview Press.

Des Forges, A. (2007) 'Call to Genocide: Radio in Rwanda, 1994' in Thompson.

Destexhe, A. (1995) *Rwanda and Genocide in the Twentieth Century*, London: Pluto Press.

Devereaux, L. and Hillman, R. (eds) (1995) *Fields of Vision: Essays in Film Studies, Visual Anthropology and Photography*, Berkeley: University of California Press.

de Waal, A. (1994) 'African Encounters', *Index on Censorship*, 6, 14–31.

Dibbets, K. and Hogenkamp, B. (1995) *Film and the First World War*, Amsterdam: Amsterdam University Press.

Dimaggio, A. (2008) *Mass Media, Mass Propaganda: Examining American News in the 'War on Terror'*, Lanham, MD: Lexington.

Dittmar, L. and Michaud, G. (eds) (1990) *From Hanoi to Hollywood: The Vietnam War in American Film*. New Brunswick, NJ: Rutgers University Press.

Dobkin, B. (1992) *Tales of Terror: Television News and the Construction of the Terrorist Threat*, Westport, CT: Praeger.

Doherty, M. (2000) *Nazi Wireless Propaganda: Lord Haw-Haw and British Public Opinion in the Second World War*, Edinburgh: Edinburgh University Press.

Doherty, T. (1988–9) 'Full Metal Genre: Stanley Kubrick's Vietnam Combat Movie', *Film Quarterly*, 42, ii, 24–30.

Doherty, T. (1998) '*Saving Private Ryan*', *Cineaste*, XXIV, i, 68–71.

Doherty, T. (1999) *Projections of War: Hollywood, American Culture and World War II*, New York: Columbia University Press. Second edition.

Doob, L. (1995) 'Goebbels' Principles of Propaganda' in Jackall.

Dorman, W. (2006) 'A Debate Delayed Is a Debate Denied: US News Media before the 2003 War with Iraq' in Nikolaev and Hakanen.

Dorman, W. and Livingston, S. (1994) 'The Establishing Phase of the Persian Gulf Policy Debate' in Bennett and Paletz.

Douglas, S. (2006) 'The Turn Within: The Irony of Technology in a Globalized World', *American Quarterly*, 58, iii, 619–38.

Dowd, M. (2001) 'Liberties: Talkin' Ain't Fightin'', *The New York Times*, November 7.

Dowden, R. (1995) 'Covering Somalia: Recipe for Disaster' in Girardet.

Dower, J. (1986) *War Without Mercy: Race and Power in the Pacific War*, New York: Pantheon.

Dower, J. (1996a) *Japan in War and Peace: Essays on History, Culture and Race*, London: Fontana.

Dower, J. (1996b) 'The Bombed: Hiroshimas and Nagasakis in Japanese Memory,' in Hogan.

Dower, J. (1999) *Embracing Defeat: Japan in the Wake of World War II*, New York: W. W. Norton & Company.

Downing, J., Mohammadi, A. and Sreberny-Mohammadi, A. (eds) (1995) *Questioning the Media: A Critical Introduction*, London: Sage.

Doyle, M. (2007) 'Reporting the Genocide' in Thompson.

Drew, C. (2010) 'Drone Flights Leave Military Awash in Data', *The New York Times*, January 11.

Dubriwny, T. (2005) 'First Ladies and Feminism: Laura Bush as Advocate for Women's and Children's Rights', *Women's Studies in Communication*, 28, i, 84–114.

Dudziak, M. (ed.) (2003) *September 11 in History: A Watershed Moment?*, Durham, NC: Duke University Press.

Dworkin, A. (1996) 'The World in Judgement', *Index on Censorship*, 25, v, 137–44.

Eckstein, H. (ed.) (1964) *Internal War: Problems and Approaches*, New York: Free Press.

Economist, The (2001) 'Picture Perfect?', October 20, 75–6.

Economist.com (2009) 'Tolerating Abuse', July 30.

Edwards, D. and Cromwell, D. (2004) 'Mass Deception: How the Media Helped the Government Deceive the People' in Miller.

Edwards, P. (1996) *The Closed World: Computers and the Politics of Discourse in Cold War America*, Cambridge, MA: MIT Press.

Ehrenburg, I. (1964) *The War, 1942–45*, London: MacGibbon & Kee.

Eickelman, D. (2004) 'The Middle East's Democracy Deficit and the Expanding Public Sphere' in van der Veer and Munshi.

Eisenman, S. (2007) *The Abu Ghraib Effect*, London: Reaktion.

Eksteins, M. (1980) '*All Quiet on the Western Front* and the Fate of a War', *Journal of Contemporary History*, 15, 345–66.

Eksteins, M. (1990) *Rites of Spring: The Great War and the Birth of the Modern Age*, London: Black Swan.

Elasmar, Michael G. (2007) *Through Their Eyes: Factors Affecting Muslim Support for the US-Led War on Terror*, Spokane, WT: Marquette.

Eldridge, J. (1993) *Getting the Message: News, Truth and Power*, London: Routledge.

Elegant, R. (1989) 'How to Lose a War', in Sevy.

Ellul, J. (1972) *Propaganda: the Formation of Men's Attitudes*, New York: Alfred A. Knopf.

El-Nawawy, M. (2007) 'US Public Diplomacy and the News Credibility of Radio Sawa and Television Al Hurra in the Arab World' in Seib.

Elsaesser, T. (ed.) (1996) *A Second Life: German Cinema's First Decades*, Amsterdam: Amsterdam University Press.

Engelberg, S. (1989) 'Washington's War on Terrorism Captures Few Soldiers', *The New York Times*, March 5.

Entman, R. (2000) 'Declarations of Independence: The Growth of Media Power after the Cold War' in Nacos, Shapiro and Isernia.

Entman, R. (2004) *Projections of Power: Framing News, Public Opinion, and US Foreign Policy*, Chicago: University of Chicago Press.

Entman, R. and Page, B. (1994) 'The News Before the Storm' in Bennett and Paletz.

Ettema, J. (1994) 'Discourse that is Closer to Silence than to Talk: The Politics and Possibilities of Reporting on Victims of War', *Critical Studies in Mass Communication*, 11, 1–21.

Ewen, S. (1996) *PR! A Social History of Spin*, New York: Basic.

Falk, R. (1991) 'The Terrorist Foundations of Recent US Foreign Policy' in George.

Fandy, M. (2007) *(Un)Civil War of Words: Media and Politics in the Arab World*, Westport, CT: Praeger Security International.

Farber, D. (2005) *Taken Hostage: The Iran Hostage Crisis and America's First Encounter with Radical Islam*, Princeton, NJ: Princeton University Press.

Farish, M. (2001) 'Modern Witnesses: Foreign Correspondents, Geopolitical Vision, and the First World War', *Transactions of the Institute of British Geographers*, 26, i, 273–87.

Farrar, M. (1998) *News From the Front: War Correspondents on the Western Front, 1914–18*, Stroud: Sutton.

Farrell, W. (1983) 'US Allows 15 Reporters to Go to Grenada For Day', *The New York Times*, October 28.

Fay, J. (2008) *Theaters of Occupation: Hollywood and the Reeducation of Postwar Germany*, Minneapolis: University of Minnesota Press.

Feaver, P. and Gelpi, C. (1999) 'A Look At … Casualty Aversion: How Many Deaths Are Acceptable? A Surprising Answer', *Washington Post*, November 7.

Feher, M. (2000) *Powerless by Design: The Age of the International Community*, Durham, NC: Duke University Press.

Feldstein, M. (2007) 'Dummies and Ventriloquists: Models of How Sources Set the Investigative Agenda', *Journalism*, 8, v, 499–509.

Ferguson, M. (1992) 'The Mythology about Globalization', *European Journal of Communication*, 7 (1992), 69–93.

Ferguson, N. (1999) *The Pity of War*, New York: Basic.

Fialka, J. (1991) *Hotel Warriors: Covering the Gulf*, Washington, DC: Woodrow Wilson Center.

Filkins, D. (2008) *The Forever War*, New York: Alfred A. Knopf.

Fine, J. (2004) 'Indian Media Coverage of the 2003 Iraq War' in Berenger.

Finkel, D. (2009) *The Good Soldiers*, New York: Sarah Crichton.

Fishman, M. (1980) *Manufacturing the News*, Austin, TX: University of Texas Press.

Fiske, J. (1987) *Television Culture*, London: Methuen.

Fleeson, L. (2002) 'The Civilian Casualty Conundrum', *American Journalism Review*, 24, iii, 18–27.

Flichy, P. (1995) *Dynamics of Modern Communications: The Shaping and Impact of New Communication Technologies*, London: Sage.

Forest, J. (2009) *Influence Warfare: How Terrorists and Governments Fight to Shape Perceptions in a War of Ideas*, Westport, CT: Praeger.

Forest, J. and Honkus, F. (2009) 'Introduction' in Forest.

Foster, K. (1992) 'The Falklands War: A Critical View of Information Policy' in Young.

Fox News Channel (2003) 'A Look Back at Some of the Reporting From Iraq', April 22.

Fox, T. (1995) 'The Media and the Military: An Historical Perspective on the Gulf War' in Walsh.

Frankel, M. (1969) 'Agnew: A Broad Attack on TV and the Press', *The New York Times*, November 23.

Franklin, H. B. (1994) 'From Realism to Virtual Reality: Images of America's Wars' in Jeffords and Rabinowitz.

Franklin, N. (2003) 'TV Goes to War', *The New Yorker*, March 31.

Fraser, L. (1957) *Propaganda*, Oxford: Oxford University Press.

Frey, R. and Norris, C. (eds) (1991) *Violence, Terrorism, and Justice*, Cambridge: Cambridge University Press.

Friedlander, S. (1992) *Probing the Limits of Representation: Nazism and the 'Final Solution'*, London: Harvard University Press.

Friendly, J. (1983) 'Press Voices Criticism of "Off-the-Record War"', *The New York Times* November 4.

Fumento, M. (2006) 'Covering Iraq', *National Review*, November 6, 42–6.

Fussell, P. (1989) *Wartime: Understanding and Behavior in the Second World War*, New York: Oxford University Press.

Fussell, P. (2004) 'Introduction' in Burns.

Fyne, R. (1994) *The Hollywood Propaganda of World War II*, Metuchen, NJ: Scarecrow Press.

Gailey, P. (1983) 'US Bars Coverage of Grenada Action; News Groups Protest', *The New York Times*, October 27.

Galal, I., Ahmed, A. and al-Hammouri, L. (2006) 'Operation Iraqi Freedom or Invasion of Iraq: Arab Interpretation of CNN and Al-Jazeera Coverage of the 2003 Iraq War' in Berenger.

Gallimore, T. (1991) 'Media Compliance with Voluntary Press Guidelines for Covering Terrorism' in Alexander and Picard.

Gallup Organization (1944) Survey USGALLUP 012844.RK06, January 6–11.

Gallup Organization (1945) Survey USAIPO 1945-0347, May 17–23.

Gans, H. (1970) 'Since Spiro Agnew Brought Up the Subject, How Well *Does* TV Present the News?', *The New York Times*, January 11.

Gans, H. (1979) *Deciding What's News*, New York: Pantheon.

Garrard, J. and Garrard, C. (eds) (1993) *World War 2 and the Soviet People*, New York: St Martin's Press.

Garrels, A. (2004) *Naked in Baghdad: The Iraq War and the Aftermath as Seen by NPR's Correspondent*, New York: Picador.

Gary, B. (1999) *The Nervous Liberals: Propaganda Anxieties from World War I to the Cold War*, New York: Columbia University Press.

Gassman, P. (1995) 'TV Without Government: The New World Order?' in Girardet.

Gelpi, C., Feaver, D. and Reifler, J. (2009) *Paying the Human Costs of War: American Public Opinion and Casualties in Military Conflicts*, Princeton, NJ: Princeton University Press.

George, A. (ed.) (1991) *Western State Terrorism*, Oxford: Polity Press.

Gerbner, G. (1992) 'Violence and Terror in and by the Media' in Raboy and Dagenais.

Gerrits, R. (1992) 'Terrorists' Perspectives: Memoirs' in Paletz and Schmid.

Getler, M. (1991) 'Do Americans Really Want to Censor War Coverage This Way?', *Washington Post*, March 17.

Giangreco, D. (2004) '"Spinning" the Casualties: Media Strategies During the Roosevelt Administration', *SHAFR Newsletter*, December.

Gibbs, P. (1923) *Adventures in Journalism*, New York: Harper & Brothers.

Giddens, A. (1990) *The Consequences of Modernity*, Cambridge: Polity Press.

Gienow-Hecht, J. (1999) *Transmission Impossible: American Journalism as Cultural Diplomacy in Postwar Germany, 1945–55*, Baton Rouge: Louisiana State University Press.

Gilbert, P. (1992) 'The Oxygen of Publicity: Terrorism and Reporting Restrictions' in Belsey and Chadwick.

Gilboa, E. (ed.) (2002) *Media and Conflict: Framing Issues, Making Policy, Shaping Opinions*, Ardsley, NY: Transnational.

Gilboa, E. (2005) 'The CNN Effect: The Search for a Communication Theory of International Relations', *Political Communication*, 22, 27–44.

Girardet, E. (ed.) (1995) *Somalia, Rwanda and Beyond: The Role of the International Media in Wars and Humanitarian Crises*, Dublin: Crosslines Global Report.

Girardet, E. (1996) 'Reporting Humanitarianism: Are the New Electronic Media Making a Difference?' in Rotberg and Weiss.

Giroux, H. (2006) *Beyond the Spectacle of Terrorism: Global Uncertainty and the Challenge of the New Media*, Boulder, CO: Paradigm.

Gitlin, T. (1980) *The Whole World Is Watching: The Mass Media in the Making and Unmaking of the New Left*, Berkeley: University of California Press.

Glasgow University Media Group (1985) *War and Peace News*, Milton Keynes: Open University Press.

Glass, C. (2007) 'A High Price for Bad News', *New Statesman*, January 8, 17.

Gledhill, C. and Swanson, G. (1996) (eds) *Nationalising Femininity: Culture, Sexuality and Cinema in Britain in World War II*, Manchester: Manchester University Press.

Golding, P., Murdock, G. and Schlesinger, P. (1986) *Communicating Politics: Mass Communications and the Political Process*, Leicester: Leicester University Press.

Goldstein, C. (2009) *Capturing the German Eye: American Visual Propaganda in Occupied Germany*, Chicago: University of Chicago Press.

Gombrich, E. (1970) *Myth and Reality in German War-Time Broadcasts*, London: Athlone Press.

Gopsill, T. (2004) 'Target the Media' in Miller.

Government Press Releases (2009) 'South Asia Expert Sees Obama "Redefining The War on Terror"', March 30.

Gow, J. (1997) *Triumph of the Lack of Will: International Diplomacy and the Yugoslav War*, London: Hurst & Co.

Gow, J., Paterson, R. and Preston, A. (eds) (1996) *Bosnia by Television*, London: BFI.

Gowing, N. (1991) 'The Media Dimension 1: TV and the Kurds', *World Today*, 111–12

Gowing, N. (1994) 'Real-Time Television Coverage of Armed Conflicts and Diplomatic Crises: Does it Pressure or Distort Foreign Policy Decisions?', Harvard: Joan Shorenstein Barone Center, Working Paper 94-1.

Gray, C. (1997) *Postmodern War: The New Politics of Conflict*, London: Routledge.

Greenberg, B. and Gantz, W. (eds) (1993) *Desert Storm and the Mass Media*, Cresskill, NJ: Hampton Press.

Greppi, M. (2001) 'From the Battle Zone', *Electronic Media*, October 29, 4.

Grieves, K. (1996) 'War Correspondents and Conducting Officers on the Western Front from 1915' in Cecil and Liddle.

Griffin, M. (2004) 'Picturing America's "War on Terrorism" in Afghanistan and Iraq', *Journalism*, 5, iv, 381–402.

Grisewood, H. (1968) *One Thing At A Time: An Autobiography*, London: Hutchinson.

Grossman, V. (1995) *Life and Fate*, London: Harvill Press.

Grossman, V. (2007) *A Writer at War: A Soviet Journalist with the Red Army, 1941–1945*, New York: Vintage.

Guardian (2003) 'A War of Words Over Iraq Video Games', November 15.

Gurevitch, M., Levy, M. and Roeh, I. (1991) 'The Global Newsroom: Convergence and Diversities in the Globalization of Television News' in Dahlgren and Sparks.

Gutman, R. (1993) *A Witness to Genocide: The First Inside Account of the Horrors of 'Ethnic Cleansing' in Bosnia*, Shaftesbury: Element.

Hackworth, D. (1992) 'The Gulf Crisis: The Media Point of View' in Young.

Haigh, M. *et al.* (2006), 'A Comparison of Embedded and Nonembedded Print Coverage of the US Invasion and Occupation of Iraq', *Harvard International Journal of Press/Politics*, 11, ii, 139–53.

Hale, O. (1964) *The Captive Press in the Third Reich*, Princeton, NJ: Princeton University Press.

Hall, T. (1993) 'Why the Broadcasting Ban Should Go', *Index on Censorship*, 8/9, 4–6

Hallin, D. (1989) *The 'Uncensored War': the Media and Vietnam*, New York: Oxford University Press.

Hallin, D. (1994a) *We Keep America On Top of the World: Television Journalism and the Public Sphere*, London: Routledge.

Hallin, D. (1994b) 'Images of Vietnam and the Persian Gulf Wars in US Television' in Jeffords and Rabinowitz.

Hallin, D. and Gitlin, T. (1994) 'The Gulf War as Popular Culture and Television Drama' in Bennett and Paletz.

Hamelink, C. (1994) *The Politics of World Communication: A Human Rights Perspective*, London: Sage.

Hamilton, R. (1989) 'Image and Context: The Production and Reproduction of *The Execution of a VC Suspect* by Eddie Adams' in Walsh and Aulich.

Hammock, J. and Charny, J. (1996) 'Emergency Response as Morality Play: The Media, the Relief Agencies and the Need for Capacity Building' in Rotberg and Weiss.

Hammond, P. (2007) *Framing Post-Cold War Conflicts: The Media and International Intervention*, Manchester: Manchester University Press.

Hammond, P. and Herman, S. (eds) (2000) *Degraded Capability: The Media and the Kosovo Crisis*, London: Pluto Press.

Hammond, W. (1989) 'The Press in Vietnam as Agent of Defeat: A Critical Examination', *Reviews in American History*, 17, ii, 312–23.

Hammond, W. (1998) *Reporting Vietnam: Media and Military at War*, Lawrence, KA: University of Kansas Press.

Hannerz, U. (1996) *Transnational Connections: Culture, People, Places*, London: Routledge.

Harper, J. (1991) 'The Italian Press and the Moro Affair' in Serfaty.

Harper, S. (1988) 'The Representation of Women in British Feature Films, 1939–45' in Taylor.

Harris, P. (1992) *Somebody Else's War: Frontline Reports From the Balkan Wars, 1991–2*, Stevenage: Spa.

Harris, R. (1983) *Gotcha! The Media, the Government and the Falklands Crisis*, London: Faber & Faber.

Hart, K. (2005) 'Quitting Kabul', *American Journalism Review*, February/March, 12–13.

Hartford Courant, The (1902) 'Stern Measures Against Filipinos', February 5, 1.

Haste, C. (1977) *Keep the Home Fires Burning: Propaganda in the First World War*, London: Allen Lane.

Hawkins, V. (2002) 'The Other Side of the CNN Factor: The Media and Conflict', *Journalism Studies*, 3, ii, 225–40.

Hawaleshka, D. (2004) 'What Bush Didn't Want Americans to See', *Maclean's*, May 3, 34–5.

Hedges, C. (2003) *War Is a Force that Gives Us Meaning*, New York: Anchor.

Henderson, L., Miller, D. and Reilly, J. (1990) *Speak No Evil: The British Broadcasting Ban, the Media and the Conflict in Ireland*, Glasgow: Glasgow University Media Group.

Herf, J. (1997) *Divided Memory: The Nazi Past in the Two Germanies*, Cambridge, MA: Harvard University Press.

Herf, J. (2006) *The Jewish Enemy: Nazi Propaganda During World War II and the Holocaust*, Cambridge, MA: Belknap Press.

Herman, E. (1982) *The Real Terror Network: Terror in Fact and Propaganda*, Boston: South End Press.

Herman, E. and Chomsky, N. (1988) *Manufacturing Dissent: the Political Economy of the Mass Media*, New York: Pantheon.

Herr, M. (1978) *Dispatches*, London: Pan.

Hersh, S. (2004) 'Torture at Abu Ghraib', *The New Yorker*, May 10.

Herzstein, R. (1979) *The War That Hitler Won: The Most Infamous Propaganda Campaign in History*, London: Hamish Hamilton.

Hess, S. and Kalb, M. (2003) *The Media and the War on Terrorism*, Washington, DC: Brookings Institution Press.

Hickey, N. (2002) 'Perspectives on War: Different Cultures, Different Coverage', *Columbia Journalism Review*, March/April, 40–3.

Higiro, J.-M. (2007) 'Rwandan Private Print Media on the Eve of the Genocide' in Thompson.

Hill, C. (1974) *Behind the Screen: The Broadcasting Memoirs of Lord Hill of Luton*, London: Sidgwick & Jackson.

Hill, C. (1996) 'World Opinion and the Empire of Circumstance', *International Affairs*, 72, i, 109–32.

Hilsum, L. (1995) 'Where is Kigali?' *Granta*, 51, 145–79.

Hilsum, L. (2007) 'Reporting Rwanda: the Media and the Aid Agencies' in Thompson.

Hirano, K. (1992) *Mr Smith Goes to Tokyo: Japanese Cinema Under the American Occupation, 1945–52*. Washington, DC: Smithsonian Institution Press.

Hitler, A. (1992) *Mein Kampf* (trans. Ralph Manheim), London: Pimlico.

Hoagland, J. (1992) 'Simpson's Scud Attack' in Smith.

Hobsbawm, E. (1995) *Age of Extremes: The Short Twentieth Century, 1914–1991*, London: Abacus.

Hocking, J. (1984) 'Orthodox Theories of "Terrorism": The Power of Politicised Terminology', *Politics*, 19, ii, 103–10.

Hocking, J. (1992) 'Governments' Perspectives' in Paletz and Schmid.

Hodierne, R. (1970) 'How the GIs in Vietnam Don't Learn About the War', *New York Times Magazine*, April 12.

Hoffman, B. (2009) 'Foreword' in Forest.

Hoffmann, H. (1996) *The Triumph of Propaganda: Film and National Socialism, 1933–45*, Providence, RI: Berghahn.

Hofstetter, C. and Moore, D. (1979) 'Watching TV News and Supporting the Military, A Surprising Impact of the News Media', *Armed Forces and Society*, 5, i, 261–9.

Hogan, M. (ed.) (1996) *Hiroshima in History and Memory*, Cambridge: Cambridge University Press.

Hollinger, D. (1993) 'How Wide the Circle of "We"? American Intellectuals and the Problem of Ethnos since World War II', *American Historical Review*, 98, 317–37.

Holmes, J. (2009) 'US Military is Meeting Recruitment Goals with Video Games: But At What Cost?', *Christian Science Monitor*, December 28.

Holton, R. (1998) *Globalization and the Nation-State*, London: Macmillan.

Hooper, A. (1982) *The Military and the Media*, Aldershot: Gower.

Hopkin, D. (1970) 'Domestic Censorship in the First World War', *Journal of Contemporary History*, V, iv, 151–70.

Hornblower, M. (1982) 'Propaganda Blurs War News in Buenos Aires', *Washington Post*, May 17, A1.

Howard, G. (1982) 'A Speech Given to the Chartered Building Societies Institute, 6 May 1982', BBC Press Release (PR/12/82).

Howe, E. (1982) *The Black Game: British Subversive Operations Against the Germans During the Second World War*, London: Futura.

Hull, D. (1969) *Film in the Third Reich: A Study of the German Cinema, 1933–45*, Berkeley: University of California Press.

Hunter, M. (1983) 'US Eases Restrictions on Coverage', *The New York Times*, October 31.

Huntington, S. (1996) *The Clash of Civilizations and the Remaking of World Order*, New York: Simon & Schuster.

Hüppauf, B. (1995) 'Modernism and the Photographic Representation of War and Destruction' in Devereaux and Hillman.

Hynes, S. (1998) *The Soldiers' Tale: Bearing Witness to Modern War*, London: Pimlico.

Ignatieff, M. (1998) *The Warrior's Honor: Ethnic War and the Modern Conscience*, London: Chatto & Windus.

Ingham, B. (1991) *Kill the Messenger*, London: HarperCollins.

Insdorf, A. (1989) *Indelible Shadows: Film and the Holocaust*, Cambridge: Cambridge University Press.

Isenberg, M. (1975) 'An Ambiguous Pacifism: A Retrospective on World War I Films, 1930–38', *Journal of Popular Film and Television*, 4, ii, 99–115.

Iskandar, A. and El-Nawawy, M. (2004) 'Al-Jazeera and War Coverage in Iraq: The Media's Quest for Contextual Objectivity' in Allan and Zelizer.

Jackall, R. (ed.) (1995) *Propaganda*, Basingstoke: Macmillan.

Jackson, R. (2005) *Writing the War on Terrorism: Language, Politics and Counter-Terrorism*, Manchester: Manchester University Press.

Jakobsen, P. (1996) 'National Interest, Humanitarianism or CNN: What Triggers UN Peace Enforcement After the Cold War?', *Journal of Peace Research*, 33, 205–15.

Jakobsen, P. (2000) 'Focus on the CNN Effect Misses the Point: The Real Media Impact on Conflict Management is Invisible and Indirect', *Journal of Peace Research*, 37, ii, 131–43.

Jamail, D. (2009) 'Cyber Warrior Resistance', *Atlantic Free Press*, October 23.

Jasperson, A. and El-Kikhia, M. (2003) 'CNN and al Jazeera's Media Coverage of America's War in Afghanistan' in Norris, Kern and Just.

Jeffords, S. (1986) 'The New Vietnam Films: Is the Movie Over?' *Journal of Popular Film and Television*, 13, 186–94.

Jeffords, S. and Rabinowitz, L. (eds) (1994) *Seeing Through the Media: The Persian Gulf War*, New Brunswick, NJ: Rutgers University Press.

Jenkins, B. (1988) 'Future Trends in International Terrorism' in Slater and Stohl.

Johnson, C. (2000) *Blowback: The Costs and Consequences of American Empire*, New York: Henry Holt & Co.

Johnson, T. and Kaye, B. (2006) 'Blog Day Afternoon: Are Blogs Stealing Audiences Away from Traditional Media Sources?' in Berenger.

Jordan, W. (2001) *Black Newspapers and America's War for Democracy, 1914–1920*, Chapel Hill: University of North Carolina Press.

Jowett, G. and O'Donnell, V. (1992) *Propaganda and Persuasion*, London: Sage.

Junger, S. (2010) *War*, New York: Twelve.

Jurkowitz, M. (2003) 'The Media's Conflict: Experts Say Access to Troops Helped More than Hurt', *The Boston Globe*, April 22.

Kaes, A. (1989) *From 'Hitler' to 'Heimat': The Return of History as Film*, Cambridge, MA: Harvard University Press.

Kamen, A. (2009) 'The End of the Global War on Terror', *Washington Post*, March 24.

Kaplan, D., Latif, A., Whitelaw, K. and Barnes, J. (2005) 'Hearts, Minds, and Dollars', *US News & World Report*, April 25, 22–33.

Kaplan, H. (1982) 'With the American Press in Vietnam', *Commentary*, 73, v, 42–9.

Kaplan, R. (2003) 'American Journalism Goes to War, 1898–2001: A Manifesto on Media and Empire', *Media History*, 9, iii, 209–19.

Kaplan, R. (2004) 'The Media and the Military', *Atlantic Monthly*, November, 38–40.

Katovsky, B. and Carlson, T. (2003) *Embedded: The Media at War in Iraq*, Guilford, CT: Lyons Press.

Kavoor, A. and Fraley, T. (eds) (2006) *Media, Terrorism, and Theory: A Reader*, Lanham, MD: Rowman & Littlefield.

Kaye, B. and Johnson, T. (2004) 'Weblogs as a Source of Information about the 2003 Iraq War' in Berenger.

Keane, F. (1996) *Season of Blood: A Rwandan Journey*, London: Penguin.

Keane, J. (1991) 'Democracy and the Media', *International Social Science Journal*, 129, 523–40.

Keane, J. (1996) *Reflections on Violence*, London: Verso.

Keen, S. (1986) *Faces of the Enemy: Reflections of the Hostile Imagination*, San Francisco: Harper & Row.

Keenan, T. (1994) 'Live From …' in Déotte *et al.*

Kegley, C. (1990) *International Terrorism: Characteristics, Causes, Controls*, New York: St Martin's Press.

Keller, C. (2010) 'War as the New Normal: An Interview with Andrew Bacevich', theotherjournal.com, May 11.

Kellner, D. (1992) 'Television, the Crisis of Democracy and the Persian Gulf War' in Raboy and Dagenais.

Kelly, A. (1989) '*All Quiet on the Western Front*: Brutal Cutting, Stupid Censors and Bigoted Politicos, 1930–1984', *Historical Journal of Film, Radio and Television*, 9, ii, 135–50.

Kelly, A. (1997) *Cinema and the Great War*, London: Routledge.

Kellner, D. (1992) *The Persian Gulf TV War*, Boulder, CO: Westview Press.

Kennan, G. (1993a) 'Somalia, Through a Glass Darkly', *The New York Times*, September 30.

Kennan, G. (1993b) 'If TV Drives Foreign Policy, We're in Trouble', *The New York Times*, October 24.

Kennedy, D. (1980) *Over Here: The First World War and American Society*, Oxford: Oxford University Press.

Kershaw, I. (1983) 'How Effective was Nazi Propaganda?' in Welch.

Kershaw, I. (1987) *The 'Hitler Myth': Image and Reality in the Third Reich*, Oxford: Clarendon Press.

Kershaw, I. and Lewin, M. (eds) (1997) *Stalinism and Nazism: Dictatorships in Comparison*, Cambridge: Cambridge University Press.

Khalidi, R. (2005) *Resurrecting Empire: Western Footprints and America's Perilous Path in the Middle East*, Boston: Beacon Press.

Khamis, S. (2007) 'The Role of New Arab Satellite Channels in Fostering Intercultural Dialogue: Can Al Jazeera English Bridge the Gap?' in Seib.

Khong, Y. (1992) *Analogies at War: Korea, Munich, Dien Bien Phu and the Vietnam Decisions of 1965*, Oxford: Princeton University Press.

Khoury-Machool, M. (2004) 'Propaganda and Arab Media Audiences: Resisting the "Hearts and Minds" Campaign' in Berenger.

Kimani, M. (2007) 'RTLM: The Medium that Became a Tool for Mass Murder' in Thompson.

Kimball, J. (1988) 'The Stab-in-the-Back Legend and the Vietnam War', *Armed Forces and Society*, 14, iii, 433–58.

Kincaid, C. (1995) 'Radio Talk Shows Vent Public Opinion on Bosnia', *Human Events*, December 22, 16.

Kirschenbaum, L. (2000) '"Our City, Our Hearths, Our Families": Local Loyalties and Private Life in Soviet World War II Propaganda', *Slavic Review*, 59, iv, 825–47.

Klinghoffer, A. (1998) *The International Dimension of Genocide in Rwanda*, London: Macmillan.

Knight, A. (2003) 'The Hollywoodisation of War: The Media Handling of the Iraq War', *Global Media Journal*, 2, iii, https://lass.calumet.purdue.edu/cca/gmj/fa03/gmj-fa03-knight.htm, date accessed October 26, 2009.

Knightley, P. (1991) 'Lies, Damned Lies and Military Briefings', *New Statesman and Society* (February 8), 26–7.

Knightley, P. (2004) *The First Casualty: The War Correspondent as Hero and Myth-Maker from the Crimea to Iraq*, Baltimore: Johns Hopkins University Press.

Koppes, C. and Black, G. (1977) 'What to Show the World: The Office of War Information and Hollywood, 1942–45', *Journal of American History*, LXIV, i, 87–105

Koppes, C. and Black, G. (1987) *Hollywood Goes to War: How Politics, Profits and Propaganda Shaped World War II Movies*. New York: Free Press.

Kracauer, S. (1947) *From Caligari to Hitler: A Psychological History of the German Film*, Princeton, NJ: Princeton University Press.

Krasilshcik, S. (ed.) (1985) *World War II: Dispatches from the Soviet Front*, New York: Sphinx Press.

Krimsky, G. (2002) 'The View from Abroad', *American Journalism Review*, 54–7.

Kull, A. (1985) 'Did the British Press Create the BBC Controversy?', *The Wall Street Journal*, August 7, 17.

Kull, S. and Ramsay, C. (1994a) *Christian Science Monitor*, 22 February.

Kull, S. and Ramsay, C. (1994b) *US Public Attitudes on US Involvement in Bosnia*, Program in International Policy Attitudes, University of Maryland, 1997.

Kull, S. and Ramsay, C. (2000) 'Elite Misperceptions of US Public Opinion and Foreign Policy' in Nacos, Shapiro and Isernia.

Kulman, L., Newman, R., and Mazzetti, M. (2001) 'Covering All Bases', *US News & World Report*, November 19, 44.

Kurtz, H. (1991) 'Pentagon to Ease Coverage Rules', *Washington Post*, January 5.

Lambon, T. (2001) 'No Fighting Today: It's Raining', *New Statesman*, November 12, 16.

Lang, F. and Lang, K. (1994) 'The Press as Prologue' in Bennett and Paletz.

Langguth, J. (1965) 'US Easing Curbs on Vietnam News', *The New York Times*, March 28, 3.

Lant, A. (1991) *Blackout: Reinventing Women for Wartime British Cinema*, Princeton, NJ: Princeton University Press.

Laqueur, W. (1977) *Terrorism*, London: Weidenfeld & Nicolson, London.

Larson, E. (1996) *Casualties and Consensus: The Historical Role of Casualties in Domestic Support for US Military Operations*, Santa Monica, CA: RAND.

Lasswell, H. (1927) *Propaganda Technique in the World War*, London: Kegan Paul.

Leab, D. (1995) 'Viewing the War with the Brothers Warner' in Dibbets and Hogenkamp.

Leapman, M. (1987) *The Last Days of the Beeb*, London: Coronet.

Le Bailly, L. (1983) 'The Navy and the Media,' *Naval Review*, 71, iii, 184–8.

Leiser, E. (1975) *Nazi Cinema*, New York: Macmillan.

Lerner, D. (1971) *Psychological Warfare Against Nazi Germany: The Sykewar Campaign, D-Day to VE-Day*, Cambridge, MA: MIT Press.

Lewis, J. and Brookes, R. (2004) 'How British Television News Represented the Case for the War in Iraq' in Allan and Zelizer.

Lewis, J., Brookes, R., Mosdell, N. and Threadgold, T. (2006) *Shoot First and Ask Questions Later*, New York: Peter Lang.

Li, D. (2007) 'Echoes of Violence: Considerations on Radio and Genocide in Rwanda' in Thompson.

Library of America (2000) *Reporting Vietnam: American Journalism, 1959–1975*, New York: Library of America.

Library of America (2001) *Reporting World War II: American Journalism, 1938–1946*, New York: Library of America.

Library of America (2008) *Liebling: World War II Writings*, New York: Library of America.

Lichty, L. and Carroll, R. (1988) 'Fragments of War: *Platoon* (1986)' in O'Connor and Jackson.

Lindner, A. (2009) 'Among the Troops: Seeing the Iraq War Through Three Journalistic Vantage Points', *Social Problems*, 56, i, 21–48.

Lippmann, W. (1922) *Public Opinion*, New York: Free Press.

Livingston, S. (1996) 'Suffering in Silence: Media Coverage of War and Famine in the Sudan' in Rotberg and Weiss.

Livingston, S. (2007a) 'Preface' in Bahador.

Livingston, S. (2007b) 'Limited Vision: How Both the American Media and Government Failed Rwanda' in Thompson.

Livingston, S. and Eachus, T. (1995) 'Humanitarian Crises and US Foreign Policy: Somalia and the CNN Effect Reconsidered', *Political Communication*, 12, 413–29.

Lobe, J. (2008) 'Army Breaks International Pact by Recruiting Children', *Inter Press Service*, May 13.

Lodge, J. (ed.) (1981) *Terrorism: A Challenge to the State*, Oxford: Martin Robertson.

Londoño, E. (2009) 'A High-Priced Media Campaign that Iraqis Aren't Buying', *Washington Post*, June 7.

Lonsdale, J. (1990) 'Mau Maus of the Mind: Making Mau Mau and Remaking Kenya', *Journal of African History*, 31, 393–421.

Lorch, D. (1995) 'Genocide versus Heartstrings' in Girardet.

Lorde, A. (1984) *Sister Outsider: Essays and Speeches by Audre Lorde*, Freedom, CA: Crossing Press.

Los Angeles Times (1983) Poll USLAT.73.R90, November 12–17.

Louvre, A. and Walsh, J. (1988) *Tell Me Lies About Vietnam: Cultural Battles for the Meaning of the War*, Milton Keynes: Open University Press.

Low, R. and Bishop, P. (1982) 'Crisis in South Atlantic Starts Fight Over News', *The Observer*, May 9.

Loyd, A. (2000) *My War Gone By, I Miss It So*, London: Transworld.

Lyman, R. (1995) 'Occupational Hazards' in Girardet.

Lynch, M. (2007) 'Arab Arguments: Talk Shows and the New Arab Public Sphere' in Seib.

Lytton, N. (1921) *The Press and the General Staff*, London: W. Collins Sons & Co.

MacArthur, J. (ed.) (1991) *Despatches from the Gulf War*, London: Bloomsbury.

MacArthur, J. (1993) *Second Front: Censorship and Propaganda in the Gulf War*, Berkeley, CA: University of California Press.

MacKenzie, L. (1993) *Peacekeeper: The Road to Sarajevo*, Toronto: Douglas & McIntyre.

Mackinnon, S. (1995) 'Remembering the Nanjing Massacre: *In the Name of the Emperor* (1995)', *Historical Journal of Film, Radio and Television*, 15, iii, 431–3.

Macomber, S. (2006) 'Embedded in Sunni Iraq', *American Spectator*, May, 28–34.

Magaš, B. (1993) *The Destruction of Yugoslavia: Tracking the Break-Up, 1980–92*, London: Verso.

Maier, C. (1988) *The Unmasterable Past: History, Holocaust and German National Identity*, Cambridge, MA: Harvard University Press.

Malcolm, N. (1996) *Bosnia: A Short History*, London: Papermac.

Mamdani, M. (1996) 'From Conquest to Consent as the Basis of State Formation: Reflections on Rwanda', *New Left Review*, 216, 3–36.

Mamdani, M. (2005) *Good Muslim, Bad Muslim: America, The Cold War, and the Roots of Terror*, New York: Doubleday.

Mamdani, M. (2009a) *Saviors and Survivors: Darfur, Politics, and the War on Terror*, New York: Pantheon.

Mamdani, M. (2009b) 'Darfur: The Feelgood Conflict: Coalition Puts Action before Understanding', *Le Monde Diplomatique*, August 1.

Mandelbaum, M. (1982) 'Vietnam: The Television War', *Daedalus*, 3, iv, 157–69.

Manheim, J. (1994) 'Strategic Public Diplomacy' in Bennett and Paletz.

Manvell, R. (1974) *Films and the Second World War*, Cranbury, NJ: A. S. Barnes.

Marling, K. and Wetenhall, J. (1991) *Iwo Jima: Monuments, Memories and the American Hero*, Cambridge, MA: Harvard University Press.

Marquis, A. (1978) 'Words as Weapons: Propaganda in Britain and Germany during the First World War', *Journal of Contemporary History*, 13, 467–98.

Martin, L. (1990) 'The Media's Role in Terrorism' in Kegley.

Marx, C. (2008) 'Using the Past to Support Future Intervention', *The Boston Globe*, October 4.

Massing, M. (2004) *Now They Tell Us: The American Press and Iraq*, New York: New York Review of Books.

Massing, M. (2008a) 'Embedded in Iraq', *New York Review of Books*, July 17, 33–6.

Massing, M. (2008b) 'Blind Spot', *Columbia Journalism Review*, September/October, 14–16.

Mathews, J. (1957) *Reporting The Wars*, Minneapolis: University of Minnesota Press.

Matthews, L. (1991) *Newsmen and National Defense: Is Conflict Inevitable?*, Washington, DC: Brassey's.

Matthews, M. (1994) 'Television Shifts Focus of US Foreign Policy', *Baltimore Sun*, February 11.

Matthews, O. (2001) 'It's Like "War of the Worlds"', *Newsweek*, October 22, 48.

Mayall, J. (ed.) (1996) *The New Interventionism 1991–1994: United Nations Experience in Cambodia, Former Yugoslavia and Somalia*, Cambridge: Cambridge University Press.

McAlister, M. (2003) 'Saving Private Lynch', *The New York Times*, April 6.

McAlister, M. (2005) *Epic Encounters: Culture, Media, and US Interests in the Middle East Since 1945*, Berkeley: University of California Press.

McCoy, A. (2006) *A Question of Torture: CIA Interrogation, From the Cold War to the War on Terror*, New York: Owl.

McCullin, D. (1992) *Unreasonable Behaviour: An Autobiography*, London: Vintage.

McEwen, J. (1982) 'The National Press during the First World War: Ownership and Circulation', *Journal of Contemporary History*, 17, iii, 459–86.

McGirk, T. (2001) 'Waiting Games', *Time Europe*, October 8, 59.

McInnes, C. and Sheffield, G. (eds) (1988) *Warfare in the Twentieth Century: Theory and Practice*, London: Unwin Hyam.

McLaine, I. (1979) *Ministry of Morale: Homefront Morale and the Ministry of Information in World War II*, London: Allen & Unwin.

McLane, B. (2004) 'Reporting from the Sandstorm: An Appraisal of Embedding', *Parameters*, Spring 2004, 77–88.

McLaughlin, G. (2002) *The War Correspondent*, London: Pluto Press.

McLeary, P. (2008) 'Blogging the Long War', *Columbia Journalism Review*, March/April, 36–40.

McNair, B. (1991) *Glasnost, Perestroika, and the Soviet Media*, London: Routledge.

McQuail, D. (1992) *Media Performance: Mass Communication and the Public Interest*, London: Sage.

McQuail, D. (1994) *Mass Communication Theory: An Introduction*, London: Sage.

McReynolds, L. (1995) 'Dateline Stalingrad: Newspaper Correspondents at the Front' in Stites.

Médecins Sans Frontières (1993) *Life, Death and Aid*, London: Routledge.

Melber, A. (2008) 'Web War', *The Nation*, September 15, 25–7.

Melvern, L. (2007) 'Missing the Story: The Media and the Rwanda Genocide' in Thompson.

Mercer, D. (1984) 'Is Press Freedom a Threat during National Crises?', *Royal United Services Institute Journal*, 129, iii, 38–42.

Mercer, D., Mungham, G. and Williams, K. (1987) *The Fog of War: The Media on the Battlefield*, London: Heinemann.

Mermin, J. (1997) 'Television News and American Intervention in Somalia: The Myth of a Media-driven Foreign Policy', *Political Science Quarterly*, 112, iii, 385–403.

Mermin, J. (1999) *Debating War and Peace: Media Coverage of US Intervention in the Post-Vietnam Era*, Princeton, NJ: Princeton University Press.

Messinger, G. (1992) *Propaganda and the State in the First World War*, Manchester: Manchester University Press.

Messinger, G. (1993) 'An Inheritance Worth Remembering: The British Approach to Official Propaganda during the First World War', *Historical Journal of Film, Radio and Television*, 13, ii, 117–27.

Meštrovic, S. (1996) *Genocide After Emotion: The Postemotional Balkan War*, London: Routledge.

Meyerson, J. (1995) 'Theater of War: American Propaganda Films During the Second World War' in Jackall.

Michalski, M. and Gow, J. (2007) *War, Image and Legitimacy: Viewing Contemporary Conflict*, London: Routledge.

Miller, A. (ed.) (1982) *Terrorism, the Media and the Law*, New York: Transnational.

Miller, D. (1993) 'Official Sources and "Primary Definition": The Case of Northern Ireland', *Media, Culture and Society*, 15, iii, 385–406.

Miller, D. (1994) *Don't Mention the War: Northern Ireland, Propaganda and the Media*, London: Pluto Press.

Miller, D. (2004) *Tell Me Lies: Propaganda and Media Distortion in the Attack on Iraq*, London: Pluto Press.

Miller, D. B. (2007) *Media Pressure on Foreign Policy: The Evolving Theoretical Framework*, New York: Palgrave Macmillan.

Millis, W. (1931) *The Martial Spirit*, Cambridge, MA: Riverside Press.

Milne, A. (1988) *DG: The Memoirs of a British Broadcaster*, London: Coronet.

Milne, S. (2001) 'Imperial Nightmare: The New Appetite for Intervention Will Only Increase The Likelihood of Anti-Western Terror', *Guardian*, November 7.

Minear, L., Scott, C. and Weiss, T. (1996) *The News Media, Civil War and Humanitarian Action*, Boulder, CO: Lynne Rienner.

Mironko, C. (2007) 'The Effect of RTLM's Rhetoric of Ethnic Hatred in Rural Rwanda' in Thompson.

Mitchell, G. (2004) 'Giving a Name and a Face to the Fallen', *Editor & Publisher*, June, 22.

Mitgang, H. (1970) 'It's Not the War News; It's the Vietnam War', *The New York Times*, January 12, 28.

Moeller, S. (1989) *Shooting War: Photography and the American Experience of Combat*, New York: Basic.

Moeller, S. (1999) *Compassion Fatigue: How the Media Sell Disease, Famine, War and Death*, New York: Routledge.

Mohr, C. (1965) 'War and Misinformation: American Briefing Officers in Saigon Give Accounts Unsubstantiated in Field', *The New York Times*, November 26, 2.

Moloney, E. (1991) 'Closing Down the Airwaves: The Story of the Broadcasting Ban' in Rolston.

Molotch, H. and Lester, M. (1997) 'News as Purposive Behaviour: On the Strategic Use of Routine Events, Accidents and Scandals' in Berkowitz.

Morgan, M., Lewis, J. and Jhally, S. (1992) 'More Viewing, Less Knowing' in Mowlana, Gerbner and Schiller.

Morrison, D. (1992) *Television and the Gulf War*, London: John Libbey.

Morrison, D. (1994) 'Journalists and the Social Construction of War', *Contemporary Record*, 8, ii, 305–20.

Morrison, D. and Tumber, H. (1988) *Journalists at War: The Dynamics of News Reporting During the Falklands Conflict*, London: Sage.

Mosco, V. (1996) *The Political Economy of Communication: Rethinking and Renewal*, London: Sage.

Mosse, G. (1990) *Fallen Soldiers: Reshaping the Memory of the World Wars*, Oxford: Oxford University Press.

Mould, D. (1996) 'Press Pools and Military–Media Relations in the Gulf War: A Case Study of the Battle of Khafji, January 1991', *Historical Journal of Film, Radio and Television*, 16, ii, 133–59.

Mowlana, H. (1996) *Global Communication in Transition: The End of Diversity?*, London: Sage.

Mowlana, H., Gerbner, G. and Schiller, H. (eds) (1992) *Triumph of the Image: The Media's War in the Gulf, a Global Perspective*, Boulder, CO: Westview Press.

Mueller, J. (1973) *War, Presidents and Public Opinion*, New York: John Wiley.

Mueller, J. (1989) *Retreat from Doomsday: The Obsolescence of Major War*, New York: Basic.

Mueller, J. (1994) *Policy and Opinion in the Gulf War*, Chicago: University of Chicago Press.

Mühl-Benninghaus, W. (1996) 'Newsreel Images of the Military and War, 1914–1918' in Elsaesser.

Mungham, G. (1985) 'The Eternal Triangle: Relations Between Governments, Armed Services and the Media', *Army Quarterly*, 115, i, 7–21.

Mydans, S. (1991) 'Travel Resurges Across US As Americans Adjust to War', *The New York Times*, February 14.

Nacos, B. (1994) *Terrorism and the Media: From the Iran Hostage Crisis to the World Trade Center Bombing*, New York: Columbia University Press.

Nacos, B., Shapiro, R. and Isernia, P. (2000) *Decisionmaking in a Glass House: Mass Media, Public Opinion, and American and European Foreign Policy in the 21st Century*, Lanham, MD: Rowman & Littlefield.

Nagl, J. (2005) *Learning to Eat Soup with a Knife: Counterinsurgency Lessons from Malaya and Vietnam*, Chicago: University of Chicago Press.

Napoli, J. (2004) 'Hating America: The Press in Egypt and France' in Berenger.

Nash, W. (1998) 'The Military and the Media in Bosnia', *Press/Politics*, 3, iv, 131–5.

Nathan, J. and Oliver, J. (1975) 'Public Opinion and US Security Policy', *Armed Forces and Society*, 2, i, 58–9.

National Public Radio (2001) 'Ahmad Sheik Discusses the Arabic Language Television News Channel Al-Jazeera', October 8.

National Security Archive (2007a), 'White Paper: "Rapid Reaction Media Team" Concept', Department of Defense, January 2003, http://www.gwu.edu/~nsarchiv/NSAEBB/NSAEBB219/iraq_media_01.pdf, date accessed June 7, 2010.

National Security Archive (2007b), 'Iraq Media Timeline', http://www.gwu.edu/~nsarchiv/NSAEBB/NSAEBB219/index.htm#timeline, date accessed June 7, 2010.

Natsios, A. (1996) 'Illusions of Influence: The CNN Effect in Complex Emergencies' in Rotberg and Weiss.

Nelson, S. (2003) 'Embedded Reporter Comes Away from Front Lines Torn', *The Boston Globe*, April 22.

Neuman, J. (1996) *Lights, Camera, War Is Media Technology Driving International Politics?*, New York: St Martin's Press.

New York Times, The (1862a) 'Brady's Photographs of the War', September 26.

New York Times, The (1862b) 'Brady's Photographs: Pictures of the Dead at Antietam', October 20.

New York Times, The (1900) 'Drastic Course Needed', November 11, 6.

New York Times, The (1917) '"State of War" Exists, Wilson is to Declare in Words to Congress', March 31, 1.

New York Times, The (1952) 'Native Terrorists Raid Kenya Mission', September 13, 2.

New York Times, The (1962) 'Foreign Reporters Warned by Saigon', September 26, 9.

New York Times, The (1963) 'Censorship in Vietnam', August 30, 20.

New York Times, The (1965) 'Newsmen Report US Impose Curbs on Coverage in Vietnam', March 18, 4.

New York Times, The (1970) 'Let's Say It Right', January 11.

New York Times, The (1983) 'Military vs Press: Troubled History', October 29, 7.

New York Times, The (2009) 'Profiling the Messengers', September 3.

Nicholas, S. (1996) *The Echo of War: Home Front Propaganda and Wartime BBC, 1939–45*, Manchester: Manchester University Press.

Nicholson, M. (1992) *A Measure of Danger: Memoirs of a British War Correspondent*, London: Fontana.

Nikolaev, A. and Hakanen, E. (2006) *Leading to the 2003 Iraq War: The Global Media Debate*, Basingstoke: Palgrave Macmillan.

Nimmo, K. (2002) '"Yes, We Censored News About Afghanistan": The Lapdog Conversion of CNN', *Counterpunch*, August 23, http://www.counterpunch. com/nimmo0823.html, date accessed June 4, 2010.

Noor, F. (2004) 'When Osama and Friends Came A-calling: The Political Deployment of the Overdetermined Image of Osama ben Laden in the Contestation for Islamic Symbols in Malaysia' in van der Veer and Munshi.

Norris, C. (1992) *Uncritical Theory: Postmodernism, Intellectuals and the Gulf War*, London: Lawrence and Wishart.

Norris, M. (1994) 'Only the Guns Have Eyes: Military Censorship and the Body Count' in Jeffords and Rabinowitz.

Norris, P., Kern, M. and Just, M. (2003) *Framing Terrorism: The News Media, the Government and the Public*, New York: Routledge.

NPR. (2009) 'Al-Jazeera English Struggles for US Audience,' February 24, http://www.npr.org/templates/story/story.php?storyId=101071599, date accessed May 20, 2010.

Oakley, R. (1991) 'Terrorism, Media Coverage and Government Response' in Serfaty.

Obajtek-Kirkwood, A.-M. (2006) '*Le Monde* on a "Likely" Iraq War' in Nikolaev and Hakanen.

O'Brien, M. (2002) 'A Growing Divide', *Quill Magazine*, January/February, 15–17.

O'Connor, J. and Jackson, M. (eds) (1988) *American History/American Film: Interpreting the Hollywood Image*, New York: Ungar.

O'Heffernan, P. (1994) 'A Mutual Exploitation Model of Media Influence in US Foreign Policy' in Bennett and Paletz.

Oliver, M., Mares, M. L., and Cantor, J. (1993) 'News Viewing, Authoritarianism, and Attitudes Toward the Gulf War' in Denton.

Omissi, D. (1990) *Air Power and Colonial Control: The RAF, 1919–39*, Manchester: Manchester University Press.

Orwell, G. (1995) 'Politics and the English Language' in Jackall.

Oshry, P. (2007) 'Bloggers Under Siege', *Atlas Shrugs*, May 2.

O'Sullivan, N. (ed.) (1986) *Terrorism, Ideology and Revolution: The Origins of Modern Political Violence*, Brighton: Wheatsheaf.

Owen, J. (2001) 'Training Journalists to Report Safely in Hostile Environments', *Nieman Reports*, Winter, 25–7.

Page, C. (1996) *US Official Propaganda during the Vietnam War, 1965–73*, London: Cassell.

Paletz, D. and Boiney, J. (1992) 'Researchers' Perspectives' in Paletz and Schmid.

Paletz, D. and Schmid, A. (1992) *Terrorism and the Media: How Researchers, Terrorists, Government, Press, Public, Victims View and Use the Media*, Newbury Park, CA: Sage.

Paletz, D. and Tawney, L. (1992) 'Broadcasting Organizations' Perspectives' in Paletz and Schmid.

Parenti, M. (1993) *Inventing Reality: The Politics of News Media*, New York: St Martin's Press.

Paret, P. (1996) '*Kolberg* (Germany, 1945): As Historical Film and Historical Document' in Chambers and Culbert.

Parker, R. (1995) 'The Future of "Global" Television News: An Economic Perspective', *Political Communication*, 12, iv, 431–46.

Paul, C. and Kim, J. (2004) *Reporters On the Battlefield: The Embedded Press System in Historical Context*, Santa Monica, CA: RAND.

Pearson, D. and Anderson, J. (1967) 'Whitten Blocks Food for Miss. Negroes', *Washington Post*, May 9.

Pedelty, M. (1995) *War Stories: The Culture of Foreign Correspondents*, New York: Routledge.

Peer, L. and Chestnut, B. (1995) 'Deciphering Media Independence: The Gulf War Debate in Television and Newspaper News', *Political Communication*, 12, 81–95.

Penley, C. and Ross, A. (1991) 'Couch Potatoes Aren't Dupes', *The New York Times*, March 11.

Penrod, G. (2004) 'Letting Loose the Images of War', *News Media & The Law*, Summer, 7–9.

Peterson, H. (1939) *Propaganda for War: The Campaign Against American Neutrality, 1914–17*, Norman: University of Oklahoma Press.

Peterson, S. (2001a) *Me Against My Brother: At War in Somalia, Sudan, and Rwanda*, New York: Routledge.

Peterson, S. (2001b) 'In a Lawless Land, Hazards Mount for Reporters', *Christian Science Monitor*, November 29, 1.

Petrie, J. (ed.) (1994) *Essays on Strategy XII*, Washington, DC: National Defense University Press.

Pew Global Attitudes Project (2009) 'Support for War in Afghanistan' http://pewglobal.org/database/?indicator=9&mode=chart, date accessed June 4, 2010.

Pew Research Center for the People and the Press (2003) Poll USPSRA.303WAR7.QP07 March 28–April 1.

Phillips, T. (1967) 'Vietnam Blues', *The New York Times*, October 8.

Philo, G. (1993) 'From Buerk to Band Aid: The Media and the 1984 Ethiopian Famine' in Eldridge.

Philo, G. (1995) *Glasgow Media Group Reader, Volume 2: Industry, Economy, War and Politics*, London: Routledge.

Piety, M. and Foley, B. (2006) 'Their Morals Are Ours: The American Media on the Doctrine of "Preemptive War"' in Nikolaev and Hakanen.

Pilger, J. (1991) 'Video Nasties', *New Statesman and Society*, January 25, 6–7.

Pilger, J. (1994) *Distant Voices*, London: Vintage.

Pilkington, E. (1993) 'Shots That Shook The World', *Guardian*, October 11.

Pincus, W. (2010) 'Pentagon Tries to Steer Media Coverage on Iraq', *Washington Post*, May 25.

Platt, S. (1991a) 'Paper Flags', *New Statesman and Society*, January 25, 13–14.
Platt, S. (1991b) 'Casualties of War', *New Statesman and Society*, February 22, 12–13.
Ponsonby, A. (1928) *Falsehood in Wartime*, London: George Allen & Unwin.
Ponting, C. (1998) *Progress and Barbarism: The World in the Twentieth Century*, London: Chatto & Windus.
Porton, R. (2005) 'Film and the Anarchist Peril' in Slocum.
Postman, N. (1987) *Amusing Ourselves to Death: Public Discourse in the Age of Show Business*, London: Methuen.
Potter, D. (2002) 'At What Price Publicity?', *American Journalism Review*, March, 72.
Pottier, J. (2002) *Re-Imagining Rwanda: Conflict, Survival and Disinformation in the Late Twentieth Century*, Cambridge: University of Cambridge Press.
Powers, S. and Gilboa, E. (2007) 'The Public Diplomacy of Al Jazeera' in Seib.
Pratkansis, A. and Aronson, E. (1992) *Age of Propaganda: The Everyday Use and Abuse of Persuasion*, New York: W. H. Freeman.
Preston, A. (1996) 'Television News and the Bosnian Conflict: Distance, Proximity, Impact' in Gow, Paterson and Preston.
Prince, S. (2009) *Firestorm: American Film in the Age of Terrorism*, New York: Columbia University Press.
Pronay, N. (1988) 'The British Post-bellum Cinema: A Survey of the Films Relating to World War II made in Britain between 1945 and 1960', *Historical Journal of Film, Radio and Television*, 8, i, 39–54.
Pronay, N. and Croft, J. (1983) 'British Film Censorship and Propaganda Policy during the Second World War' in Curran and Porter.
Pronay, N. and Spring, D. (1982) *Propaganda, Politics and Film, 1918–45*, London: Macmillan.
Pronay, N. and Wilson, K. (1985) *The Political Re-education of Germany and Her Allies After World War II*, London: Croom Helm.
Protheroe, A. (1982) 'Why We have Lost the Information War', *The Listener*, June 3, 2–3.
Prunier, G. (1997) *The Rwanda Crisis: History of a Genocide*, London: Hurst & Co.
Purcell, V. (1954) *Malaya: Communist or Free?*, London: Victor Gollancz.
Purdum, T. and Rutenberg, J. (2003) 'Reporters Respond Eagerly to Pentagon Welcome Mat', *The New York Times*, March 23.
Quart, A. (2008) 'Flickring Out', *Columbia Journalism Review*, 47, ii, 14–17.
Quart, L. (1990), '*The Deer Hunter*: The Superman in Vietnam' in Dittmar and Michaud.
Quill Magazine (2004) 'Despite Ban, Newspapers Publish Coffin Photos', June/July, 6–7.
Quinn, S. and Walters, T. (2004) 'Al-Jazeera: A Broadcaster Creating Ripples in a Stagnant Pool' in Berenger.
Raboy, M. and Dagenais, B. (eds) (1992) *Media, Crisis and Democracy: Mass Communication and the Disruption of Social Order*, London: Sage.

Ramet, P. (1992) *Balkan Babel*, Boulder, CO: Westview Press.

Rampton, S. and Stauber, J. (2003) *Weapons of Mass Deception: The Uses of Propaganda in Bush's War on Iraq*, New York: Tarcher/Penguin.

Rather, D. (1993) 'Don't Blame TV for Getting Us into Somalia', *The New York Times*, October 14.

Rather, D. (1995) 'The United States and Somalia: Assessing Responsibility for the Intervention' in Girardet.

Raymond, J. (1966) 'It's A Dirty War For Correspondents, Too', *The New York Times*, February 13.

Read, D. (1992) *The Power of News: The History of Reuters*. Oxford: Oxford University Press.

Read, J. (1941) *Atrocity Propaganda, 1914–19*. New Haven, CT: Yale University Press.

Reed. C. (2009) 'Journalists' Recent Work Examined Before Embeds', *Stars and Stripes* (Mideast edition), August 24.

Reese, S. (2004) 'Militarized Journalism: Framing Dissent in the Gulf Wars' in Allan and Zelizer.

Reeves, N. (1983) 'Film Propaganda and its Audience: The Example of Britain's Official Films during the First World War', *Journal of Contemporary History*, 18, 463–94.

Reeves, N. (1986) *Official British Film Propaganda in the First World War*, London: Croom Helm.

Reeves, N. (1993) 'The Power of Film Propaganda: Myth or Reality?', *Historical Journal of Film, Radio and Television*, 13, ii, 181–201.

Reeves, N. (1997) 'Cinema, Spectatorship and Propaganda: *Battle of the Somme* and its Contemporary Audience', *Historical Journal of Film, Radio and Television*, 17, i, 5–28.

Reich, W. (ed.) (1990) *Origins of Terrorism: Psychologies, Ideologies, Theologies, States of Mind*, Cambridge: Cambridge University Press.

Renshon, S. (ed.) (1993) *The Political Psychology of the Gulf War: Leaders, Publics and the Process of Conflict*, London: University of Pittsburgh Press.

Rentschler, C. (2004) 'Witnessing: US Citizenship and the Vicarious Experience of Suffering', *Media, Culture & Society*, 26, ii, 296–304.

Rentschler, E. (1996) *The Ministry of Illusion: Nazi Cinema and Its Afterlife*, Cambridge, MA: Harvard University Press.

Reuth, R. (1995) *Goebbels*, London: Constable.

Ricchiardi, S. (2006) 'The Forgotten War', *American Journalism Review*, August/September, 4–55.

Ricchiardi, S., and Cirillo, M. (2004) 'Missed Signals', *American Journalism Review*, August/September, 22–9.

Ricchiardi, S. and Clark, S. (2005) 'Short Attention Span', *American Journalism Review*, August/September, 52–9.

Rich, F. (2005) 'On Television, Torture Takes a Holiday', *The New York Times*, January 23.

Richards, J. (1988) 'National Identity in British Wartime Films' in Taylor.

Richards, J. (1997) *Films and British National Identity, from Dickens to Dad's Army*, Manchester: Manchester University Press.

Richards, J. and Sheridan, D. (1987) *Mass-Observation at the Movies*, London: Routledge & Kegan Paul.

Ricks, T. (2006) *Fiasco: The American Military Adventure in Iraq*, New York: Penguin.

Rid, T. (2007) *War and Media Operations: The US Military and the Press from Vietnam to Iraq*, New York: Routledge.

Rigg, R. (1969) 'How Not to Report a War', *Military Review*, 49, vi, 14–24.

Ripley, A. and Thompson, M. (2004) 'An Image of Grief Returns', *Time*, May 3, 28–9.

Roach, C (ed.) (1993) *Communication and Culture in War and Peace*, London: Sage.

Robertson, J. (1982) 'British Film Censorship Goes to War', *Historical Journal of Film, Radio and Television*, 2, i, 49–64.

Robertson, L. (2003) 'Whatever Happened to Afghanistan?' *American Journalism Review*, June/July, 24–31.

Robinson, L. and Livingston, S. (2006) 'Strange Bedfellows: The Emergence of the Al Qaeda–Baathist News Frame Prior to the 2003 Invasion of Iraq' in Nikolaev and Hakanen.

Robinson, P. (1999) 'The CNN Effect: Can the News Media Drive Foreign Policy?', *Review of International Studies*, 25, i, 301–9.

Robinson, P. (2002) *The CNN Effect: The Myth of News, Foreign Policy and Intervention*, London: Routledge.

Roeder, G. (1985) 'A Note on US Photo Censorship in WWII', *Historical Journal of Film, Radio and Television*, 5, ii, 191–8.

Roeder, G. (1993) *The Censored War: American Visual Experience During World War Two*, London: Yale University Press.

Roetter, C. (1974) *Psychological Warfare*, London: Batsford.

Rollings, P. (ed.) (1983) *Hollywood as Historian: American Film in a Cultural Context*, Lexington: University of Kentucky Press.

Rolston, B. (ed.) (1991) *The Media and Northern Ireland: Covering the Troubles*, London: Macmillan.

Rolston, B. and Miller D. (eds) (1996) *War and Words: The Northern Ireland Media Reader*, Belfast: Beyond the Pale.

Roper Organization (1983) Roper Report 84-1, December 3–10.

Rose, M. (1998) *Fighting for Peace: Bosnia, 1994*, London: Harvill.

Rose, T. (1995) *Aspects of Political Censorship, 1914–18*. Hull: Hull University Press.

Roselle, L. (2006) *Media and the Politics of Failure: Great Powers, Communication Strategies, and Military Defeats*, New York: Palgrave Macmillan.

Rosenau, J. (1997) *Along the Domestic–Foreign Frontier: Exploring Governance in a Turbulent World*, Cambridge: Cambridge University Press, 1997.

Rosenblatt, L. (1996) 'The Media and the Refugee' in Rotberg and Weiss.

Rosenblum, M. (1993) *Who Stole the News? Why We Can't Keep Up With What Happens in the World and What We Can Do About It*, New York: John Wiley.

Rosenstone, R. (1995) *Revisioning History: Film and the Construction of a New Past*, Princeton, NJ: Princeton University Press.

Ross, A. (1992) 'The Ecology of Images', *The South Atlantic Quarterly*, 91, i, 215–38.

Ross, S. (1996) *Propaganda for War: How the US was Conditioned to Fight the Great War of 1914–18*, Jefferson, NC: McFarland.

Rotberg, R. and Weiss, T. (eds) (1996) *From Massacres to Genocide: the Media, Public Policy and Humanitarian Crises*, Washington, DC: Brookings Institution.

Röther, R. (1996) 'Learning from the Enemy: German Film Propaganda in World War I' in Elsaesser.

Rowe, C. (1991) 'The "Vietnam Effect" in the Persian Gulf War', *Cultural Critique*, 19, 121–39.

Rowe, C. and Berg, R. (1991) *The Vietnam War and American Culture*, New York: Columbia University Press.

Roxburgh, A. (1987) *Pravda: Inside the Soviet News Machine*, New York: George Braziller.

Royle, T. (1989) *War Report*, London: Grafton.

Rubin, E. (2001) 'On the Road', *The New Republic*, October 29, 25–7.

Rutenberg, J. (2001a) 'Hollywood Seeks Role in the War', *The New York Times*, October 20.

Rutenberg, J. (2001b) 'Fox Portrays a War of Good and Evil, and Many Applaud,' *The New York Times*, December 3.

Said, E. (1996) *Covering Islam: How the Media and Experts Determine How We See the Rest of the World*, London: Vintage.

Said, E. and Hitchens, C. (eds) (1988) *Blaming the Victims: Spurious Scholarship and the Palestinian Question*, London: Verso.

Saint, N. (2009) 'US Army Spent $32.8 Million on a Video Game', *Business Insider*, December 9.

Sakmyster, T. (1996) 'Nazi Documentaries of Intimidation: *Felzug in Polen* (1940), *Feuertaufe* (1940) and *Sieg im Westen* (1941)', *Historical Journal of Film, Radio and Television*, 16, iv, 485–514.

Salt, J. (2008) *The Unmaking of the Middle East: A History of Western Disorder in Arab Lands*, Berkeley: University of California Press.

Sanders, M. and Taylor, P. (1982) *British Propaganda during the First World War*, Basingstoke: Macmillan.

Scarry, E. (1987) *The Body in Pain: The Making and Unmaking of the World*, New York: Oxford.

Schechter, D. (2003) *Embedded: Weapons of Mass Deception: How the Media Failed to Cover the War on Iraq*, Amherst, NY: Prometheus.

Schechter, D. (2006) *When News Lies: Media Complicity and the Iraq War*, New York: Select.

Schell, O. (2004) 'Preface' in Massing.

Schiffrin, A. (2009) *Dr Seuss & Co. Go to War: The World War II Editorial Cartoons of America's Leading Comic Artists*, New York: New Press.

Schiller, H. (1996) *Information Inequality: The Deepening Social Crisis in America*, New York: Routledge.

Schlesinger, P. (1987) *Putting 'Reality' Together: BBC News*, London: Methuen.

Schlesinger, P. (1991) *Media, State and Nation: Political Violence and Collective Identities*, London: Sage.

Schlesinger, P. (1995) 'Terrorism' in Smith.

Schlesinger, P., Murdock, G. and Elliott, P. (1983) *Televising 'Terrorism': Political Violence in Popular Culture*, London: Comedia.

Schmid, A. (1992) 'Editors' Perspectives' in Paletz and Schmid.

Schmid, A. and de Graaf, J. (1982) *Violence as Communication: Insurgent Terrorism and the Western News Media*, London: Sage.

Schmid, A. and Jongman, A. (1988) *Political Terrorism: A New Guide to Actors, Authors, Concepts, Data Bases, Theories and Literature*, Amsterdam: North Holland.

Schudson, M. (1995) *The Power of News*, Cambridge, MA: Harvard University Press.

Schull, M. and Wilt, D. (1996) *Hollywood War Films, 1937–1945: An Exhaustive Filmography of American Feature-Length Motion Pictures Relating to World War II*, Jefferson, NC: McFarland & Co.

Schulte, S. (2008) '"The War Games Scenario": Regulating Teenagers and Teenaged Technology (1980–1984)', *Television and New Media*, 9, vi, 487–513.

Seaver, B. (1998) 'The Public Dimension of Foreign Policy', *Press/Politics*, 3, i, 65–91.

Segaller, S. (1987) *Invisible Armies: Terrorism into the 1990s*, Orlando, FL: Harcourt Brace Jovanovich.

Seib, P. (1997) *Headline Diplomacy: How News Coverage Affects Foreign Policy*, Westport, CO: Praeger.

Seib, P. (2005) 'Hegemonic No More: Western Media, the Rise of Al-Jazeera, and the Influence of Diverse Voices', *International Studies Review*, 7, 601–15.

Seib, P. (2007a) *New Media and the New Middle East*, New York: Palgrave Macmillan.

Seib, P. (2007b) 'New Media and Prospects for Democratization' in Seib.

Seib, P. (2008) *The Al Jazeera Effect: How the New Global Media Are Reshaping World Politics*, Washington, DC: Potomac.

Sengupta, S. and Masood, S. (2005) 'Guantánamo Comes to Define US to Muslims', *The New York Times*, May 21.

Sennott, C. (2007) 'Foreign Reporting: Adding Layers to What Goes in the Notebook', *Nieman Reports*, Spring, 24–7.

Serfaty, S. (ed) (1991) *The Media and Foreign Policy*, New York: St Martin's Press.

Sevy, G. (ed.) (1989) *The American Experience in Vietnam: A Reader*, London: University of Oklahoma Press.

Shadid, A. (2005) *Night Draws Near: Iraq's People in the Shadow of America's War*, New York: Henry Holt & Co.

Shafer, D. (ed.) (1990) *The Legacy: The Vietnam War in the American Imagination*, Boston, MA: Beacon Press.

Shales, T. (1982) 'The War You Can't See ...', *Washington Post*, May 7.

Shanker, T. (2004) '6 GIs in Iraq Are Charged with Abuse of Prisoners', *The New York Times*, March 21.

Sharkey, J. (1991) *Under Fire: US Military Restrictions on the Media from Grenada to the Persian Gulf*, Washington, DC: Center for Public Integrity.

Shattuck, J. (1996) 'Human Rights and Humanitarian Crises: Policymaking and the Media' in Rotberg and Weiss.

Shaw, M. (1992) 'Global Society and Global Responsibility: The Theoretical, Historical and Political Limits of "International Society"', *Millennium: Journal of International Studies*, 21, iii, 421–34.

Shaw, M. (1994) 'Civil Society and Global Politics: Beyond a Social Movements Approach', *Millennium: Journal of International Studies*, 23, iii, 647–67.

Shaw, M. (1996) *Civil Society and Media in Global Crises: Representing Distant Violence*, London: Pinter.

Shaw, M. and Carr-Hill, R. (1992) 'Public Opinion and Media War Coverage in Britain' in Mowlana, Gerbner and Schiller.

Shepherd, L. (2006) 'Veiled References: Constructions of Gender in the Bush Administration Discourse on the Attacks on Afghanistan Post-9/11', *International Feminist Journal of Politics*, 8, i, 19–41.

Sherry, M. (1995) *In the Shadow of War: The United States Since the 1930s.*,New Haven, CT: Yale University Press.

Shindler, C. (1979) *Hollywood Goes to War: Films and American Society, 1939–52*, London: Routledge & Kegan Paul.

Shoemaker, P. (1991) *Gatekeeping*, London: Sage.

Shoemaker, P. and Reese, S. (1996) *Mediating the Message: Theories of Influence on Mass Media Content*, White Plains, NY: Longman.

Short, K. (ed.) (1983a) *Film and Radio Propaganda in World War Two*, Knoxville: University of Tennessee Press.

Short, K. (ed.) (1983b) 'Washington's Information Manual for Hollywood', *Historical Journal of Film, Radio and Television*, 3, ii, 171–80.

Short, K. (ed.) (1985) 'Hollywood: An Essential War Industry', *Historical Journal of Film, Radio and Television*, 5, i, 90–9.

Short, K. (ed.) (1996) *Catalogue of Forbidden German Feature and Short Film Productions held in Zonal Film Archives of Film Section, Information Services Division, Control Commission for Germany*, Westport, CT: Greenwood Press.

Sides, H. (2003a) 'Unembedded', *The New Yorker*, March 24.

Sides, H. (2003b) 'A Centcom Star', *The New Yorker*, April 21.

Sifry, M. and Cerf, C. (eds) (1991) *The Gulf War Reader: History, Documents, Opinions*, New York: Times.

Simon, E. (2004) 'Digital Amateurs Amid the Struggle: Unembedded – And Snap-Happy', *Associated Press*, May 9.

Simpson, J. (1991a) 'Enemies Within', *The Spectator*, February 23, 11–12.

Simpson, J. (1991b) *From the House of War: John Simpson in the Gulf*, London: Arrow.

Simpson, J. (1991c) 'Worse than Saddam', *The Spectator*, February 9, 17–19.

Sims, J. (2004) 'When Reality is Just an Illusion', *The Independent*, March 29.

Sinclair, J., Jacka, E. and Cunningham, S. (1996) *New Patterns in Global Television: Peripheral Vision*, Oxford: Oxford University Press.

Sklar, R. (1975) *Movie-Made America: A Cultural History of American Movies*, New York: Random House.

Slater, R. and Stohl, M. (eds) (1988) *Current Perspectives on International Terrorism*, London: Macmillan.

Slocum, J. (ed.) (2005) *Terrorism, Media, Liberation*, New Brunswick, NJ: Rutgers University Press.

Slocum, J. (ed.) (2006) *Hollywood and War, The Film Reader*, New York: Routledge.

Slotkin, R. (2000) *Regeneration through Violence: The Mythology of the American Frontier, 1600–1860*, Norman: University of Oklahoma Press.

Small, M. (1994) *Covering Dissent: The Media and the Anti-Vietnam War Movement*, Brunswick, NJ: Rutgers University Press.

Smith, A. (1990) 'Towards a Global Culture?' *Theory, Culture and Society*, 7, 171–91.

Smith, A. (1995) *Television: An International History*, Oxford: Oxford University Press.

Smith, H. (ed.) (1992) *The Media and the Gulf War: The Press and Democracy in Wartime*, Washington, DC: Seven Locks Press.

Smith, T. (1994) *America's Mission: The United States and the Worldwide Struggle for Democracy in the Twentieth Century*, Princeton, NJ: Princeton University Press.

Smither, R. (1993) '"A Wonderful Idea of the Fighting": The Question of Fakes in *The Battle of the Somme*', *Historical Journal of Film, Radio and Television*, 13, ii, 149–68.

Smolkin, R. (2004) 'Photos of the Fallen', *American Journalism Review*, June/July, 14–15.

Snow, N. (2006) 'Terrorism, Public Relations, and Propaganda' in Kavoor and Fraley.

Sobchack, V. (ed.) (1996) *The Persistence of History: Cinema, Television, and the Modern Event*, New York: Routledge.

Sobel, R. (1998) 'Portraying American Public Opinion toward the Bosnia Crisis', *Press/Politics*, 3, ii, 16–33.

Sontag, S. (1979) *On Photography*, Harmondsworth: Penguin.

Sontag, S. (2003) *Regarding the Pain of Others*, New York: Picador.

Sorlin, P. (1980) *The Film in History: Restaging the Past*, Oxford: Blackwell.

Sorlin, P. (1991) *European Cinemas, European Societies, 1939–1990*, London: Routledge.

Sorlin, P. (1994) 'War and Cinema: Interpreting the Relationship', *Historical Journal of Film, Radio and Television*, 14, iv, 357–66.

Souri, H. (2007) 'The Political Battlefield of Pro-Arab Video Games on Palestinian Screens', *Comparative Studies of South Asia, Africa and the Middle East*, 27, iii, 536–51.

Spector, M. (2006) 'Cry Bias, and Let Slip the Blogs of War', *The Wall Street Journal*, July 26.

Spencer, G. (2005) *The Media and Peace: From Vietnam to the 'War on Terror'*, Basingstoke: Palgrave Macmillan.

Spigel, L. (2004) 'Entertainment Wars: Television Culture after 9/11', *American Quarterly*, 56, ii, 235–70.

Spillman, K. and Spillman, K. (1991) 'On Enemy Images and Conflict Escalation,' *International Social Science Journal*, 127, 57–76.

Squires, J. (1935) *British Propaganda at Home and in the United States from 1914 to 1917*, Cambridge, MA: Harvard University Press.

Stead, P. (1988) 'The People as Stars' in Taylor.

Stech, F. (1994) 'Preparing for More CNN Wars' in Petrie.

Sterba, J. (1970a) 'GIs Outburst Widens Censorship Issue', *The New York Times*, January 5, 1.

Sterba, J. (1970b) 'Army's Newsmen Want to "Tell It Like It Is"', *The New York Times*, January 11, 167.

Sterling, C. (1981) *The Terror Network: The Secret War of International Terrorism*, London: Weidenfeld & Nicolson.

Stern, J. (1975) *Hitler: The Führer and the People*, London: Fontana.

Stevenson, N. (1995) *Understanding Media Cultures: Social Theory and Mass Communication*, London: Sage.

Stewart, B. (1993) *Broken Lives: A Personal View of the Bosnian Conflict*, London: HarperCollins.

Stewart, I. and Carruthers, S. (eds) (1996) *War, Culture and the Media: Representations of the Military in Twentieth Century Britain*, Trowbridge: Flicks.

Stites, R. (ed.) (1995) *Culture and Entertainment in Wartime Russia*, Bloomington: Indiana University Press.

Stohl, M. (1990) 'Demystifying the Mystery of International Terrorism' in Kegley.

Strobel, W. (1994) 'TV Images May Shock but Won't Alter Policy', *Christian Science Monitor*, December 14.

Strobel, W. (1997) *Late-Breaking Foreign Policy: The News Media's Influence on Peace Operations*, Washington, DC: United States Institute of Peace Press.

Strobel, W. and Landay, J. (2001) 'Pentagon Gets Help With PR: Firm Is to Help Explain Military Strikes to Foreign Audiences', *Charlotte Observer*, October 19.

Strong, P. (1999) *Captive Selves, Captivating Others: The Politics and Poetics of Colonial American Captivity Narratives*, Boulder, CO: Westview Press.

Sulzberger, C. (1966) 'Foreign Affairs: A Distorted Mirror of War', *The New York Times*, May 29.

Sulzberger, C. (1970) 'Foreign Affairs: Danger of the Private Eye', *The New York Times*, April 29, 39.

Summers, H. (1993) 'Scapegoating the Power of the Press for Gaffes?', *Washington Times*, November 19.

Swanson, D. (2009) 'The Army Experience Center's Bad Experience: Turns Out Training Kids to Kill Not Popular with Public', *Humanist*, November/December.

Sweeney, M. (2001) *Secrets of Victory: The Office of Censorship and the American Press and Radio in World War II*, Chapel Hill: University of North Carolina Press.

Sweeney, M. (2006) *The Military and the Press: An Uneasy Truce*, Evanston: Northwestern University Press.

Swinton, E. (1933) *Eyewitness: Being Personal Reminiscences of Certain Phases of the Great War, Including the Genesis of the Tank*, Garden City, NY: Doubleday, Doran & Co.

Swofford, A. (2003) *Jarhead: A Marine's Chronicle of the Gulf War and Other Battles*, New York: Scribner's.

Szumski, B. (ed.) (1986) *Terrorism: Opposing Viewpoints*, St Paul, MN: Greenhaven Press.

Tait, S. (2008) 'Pornographies of Violence? Internet Spectatorship on Body Horror', *Critical Studies in Media Communication*, 25, i, 91–111.

Talev, M. (2007) 'Hyped Tales of Heroism: Lynch Wonders Why They Lied', *Kansas City Star*, April 25.

Tatham, S. (2006) *Losing Arab Hearts and Minds: The Coalition, Al-Jazeera and Muslim Public Opinion*, Rockville Centre, NY: Front Street Press.

Taylor, J. (1991) *War Photography: Realism in the Press*, London: Routledge.

Taylor, J. (1998) *Body Horror: Photojournalism, Catastrophe and War*, Manchester: Manchester University Press.

Taylor, P. (1981) 'Techniques of Persuasion: Basic Ground Rules of British Propaganda during the Second World War', *Historical Journal of Film, Radio and Television*, 1, i, 57–65.

Taylor, P. (1983) 'Propaganda in International Politics, 1919–1939' in Short.

Taylor, P. (1988) *Britain and the Cinema during the Second World War*, London: Macmillan.

Taylor, P. (1992) *War and the Media: Propaganda and Persuasion in the Gulf War*, Manchester: Manchester University Press.

Taylor, P. (1995) *Munitions of the Mind: War Propaganda from the Ancient World to the Nuclear Age*, Manchester: Manchester University Press.

Taylor, P. (1997) *Global Communications, International Affairs and the Media since 1945*, London: Routledge.

Taylor, Peter (1986) 'The Semantics of Political Violence' in Golding, Murdoch and Schlesinger.

Taylor, R. (1979) *Film Propaganda: Soviet Russia and Nazi Germany*, London: I. B. Tauris.

Taylor, R. (1983) 'Goebbels and the Function of Propaganda' in Welch.

Taylor, S. (1983) 'In Wake of Invasion, Much Official Misinformation by US Comes to Light', *The New York Times*, November 6, 20.

Terrell, R. and Ross, K. (1991) 'The Voluntary Guidelines' Threat to US Press Freedom' in Alexander and Picard.

Tester, K. (1994) *Media, Culture and Morality*, London: Routledge.

Thatcher, M. (1993) *The Downing Street Years*, London: HarperCollins.

Thayer, C. (1992) 'Vietnam: A Critical Analysis' in Young.

Thayer, N. (2001) 'Freelancers' Vital Role in International Reporting', *Nieman Reports*, Winter, 28–30.

Thies, J. (1983) 'Nazi Architecture: A Blueprint for World Domination: The Last Aims of Adolf Hitler' in Welch.

Thomas, E. (1979) *Collected Poems*, London: Faber & Faber.

Thompson, A. (ed.) (2007) *The Media and the Rwanda Genocide*, London: Pluto Press.

Thompson, C. (2006) 'Saving the World, One Video Game at a Time', *The New York Times*, July 23.

Thompson, J. Lee (1999) *Politicians, the Press and Propaganda: Lord Northcliffe and the Great War*, Kent, OH: Kent State University Press.

Thompson, M. (1992) *A Paper House: The Ending Of Yugoslavia*, London: Vintage.

Thompson, M. (1994) *Forging War: The Media in Serbia, Croatia and Bosnia-Hercegovina*, London: Article 19.

Thomson, A. (1992) *Smokescreen: The Media, the Censors, the Gulf*, Tunbridge Wells: Laburnham & Spellmount.

Thomson, G. (1947) *Blue Pencil Admiral: The Inside Story of Press Censorship*, London: Sampson Low, Marston & Co.

Thorpe, F. and Pronay, N. (1980) *British Official Films in the Second World War*, Oxford: Oxford University Press.

Thussu, D. and Freedman, D. (2003) *War and the Media: Reporting Conflict 24/7*, London: Sage.

Timms, E. (2004) 'Echoes of Somalia, But Will US React the Same?', *Dallas Morning News*, April 1.

Toplin, R. (1996) *History By Hollywood: The Use and Abuse of the American Past*, Urbana: University of Illinois Press.

Towle, P. (1975) 'The Debate on Wartime Censorship in Britain, 1902–14' in Bond and Roy.

Townshend, C. (1975) *The British Campaign in Ireland, 1919–21: The Development of Political and Military Policies*, Oxford: Oxford University Press.

Townshend, C. (1983) *Political Violence in Ireland: Government and Resistance since 1848*, Oxford: Clarendon Press.

Townshend, C. (1986a) *Britain's Civil Wars: Counterinsurgency in the Twentieth Century*, London: Faber & Faber.

Townshend, C. (1986b) 'The Process of Terror in Irish Politics' in O'Sullivan.

Trevor-Roper, H. (ed.) (1978) *The Goebbels Diaries: The Last Days*, London: Secker & Warburg.

Truman, H. (1947) 'Aid to Greece and Turkey', *Vital Speeches of the Day*, March 15, 322–4.

Tuchman, G. (1985) *Making News: A Study in the Construction of Reality*, New York: Free Press.

Tuchman, G. (1997) 'Making News by Doing Work: Routinizing the Unexpected' in Berkowitz.

Tumber, H. (1997) 'Bystander Journalism, or the Journalism of Attachment?', *Intermedia*, 25, i, 4–7.

Tumber, H. and Webster, F. (2006) *Journalists Under Fire: Information War and Journalistic Practices*, London: Sage.

Tunstall, J. (1996) *Newspaper Power: The New National Press in Britain*, Oxford: Clarendon Press.

Turner, I. (ed.) (1989) *Reconstruction in Post-War Germany: British Occupation Policy and the Western Zones, 1944–55*, Oxford: Berg.

Turner, K. (1985) *Lyndon Johnson's Dual War: Vietnam and the Press*, Chicago: University of Chicago Press.

Tyson, A. (2004) 'US Soldiers Face Charges of Prisoner Abuse', *Christian Science Monitor*, March 26.

Tyson, A. (2009a) 'Military Prepares Profiles on Reporters Visiting War Zones', *Washington Post*, August 28.

Tyson, A. (2009b) 'Military Limits Publishing Images of US Casualties in Afghanistan', *Washington Post*.

US Army Marine Corps (2007) *Counterinsurgency Field Manual*, Chicago: University of Chicago Press.

van Ginneken, J. (1998) *Understanding Global News: A Critical Introduction*, London: Sage.

van der Veer, P. and Munshi, S. (eds) (2004) *Media, War, and Terrorism: Responses from the Middle East and Asia*, London: RoutledgeCurzon.

Viereck, G. (1931) *Spreading Germs of Hate*, London: Duckworth.

Virilio, P. (1989) *War and Cinema: The Logistics of Perception*, London: Verso.

Virilio, P. (2000) *The Information Bomb*, London: Verso.

Vlastos, S. (1991) 'Revisionist Vietnam History' in Rowe and Berg.

von Geldern, J. (1995) 'Radio Moscow: The Voice from the Center' in Stites.

Voss, F. (1994) *Reporting the War: The Journalistic Coverage of World War II*, Washington, DC: Smithsonian Institution Press.

Vulliamy, E. (1994) *Seasons in Hell: Understanding Bosnia's War*, London: Simon & Schuster.

Wagner-Pacifici, R. (1986) *The Moro Morality Play: Terrorism As Social Drama*, Chicago: University of Chicago Press.

Wall, M. (1997) 'A "Pernicious New Strain of the Old Nazi Virus" and an "Orgy of Tribal Slaughter"': A Comparison of US News Magazine Coverage of the Crises in Bosnia and Rwanda', *Gazette: The International Journal for Communications Studies*, 59, vi, 411–28.

Wall, M. (2006a) 'Blogs over Baghdad: A New Genre of War Reporting' in Berenger.

Wall, M. (2006b) 'Blogging Gulf War II', *Journalism Studies*, 7, i, 111–26.

Wall, M. (2009) 'The Taming of the Warblogs: Citizen Journalism and the War in Iraq' in Allan and Thorsen.

Wallach, J. (1991) 'Leakers, Terrorists, Policy Makers and the Press' in Serfaty.

Wallis, R. and Baran, S. (1990) *The Known World of Broadcast News: International News and the Electronic Media*, London: Routledge.

Walsh, J. (1995) *The Gulf War Did Not Happen: Politics, Culture and Warfare Post-Vietnam*, Aldershot: Arena.

Walter, E. (1969) *Terror and Resistance: A Study of Political Violence with Case Studies of Some Primitive African Communities*, Oxford: Oxford University Press.

Walzer, M. (1992) *Just and Unjust Wars: A Moral Argument with Historical Illustrations*, New York: Basic.

Ward, S. (1998) 'An Answer to Martin Bell: Objectivity and Attachment in Journalism', *Press/Politics*, 3, iii, 121–5.

Wardlaw, G. (1989) *Political Terrorism: Theory, Tactics, and Counter-Measures*, Cambridge: Cambridge University Press.

Washburn, P. (1986) *A Question of Sedition: The Federal Government's Investigation of the Black Press during World War II*, New York: Oxford University Press.

Washington Post. (1899) 'Is The War Popular? It Will Be if It Wins Speedily, but Unpopular if It Drags', August 24, 6.

Washington Post. (1952) 'Kenya Battles White-Hating Secret Society', September 8, 3.

Wasserman, E. (2001) 'The Video Phone War', *American Journalism Review*, November, 22–3.

Waterman, S. (2005) 'Army Will Crack Down on Military Bloggers', *UPI International Intelligence*, August 30.

Waters, M. (1995) *Globalization*, London: Routledge.

Watson, R. (2009) 'Bare Knuckles: A Half-Billion Reasons to Marvel at MW2', *Philadelphia Inquirer*, November 20.

Waugh, E. (1943) *Scoop: A Novel About Journalists*, Harmondsworth: Penguin.

Weart, S. (1988) *Nuclear Fear: A History of Images*, Cambridge, MA: Harvard University Press.

Weaver, T. (1995) 'Prostituting the Facts in Time of War and Humanitarian Crisis' in Girardet.

Weber, C. (2006) *Imagining America at War: Morality, Politics and Film*, London: Routledge.

Weimann, G. (2009) 'When Fatwas Clash Online: Terrorist Debates on the Internet' in Forest.

Weinberg, S. (1968) 'What to Tell America: The Writers' Quarrel in the OWI', *Journal of American History*, LV, i, 73–89.

Weinberg, S. (1984) 'Approaches to the Study of Film in the Third Reich: A Critical Appraisal', *Journal of Contemporary History*, 19, i, 105–26.

Weinstock, D. and Boudreau, T. (2006) 'Online Iraq War News: Why It Had as Much Appeal as Spinach and Liver to Younger Audiences' in Berenger.

Weiss, M. (2007) 'Johnny Close Your Laptop', *Slate*, May 4.

Welch, D. (1983a) *Nazi Propaganda: The Power and the Limitations*, London: Croom Helm.

Welch, D. (1983b) *Propaganda and German Cinema, 1933–45*, Oxford: Clarendon University Press.

Welch, D. (1983c) 'Nazi Wartime Newsreels Propaganda' in Short.

Welch, D. (1993) *The Third Reich: Politics and Propaganda*, London: Routledge.

Wells, M. (2005) 'Paxman Answers the Questions', *Guardian*, January 31.

Weschler, L. (2005) 'Valkyries Over Iraq', *Harper's Magazine*, November, 65–77.

West, W. (ed.) (1987a) *Orwell: The War Broadcasts*, Harmondsworth: Penguin.

West, W. (1987b) *Truth Betrayed*, London: Duckworth.

Western, J. (2005) *Selling Intervention and War: The Presidency, the Media, and the American Public*, Baltimore: Johns Hopkins University Press.

Westmoreland, W. (1979) 'Vietnam in Perspective', *Military Review*, 59, i, 34–43.

Wijadi, T. (2004) 'The WTC Tragedy and the US Attack on Afghanistan: The Press Joins Hands in Beating the War Drums' in van der Veer and Munshi.

Wilkinson, P. (1986) *Terrorism and the Liberal State*, New York: New York University Press.

Wilkinson, P. (1997) 'The Media and Terrorism: A Reassessment', *Terrorism and Political Violence*, 9, ii, 51–64.

Wilkinson, P. and Stewart, A. (eds) (1987) *Contemporary Research on Terrorism*, Aberdeen: Aberdeen University Press.

Willcox, T. (1983) 'Projection or Publicity? Rival Concepts in the Pre-War Planning of the British Ministry of Information', *Journal of Contemporary History*, 18, i, 97–116.

Williams, D. (2001) 'Pulverised by the Daisy Cutter: Taliban Face the Biggest Bomb in the World', *Daily Mail*, November 7.

Williams, K. (1992) 'Something More Important than Truth: Ethical Issues in War Reporting' in Belsey and Chadwick.

Williams, K. (1993) 'The Light at the End of the Tunnel: The Mass Media, Public Opinion and the Vietnam War' in Eldridge.

Williams, P. (1992) 'Statement Before the US Senate Committee on Governmental Affairs' in Smith.

Williams, T. (1991) 'Narrative Patterns and Mythic Trajectories in Mid-1980s Vietnam Movies' in Anderegg.

Wilson, T. (1979) 'Lord Bryce's Investigation into Alleged German Atrocities in Belgium, 1914–15', *Journal of Contemporary History*, 14, 369–83.

Wiltenburg, M. (2003) 'More Than Playing Games', *Christian Science Monitor*, April 3.

Winkler, A. (1978) *The Politics of Propaganda: the Office of War Information, 1942–45*, New Haven, NJ: Yale University Press.

Winn, A. and Zakem, V. (2009) 'Jihad.com 2.0: The New Social Media and the Changing Dynamics of Mass Persuasion' in Forest.

Winter, J. (1989) *The Experience of World War One*, New York: Oxford University Press.

Winter, J. (1995) *Sites of Memory, Sites of Mourning: The Great War in European Cultural History*, Cambridge: Cambridge University Press.

Wolfsfeld, G. (1997) *Media and Political Conflict: News from the Middle East*, Cambridge: Cambridge University Press.

Woodward, B. (1992) *The Commanders*, London: Simon & Schuster.

Wright, E. (2008) *Generation Kill: Devil Dogs, Iceman, Captain America, and the New Face of American War*, New York: Berkeley Caliber.

Wyatt, C. (1993) *Paper Soldiers: The American Press and the Vietnam War*, New York: W. W. Norton.

Young, M. (1991) *The Vietnam Wars, 1945–1990*, New York: HarperPerennial.

Young, P. (ed) (1992) *Defence and the Media in Time of Limited War*, London: Cassell.

Young, P. and Jesser, P. (1997) *The Media and the Military: From the Crimea to Desert Strike*, Basingstoke: Macmillan.

Youngblood, D. (1996) '*Ivan's Childhood* (USSR, 1962) and *Come and See* (USSR, 1985): Post-Stalinist Cinema and the Myth of World War II' in Chambers and Culbert.

Youngblood, D. (2001) 'A War Remembered: Soviet Films of the Great Patriotic War', *American Historical Review*, 106, iii, 839–56.

Zaller, J. (1992) *The Nature and Origins of Mass Opinion*. Cambridge: Cambridge University Press.

Zaller, J. and Chiu, D. (2000) 'Government's Little Helper: US Press Coverage of Foreign Policy Crises, 1946–1999' in Nacos, Shapiro and Isernia.

Zednick, R. (2002) 'Perspectives on War: Inside Al Jazeera', *Columbia Journalism Review*, March/April, 44–7.

Zelizer, B. (1998) *Remembering to Forget: Holocaust Memory Through the Camera's Eye*, Chicago: University of Chicago Press.

Zeman, Z. (1973) *Nazi Propaganda*, London: Oxford University Press.

Zulaika, J. and Douglas, W. (1996) *Terror and Taboo: The Follies, Fables and Faces of Terrorism*, London: Routledge.

Index

313

Lightning Source UK Ltd.
Milton Keynes UK
UKHW02f2012231217
314934UK00007B/332/P

9 780230 244573